Richard Briers

Box of Delights

also by Hilary Kingsley

SOAPBOX

Box of Delights

HILARY KINGSLEY
and
GEOFF TIBBALLS

MACMILLAN
LONDON

to Carol and Peter

First published in 1989 by
MACMILLAN LONDON LIMITED
4 Little Essex Street London WC2R 3LF
and Basingstoke

Associated companies in Auckland, Delhi, Dublin, Gaborone,
Hamburg, Harare, Hong Kong, Johannesburg, Kuala Lumpur,
Lagos, Manzini, Melbourne, Mexico City, Nairobi,
New York, Singapore and Tokyo

ISBN 0–333–51812–8

A CIP catalogue record for this book is available from the British Library.

Printed in Italy

Contents

Acknowledgements

Our thanks are due to: BBC Written Archives; Daily Mirror Library; IBA Library; ITVA; Maggie Shrubsall; TV Times; and the numerous stars and producers who kindly dug deep into their memories.

Picture Acknowledgements

Robert Beatty: 270 right. Barry Bucknell: 271 right. BBC Enterprises Ltd: *What's My Line* 11; *The Quatermass Experiment* 13; *1984*; *On Safari* 18; *Sportsview* 20; *Dixon of Dock Green* 22; *Six-Five Special* 33; Pinky and Perky 35; *Black and White Minstrel Show* 38; *Juke Box Jury* 44; *Face to Face* 45; *The Third Man* 47; *It's a Square World* 57; *The Rag Trade* 63; *TW3* 67; *Compact* 69; *Dr Who* 72; *Telegoons* 74; *Marriage Lines* 74; *Top of the Pops* 79; *United* 83; *Till Death Us Do Part* 88; *Cathy Come Home* 88; *Troubleshooters* 91; *The Forsyte Saga* 92; *Pan's People* 93; *Dad's Army* 99; *Braden's Week* 100; *Monty Python* 104; *The Liver Birds* 105; *Z Cars* 111; *The Six Wives of Henry VIII* 117; *Elizabeth R* 121; *Colditz* 129; *The Brothers* 132; *Some Mothers Do 'Ave 'Em* 137; *Porridge* 145; *The Family* 148; *Churchill's People* 149; *Fawlty Towers* 152; *Pennies from Heaven* 172; *The Generation Game* 173; *Tinker Tailor Soldier Spy* 178; *Shoestring* 180; *Not the Nine O'Clock News* 180; *The Good Life* 187; Barbara Woodhouse 194; *Tenko* 199; *The Borgias* 200; *Only Fools and Horses* 202; *The Young Ones* 205; *Boys from the Blackstuff* 206; *Black Adder* 212; *Edge of Darkness* 229; *Howards' Way* 230; *Monocled Mutineer* 236; *The Life and Loves of a She-Devil* 237; *Tutti Frutti* 241; *Fortunes of War* 244; *Tumbledown* 249; *Jumping the Queue* 257; *The Singing Detective* 263. Central Independent Television Ltd: *Crossroads* 77; *New Faces* 140; *OTT* 209; *Auf Wiedersehen Pet* 215; *The Price is Right* 221; *Spitting Image* 223; *Yesterday's Dreams* 243; *The 19th Hole* 259. Russ Conway: 272 below right. Michaela Denis: 273 left. Patricia Driscoll: 273 right. Keith Fordyce: 274 left. Eileen Fowler: 274 right. Glasgow Herald: Robin Hall 275 below left. Granada Television Ltd: *The Army Game* 34; *Coronation Street* 56; *The Lovers* 117; *The Comedians* 124; *Sam* 139; *Brideshead Revisited* 201; *Jewel in the Crown* 220. Simon Groom: 275 above left. Grundy Television: *Neighbours* 248. Jeremy Hawk: 276 left. Henson Associates Inc 1976: Muppets 159. Pip Hinton: 276 above right. Tony Holland: 277 left. ITC Library Sales Ltd: Robin Hood 25; Sir Lancelot 30; Arthur Haynes 31; *Emergency – Ward 10* 34; *Sunday Night at the London Palladium* 38; *The Larkins* 39; *The Invisible Man* 46; *Danger Man* 57; *Morecambe and Wise* 62; *Police 5* 68; *The Saint* 68; *Thunderbirds* 86; *Mrs Thursday* 91; *The Champions* 102; *Randall and Hopkirk (Deceased)* 118; Father Brown 146; Jesus of Nazareth 161. Lorimar Television: *Dallas* 169. LWT: *Upstairs Downstairs* 120; *Budgie* 123; *Within These Walls* 144; *The Fosters* 157; *The Professionals* 163; *Dempsey and Makepeace* 231; *Beauty and the Beast* 250; *Trick or Treat* 256; *John Freeman* 274 below right. Jimmie Macgregor: 275 below left. Mirror Group Newspapers: Coronation 9; Richard Dimbleby 10; *The Grove Family* 17; Billy Cotton 29; Oxo Ad 40; *Mash* 136; *All Creatures Great and Small* 166; *Death of a Princess* 192; *Coronation Street* 216; *Eastenders* 228; *Emmerdale Farm* 235; *The Paradise Club* 258; Shirley Abicair 269 left; Anne Aston 269 right; Raymond Baxter 270 left; Terry Brooks 271 below left; Gerald Campion 272 left; Jillian Comber 272 above right; Hans and Lotte Hass 275 right; Mary Holland 276 below left; Mary Malcolm 277 right; Ray Martine 278 left; Janice Nicholls 278 above right; Anthea Redfern 281 above left; Jonathan Routh 282 left; Sabrina 282 right; Jack Scott 283 left; Christopher Trace 283 above right; Leila Williams 284 right; Jess Yates 285 right. John Noakes: 279 left. Sylvia Peters: 279 right. Conrad Phillips: 280 left. Leslie Randall: 280 right. Joan Regan: 281 below left. Scope Features: *Take Your Pick* 23; Fanny and Johnny Cradock 24; Brooke Bond chimps 28; *No Hiding Place* 49; *77 Sunset Strip* 59; Avengers 65; *Rawhide* 64; *Ready Steady Go!* 71; *The Beverly Hillbillies* 77 below; Dulux Dog 78; Kennomeat Ad 84; Callan 94; *At Last the 1948 Show* 95; *Do Not Adjust Your Set* 101; *Special Branch* 106; *Family at War* 116; Hovis Ad 153; *Rock Follies* 156; Cinzano Ad 195; *Bernie the Bolt* 271 above left; Monica Rose 281 right; Wally Whyton 284 left. Aaron Spelling: *Dynasty* 208. Thames Television: *Rainbow* 133; *The Naked Civil Servant* 152; *Edward and Mrs Simpson* 171; *Minder* 177; *Widows* 213; *The Bill* 222; *Jack the Ripper* 252. J. Walter Thompson: Yorkie Ad 165. Touchstone Television: *The Golden Girls* 236. Twentieth Century Fox Television: *Peyton Place* 82; *Starsky and Hutch* 158. Bert Weedon: 283 above right. Kenneth Wolstenholme: 285 left. Yorkshire Television: *Hadleigh* 108; *Emmerdale Farm* 128; Arthur C. Clarke 192; *High and Dry* 240. Muriel Young: 286.

Box of Delights

THE EARLY DAYS

Dirty Den, Alf Garnett and Arthur Daley all owe their place in history to the efforts of one man: Scotsman John Logie Baird. It was his determination to add pictures to wireless that brought about the invention of television, and without him we would never have known which half of Morecambe and Wise had the short fat hairy legs, who shot JR and what was in Box 13.

Baird gave the world's first demonstration of true television in 1926, and three years later the BBC was persuaded to let Baird's company use its London transmitter; but until the opening of a second transmitter in 1930 there could be no simultaneous broadcasts of sound and vision. That year, the first publicly televised play in Britain was broadcast from the Baird studio in London's Long Acre. It was called 'The Man with a Flower in His Mouth' and was organised by the BBC. Inevitably it was fairly basic; indeed, only one actor's face could be seen at a time because the performing area was so restricted. Among those who appeared in these early days of television were Gracie Fields, George Robey, Stanley Holloway and Arthur Askey, and in 1931 and 1932 Baird televised the Derby live.

As the interest in the new invention increased, the BBC became more involved and installed Baird equipment in the newly opened Broadcasting House in Portland Place from where they put on fashion shows, ballet and boxing. In August 1936, Alexandra Palace was the setting for a public demonstration of television at the annual Radiolympia Exhibition. Transmissions alternated daily between Baird's system and that of his rival, Marconi-EMI. The BBC chose three hosts who became the first television personalities: Jasmine Bligh, Elizabeth Cowell and Leslie Mitchell. Jasmine and Elizabeth were selected from 1,222 applicants, and all candidates had to be unmarried and not have red hair. The successful pair were entitled to a dress allowance of £25 per annum whereas Mitchell was expected to provide his own clothes. Leslie Mitchell's famous opening words to herald a new age were: 'Good afternoon, ladies and gentlemen. It is with great pleasure that I introduce you to the magic of television.'

In October, after the exhibition, test transmissions began, including the magazine programme 'Picture Page' where guests were introduced to viewers by Canadian actress Joan Miller via a mock telephone switchboard. The official opening of the service took place on 2 November, first with the Baird system then with Marconi-EMI. It featured speeches, a newsreel and a variety performance starring American comedy dancers Buck and Bubbles, Chinese jugglers the Lai Founs and even including a specially composed song entitled

'Television', sung by Adele Dixon. Among other programmes scheduled for that historic first week was variety with Bebe Daniels and Ben Lyon, a display by Alsatian dogs, excerpts from the West End play *Marigold*, an item on breeding silver foxes, a tap-dancing demonstration, a feature on prize chrysanthemums, and bus driver Mr L. A. Stock describing the model he had made of Drake's ship, *Golden Hind*! Cecil Madden, programme organiser and senior producer at Alexandra Palace, was allocated £1,000 for his entire week's output but, then, television was limited to one hour in the afternoon and one hour in the evening with nothing on Sundays. It is estimated that the opening ceremony was seen on a maximum of 400 sets – hardly surprising as they each cost up to £100, the price of a small car at the time. For all Baird's enthusiasm and pioneering, Marconi won the day, and it was that system which came to be adopted. To add insult to injury, much of Baird's equipment was destroyed in the Crystal Palace fire at the end of November.

Between 1936 and 1939, the BBC screened 326 plays, among them the 1937 production of *How He Lied to Her Husband* in which the cast, led by Greer Garson, were visited by its author George Bernard Shaw. In the same year, the coronation of George VI drew an estimated audience of as high as 50,000. By 1938, 5,000 sets had been sold, but reception was still confined to the London area. The BBC gave Londoners, already under the threat of war, a terrible shock one night. Terrified residents phoned the police after hearing heavy gunfire from Alexandra Palace. They thought it was a German invasion and began digging holes in their back gardens. They were informed that the guns were blank rounds fired by the Territorials for the play 'The White Château'. When the play was repeated a few days later, the BBC decreed no guns and used fireworks instead; but a huge crowd turned up to see the guns, and on discovering that there weren't any this time started booing. The microphones picked all this up, and the producer had to cut back to the studio. The play was ruined.

Prewar television ended as it had started, during Radiolympia. On 1 September 1939, the screen simply went blank (there was no announcement) during a Mickey Mouse cartoon. It was felt that the signals from the mast at Alexandra Palace would attract enemy aircraft. The service reopened on 7 June 1946 with the same Mickey Mouse cartoon that had been interrupted seven years earlier. Jasmine Bligh opened with 'Hello . . . do you remember me?' and Leslie Mitchell added: 'As I was saying before we were so rudely interrupted . . .' There was music from Mantovani, dancing from Margot Fonteyn, and on the next day a major outside broadcast: the Victory Parade through London to celebrate the end of war. The commentators were Richard Dimbleby and Freddie Grisewood, and up to 100,000 watched with delight on television.

However, television still had many opponents. The Stoll Theatre would not let Ivy Benson and her all-girl band appear on television, and big variety agencies threatened to blacklist artists who were seen on the small screen. Also, the severe winter of 1946–7 resulted in a fuel crisis and the Government closed down television for a month. Because of government restrictions on expenditure, television was slow to spread beyond the London area. It eventually reached the Midlands in 1949, Manchester in 1951 and Scotland, Wales and the West Country in 1952. By 1950, there were 343,882 sets in Britain – less than one home in twenty.

Those who did possess sets were able to watch Sylvia Peters, Mary Malcolm and McDonald Hobley introduce such delightful postwar shows as Joan Gilbert's 'Picture Page' (début 1936), 'Muffin the Mule' (1946), 'Café Continental' (1947), 'Rooftop Rendezvous' with Jack Jackson (1948), Norman Wisdom in 'Wit and Wisdom' (1948), 'The Charlie Chester Show' (1949), 'Come Dancing' (1950), Terry-Thomas in 'How Do You View?' (1950) and – not to be forgotten – 'For the Housewife' (1950), an afternoon programme which instructed the lady of the house on such everyday matters as how to renovate a chest of drawers, how to cook whale meat and how to cure home-grown tobacco. (It is hard to envisage Alexis from 'Dynasty' curing tobacco!) That year also saw the first general election coverage with Chester Wilmot as anchorman and David Butler, who went on to become an election regular, as chief pundit. And the Woman Television Personality of the Year was eighteen-year-old Petula Clark.

The early fifties continued with 'What's My Line?' (1951), 'The Betty Driver Show' (1952), Frankie Howerd in 'The Howerd Crowd' (1952), and in the same year 'Hit Parade', an early 'Top of the Pops' with Cyril Stapleton and his Augmented Orchestra. Television was building up a vast army of talent. It was ready to take the country by storm in 1953: coronation year.

THE
FIFTIES

1953

On 2 June, Elizabeth II was crowned in Westminster Abbey. □ On the same day, news came through that a British expedition led by New Zealander Edmund Hillary had become the first to conquer Everest. □ The Korean War ended. □ Stalin died. □ Colour television came to America. □ Blackpool beat Bolton in the 'Stanley Matthews' Cup Final. □ Ian Fleming introduced James Bond in the book Casino Royale. *□ Christian Dior brought the bosom back into women's clothes with the 'sweater girl' bra. □ Hugh Hefner launched* Playboy. *□ To combat smogs, 6½d (3p) mouth-masks could be purchased from chemists (6½d was also the price of a pint of milk). □ The cost of a three-bedroom semi was just over £2,000. □ The world went flying-saucer crazy – several thousand sightings were officially reported in America alone. □ Over 100,000 Londoners were waiting to have telephones installed. □ Frankie Laine was the top recording artist. □ And one of the most popular songs was Lita Roza's 'How Much Is That Doggie in the Window?'*

The coronation of Elizabeth II marked the start of television's superiority over radio.

The British nation came to a standstill on that great day in June. Thousands lined the streets of London, while in homes and offices the length and breadth of the country colleagues, neighbours and relatives huddled in corners, all peering avidly at a small piece of furniture with a grey screen, watching magic pictures of the coronation of Elizabeth II. For many, it was their first glimpse of an invention that has gone on to change the face and behaviour of the world: television.

The vigil lasted all day. Mealtimes were slotted in around crucial moments as girls gossiped about the merits of the Queen's dress and grandmothers said they had had none of this when George V became King. It was an occasion none would forget. They shed tears at the shot of the boy Prince Charles in the royal box watching his mother being crowned, reflected in a moment's silence at that solitary shot of her handbag lying on the seat of the state coach and cheered wildly as the new Queen emerged from Westminster Abbey. Television had arrived.

Of course, the coronation was only one of the splendid programmes screened by the BBC in 1953, but at the start of the year the television programmes were tucked away in *Radio Times*, very much the poor relation. Fewer than 2 million homes had television, and these were mainly grouped around the cities of London, Birmingham, Manchester, Glasgow and Cardiff. However, in the build-up to the great day 526,000 sets were sold as coronation fever swept the country. Temporary transmitters were put up in areas not yet able to receive programmes, and 3,000 tickets for a large-screen showing at the Festival Hall went in under an hour. Although there were still only 2½ million sets in Britain (a new set cost around £85), somehow 20 million contrived to watch the occasion on television. This figure represented 56 per cent of the population and compared extremely favourably with radio's audience of only 12 million. Quite simply, the coronation was the biggest event in television history to date. It was also broadcast in France, Holland and Germany, and film recordings were sent all over the world. It is estimated that the world audience was a staggering 277 million.

What made the coverage so special was that, unlike George VI's coronation in 1937, cameras were actually allowed inside Westminster Abbey for the service itself. Permission to do this was initially refused, but the BBC managed to persuade the royal advisers that nobody was going to faint under the lights nor would the cameras be in any way obtrusive. The Prime Minister, Winston Churchill, was the principal objector. Ultimately, it was the Queen's decision to screen the coronation.

The broadcast began just after 10 a.m. with Sylvia Peters introducing Berkeley Smith, the commentator outside Buckingham Palace, and it ended at 11.30 p.m. when Richard Dimbleby, who was commentating on the ceremony, said goodnight from the empty Abbey. The day was of course a tremendous personal triumph for Richard Dimbleby, who thus established himself as the man for all great state occasions. Dimbleby had been a radio correspondent during the war and had made broadcasts from an RAF bomber over Germany, but the coronation was probably his finest hour – or nineteen, for he arrived at the Abbey at 5.30 a.m. and left at 12.30 a.m. the following morning, a marathon stint. He later admitted that he had never been so tired as when he finally left the Abbey and had never felt so acutely the strain of describing such a great public occasion or been so proud to be able to contribute to it. He added: 'I was deeply conscious not only of the responsibility upon my own shoulders but of the tremendous duty that rests upon the Television Service as a whole.'

The whole event cost the BBC £44,000, which these days wouldn't go anywhere near buying a single episode of a third-rate situation comedy, but it changed the nation's

Richard Dimbleby, the voice of the BBC.

appreciation of the medium. The likes of politicians who had previously scorned it were now desperate to appear and promote themselves, and the sale of sets increased by a further 50 per cent over the next year.

Even though television was still in its infancy, some of the most popular programmes of 1953 had been going for a few years. One of the most colourful characters (although he could only be seen in black and white) was 'the rudest man in Britain': the legendary Gilbert Harding. A former Bradford police constable, Harding was the radio questionmaster of 'Round Britain Quiz' and 'The Brains Trust' before becoming the grumpy intellectual on **'What's My Line?'** His habit of bullying innocent challengers if they gave evasive answers or didn't speak perfect English appalled viewers. He made Robin Day look like a boy scout. After one clash between Harding and chairman Eamonn Andrews, the BBC was swamped with 175 phone calls and six telegrams, all protesting about his behaviour. (Later they became friends but faked rows for the viewers.) On another occasion, Harding even argued with puppet Archie Andrews. Ironically, Harding's father had once suggested that young Gilbert might become a comedian!

'What's My Line?' began in 1951, and the original intention was for Eamonn Andrews and Gilbert Harding to

chair the programme on alternate weeks. Eamonn later recalled Gilbert's memorable début as chairman: 'Gilbert had this challenger who was a male nurse but unfortunately Gilbert had the cards out of order and he had "motor mechanic" written down. When the challenger was asked if he used instruments in his job, the poor fellow said "yes" but Gilbert insisted "no, no you DON'T". It blew up into such chaos that Gilbert said he would never do it again and he went on to the panel where he was much better.'

It was estimated that in 1952 an incredible 90 per cent of people with television sets watched 'What's My Line?', making it easily the most popular programme in the country. Each week, the show received over 200 letters from would-be challengers. The most frequent applicants were sub-postmasters and undertakers who thought they looked more like bookmakers or publicans. The most celebrated occupation was that of saggar maker's bottom-knocker in the pottery industry. However, not everyone benefited from the exposure of television. One challenger, giving his job as frogman, was recognised by a bank manager who promptly phoned the police. The man was gaoled for fifteen months for passing dud cheques.

'What's My Line?' was front-page news. When Barbara Kelly lost an ear-ring on the show and when Bob Monkhouse appeared wearing an eye-patch (a blood vessel had burst), the papers gave the stories the same prominence as they gave the exploits of Dirty Den in the

Regulars on the 'What's My Line?' panel in 1953 besides Gilbert Harding were (*from left*) Ghislaine Alexander, Jerry Desmonde and Barbara Kelly.

eighties. The series ran until 1963 and was briefly revived ten years later with David Jacobs in the chair before earning a more permanent comeback in 1984. Eamonn Andrews and Barbara Kelly were the sole survivors from the early days, George Gale taking over Gilbert Harding's rôle. First Penelope Keith and then Angela Rippon took charge following Eamonn Andrews's death in 1987. What of another popular panellist, Lady Barnett? The wife of Leicester's Lord Mayor committed suicide in 1980 after being fined for shoplifting goods worth just 87p.

Richard Dimbleby's high spot of the year had to be the coronation, but he was to become firmly associated with a programme that began its long history at the tail end of 1953: **'Panorama'**. In truth, the only thing the early editions had in common with the political powerhouse which subsequently developed was the title. Presented at first by Max Robertson, it was more of a magazine with Malcolm Muggeridge on hand to interview the famous. Muggeridge had a highly individual manner of interrogation. He once asked a celebrated brain surgeon who had just completed the separation of Siamese twins whether, if requested to do so, he could join them together again.

'Panorama' was transformed into the programme we know today by the arrival of Richard Dimbleby as anchorman a few years later. Described as 'the window on the world', 'Panorama' turned Dimbleby into a father-figure upon whom people felt they could rely. He used to be sent letters like 'Our local hall needs a new roof – can you find us the money?' or 'They're building a road through our village – can you stop it?' In 1962, at the height of the Cuban crisis, a worried mother phoned the BBC to say: 'I won't send my children to school tomorrow unless Mr Dimbleby can promise me there will be no war.' Dimbleby said: 'They think I'm a sort of national doctor who can cure all ills.' He was also constantly in the newspapers. Demonstrating the dangers of children's nightclothes, he singed his eyebrows. The sensational headline the following morning was 'Whoosh – and Dimbleby Catches Fire'. And when an intended aside, 'Jesus wept', was heard by millions he was chastised for blasphemy.

Other notable occupants of the 'Panorama' hot seat have been Robin Day, Alastair Burnet, Robert Kee and Richard Dimbleby's son David who took over in 1974.

One of the first postwar broadcasts had been an Edwardian music-hall from the Players' Theatre beneath London's Charing Cross arches. The cast included Hattie Jacques, and the chairman was a gentleman by the name of Leonard Sachs. Some years later, BBC producer Barney Colehan made a programme on the life of the music-hall. There was an audience of only about eight people, but they so enjoyed dressing up for the part that they wanted to do some more – and bring their friends. So, in July 1953, **'The Good Old Days'** began at the City Varieties Theatre, Leeds, and Leonard Sachs was to become the celebrated chairman of a show that lasted for thirty years and featured 2,000 artists.

Barney Colehan had also produced radio's hugely successful 'Have a Go' (he was the Barney in Wilfred Pickles's catchphrase 'Give 'em the money, Barney') and realised that audience participation was the keynote. So the assembled throng not only wore period clothes like the artists; they were encouraged to join in the songs, too. All the money for their outfits, false beards, stick-on moustaches and side-whiskers came out of their own pocket, although some were known to cheat by only wearing costume from the waist up since only their top halves were visible on television. Authenticity was an important factor. Before the curtain went up, Colehan used to tell them: 'Ladies, please don't smoke – you didn't in public in the 1900s. And don't flash cigarette-lighters – they hadn't been invented!'

The other splendidly individual feature about 'The Good Old Days' was the performance of Leonard Sachs. No act ever had a bigger build-up as he reeled off a list of sesquipedalian provincialisms (long words) with the audience reaching a crescendo of oohs and aahs as Sachs sounded increasingly constipated. Finally, as the atmos-

phere reached fever pitch, he would activate his gavel, shriek 'Your own, your very own . . .' and often introduce an act that nobody had ever heard of.

One of the great children's favourites of 1953 was good old **'Muffin the Mule'**. Partnered by Annette Mills, sister of actor John Mills, he actually started life in 1946 and was really the first television character to capture the hearts of children. Muffin used to clank around energetically on the piano-top while Annette played the music. He was worked by Ann Hogarth, who stood on the piano behind a screen, and he had a number of unlikely companions including Mr Peregrine the penguin, Sally the sea-lion and Louise the lamb. Annette Mills also created Prudence Kitten in 1951. Muffin bowed out on 2 January 1955, and the following week, on the 10th, Annette Mills died at the age of sixty-one after an operation.

Back in 1953, Muffin was facing fierce competition from a little orange bear who delighted in squirting his master with a water-pistol or covering him in flour. **Sooty** was every child's hero, able to misbehave with impunity and torment the life out of poor old Harry Corbett; but Sooty was born in unlikely circumstances. A Bradford business-man with a degree in engineering, Harry was holidaying in Blackpool in 1948 when he saw this glove puppet in a shop window on a miserable afternoon. He bought it for just 7s 6d (37½p) to entertain his children and turned it into one of television's greatest-ever characters. There is even a Sooty Museum in Shipley, Yorkshire.

Sooty first appeared in 1952 (Harry was paid £10 per programme), and his series has been transmitted every year since – a unique achievement. Harry's fingers were his fortune and were reportedly insured for £20,000. Sooty began as a solo performer but was joined after five years by the even naughtier Sweep. They were a great double act, Sooty with his Oofle Dust and magic spell 'Izzy whizzy, let's get busy' and Sweep with his endless strings of sausages. An early high spot for Sooty was when he turned his water-pistol on no less a person than Prince Philip. In the sixties, Soo the panda arrived as Sooty's girlfriend. There were a few raised eyebrows at Soo's arrival, particularly as she and Sooty appeared to be cohabiting. The BBC was worried that giving Sooty a girlfriend would be introducing sex to children's television.

Further characters followed, such as Kipper the cat, Butch the dog and Ramsbottom, a snake with a broad Northern accent, and in 1968 Sooty switched to ITV. Eventually, ill health forced Harry to hand over the reins to son Matthew who, born in 1948, is the same age as Sooty. These days Soo's voice has finally broken, while Sweep has got a different-shaped face, clearly the result of plastic surgery. And of course there's no longer Harry's familiar weary voice to say: 'Bye-bye, everyone. Bye-bye.' But Sooty is as popular as ever. Reflecting on that initial outlay of 7s 6d, Matthew Corbett says: 'I think we've got our money back . . .'

The early fifties really were a great time to be a child, providing you were fortunate enough to have access to a television set. In addition to Muffin and Sooty, there was **'Watch with Mother'**. The title 'Watch with Mother' was adopted in 1950 with the advent of **'Andy Pandy'**. Andy was created by Mary Adams, the Head of Television Talks at the BBC. Maria Bird used to bring Andy out to play, opera singer Gladys Whitred sang the songs, and Audrey Atterbury and Molly Gibson pulled the strings. In those days, the strings were not only visible; they were positively intrusive. But nobody minded as Andy was jerked around the screen to perfect a silly walk years before John Cleese. Andy was by himself at first, but after a few months he was joined by Teddy and Looby Loo with whom he shared a basket. Andy's attire was always somewhat effeminate with his blue and white striped jogging-suit and matching floppy hat. Indeed there is a school of thought that believes he inspired Quentin Crisp. Incredibly, only twenty-six shows were ever made, but they were repeated right up until 1970. And they all ended

with the song: 'Time to go home, time to go home. Andy is waving goodbye, goodbye.'

In 1952 we saw what really goes on behind the potting-shed with those controversial characters Bill and Ben, **'The Flowerpot Men'**. The controversy arose from their peculiar language, which parents claimed was impairing children's speech development. Bill and Ben were worked by the same team as Andy Pandy, but with the versatile Peter Hawkins doing the voices. Hawkins was later responsible for the distinctive sounds of Captain Pugwash and assorted Daleks. The Flowerpot Men lived in constant fear of the Gardener, a sort of mysterious Mafioso figure who was never seen. In truth, the programme was an early whodunnit:

> *Was it Bill or was it Ben*
> *Fed paraquat to Little Weed just then?*

By the end of 1953, 'Andy Pandy' was being shown on Tuesdays, 'The Flowerpot Men' on Wednesdays, and the year's new addition, **'Rag, Tag and Bobtail'** (the enchanting tales of a hedgehog, a mouse and a rabbit respectively) went out on Thursdays. As every discerning child knows, the line-up was completed in 1955 by **'Picture Book'** on Mondays and **'The Woodentops'** on Fridays. 'Watch with Mother' was eventually dropped in 1980 and the title changed to 'See-Saw'. The BBC explained that mothers were no longer around to watch – most children in the eighties saw television with a play group, a child-minder or a nanny. But the memory lingers on, and to prove it a compilation of the old 'Watch with Mother' favourites quickly became a best-selling video tape in 1988.

While younger children were enthralled by Andy Pandy in 1953, their older brothers were tucking into the adventures of **'Billy Bunter of Greyfriars School'**. Bunter was also popular with adults; in fact the show used to go out live twice every Friday, at 5.25 p.m. for children and two hours later for their parents. Written by Frank Richards and based on his books, Bunter came to television in 1952 and ran (or, rather, waddled) intermittently for ten years. Producer Joy Harington had great difficulty in finding someone suitable to play the 'Fat Owl'. She said at the time: 'Every fat boy in England came for the part but none was right. Then a friend suggested Gerald Campion. Of course, he isn't fat enough in the tummy – we'll have to arrange that. But he's got the face for it.' And so Gerald Campion became Bunter. At 11 stone 12 pounds, he wasn't really fat; and at twenty-nine years of age, married with two children, he certainly wasn't a schoolboy. But he did read the *Magnet* in which the Bunter stories appeared and was confident he could solve his weight problem. 'They called me Fatty at school,' he confessed in 1952, 'but I've since been dieting to keep my weight down. I shan't bother any more. And I love jam tarts – I even make them myself.'

Without doubt the most disturbing serial of the time was 'The Quatermass Experiment', a prophetic science-fiction thriller by Manx writer Nigel Kneale. The hero, Professor Bernard Quatermass, was confronted with a space ship which, having drifted off course, returned to Earth with just one surviving crew-member. And that astronaut had something of a problem – an infection that slowly turned him into a vegetable monster slightly more sinister than a rampaging radish. Reginald Tate played the Professor (*left of picture*) with Duncan Lamont as the hapless spaceman in a memorable production that gripped the nation for six weeks on Saturday nights.

Bunter's vocabulary sounds pretty dated now, with phrases like 'I say, you fellows' and exclamations such as 'Beast!', 'Blimey!' and 'Crikey!', but the use of 'Crikey!' got the series into trouble when an Enfield vicar criticised it for bad language. He counted Bunter saying 'Crikey!' thirteen times in one episode and pointed out that the dictionary defines the word as 'vulgar'. Bunter's great adversary was the form-master of the Remove, Mr Quelch, played in the fifties by Kynaston Reeves and in the sixties by Frank Melford. Bunter's chums included Nugent, Cherry and Wharton, and among those who appeared as boys were Melvyn Hayes, David Hemmings and Michael Crawford.

The best-known faces of 1953 belonged to the three BBC programme-announcers: McDonald Hobley, Mary Malcolm and Sylvia Peters. The trio first appeared in 1946 and quickly became immensely popular with viewers. The late Mac Hobley was naturally calm and debonair, but even he was ruffled when, before a 1951 political broadcast, he introduced Sir Stafford Cripps by announcing: 'And now, the moment you have been waiting for – the Chancellor of the Exchequer, Sir Stifford Crapps.'

Mary Malcolm, granddaughter of Lily Langtry, had been a wartime radio announcer; then a friend asked Mary to model some clothes for a television programme about dress design, she was remembered from that and was offered the announcer's job. As with the other female announcers, Mary's clothes had to fit the programmes. The BBC stated: 'In the main, an evening gown is suitable for many evenings, especially as it can be simple or elaborate according to whether the programmes are straightforward or of specially grand moment. But there are special occasions which require a quiet dignity of dress, just as there are others needing an announcer to look as glamorous and as scintillating as she can. It would not be the thing to have a woman announcer introducing a Sunday religious programme in a ravishing gown nor would it do to have a gala variety show introduced by a woman wearing a skirt and jumper.'

Sylvia Peters got the job by reciting 'Goldilocks' to her interview board who later described her as 'winsome'. She was also a great sport. She recalls: 'Everybody in the studio used to make me laugh. One of them used to throw nuts at me, trying to get one down my cleavage just as I

Also Shown in 1953

'**The Man in the Kitchen**' was Philip Harben, resplendent as always in his blue-striped butcher's apron; he used to cook with his family's rations, so if he burned a joint on television there would be no Sunday lunch for the Harben family. '**Inventor's Club**' was a sort of do-it-yourself version of 'Tomorrow's World'; and '**Café Continental**' was described as 'Gay International Cabaret'. There were also '**The Passing Show**', a series of five shows of the same title made to reflect the history of popular entertainment from the turn of the century; '**Music for You**', a series begun in 1951 and priding itself on inviting major overseas operatic stars to take part; '**Face the Music**'; and the Television Toppers, whose principal show of the year was '**Toppers about Town**' in which the twelve leggy dancers visited some of London's most celebrated rendezvous. Another famous sight was that of Australian **Shirley Abicair** with her zither.

Other variety shows included '**Re-Turn It Up**' with Jimmy Jewel and Ben Warriss; '**Music Hall**'; '**Quite Contrary**' with Viscountess (Katie) Boyle; '**Before Your Very Eyes**', starring Arthur Askey, Diana Decker and Dickie Henderson; an October edition of '**Variety Parade**', which introduced a couple of newcomers called Morecambe and Wise; '**The Eric Barker Half-Hour**' led by Eric and his wife Pearl Hackney; and a mystifying demonstration

of psycho-magic from **Chan Canasta**. Then there were the '**Interludes**', fourteen of them, the potter's wheel, the speeded up train journey and the kitten and its ball of wool among the favourites.

An essential part of afternoon viewing for many women was '**About the Home**' which frequently did things with raffia. Whatever happened to raffia?

Among the quiz shows were '**Animal, Vegetable, Mineral?**', which presented distinguished archaeologists attempting to guess the nature of museum exhibits (the Queen liked it); '**The Balloon Game**', an idea based on the premiss that a balloon containing three historically famous people was plummeting rapidly towards the sea (who would you have thrown out to save the others and why?); '**Why?**', a new family game with the curious format of adult panellists pretending to be children and parents (after just one show, the BBC were inundated with viewers' calls demanding that it be taken off); and a news quiz called '**Guess My Story**'.

Children could enjoy Richard Hearne as the accident-prone **Mr Pastry**, '**The Appleyards**', '**Billy Bean and his Funny Machine**' or go '**Looking at Animals**' with George Cansdale. Do you remember Hank the cowboy or Mr Turnip? They were both to be found on '**Whirligig**'. And who could forget **Bengo**, the lovable boxer puppy whose stories were narrated by Sylvia Peters?

said, "Good evening". Sometimes he succeeded, and I'm sure that's why I always looked so jolly.' Sylvia also presented a programme that is now, thirty-nine years after its inception, the longest-running musical show on television – **'Come Dancing'**. The idea stemmed from Mecca's Eric Morley, who suggested to the BBC the possibility of a dance show with a few added gimmicks. One of these was roller-skating. (In view of Mr Morley's subsequent tendency to do everything in reverse order, it is surprising that another wasn't dancing backwards.) In those early days, the men had to wear a huge cardboard number on their back, which made them appear to be carrying sandwich-boards instead of dancing; but they still managed to glide across the floor in style, and early champions were Syd Perkins and Edna Duffield. Ah, who could forget Syd and Edna?

The list of 'Come Dancing' compères reads like a Who's Who of Television: alongside Sylvia Peters are Peter West, Pete Murray, Michael Aspel, David Jacobs, Judith Chalmers, Terry Wogan, Peter Marshall and Angela Rippon. Peter West gives an insight into the ferocious competition that goes on behind the painted smiles.

'Viewers don't see the intense rivalry between the regions but passions ran very high. Scotland always used to get worked up. The people involved were extremely competitive and I was often accused of cooking the books. We got a lot of nasty letters.'

'Come Dancing' certainly didn't always get it right. In 1963, Eric Morley launched a new dance called the Golli Golli on the show. 'This is a brand-new party dance which we believe will sweep the country,' enthused the Bryl-creemed one. Can anyone remember the Golli Golli? But the wonderful thing about the programme is that you don't have to be a dancer to enjoy it. Peter West admits: 'I've got two left feet. Every time my wife dances with me, she has to wear shin-pads.' But does she sew all her own sequins?

A final thought for 1953 is that, over thirty years before live football came to television on a regular basis, Cliff Michelmore was commentating on the second half of a match that the BBC cameras don't seem to cover any more: the Mitcham Primary Schools Cup Final, between Fortescue Road and Bond Road . . .

1954

Rationing ended on butter, fats, bacon and meat. □ America tested an H-bomb at Bikini Atoll. □ Roger Bannister ran the first sub-four-minute mile. □ Lester Piggott won his first Derby on Never Say Die. □ American evangelist Billy Graham preached for seventy-two consecutive nights on his British tour, culminating in over 120,000 people flocking to Wembley Stadium. □ Ten thousand West Indians arrived in Britain in search of a better life. □ Marlon Brando starred in the film The Wild One, *and* The Belles of St Trinian's *was also released. □ Significant novels were Kingsley Amis's* Lucky Jim *and J. R. R. Tolkien's* Lord of the Rings. □ *Popular songs included 'Oh, Mein Pa-Pa' by Eddie Calvert and Frank Sinatra's 'Three Coins in the Fountain'. □ The game of Scrabble was launched. □ And a new Morris Minor cost £439 10s 0d (£439.50).*

Many of the formats for the successful programmes of the eighties are loosely based on shows from the fifties. 'Jim'll Fix It', 'Surprise! Surprise!' and 'That's Life' all owe a considerable debt to by far the most popular new series of 1954, **'Ask Pickles'**. Beginning in May and presented by professional Yorkshireman Wilfred Pickles and his wife Mabel, it contained elements later to be seen in each of the aforementioned shows. 'Ask Pickles' made dreams come true, it reunited folk with long-lost relatives and it had talking dogs.

Formerly a builder, Pickles had entered radio broadcasting in 1931, and by reading the news during the war he helped boost national solidarity. Whereas the other newsreaders had regulation BBC Home Counties South accents, Pickles deliberately set out to comfort Northerners by wishing them 'Good neet, everybody'. Pickles loved sentimentality: the more people that burst into tears in the studio each week, the better the show. They cried when they were confronted with former classmates or workmates and they were completely overcome with emotion when faced with relations they thought (or perhaps hoped) they'd never see again. Viewers in their millions wept, too. The show topped the ratings for two years; everyone was having a bawl. Well, almost everyone. Cynics accused Pickles of being shamelessly sentimental, of exploiting suffering; and a Mrs Sybil Dickinson of Strood in Kent had an experience she would rather forget. She wrote to 'Ask Pickles', saying she would like to fondle a lion. She was expecting to stroke a tiny cub but instead came face to face with a half-grown ten-month-old monster which promptly snapped at the studio manager's legs, then savaged the sleeve of Mrs Dickinson's dress. Still, as long as she cried. . .

The year of 1954 was an important one for fans of soap opera with the arrival of the fifties equivalent of 'EastEnders', **'The Grove Family'**. Named after the BBC's Lime Grove studios, 'The Grove Family' was Britain's first soap for adults. The first twenty-minute story went out on Friday, 2 April at 7.50 p.m. and showed a lower-middle-class couple who'd worked hard to build a home for themselves and their family after the war and were just beginning to feel comfortably off after years of hardship.

By the end of the year, the Groves had built up a following of nearly 9 million people, a quarter of the population. It was second in popularity only to 'Ask Pickles'. Viewers of all ages wrote angry letters to the BBC about the atrociously ungrateful Gran; asked for estimates for building work from Bob Grove; advised Gladys about slimming, Jack about his girlfriends and Pat about her admirers. They held their breath when actress Ruth Dunning was rushed to hospital with appendicitis. The show even had royal patronage. On a visit to the studios, the Queen Mother declared herself a fan, calling the family 'so English, so real'.

Then suddenly in June 1957, the series was scrapped after a row between the BBC and the father and son

'The Grove Family': Dad, played by Edward Evans, was a jolly, although sometimes harassed, jobbing builder. Mum (Ruth Dunning) was a warm and forthright housewife. Their children were Lenny, bright but a fibber, played by twelve-year-old Christopher Beeny; Daphne, two years older, played by Margaret Downs; Pat, a twenty-year-old assistant librarian who turned actress Sheila Sweet into the country's dream girl-next-door; and Jack who was doing National Service. Grandma, played by Nancy Roberts, was always complaining: 'I'm starved for want of nourishment.'

writing team of Roland and Michael Pertwee. Exhausted from three years of writing, the Pertwees wanted a break and asked instead whether they could oversee the scripts of other writers. The BBC wouldn't agree to this, hired new writers but then axed the Groves altogether. Recently Michael Pertwee reflected: 'The people at the BBC then didn't have the foresight, the commercial sense, to see what the people making "Coronation Street" saw – that these series can go through quiet spells but they can survive and last and be important.' It was a sad end for the Groves. Edward Evans and Ruth Dunning never again achieved such stardom. Only Christopher Beeny prospered, as the accident-prone under-butler in 'Upstairs Downstairs' and the gormless nephew in the funeral-parlour comedy 'In Loving Memory'. All that remains of 'The Grove Family' is a short film. No copies of the series exist.

The British viewing public of 1954 had been largely raised on a diet of gentle parlour games, jolly comedics and afternoon programmes on flower-arranging, so anything likely to shock immediately led to that great television phenomenon: the jammed switchboard. Just a year after 'The Quatermass Experiment' had sent shivers down the backbone of Britain, the same author, Nigel Kneale,

adapted Orwell's classic '1984' for screening on Sunday, 12 December. And what an outcry it caused! Nearly a thousand irate callers besieged the BBC to complain, many of them further incensed by the fact that a horror programme was being shown on a Sunday – although this was then the BBC's regular night for drama. At that time the custom was to show a play live on the Sunday and then have a repeat performance on Thursday. There was a determined but vain attempt to have the repeat of '1984' cancelled, and four motions were tabled in Parliament accusing the Corporation of unnecessarily frightening the audience. Yet the piece received backing from an unlikely source: the royal family. Prince Philip is reported to have said: 'The Queen and I watched the play and thoroughly enjoyed it.'

The adaptation starred Peter Cushing as Winston Smith, supported by Yvonne Mitchell, André Morell and even Leonard Sachs from 'The Good Old Days'. It brought the phrase 'Big Brother is watching you' into everyday conversation. The producer was Rudolph Cartier, a master-craftsman and utter perfectionist. For the scene with the rats, he had insisted they use genuine sewer rats; but so many technical lights were needed in those days that when the creatures got into the studio they passed out from the heat, so the crew had to get whatever rats they could from the local pet shop. Unfortunately, the shop only had white ones, so these were made up to look brown!

Peter Cushing hoped Yvonne Mitchell's Big Brother was not watching this moment in '1984'.

It would take more than a few tanned rats to worry those intrepid travellers Armand and Michaela Denis, the first people to make wildlife films. This was the year they made their début on television with two programmes, **'Filming Wild Animals'** and **'Filming in Africa'**. In 1955 they switched to ITV for a series entitled 'Michaela and Armand Denis' before returning to the BBC for their hugely popular 'On Safari' in 1958.

Armand, an imposing Belgian, first joined forces with London-born Michaela when they were on separate expeditions in South America. Michaela recalls: 'It was 1948, and I was on a solo safari. In those days, women weren't allowed on expeditions – they were too much worry and trouble. The only way for a woman to get on one was to marry the leader. And, although that was certainly not my intention, that was exactly what happened. For a friend had said, "You must meet Armand Denis," and when I saw him my legs melted – it was love at first sight. He proposed in the Andes and we were married in Bolivia.' Their individual style of presentation (they spoke alternately), their wonderful accents (she was trilingual as a child and acquired her foreign dialect through conversation) and of course their marvellous photography turned Armand and Michaela into two of the best-loved characters on screen. Remember Armand's excitement at meeting 'our old friend the aardvark'?

Michaela's beautiful blonde hair turned her into a pinup. 'People were used to safari-goers looking rough but I changed all that. I insisted on looking glamorous. If I lived on a desert island, I would manage to find a pool to do my lips and discover some way of combing my hair! I think part of our appeal was that we came across as an ordinary couple on safari. I believe we started the boom in safaris and possibly even overseas holidays as a whole.'

Naturally, there were some hair-raising moments during filming, although few were caused directly by animals. 'We had feelings about animals,' says Michaela. 'We could tell when a creature didn't want to be photographed.' They had a lucky escape when they were filming sea-lions on a remote rocky island. 'Armand wanted to land on the island alone,' says Michaela,

but I insisted on joining him. I felt we had to face danger together. The landing was hazardous in the choppy seas and I was sick with fright, mainly because I am a poor swimmer. I vanished below the water at one point before Armand hauled me spluttering on to the rocks. Once there, we became so absorbed in filming the sea-lions at such close quarters that we did not notice the tide had turned and the sea was starting to submerge our rock. As we tried to scramble to safety, our clothes were ripped to shreds and our hands were bleeding. Then a giant wave swept me off my feet, but thankfully Armand dragged me back. There was no sign of our rescue boat. As night fell, our limbs grew numb with the cold. Then out of the darkness we finally heard the motor of the boat. It had broken down, which was why it was so late. We were safe – our twelve-hour ordeal on the rock was over.

The couple were once arrested in Bolivia. Michaela saved the day. 'I told the guards I knew Rita Hayworth, which was a lie. I had to promise them an autographed photo of her which I duly sent, signed by myself.'

David Attenborough also had an alarming experience during the filming of **'Zoo Quest'**, a series in which he filmed wild animals and brought them back for London Zoo.

We were in New Guinea marching into a valley which was largely unexplored, accompanied by nearly a hundred half-naked tribesmen with pierced noses, painted faces and spectacular head-dresses. Then the men stopped, refusing to go any further because they were entering the territory of another tribe who were 'badfolk too much; im i kai-kai man'. This was calmly translated to me as 'cannibals'.

Suddenly, with ear-splitting yells, a horde of men leaped out from behind boulders and rushed towards us, brandishing knives and axes. My only conscious thought was that I must urgently convince them we were friendly. I walked towards them, stretched out my hand and said loudly in what seemed like absurdly cultured tones: 'Good afternoon.' This had no effect, for they couldn't hear it above their own ferocious yells. Within seconds they were upon me. To my astonishment, several of them

Armand and Michaela Denis took viewers 'On Safari' and rescued, among other things, a baby spring hare.

seized my right hand and pumped it up and down. Others patted me violently on the shoulder. With enormous relief, I realised that what I had taken to be an all-out attack was no more than a standard show of strength – the usual welcome given to strangers. I had never been so frightened in my life. I thought my heart was going to knock a hole in my ribs.

One of David Attenborough's avowed intentions at the time was to avoid any type of celebrity status which would mean having to appear on the likes of **'What's My Line?'** Another person who must have wished he had steered clear of the game in 1954 was its temporary chairman, Australian Ron Randall. Over 1,200 letters in just two weeks complained about Ron's amorous behaviour. He blew a kiss to viewers at the end of one show, on another occasion he kissed a challenger and he even promised to kiss Barbara Kelly. Whatever next? The television critic of the *Daily Express* felt the kissing had to stop, adding: 'The BBC is bound to regard it as extremely unofficial and quite irregular.' Fortunately, Eamonn Andrews returned before the whole thing degenerated into an orgy.

If it is any consolation to poor Ron, he wasn't the only one to fall foul of the critics that year. An up-and-coming comedy duo, Morecambe and Wise, starred in their own series, **'Running Wild'**; but after the reviews they were running scared. One said: 'How do two commonplace performers such as these get elevated to the position of having a series built round them?' And a fellow-scribe denounced: 'How dare they put such mediocre talent on television!'

A comedy series that fared considerably better was **'Fast and Loose'** starring Bob Monkhouse and Denis Goodwin. Lasting forty-five minutes, instead of the usual half-hour, each show consisted of lengthy sketches. It has been hailed as the first programme to make situation comedy work as the sketches were long enough to allow the situations to develop through the characters. Bob Monkhouse had begun his writing career in 1943 when, as a fifteen-year old schoolboy, he sold a joke to Max Miller, then appearing at the Penge Emporium, for *2s 6d* (12½p). He went on to team up with Denis Goodwin, who had been at the same school as Bob although they were in different years and had never actually met there. 'Fast and Loose' was to have been called 'The Bob Monkhouse Show', but Goodwin was not too keen on that idea. Bob says: 'The programme was an absolute smash, the best reviews I've ever got.' But the pair needed time to recharge their batteries for a second run, so Bob faked a collapse at the end of the series. The papers carried pictures of him 'recovering', and he and Denis thus had the opportunity to prepare future material. 'I never told anybody that it was a fake,' confesses Bob.

Charlie Drake still bears the scars of 'Fast and Loose' to this day. Bob says:

On one show, I blew off half of Charlie's left ear. He was supposed to be a Russian spy, hiding in a cupboard, but as I fired a gun loaded with blanks it blew the packing out of the cylinder of the revolver. Charlie emerged gushing blood, his ear hanging off and his face peppered with gunpowder. This was all live and there was still a minute and a half to go on the sketch, which isn't long but is an age when you're bleeding. Bravely, Charlie carried on, keeping his right side to the audience – and still being funny. As we finished the sketch, he collapsed and the doctor mopped up the blood and stitched his ear. Incredibly, Charlie came back for the walkdown at the end, wearing a hat at a rakish angle to cover the wound!

Another sketch that went wrong involved a glass door that steadfastly refused to smash. Throughout the sketch, actor Alexander Gauge had been singing the praises of his lovely glass door. At the end, in a complicated piece of business, Bob's coat was supposed to get caught on a hat-stand and the stand shatter the lovely glass door. It called for immaculate timing and execution. Bob recalls:

It worked perfectly in rehearsals, and when we performed it live in the evening I did everything as planned. I propelled the stand towards the door, but it simply bounced off the glass. The audience, who had been waiting for the pay-off, howled – I've never heard such laughter. So I picked up this six-foot hat-stand and hammered it at the door like the man with the gong in the Rank films. Still it didn't break. Eventually, at the third attempt, to a huge cheer, the glass broke. As I came off, I said to Bill King, who was in charge of props, 'What on earth happened to that door?' 'I know,' he said, 'but when it smashed this afternoon I thought I'd better put in shatter-proof glass so it didn't break again. But you did hit it bloody hard, mate!' Bill was a marvellous man. He could build you anything but he never saw the point of the joke.

Television's great scoop of 1954 was achieved by the new series **'Sportsview'**. On 6 May their cameras covered a minor athletics meeting at Oxford and captured Roger Bannister becoming the first man to run a mile in under four minutes. For years the programme was a mid-week must for sports enthusiasts, coming up with all sorts of gimmick to bring the action right into your living-room. They mounted cameras everywhere – on a sports-car at Le Mans, on a motor-cycle at the Isle of Man TT races, and on a bobsleigh at the Cresta Run. It was also in 1954 that the BBC began its Sports Personality of the Year Award, the first winner being athlete Chris Chataway.

It was also a significant year for news and weather broadcasts. At 7.30 p.m. on 5 July, **'Television News and Newsreel'** brought Britain's first daily television news service. It was introduced by Richard Baker, who was heard but not seen, the BBC fearing that if

The anchorman on 'Sportsview' was former RAF pilot, horse-racing commentator and a key figure in BBC's coronation coverage Peter Dimmock – seen here with Donald Campbell.

"Television's girl of '48",' says Eileen, 'and the response to my first show was staggering. The BBC had to draft in extra staff to send the viewers my sheet drawings which showed pin figures doing the exercises.'

Finally, we must not forget a programme called '**All Your Own**' which gave children an opportunity to display their own individual talents. Introduced by Huw Wheldon, later to become BBC Director of Television, and frequently produced by Cliff Michelmore, 'All Your Own' guided a young guitarist by the name of John Williams on his first step to stardom. And it did the same for the King Brothers, a popular middle-of-the-road group of the sixties. One guest who did not, however, enjoy a fruitful – or, indeed, lengthy – career was a pet mouse brought along by a schoolboy in company with the lad's other pet, an eagle. While Wheldon was enthusing about how amazing it was that in the wild the mouse would be the eagle's natural prey yet in captivity they were the best of friends, the eagle let his instincts get the better of him and suddenly swooped from his studio perch and ate the mouse. Ah, well, that's showbusiness.

newsreaders were in vision their personalities would affect the impartiality of the news. Instead Baker's voice was heard over a view of Nelson's Column. The first weather chart had been shown as far back as 1936, but it was on 11 January 1954 that the first professional meteorologist presented the weather forecast. His name was George Cowling.

Someone who was soon to become one of the most famous faces on television was forty-eight-year-old **Eileen Fowler**, queen of the tummy-tighteners. After her first keep-fit programme in 1954, the BBC was swamped with no fewer than 10,000 letters as women tried to work off the extra food they were able to eat following the end of rationing. 'The *Radio Times* called me

Also Shown in 1954

Other shows of the year included '**Amos 'n' Andy**', an early American comedy import; '**Fabian of the Yard**' which featured Patrick Barr in semi-fictional re-creations of famous police cases; '**Top Town**', a relatively sane predecessor of 'It's a Knockout'; and '**War in the Air**', a fifteen-part series on the history of air power.

The most original children's programme was Michael Bentine's '**The Bumblies**': these creatures came from the planet Bumble and resembled large pears. From America came the juvenile Western '**The Cisco Kid**', starring Duncan Renaldo with Leo Carillo as Pancho.

1955

That Was the Year When...

September saw the start of Independent Television – but only in the London area. □ Churchill resigned, and Sir Anthony Eden became Prime Minister. □ Russia and other Eastern European countries signed the Warsaw Pact. □ Ruth Ellis was executed. □ Albert Einstein died. □ 'Archers' fans mourned the death of Grace Archer in a fire. □ Luncheon vouchers were introduced. □ The first Wimpy Bar was opened at Lyons Corner House, London. □ Fish fingers were created. □ Ruby Murray had five hits in the Top Twenty at the same time. □ Slim Whitman spent eleven weeks at number one with 'Rose Marie'. □ Mary Quant opened Bazaar, the country's first boutique, in King's Road, Chelsea. □ And the film Rebel without a Cause was released two weeks after the death in a car crash of its young hero, James Dean. A legend was born.

On 22 September 1955 – ITV began. The brash new station which would soon steal nearly 70 per cent of viewers ensured that Aunty's life was never the same again. Whereas the BBC presented nice quiet panel games, ITV – dismissed by Churchill as 'this tuppenny Punch and Judy Show' even before it had started – burst forth with boisterous quizzes like 'Double Your Money' and 'Take Your Pick', the first British game shows to give cash prizes. And ITV had commercials – something which, to this day, the BBC finds abhorrent.

Before switching to the brave new world of ITV, let us look at a couple of BBC programmes which began in 1955 and have justifiably secured a place in television history. One was 'This Is Your Life' and the other a show that was the very epitome of all that the BBC stood for, **'Dixon of Dock Green'**.

The character of Dixon, played by Jack Warner, first appeared in the 1950 film *The Blue Lamp*, and he was shot dead after a mere twenty-one minutes by Dirk Bogarde. Five years later, on 7 July 1955, Ted Willis revived him and created a series that was to span twenty-one years and 367 episodes, always opening with Dixon's matey greeting, 'Evenin' all'. It was the first television programme to be based on a film. After being commissioned to write the initial six-part series, Willis was worried. 'I didn't know how I'd be able to find six good stories,' he said. But eventually he had 250 policemen on his payroll who fed incidents and true stories to him for the scripts. Dixon was based on a real policeman once stationed at Leman Street in the East End of London. Dixon reflected the public's image of the police at the time: he was the friendly local bobby with a kind word for everyone. There was very little serious crime in Dock Green and therefore precious little action as we know it today. It would have been inappropriate for old George to Rugby-tackle a suspect, spreadeagle him against the wall and bellow 'You're nicked' just for riding a bicycle without a rear light.

George Dixon started off as a constable before being promoted to sergeant. Detective Andy Crawford, played by Peter Byrne, was Dixon's son-in-law, being married to his daughter Mary, which allowed for cosy family scenes away from the station. Then there was Geoffrey Adams as PC Lauderdale (known to all as 'Laudy') and Arthur Rigby as Desk Sergeant Flint. Apparently, Rigby used to write his lines on the desk sergeant's blotting-pad. Jack had the perfect copper's walk – like a penguin's – thanks to a back injury sustained while playing a train driver earlier in his career. He made sure other details were authentic too – a policeman was not supposed to remove his helmet when entering a house but he should take it off when asking an old lady about her dog licence. And the helmet had to be held under the arm when addressing a bishop! Jack Warner died in 1981 at the age of eighty-five. At his funeral was a wreath in the shape of a blue lamp, and the show's theme tune, 'An Ordinary Copper', was played over the public-address system. The coffin-bearers were from the Metro-

Jack Warner, here as Dixon of Directory Enquiries.

politan Police, a tribute to the enormous affection in which Jack Warner and George Dixon were, and are still, held.

The same month of July 1955 that Dixon started pounding the beat, Eamonn Andrews and **'This is Your Life'** also began. The show ran on the BBC until 1964 and then, after a five-year rest, re-emerged on ITV where it has stayed ever since. When Eamonn died in 1987, Michael Aspel took over in the following year.

The meticulously secret planning for the first programme failed miserably when the *Daily Sketch* revealed in advance that footballer Stanley Matthews was to be the victim. So they had to find a last-minute substitute. Eamonn was led to believe that it would be boxer Freddie Mills, but the tables were turned on the show itself and Eamonn was the subject. Wilfred Pickles would have been proud of him as he burst into tears when his mother Margaret was brought on. Eamonn said afterwards: 'I had no idea that my mother was anywhere but miles away in Ireland. When I saw her, it just brought tears to my eyes.'

Over the years, Eamonn, his perspiration and his big red book underwent a number of disguises to trap the unwary. He dressed as an airline steward to catch Shirley Bassey; as a wine waiter for David Frost; as a petrol-pump attendant for John Alderton; as Hudson from 'Upstairs Downstairs' for Alderton's wife Pauline Collins; as an astronaut for Patrick Moore; as a Scottish soldier for Andy Stewart; and he was tied up in a sack to surprise David

Nixon. More famous than the successes are the two that got away. As Eamonn proclaimed the immortal words 'Tonight, Danny Blanchflower, This Is Your Life,' the Spurs footballer calmly replied, 'Oh, no, it's not,' and refused to have anything to do with the show. The other refusal came from Richard Gordon, author of the 'Doctor' books. And not everyone approved of the methods used for luring the victims to the chosen venue. The Reverend Brian Hesslon from Bournemouth had survived an operation for cancer after being told he had only a few hours to live. It was thought he would make a suitably moving subject, but he complained at being 'tricked' into appearing on the programme. In a letter to parishioners, he wrote: 'To those who wondered why I looked surprised or annoyed, I would say that I had been tricked, deceived and dragged there, imagining I was going to do a serious radio recording about cancer.'

The vast majority of early fifties comedians had transferred their talents to television following successful radio shows – people like Arthur Askey, Bob Monkhouse and Charlie Chester; but the year saw the emergence of the first comic to be purely a product of television. He made an immediate impact then and he is still as popular now. His name is Benny Hill. **'The Benny Hill Show'** is a British institution like the naughty seaside postcard, but his humour has become international, encompassing over a hundred countries with such diverse tastes as America, Norway, Australia, Yugoslavia, France and Greece. Even the Russians tune in by pointing their aerials towards Finland, and in Beirut the shooting stops on both sides when Benny is on television.

The nation soon warmed to Benny's cheeky cherubic grin which over the years has enabled him to get away with material that in other hands would have been considered offensive. He was always at his best sending up television itself, particularly commercials for soap powder and washing-up liquid. Not everyone saw the funny side. Television chef Philip Harben once walked out on the show after reading the script. He complained at the time: 'They submitted a sketch to me which I considered degrading. It seemed devised to make me appear professionally incompetent. I was supposed to be half-tight and the whole thing indicated that I couldn't cook. That's no joke to me.'

Even in the fifties, Benny used to buy sixty wigs a year to enable him to impersonate stars of the day like Shirley Abicair, Isobel Barnett and Diana Dors. Besides Benny's own female creations, a feature of his shows has always been the presence of numerous skimpily clad girls, the most notable collection being Hill's Angels. His stooges have stayed with him for years – men such as Jack Wright, Bob Todd and Henry McGee. There are certainly few surprises in a 'Benny Hill Show'. You know it's going to be the same diet of innuendo – they don't call him 'King Leer' for nothing – but by rationing his appearances to just a few per year Benny has managed to stay at the top while others have fallen by the wayside. And even his critics had to stand up and take notice when in 1979, at the age of fifty-four, he suddenly conquered America. His fame in the States is such that a 1988 survey of Florida schoolchildren revealed that, although many of them did not know London was our capital, they all associated one person with Britain: Benny Hill. A riot broke out in a California gaol when prisoners were prevented from watching his show, and a Mafia boss only agreed to do a documentary interview with Thames Television on condition that they got Benny to do a stint at the mobster's Las Vegas casino.

There were 4½ million television-licence holders in 1955, and 95 per cent of the population could receive television; but only 12½ per cent could get the new ITV channel – and they all lived around the capital. In that first ITV week at the end of September, lucky old London was able to witness two of the most popular yet nauseating game shows ever: **'Take Your Pick'** and 'Double Your Money'.

'Take Your Pick' was the lesser of the two evils, if only because it didn't feature Hughie Green. The host of 'Take Your Pick' was 'your quiz inquisitor' Michael Miles, an amiable New Zealander who was originally only taken on as a late-night announcer in his native country after he had pestered the station every day for six weeks. He graduated to Radio Luxembourg where 'Take Your Pick' was heard for three years before the switch to television. Miles masterminded the show, hiring a staff of six and earning £20,000 a year for it. An 'open secret' in showbusiness was that he drank heavily. In fact he was an epileptic who would lock himself in his dressing room, ashamed of his condition, preferring to be thought drunk.

The contestants were chosen from the studio audience just minutes before the show. Miles described the scene thus: 'When the audience is seated, I ask for volunteers to stand up, and from the response you'd think we had played the National Anthem.' The poor unfortunates then had to face the infamous yes no interlude, where Alec Dane would be poised with his gong, before going on to the serious business of winning prizes. These were announced by booming Bob Danvers-Walker, accompanied by a quick burst from Harold Smart on the organ. There were always three booby prizes like a prune or, worse still, a ticket for next week's show. And there was the mysterious Box 13, the contents of which were unknown even to Miles, the treasure-chest of money and 'tonight's star prize', which was greeted with a crescendo of oohs from the audience as if they'd never seen a three-piece suite before. Miles would offer cash to induce the contestant to part with the key to his particular box (in which details of the prize were hidden), whipping the throng into a frenzy with that emotive plea: 'What shall he do – open the box or take the money?' The sensible prizes were of a high standard. One of the best was asking two competitors to meet on Sydney

'Take Your Pick' brought you Quiz Inquisitor Michael Miles (*right*), gongsman Alec Dane (*left*) and prizes-announcer Bob Danvers-Walker.

Harbour Bridge, having flown in opposite directions around the world, and then to collect a sum of money placed in a joint account at a Sydney bank.

As if aware that there was only so much excitement a nation could take, ITV dropped 'Take Your Pick' in 1968. Miles returned with 'Wheel of Fortune' but died in 1971. Shortly before his death, he calculated that he had given away £500,000 in prizes.

Presented by Canadian ex-pilot Hughie Green, **'Double Your Money'** also took off from Radio Luxembourg. The quiz itself was quite passable but was marred by Green's showmanship which frequently reduced it to little more than a farce. His speciality was the most contrived of gags, usually with his female assistant as a willing foil and invariably accompanied by a pained grimace into the camera. There was a place for a gag on the show – over Hughie's mouth.

The hostesses on 'Double Your Money' were certainly a mixed crew. In 1957 there was leggy eighteen-year-old Valerie Drew, and three years later came a girl by the name of Jean Clarke who was famous for wiggling her bottom. When asked why she did it, she replied profoundly: 'I just can't help it.' She was succeeded by seventy-seven-year-old charlady Alice Earrey, who was brought back by popular demand after winning £4 as a contestant

Commercial Break

With the birth of ITV came commercials, or 'natural breaks' as they were then known. The very first commercial was transmitted on 22 September at 8.12 p.m. and was for Gibbs SR toothpaste. Viewers saw a tube of toothpaste embedded in a block of ice, a lady by the name of Meg Smith brushing her teeth 'up and down and round the gums' and heard BBC presenter Alex Mackintosh declare in immaculate BBC tones: 'It's tingling fresh. It's fresh as ice. It's Gibbs SR toothpaste.' It was chosen to be first by drawing lots with the other twenty-three opening-night offerings which included Guinness, Surf, National Benzole, Brown & Polson custard, Lux, Summer County margarine, Batchelor's peas and Brillo. But probably the best commercial of 1955 was John Halas and Joy Batchelor's animated promotion of Murraymints where the Murraymints characters were Guardsmen in bearskins.

famous revolve at the end. The revolve caused a few problems as well. Judy Garland was too emotionally upset to go on it, and in the sixties the Rolling Stones refused because it wouldn't fit their rebellious image. Another feature in the latter years was Italian puppet mouse Topo Gigio, who frequently upstaged the stars. In all the Palladium show ran for twelve years. In addition to Tommy Trinder and Hughie Green, other compères were Dickie Henderson, Bob Monkhouse, Alfred Marks, Robert Morley, Bruce Forsyth, Don Arrol, Arthur Haynes, Norman Vaughan, Des O'Connor, Roger Moore and Jimmy Tarbuck. The best-known was Bruce Forsyth, who took over in 1958. His handling of Beat the Clock was brilliant and his catchphrase, 'I'm in charge', was the first of many he has used throughout his career.

There were numerous odd occurrences: Frankie Howerd sparked off protests by walking on stage with a Union Jack carried upside-down; Norman Vaughan dropped a rifle and nearly broke his toe; the orchestra once played the closing tune covered in straw after a Jewel and Warriss sketch got out of hand; and Harry Secombe fell through a trapdoor. Jimmy Tarbuck made his début in 1963 as an unknown twenty-three-year-old comic. 'I was meant to go on for six minutes and carried on for nine, but I was just a boy and had no idea.' As a result, Xavier Cugat

on the show answering questions on cookery. Another former contestant to become a hostess was the elfin Monica Rose. This cheeky cockney won £8 on famous women in 1964, and created such an impression that Hughie made her a permanent fixture. Probably the most famous contestant was young footballer Bobby Charlton, who won £1,000 on pop music although he flouted the rules by refusing to go in the soundproof glass box to answer the jackpot question.

When the show was axed along with its partner in crime 'Take Your Pick' in 1968, Hughie was characteristically bitter: 'For thirteen years we have been consistently in the Top Ten. My only crime, apparently, is I have been popular for a long time. They say they want more culture and that "Double Your Money" is too trivial. But do people really want more culture? I very much doubt it.'

That they didn't was evidenced by the fact that Hughie soon bounced back with the equally banal 'The Sky's the Limit' as well as continuing with 'Opportunity Knocks'.

Hughie Green was also temporarily associated with that classic variety show **'Sunday Night at the London Palladium'**. He certainly made an impact, because just as he was about to introduce Gracie Fields the scenery fell on his head!

Launched by Val Parnell, the first Palladium show was presented by Tommy Trinder and starred Gracie Fields. Regular ingredients were the high-kicking Tiller Girls at the start, the game Beat the Clock in the middle and the

The incomparable Fanny and Johnny Cradock – Bon Viveur husband and wife cookery team of 'Kitchen Magic' on BBC and 'Fanny's Kitchen' on ITV. Fanny always came across as a domineering woman who ruled her kitchen with a rolling-pin of iron. The monocled Johnny was somewhat jollier. The pair were often hilariously sent up by Benny Hill and Bob Todd, the latter portraying Johnny as one who had over-indulged with the cooking sherry.

and his band, who topped the bill with singer Abbe Lane, had to cut their act to make time for him. Two years later, Tarbuck was Palladium compère. He once completely forgot Petula Clark's name and introduced her as 'someone who needs no introduction'.

The show was reincarnated in 1973 with Jim Dale as host, yet it only lasted one short series; but in its day it was quite simply the best of its kind.

Youngsters of 1955 saw the creation of one of the most celebrated children's programmes of all time: the BBC's **'Crackerjack'**. It had everything: corny jokes, the coveted 'Crackerjack' (yes, 'Crackerjack') pencils, the pop songs of the day and Double or Drop, a game where kids' arms were piled high with prizes if they answered questions correctly or with cabbages if they got them wrong. And it was a disaster if they dropped anything.

It was also a show that had the royal seal of approval as Leslie Crowther discovered. 'After one show, we were told that the Queen had been to see us. Apparently, she wanted to see "Crackerjack" because her children, Charles and Anne, liked it and she watched it whenever

---

Robin Hood (Richard Greene) did battle with evil Patrick Cargill, while the lily-livered Sheriff of Nottingham (Alan Wheatley) cowered again.

---

she could.' Crowther's own family of five children were fans of the show, too.

> *It was handy having a big family because the children sometimes came up with comedy ideas. One of the great things about 'Crackerjack' was that we never played down to the audience just because they were young. We tried to appeal to an audience of all ages. What a lot of people forget is the sheer volume of pop stars of the day who, in the sixties, used to regard 'Crackerjack' as second only in terms of exposure to 'Top of the Pops'. I introduced countless big names: Roy Orbison; Cliff Richard; Dave Dee, Dozy, Beaky, Mick and Tich. And Tom Jones made his second-ever TV appearance on 'Crackerjack'.*

Leslie Crowther was involved with the show for eight years from 1960, first as comic then as compère. Other hosts have included Eamonn Andrews, Michael Aspel, Ed Stewart and Stu Francis, while among the comedians have been Rod McLennan, Don MacLean, Little and Large and the daddy of them all, Peter Glaze.

The year 1955 also marked the beginning of **'The Adventures of Robin Hood'**, a series made for the American market and one of Lew Grade's first big moneyspinners. Richard Greene played the title rôle and it lasted for 143 episodes after which Greene lived in

Also Shown in 1955

That doyen of the dahlia, Percy Thrower, set off down the path for a twelve-year run of **'Gardening Club'**, and Peter Scott introduced a new wildlife series called **'Look'**. **'The Burns and Allen Show'** continued the stage partnership of American comedian George Burns and his wife Gracie Allen that had been going for nigh on thirty years; **'Is This Your Problem?'** was television's first agony column; John Robinson starred as the Professor in **'Quatermass II'**; and Derek Roy presented **'People Are Funny'**, an embryonic 'Game for a Laugh'.

On a loftier plane there was the conversion from radio of **'The Brains Trust'**; but there was also **'I Love Lucy'**, an excuse for Lucille Ball to screech incessantly, and **Liberace** whose teeth shone as brightly as his jackets. The forerunner of endless disabled cops was **'Colonel March of Scotland Yard'** played by Boris Karloff, who would have been no match for Sergeant Joe Friday, tough laconic hero of **'Dragnet'**.

One of the first adult Westerns to come to Britain was **'Gun Law'** starring six-foot-six-inch sixteen-stone James Arness as Marshal Matt Dillon of Dodge City; Marius Goring was that master of disguise **'The Scarlet Pimpernel'**; **'Douglas Fairbanks Junior Presents'** was a series of over 120 half-hour plays produced by and occasionally starring the American actor; boxing promoter Jack Solomons introduced big-fight action from **'Jack Solomons' Scrapbook'**; Lord Boothby, Michael Foot, A. J. P. Taylor and W. J. Brown teamed up for the political debate **'Free Speech'**; and ITV unveiled its first daily serial, **'Sixpenny Corner'**, a fifteen-minute drama shown on weekday mornings.

Among other children's series for the year were Charlie Drake and Jack Edwardes in **'Mick and Montmorency'**, **'The Adventures of Noddy'** and three Westerns: **'Hopalong Cassidy'** starring fifty-seven-year-old William Boyd, **'Roy Rogers and Trigger'**, and **'The Range Rider'** with Jock Mahoney and Dick Jones as the 'all-American boy'. And for younger children there was **'Picture Book'** and the advent of that remarkable family **'The Woodentops'**, complete with Spotty Dog.

semi-retirement. He was ably supported in the show by Alexander Gauge as Friar Tuck, first Bernadette O'Farrell then Patricia Driscoll as Maid Marian, Archie Duncan as Little John, Paul Eddington as Will Scarlet and Alan Wheatley as the evil Sheriff of Nottingham. In fact the Sheriff was so detested that poor Alan Wheatley used to find his car scratched! Archie Duncan was also a hero in real life – he received a gallantry award after dragging a boy out of the path of a stampeding horse.

Perhaps the real star was a twenty-foot hollow tree-trunk on wheels which, because of its mobility, played most of Sherwood Forest. Much of the series was shot in the studio, but with careful camera angles that one tree gave a reasonably effective impression of a forest. To keep it company, the producers later built another tree. It gave a whole new meaning to wooden acting.

1956

President Nasser seized the Suez Canal; and Britain's Prime Minister, Sir Anthony Eden, ordered an invasion of Egypt. □ *John Osborne's* Look Back in Anger *opened at London's Royal Court Theatre.* □ *England's Jim Laker set a world record of nineteen wickets in a Test match.* □ *Steeplechaser Chris Brasher, swimmer Judy Grinham and boxers Terry Spinks and Dick McTaggart struck gold for Britain at the Melbourne Olympics.* □ *The new high-street trend was for self-service shops – fifty opened each month.* □ *The first yellow no-parking lines were painted, in Slough.* □ *Premium bonds went on sale.* □ *ITV spread to the Midlands and the North.* □ *A new Ford Zephyr cost around £900.* □ *There were 300,000 people out of work in Britain – but there were ten vacancies for each of them.* □ *And American-style rock 'n' roll hit Europe with numbers like 'Rock around the Clock' by Bill Haley and 'Hound Dog' by Elvis Presley.*

Just as rock 'n' roll was to change the whole course of popular music, a television announcement of 1956 was to alter viewing habits for the next five years and have a profound effect to this very day. It was short and to the point. It went: 'BBC Television presents Tony Hancock in . . . **"Hancock's Half-Hour".**'

Transferring from radio where it had started two years earlier, 'Hancock's Half-Hour' swiftly established Tony Hancock as Britain's top comic. The show became a way of life for over 10 million people. Fish-and-chip shops complained to the BBC that they had no customers for thirty minutes every Friday night when the show was on. Of course, much of the subsequent fascination with Hancock lies not only in his unsurpassed skills as a comic actor but also in a complex personality which resulted in his 1968 suicide in an Australian hotel at the age of forty-four. Hancock was one of the few showbusiness talents genuinely to warrant the description 'genius', although he owed much to his sparring partner Sidney James and even more to the writers Ray Galton and Alan Simpson.

Set at the immortal address of 23 Railway Cuttings, East Cheam, the television series saw Anthony Aloysius Hancock constantly dreaming of rising above his humble station, only to be deflated by his pal Sid. Many episodes were classics: 'Twelve Angry Men' where he berates his fellow-jurors, 'Does Magna Carta mean nothing to you? Did she die in vain?'; 'The Missing Page' when Hancock reaches the final page of a thriller, *Lady Don't Fall Backwards*, only to find that it has been vandalised; 'The Radio Ham' ('Yes, I know it's raining in Tokyo'); probably the best-known of all, 'The Blood Donor'; and 'The Bowmans', a wonderful send-up of 'The Archers' with Peter Glaze as the family dog.

By 1960, Hancock had become irritated at being thought of as just one half of a double act with Sid James and he also wanted to branch out into films. So he and Sid went their separate ways. It is a common myth that Hancock's career went downhill from the moment of parting, but 'The Radio Ham', 'The Blood Donor' and 'The Bowmans' were all made after Sid's exit – by which time, incidentally, the title had been shortened to just 'Hancock'. 'The Blood Donor' is remarkable in that Hancock was able to give a superb performance without knowing any of his lines. He had been involved in a car crash and hadn't had time to learn the script, and so idiot cards were strategically placed all over the set. Ray Galton once said: 'If you look at "The Blood Donor", you'll see Hancock's not looking at June Whitfield or anyone else – he's looking over their shoulder and he's reading it all. And he thought "This is marvellous, isn't it? Why have I been flogging my guts out for the last ten years learning scripts when I can do it this way?" So he continued like that.'

After seven series with the BBC, Hancock went to ITV

(although he had previously made **'The Tony Hancock Show'** for ITV in 1956). No longer bothering to learn his lines, his work deteriorated steadily as he sadly missed the sharp scripts of Galton and Simpson who had gone on to write 'Steptoe and Son'. Hancock finished a broken man; but, thanks to repeats, his genius remains intact.

It is comforting to know that there is still a place on television for amateurs (witness 'Santa Barbara'), and the show that put more mediocrity on screen than any other over the years was **'Opportunity Knocks'**. Between 1956 and 1977, it produced acts of the calibre of Bobby Crush, Bonnie Langford, Peters and Lee, the singing miners Millican and Nesbitt, Neil Reid and Lena Zavaroni. Out of the thousands of acts auditioned, only a handful have proved bearable – like Les Dawson, Freddie Star, Frank Carson, Ken Goodwin, Little and Large, Freddie Davies and Mary Hopkin. Nevertheless, 'Opportunity Knocks' fulfilled a vital rôle in bringing new artists to television. It was extremely worthy and was even worthier if you didn't have to watch it.

Recently revived in a more palatable form with Bob Monkhouse, 'Op Knocks' used to be a showcase for the indefatigable Hughie Green, who meant everything 'most sincerely, friends'. One of the first contestants was buxom Gladys Brocklehurst, a Lancashire cotton-mill girl who, while singing her number, used to grab husband Norman by the hair and slap him. When asked about her unusual act, mad Glad replied: 'We do this for the fun of it.' Barbara Castle's cook and housekeeper, sixty-three-year-old Mildred Bracey, combined playing the piano with a voice that would have frightened King Kong. She was known as 'Bristol's phenomenal lady tenor'. 'We wanna hear it for her,' said Hughie in his introduction. Fortunately, the public neither wanted to hear it or her again. Su Pollard was beaten by a singing dog, and after winning at the age of six Bonnie Langford was unable to appear for the second week as she had to appear in concert at her mother's dancing school. One that didn't pass the show's auditions was a singer called Gerry Dorsey (he later changed his name to Engelbert Humperdinck), but there was never any doubt in Hughie's mind about the ability of one particular comic. Hughie recalled: 'A man came to me one day and said, "I promised my missus that if I didn't get on your show and pass your audition, I'd quit trying to get places in showbusiness. Can I have a try?" He changed into the lousiest dress suit I've ever seen, sat at the piano and made me and the rest of the auditioners fall about laughing. His name? Les Dawson.'

Whatever its faults, 'Opportunity Knocks' was not a cruel show and genuinely cared for the acts – a point illustrated by the story of James Conaghan, an Irishman who played the ivy leaf by placing it between his fingers and blowing it. When he flew over for the show, his leaves shrivelled up under the studio lights (it was probably nerves), rendering them musically useless. He rushed off

Commercial Break

If mum's idea of heaven was a leisurely cup of tea, she wouldn't have fancied sharing it with the outrageous Brooke Bond chimps who first appeared that year to promote PG Tips. The chimps have since become television legends, and the famous commercial with removal men grappling with a piano has been screened over a thousand times. More than forty personalities have provided the voices, among them Stanley Baxter, Bruce Forsyth, Irene Handl, Bob Monkhouse and Kenneth Williams. The very first chimp commercial was set in an elegant country house and showed an immaculately dressed 'boy' and 'girl' sitting at a Regency table and drinking tea from a silver service in dainty china cups. The voiceover came from Peter Sellers, who was paid £100 for his work.

Also in 1956, Sooty promoted Oxo and we were told 'Don't say brown, say Hovis'. One of the most whistled jingles was 'You'll wonder where the yellow went when you brush your teeth with Pepsodent'. Where did Pepsodent go?

to a Manchester park but found that he couldn't get a note out of English ivy leaves. Not to be denied this feast of entertainment, Hughie Green arranged for a dozen Irish ivy leaves to be flown in specially from Dublin, and James was able to enjoy his fleeting moment of fame. And that, friends, was what 'Opportunity Knocks' was all about.

'Opportunity Knocks' turned into one of ITV's most successful programmes and among the other popular new series they launched that year were two major game shows, **'The 64,000 Question'** and 'Spot the Tune'. In America the former was known as 'The 64,000 Dollar Question', but in Britain the figure represented sixpence instead of dollars so initially the top prize was £1,600, although this was soon doubled. The principal compère was Jerry Desmonde (Robin Bailey also had a stint), who had previously been a stooge to Arthur Askey. But Desmonde treated this rôle very seriously, to such an extent that critics dubbed him 'the Hanging Judge' or 'a character out of "Dragnet"'. To ensure fair play, the questions were kept in a safe and guarded by retired Detective Superintendent Robert Fabian. There were some interesting contestants. Kenneth Tynan answered questions on jazz, and sixty-eight-year-old Lady Cynthia Asquith, daughter-in-law of Lord Asquith, the Prime Minister at the outbreak of the First World War, chose as her subject the novels of Jane Austen. By the time she reached the jackpot round, she had read each book six times. The producers once narrowly escaped total humiliation when a little old lady hatched a plot to make the nation blush. She was appearing on an all-champions programme against a young housewife and was so sure of winning that she offered the housewife £1,000 to take all her clothes off when the lights were dimmed for the tense finale. So when the lights came back up, the girl would be standing there stark naked. Apparently, the old lady thought it would be a huge joke, but after careful deliberation the housewife rejected the offer. She lost not only her chance of notoriety but the quiz as well, for the little old lady duly went on to win.

'Spot the Tune' had a moment of high drama, too, concerning a lady by the name of Norma Longbottom who was going for the £600 jackpot. Host Ken Platt wasn't sure whether she had given the correct tune-title within the time-limit. He appealed to the floor manager, who in turn consulted the director. In the end they decided that an answer would be given after the director had heard a recording of the show. Switchboards were jammed as viewers waited anxiously for the outcome while the production team sat round a tape-recorder. Eventually, they agreed that Norma had won. The nation rejoiced. The show, a forerunner of 'Name That Tune', ran for 209 editions, other compères including Jackie Rae and Ted Ray. The resident singer was Marion Ryan, mother of sixties pop stars Paul and Barry Ryan. Marion always looked glamorous and for the 1958 season had no fewer than a hundred dresses on order, ranging in price from 325 guineas (£341.25) to £7 10s (£7.50). She predicted, 'I'll defy most people to tell which are the cheap ones and which are the expensive' – in which case somebody somewhere wasted a lot of money.

The leading showman of the time was the rotund fifty-six-year-old Billy Cotton, and the lively **'Billy Cotton Bandshow'** became a Saturday-evening favourite for many years. Beginning with his familiar bellow of 'Wakey wakey' and dashing through the signature tune 'Somebody Stole My Girl', the show continued at a relentless pace dictated by the effervescent Cotton. Billy Cotton began his career as a drummer boy in the First World War and he became a band leader in the twenties. His sporting prowess encompassed boxing, playing centre forward for Brentford and motor racing. In fact he bought Sir Malcolm Campbell's first Bluebird. The same energy that he displayed at sport he used in showbusiness. He loved clowning around on his show, and despite his seventeen-stone frame was not averse to rolling up his trousers and dancing a hornpipe or even doing a cartwheel. A critic on the *Financial Times* described him as having a centre of gravity somewhere near his knees.

The show's relatively small budget meant that it couldn't hope to compete with 'Sunday Night at the London Palladium' but it still managed to attract performers like Tom Jones, Cliff Richard, Ted Rogers, Alma Cogan, Terry Scott and Hugh Lloyd. And Cotton was regularly assisted by pinup pianist Russ Conway, Kathie Kay and Alan Breeze. Conway collapsed on stage in 1962, reportedly suffering from a breakdown, and there was more drama

---

Wakey, way-kee! No need to turn up the volume for Billy Cotton.

two years later when a special-effects piano exploded injuring a technician and three girl extras. Then, in 1966, Alan Breeze was sensationally sacked by the producer, Bill Cotton, Jnr, Billy's son, after thirty-four years with the band. We remember Breeze for such cultured contributions as 'I Can't Do My Bally Bottom Button Up', a song about trouser-flies. Billy Cotton died in 1969, and there has never been anyone quite like him since.

Although Hancock stole the comedy honours for 1956, the nation's funny bone was tickled by a whole host of new shows, notably **'Whack-O'**, starring the late Jimmy Edwards. Written by Frank Muir and Denis Norden, who also scripted Edwards's long-running radio series 'Take It from Here', 'Whack-O' was set at Chiselbury School with Edwards as the demon headmaster. Edwards was a wartime fighter pilot and won the Distinguished Flying Cross after being badly burned when his Dakota was shot down over Arnhem. His injuries were such that half of his face had to be rebuilt, hence his famous handlebar moustache. He was nicknamed 'Professor' because of his Cambridge MA and positively revelled in the rôle of headmaster. 'It's no effort for me to play this frightful character,' he said, 'no effort at all.' His assistant at Chiselbury was the limp science master Oliver Pettigrew, who used to be forced to double up as boxing instructor, model for the art class, relief boilerman and left-hand goal-post in inter-house soccer matches. For his pains, he was paid the princely sum of £3 a week. He was played by Arthur Howard, brother of film star Leslie Howard, and Arthur received similar treatment to Mr Pettigrew when Leslie made *The Scarlet Pimpernel*. The film included a tough violent mob scene, and the producers refused to allow Leslie to fight his way through the brawling crowds in case he was injured. So poor Arthur had to stand in for him. It clearly didn't matter if *he* was maimed!

December 31st heralded the arrival of British television's first pop-music programme, **'Cool for Cats'**. Introduced by Kent Walton, later famed for his wrestling commentaries, 'Cool for Cats' showed dancers performing to popular records of the day. And there was definitely no grunt and groan from the likes of Rosemary Clooney. The programme budget was only £200 per show, so the dance routines were staged all over London's Television House, home of Associated Rediffusion, in the foyer, along corridors and up staircases. At first, only five shows were made, but it soon became so popular that it was screened three times a week. Not everybody approved – a group calling themselves 'serious music lovers' sent Kent Walton a card bearing the highly original message: 'Drop dead, please.'

Still on a musical note, you can always guarantee the quality of the **'Eurovision Song Contest'** – there isn't any. It was back in 1956 that some bright spark came up with the idea for this epic which was won, in its inaugural year, by Switzerland with 'Refrains'. It was an appropriate

William Russell as Sir Lancelot in the natty headgear that won the hearts of Camelot's ladies. (Was it a washing-up glove inside out?)

title as the United Kingdom (or Royaume-Uni as we are known once a year) wisely refrained from entering. The contest has given the world such lyrical masterpieces as 'La, La, La, Ding Ding A Dong', 'A-Ba-Ni-Bi' and our own 'Boom Bang-a-Bang'. The organisers defend the contest by saying that the songs are catchy. So was the plague.

The year saw the development of a series that was to do for drama what 'Opportunity Knocks' did for entertainment – only with style. **'Armchair Theatre'** was a collection of single plays which became compulsive Sunday-night viewing, running periodically right up until 1974. It introduced young British writers like Harold Pinter and Alun Owen and new performers such as Tom Courtenay, Tom Bell and Diana Rigg. One of the plays led directly to the powerful series 'Callan'. The very first play was a medical tale, 'The Outsider', with Adrienne Corri and David Kossoff. In spite of the general high standard, 'Armchair Theatre' was a bit too realistic for some, and various seamy scenes led to it being dubbed 'Armpit Theatre'.

Party political broadcasts were just as much of a turn-off then as they are now. In March, BBC and ITV announced that they would be broadcast on both channels simultaneously after politicians discovered that nobody would watch them if they had a choice. When Eden had appeared for the Tories, 80 per cent of viewers switched to 'People Are Funny', and when Gaitskell followed for Labour four out of five turned to 'Jack Solomons' Scrapbook'.

A more important political event was the birth of **'This Week'**, ITV's answer to 'Panorama'. The first edition had a film about Dr Otto John's defection in West Germany and an interview with a television quiz winner and was presented by Leslie Mitchell from a restaurant in London's Lower Regent Street. Sometimes cramming as many as half a dozen topics into a thirty-minute programme, 'This Week' continued until 1978 when it was replaced by 'TV Eye'. The title was revived again eight years later. Leslie Mitchell's successors in the hot seat have included Brian Connell and Ludovic Kennedy.

Hans and Lotte Hass and their underwater exploits appeared on screen in **'Diving to Adventure'**, in 1956, and this series and its follow-up, **'The Undersea World of Adventure'**, established the German divers and naturalists as the aquatic counterparts of Armand and Michaela Denis. Indeed, Lotte and Michaela were often mistaken for one another. Their programmes were shot all over the world, including the Caribbean, the Red Sea and the Indian Ocean. Hans Hass made the films to pay for his scientific expeditions and had mixed feelings about missing out on a lot of the research. He explains: 'Much as I enjoyed making the films, they took all my time and I would have liked to have done more of the research. But we had to finance our work. I remember leaving the ship at Ceylon and flying to the BBC Natural History Unit in Bristol with six half-hour programmes. And the ship had to wait at Ceylon for me to return with the money that would enable us to continue our expedition.'

Hans and Lotte did English and German commentaries, for the respective countries. 'The series were more popular in Britain than in Germany,' says Hans. 'It appealed to the British sense of adventure.'

Arthur Haynes with the banes of his television life, Nicholas Parsons and Patricia Hayes.

Also Shown in 1956

There was a sort of early 'Mr and Mrs' called **'Do You Trust Your Wife?'**, and Arthur Askey's **'Before Your Very Eyes'** introduced the busty dumb blonde Sabrina, who was once, believe it or not, the junior breast-stroke champion of Manchester. One of the best comedies was **'The Arthur Haynes Show'**, written by Johnny Speight. The Goons made a rare foray into television with **'Idiot Weekly, Price 2d'**, and this was followed later in the year by **'A Show Called Fred'** and **'Son of Fred'**. Husband and wife comedy team the Randalls starred in **'Joan and Leslie'**; Alan Melville was one of the funniest men on television in his series **'A-Z'**; perhaps the most charming and elegant was Michael Denison's Richard Boyd in **'Boyd QC'**.

One man who didn't set women's hearts pounding in 1956 was Broderick 'Ten-four' Crawford of the Californian cop series **'Highway Patrol'**. The macabre Alfred Hitchcock probably had even fewer female fans, but his long-running anthology **'Alfred Hitchcock Presents'** brought his vast cinema following to television. Adventure series of the year included **'The Count of Monte Cristo'** with George Dolenz, father of Monkee Mickey; **'The Buccaneers'** starring Robert Shaw as reformed pirate Dan Tempest; and Hugh O'Brian as the famous marshal of Tombstone in **'The Life and Legend of Wyatt Earp'**.

Prior to 1956, television had closed down between 6 p.m. and 7.30 p.m. on Sunday evenings so as not to deter churchgoing. ITV's **'About Religion'** was the first show to fill that period – a time which came to be known as the God Slot. Its BBC rival was **'Meeting Point'**. **'Picture Parade'** previewed new films, while **'What the Papers Say'** reviewed old papers.

Animals ruled the roost on children's television. The canine celebrities were **Lassie** the collie (there were seven different Lassies in eighteen years) and Alsatian **Rin-Tin-Tin**, but **Champion the Wonder Horse** was also a great favourite and anything that Champion could do, **The Lone Ranger** and his horse, Silver, could do better. Desmond Morris presented **'Zoo Time'**, starring Congo the chimpanzee, such a talented artist that Picasso bought one of his paintings; and **Lennie the Lion**, with Terry Hall, was the King of the Jungle who couldn't roll his r's. **'Davy Crockett'**, played by Fess Parker, was king of the wild frontier, while sporting instruction for youngsters was popularised through **'Seeing Sport'**, hosted by Peter Lloyd.

1957

Throughout the fifties there had been sightings of strange objects from outer space, some too hideous to describe; but surely no one sitting in the comfort of his home on the evening of 26 April 1957 could have been prepared for what suddenly appeared on his television screen. It was Patrick Moore.

On that fateful date, **'The Sky at Night'** first saw the light of day and it is still going strong – a world record for the same presenter to be with a programme for over thirty years. It has deservedly made that presenter one of the best-loved personalities in Britain, for in addition to being an expert on astronomy Patrick is a genuine eccentric who doesn't take himself too seriously. It is hard to imagine anybody not liking him – except perhaps his tailor. One of Patrick's many claims to fame is that he was probably the

first person to swallow a fly on television. He remembers: 'It was during an early broadcast and it was rather a large fly. I had just opened my mouth to make some world-shattering pronouncement when in it flew. The producer said that he saw a look of glazed horror come into my eyes, after which I gave a strangled gulp and went on. My mother later summed it up beautifully: "Yes dear, it was nasty for you but so much worse for the fly." I suppose she was right.'

Patrick's proficiencies have seen him crop up on all sorts of programme over the years from serious lunar discussions to fooling around on the likes of 'The Generation Game' and 'Blankety Blank'. He has also been a popular target for impressionists and seems to view it as something of a compliment although he did once have to take issue with Mike Yarwood. 'I have been one of Mike's regular victims,' says Patrick, 'but I did once make a mild protest. Over my left eyebrow I have a pronounced scar from where I came off my motor-cycle in 1952. Mike got the scar wrong, but after I pointed this out he kindly repositioned it!'

The demise of the Toddlers' Truce in February saw ITV quickly slip adventure series such as 'Robin Hood' and 'Sir Lancelot' into the slot, while the BBC introduced a programme that was to be held in great affection by the public over the next eight years. **'Tonight'** went out every weekday, beginning with an audience of just 1 million but by the end of the year soaring past the 5 million mark. The start of 'Tonight' followed the death of the magazine *Picture Post*, and some of the show's most popular contributors came from there – among them Fyfe Robertson, Trevor Philpott, Slim Hewitt and later Kenneth Allsop. The presenter was Cliff Michelmore, and he introduced weird and wonderful stories from the above-mentioned together with Derek Hart, Macdonald Hastings, Geoffrey Johnson Smith and a new reporter named Alan Whicker. Cy Grant sang a topical calypso, written by Bernard Levin, and there was a little ditty from folk duo Robin Hall and Jimmie Macgregor.

The first woman reporter on the programme was Polly

Elwes, who recalls a typical 'Tonight' tale. 'I had to do a story about some sheep on Ilkley Moor which, because the moor wasn't fenced, were getting into people's back gardens and eating their chrysanthemums. We did a recce and there were sheep, loads of them, doing just that. Next morning when we came to film it there wasn't a sheep in sight. So we went up on the moors, found some sheep, drove them down and put them into the gardens!'

Human guests included Brigitte Bardot and Jayne Mansfield, both interviewed by the show's resident charmer, Geoffrey Johnson Smith. Cliff Michelmore recalls the arrival of La Mansfield. 'She was wearing a leopardskin affair which looked as though she had been poured into it. It hugged every bit of her body tightly down to her ankles. She shuffled across the studio floor and stood leaning against a piece of scenery. When offered a chair or a stool, she declined, informing us: "This dress ain't for sittin', this dress ain't for walkin', all this dress is for is leanin'."'

Although the title was reintroduced in 1975 for a late-night show, 'Tonight' really ceased to be ten years earlier when, after some 1,800 editions, Cliff Michelmore could no longer say: 'The next "Tonight" will be tomorrow night.'

On Saturdays the BBC were determined to fill the 6 p.m.–7 p.m. slot with a show for teenagers – something they could enjoy before they went out dancing or to the cinema. And so the **'Six-Five Special'** came down the line. Opening with a train sequence to Johnny Johnson's theme music, 'Six-Five Special' was the forerunner to many other pop shows with its studio audience of 150 kids

Groovy cats on the 'Six-Five Special' with Pete Murray (*bottom left*) **included Josephine Douglas** (*centre, striped blouse*) **and Jon Pertwee** (*top centre*).

jiving and clapping. It was introduced by Pete Murray and Josephine Douglas with Don Lang (and his Frantic Five) and former boxer Freddie Mills in support. Adam Faith made his television début on the programme, and regular performers were young Tommy Steele and the Steelmen and 'Little' Laurie London who had 'the whole world in his hands' after his first appearance. The BBC felt that the show should say something, and so a priest in a dog-collar came in and did the hand jive to prove that the Church was alive and kicking. 'Six-Five Special' soon built up a huge following of over 8 million viewers, and it led to a film, two stage shows and a concert version. It was a row over the last which led to its mentor, producer Jack Good, being sacked by the BBC. He promptly took his talents to ITV where he created 'Oh Boy!' in 1958. Ironically, it was 'Oh Boy!' that effectively killed off 'Six-Five Special'. Following Good's departure, Jim Dale assumed the mantle of host, but the show had lost much of its zest. And five years before Dr Beeching the 'Six-Five Special' was cancelled.

One programme that was certainly on the right track was television's first medicated soap, **'Emergency – Ward 10'**. This was ITV's first twice-weekly serial and it was shown on Tuesdays and Fridays. Yet both its start and its finish ten years later came about almost by accident. In 1957, Tessa Diamond, then a lowly £15-a-week Associated Television continuity writer, casually suggested to her boss that 'something about doctors and nurses' might fill an empty 7.30 p.m. slot. The plugs were finally pulled in 1967 when old age and weakness in the ratings area were diagnosed – an action subsequently rediagnosed by ATV chief Lew Grade as one of his worst mistakes. Tessa, a doctor's daughter, dreamed up a hospital called the Oxbridge and a six-week serial titled 'Calling Nurse Roberts'. The racier 'Emergency – Ward 10' title was chosen, but the emergencies were never as important as the romantic entanglements of the handsome doctors and pert young nurses. The medical staff included Charles Tingwell as surgeon Alan Dawson, twenty-one-year-old John Alderton as Dr Richard Moore, Jill Browne (who became Mrs Alderton) as Sister Carole Young, John Carlisle as Dr Lester Large, Ray Barrett as Dr Don Nolan, Desmond Carrington as Dr Chris Anderson and Richard Thorp as Dr Rennie. Thorp, later to star as Alan Turner in 'Emmerdale Farm', was once invited to watch a real operation but had to leave halfway through – shortly before he fainted.

Among those playing patients were Albert Finney, Ian Hendry and Joanna Lumley. Indeed, the patients at Oxbridge were remarkably healthy and fortunate. The number of deaths a year was set at five (later reduced to two), and no worrying or incurable illnesses were allowed. The writers did occasionally tug heart-strings. When the wife and baby of Dr Anderson died in a flood, tearful viewers protested in droves. The series won praise in a British Medical Association report for allaying people's

Before he was Fenn Street's 'Sir', John Alderton played doctors and nurses in 'Emergency – Ward 10'.

fears about hospitals, and in 1962 Enoch Powell, then Minister of Health, congratulated the soap on its 500th edition and commented on the useful job it did in reminding the public of the need for immunisation. There were critics, too, in the medical world. A Manchester St John Ambulance Brigade commissioner banned his cadets from watching it because, he claimed, it portrayed nurses as 'feather-headed flippertigibbets'.

There were two notable events in current-affairs programmes, one rather more serious than the other. ITN's **'Roving Report'** featured a relatively youthful Robin Day interrogating personalities abroad. In 1957, Egypt was still technically at war with Britain following the Suez crisis, and so it was a major coup when Day obtained an exclusive interview with President Nasser of Egypt in the garden of his home just outside Cairo. Their conversation assumed even greater significance when Nasser leaned towards the camera and invited Britain to re-establish amicable relations with his country. The other item was far more light-hearted and is still remembered today as the most effective April Fool joke ever. **'Panorama'** viewers witnessed Richard Dimbleby reporting on a bumper spaghetti harvest in southern Switzerland. Dimbleby was seen walking between spaghetti-laden trees as farmworkers loaded the crop into baskets. Hundreds of people rang the BBC, most of them wanting to know where they could obtain spaghetti plants. Producer Michael Peacock informed them that many British enthusiasts got admirable results from planting a small tin of spaghetti in tomato sauce!

It was also the year of the Queen's maiden Christmas message, from Sandringham. To help Her Majesty, Sylvia Peters made a special film for her demonstrating 'the five best ways to make a speech on TV'.

And 1957 saw the emergence of two of the best comedies of the fifties: from America **'The Phil Silvers Show'** and from Chelsea Palace 'The Army Game'. Originally entitled 'You'll Never Get Rich', 'The Phil Silvers Show' remains a classic to this day. Set in a remote army post, it starred Silvers as fast-talking Master Sergeant Ernest T. Bilko, a man whose major aim in life was to make money – and plenty of it. Created by Nat Hiken, who was later responsible for 'Car 54, Where Are You?', 'The Phil Silvers Show' featured Paul Ford as Colonel Hall, Maurice Gosfield as 'Doberman, Harvey Lembeck as Barbella, Joe E. Ross as Ritzik and Elizabeth Fraser as Sergeant Hogan. Sadly, the show has proved more durable than Silvers himself, for he was never able to repeat this success. His career steadily declined until his death in 1985.

'The Army Game' was British comedy at its best, very much in the style of the 'Carry On' films which were to start the following year. Indeed, some of the 'Army Game' cast developed into 'Carry On' regulars. William Hartnell, who in time became the first Dr Who, was the appropriately named Sergeant-Major Bullimore with Bill Fraser as the odious beady-eyed Sergeant Claude Snudge. Michael Medwin (later replaced by Harry Fowler) led as motley a crew of men as you're ever likely to meet, played by Norman Rossington, Bernard Bresslaw, Charles Hawtrey, whose character was heavily into knitting, and Alfie Bass, who took the part of Private 'Excuse Boots' Bisley.

'The Army Game' won the ratings war for ITV. Bootsie and Snudge (Alfie Bass and Bill Fraser, *right*) fought on in their own series.

Bresslaw displayed a minus IQ in the series and had a catchphrase of 'I only arsked' which became the title of a 1958 film spin-off. And in 1960 Alfie Bass and Bill Fraser marched their characters into civvy street for 'Bootsie and Snudge'. The cast were great practical jokers, which made them particularly dangerous on a live show such as this.

Commercial Break

In 1957 we were told that 'the Esso sign means happy motoring' and that Fairy Snow gives 'washday white without washday red' – a dig at powders which had been rumoured to cause skin rashes. Norman Hackforth intoned, 'Ah, Woodbine – a great little cigarette', and Omo produced the first commercial to incorporate street interviews.

An alternative method of advertising was through a genre of programmes called admags, which placed commercials within the framework of a show. The best-known of these admags was 'Jim's Inn'. Jim's Inn was a village pub run by Jimmy Hanley and his wife Maggie where the locals would gather and discuss the latest bargains over drinks. An indication of its selling power occurred when Roma, who ran the beauty salon in the imaginary village, swanned into the pub wearing a fur coat. Maggie exclaimed: 'What a lovely coat! Where did you get it?' To which Roma unashamedly replied, in a plug worthy of any chat-show guest: 'Jones & Higgins of Peckham – they've got a sale on. It was reduced from £70 to £50.' The morning after the programme, there was a queue a mile long outside Jones & Higgins. To the disgust of the public, Parliament outlawed admags in 1963, and so 'Time, gentlemen, please' was called at Jim's Inn.

There were a few faux pas. On the political programme 'Under Fire', respected journalist Kingsley Martin was cut off in mid-sentence by a commercial for Tide. But that was nothing compared to the chaos of 19 May when the wrong soundtrack accompanied the pictures. Consequently the voiceover 'clean your teeth with this' was partnered by a photo of a sausage; 'give this to your cat' produced a bottle of Babycham with the qualification 'it will love it'; 'this will make your hair gleam' coincided with a shot of a tube of toothpaste; 'lubricate your car with this' was illustrated by a bottle of beer; and finally a well-fed cat was shown on screen. 'That's my husband,' said the voiceover proudly!

On one occasion, Harry Fowler had to dash off stage and return with a haversack on his back. But the others had loaded a stage weight into his haversack, and poor Harry was forced to hump around an extra twenty-five pounds. Not everyone saw the funny side of 'The Army Game'. A real commanding officer believed it to be a corrupting influence and decreed that the men in his command should not watch it, but he relented after the cast heard about his edict and 'invaded' his headquarters!

It is stretching a point to call 'Emergency – Ward 10' a drama, so the most promising newcomer in that category was **'Murder Bag'** which introduced Raymond Francis as Detective Superintendent Tom Lockhart. Apart from good old George Dixon, Lockhart became probably the most respected television policeman over the next decade as 'Murder Bag' begat 'Crime Sheet' which in turn begat 'No Hiding Place'. Lockhart's trademark was taking snuff, something Francis enjoyed too. On the series he used a snuffbox given to him by Kenneth More. The show was done live, and Francis had a habit of hiding his lines all over

It is ironic that such worthy series as 'Emergency – Ward 10', 'Tonight' and 'Murder Bag' should be outlived by two little pigs with silly speeded-up voices. But 1957 saw the début of Pinky and Perky on BBC, and they were still hamming it up when they defected to ITV in 1968. Pinky and Perky were the sort of characters that made you think perhaps the Big Bad Wolf wasn't such a bad guy after all. These porky puppets, created by Czechs Jon and Vlasta Dalibor, used to cavort around to the popular music of the day, the sound emanating from beneath their snouts bearing an uncanny similarity to playing a Little Jimmy Osmond record at 78 r.p.m. Yet they were amazingly successful. At the height of their fame in the sixties, they received almost as much fan mail as the Beatles!

Also Shown in 1957

Game shows continued to flourish on ITV, and their hand was strengthened with the arrival of 'Criss Cross Quiz', which drew a record ITV audience of nearly 10 million, and its offspring 'Junior Criss Cross Quiz' which, curiously, ran longer than the senior version.

Other game shows of 1957 included 'Tell the Truth' under the chairmanship of David Jacobs where three people claimed to be somebody but only one was telling the truth; and there was 'Bury Your Hatchet' which had people with a mild grudge against one another in competition under the watchful eyes of Bob Monkhouse and Denis Goodwin.

Noele Gordon hosted 'Lunch Box', for which she rode an elephant, went down a mine and entered a cage of lions; new crime series were 'Mark Saber', starring one-armed actor Donald Gray, and 'Shadow Squad', while 'The New Adventures of Charlie Chan' starred J. Carroll Naish as the original Chinese detective; and Westerns included 'Annie Oakley' with Gail Davis as

the sharp-shooting heroine and 'Tombstone Territory', a series of true stories taken from the *Tombstone Epitaph*, the oldest weekly paper in America's south-west. Psychiatrist Dr Stafford-Clark featured in the medical series 'Lifeline', Carroll Levis introduced more of his talented discoveries, 'Chelsea at Nine' paraded international stars every Monday at 9 p.m. from the Chelsea Palace, Minerva Urecal played Annie with Walter Sande as her sea-faring rival Captain Bullwinkle in 'The Adventures of Tugboat Annie' and Tommy Cooper had the first series of his own, 'Cooper – Life with Tommy'.

For younger viewers, there was the birth of the most basic of all animated programmes, 'Captain Pugwash'; John Hart was Hawkeye and Lon Chaney, Jnr played Chingachgook in 'Hawkeye and the Last of the Mohicans'; 'Fury' was yet another boy-meets-animal saga starring young Bobby Diamond and Peter Graves; and Robert Newton took the title rôle in 'The Adventures of Long John Silver' alongside Kit Taylor as cabin boy Jim Hawkins.

the set. One such crib card was inside his desk drawer, and Francis used to open it slightly and glance down. One day, a technician played a joke on him by replacing the card with one which read: 'You will dry now.' And sure enough he did! 'Murder Bag' got its title from the black leather briefcase that the police used on murder enquiries and which contained over forty-two items of equipment.

The year also saw the emergence of a programme that was to be the bane of husbands for years to come. No longer could they lie in bed reading the *Sunday Pictorial*; they were expected to be dashing around the house putting shelves up with a minimal loss of blood. The culprit was Barry Bucknell, and his long-running programme 'Do It Yourself' taught men everything they never wanted to know about doing jobs around the home. From the first edition – a festive show in which Bucknell demonstrated how to make a stand for a Christmas tree as well as giving some tips on tree-lights – his popularity soared to the point where he received more mail than anybody else on television, up to 35,000 letters a week! He needed to

employ ten secretaries. Yet Bucknell only really became a television celebrity thanks to his wife. A former engineer in the car industry, he had done a few radio talks on housing and education, but it was his wife Betty, noted for her cookery programmes on radio, who made the break into television. Bucknell casually chatted to her producer about the possibilities of doing some sort of practical programme but thought no more about it; then out of the blue he got a call from the BBC to appear on the afternoon series 'About the Home' and 'Do It Yourself' duly followed.

'The show was very much a one-man effort,' says Bucknell. 'I used to build all the shelves, tables, whatever we were using on the programme, in the basement of my own house and transport them *en bloc* to the studio. Even the rehearsals used to take place in my basement. The early editions were live, and I was dependent on the floor manager to ensure that things like screws were close at hand. The whole show could fall apart without a few screws, and it didn't look very good if I had to search around for them. And it wasted valuable air-time.'

1958

The Munich air crash killed seven Manchester United footballers. ☐ Nikita Khrushchev took over in the Kremlin. ☐ Race riots hit Notting Hill. ☐ Elvis Presley was called up for military service. ☐ Chi Chi, the giant panda, arrived at London Zoo. ☐ The newly formed Campaign for Nuclear Disarmament held its first protest march from Aldermaston to London, led by Canon John Collins and Michael Foot. ☐ The first parking meter came to Britain, in London's Mayfair. ☐ The do-it-yourself craze swept the country. ☐ Mike Hawthorn became Britain's first world motor-racing champion. ☐ Donald Campbell in Bluebird *set a new world water-speed record of 248 m.p.h. ☐ Among the new films were* Room at the Top *and the first 'Carry On' film,* Carry On Sergeant. *☐ Conway Twitty sang 'It's Only Make Believe'. ☐ And the face of the year belonged to French sex kitten Brigitte Bardot.*

We now know that Cliff Richard is hardly a bad boy, but back in 1958 he was the *enfant terrible* of the music scene, considered to be a corrupting influence on teenagers and definitely too hot for television. The series that earned poor Cliff such an awful reputation was **'Oh Boy!'**, the ITV pop show which reflected the change in musical tastes and in youngsters generally. In 1957, Cliff had been an unknown £4-a-week clerk called Harry Webb, but 'Oh Boy!' rocketed him to fame and parental dis-approval. Cliff had modelled himself on Elvis, even down to the curled lip and was accused of 'smouldering on screen'. Newspapers attacked his 'crude exhibitionism' and warned: 'Don't let your daughter go out with people like this.'

Cliff explains: 'One of my front teeth was capped and the shadow from the TV lighting made it look as though I had a tooth missing. So instead of smiling I smouldered.' He cheerfully admits: 'Physically, I was a greasy slob. I was probably the first bad-taste dresser in this country. I wore pink socks and a pink jacket. I used to fluoresce!'

But the kids worshipped him – so did some posh people. Lady Jellicoe said at the time: 'I really think Cliff Richard is quite an alarmingly entertaining young man. And "Oh Boy!" is simply heavenly.' Elfrida Eden, eighteen-year-old niece of Sir Anthony Eden, drooled: 'I think Cliff's action is incredible. My mother doesn't approve, but give me "Oh Boy!" every time instead of all that debbery nonsense.'

Besides Cliff, other regulars on 'Oh Boy!' were Lord Rockingham's XI, the Dallas Boys, the Vernon Girls, Billy Fury, Marty Wilde and Cherry Wainer on electric organ. Kerry Martin left 'Six-Five Special' to join 'Oh Boy!' She was sacked from the BBC show because she wiggled too much in a dance routine and she went to the rival channel as a singer.

The musical content was slightly different in another hit of 1958, **'The Black and White Minstrel Show'**, a series that was to delight viewers for the next twenty years. Created by George Inns, 'The Minstrel Show' had been on children's television back in 1954 but now it graduated to a wider audience. In its lifetime, it combined comedy from the likes of Leslie Crowther and Stan Stennett, witty melodic offerings from Margo Henderson and medleys from the thirty-six George Mitchell Singers with soloists Dai Francis, Tony Mercer and John Boulter. There were twenty-four girl dancers from the Television Toppers. The only lack of harmony on the show was when complaints were made that the men's black facial make-up was racist.

Leslie Crowther, who in the sixties often had to change costumes in the taxi after dashing to the show from 'Crackerjack', recalls one particularly painful moment. The opening shot had him dressed as a baby, complete with nappy, hanging on a wire harness high above the stage. The programmes didn't always run to time then, and the previous one over-ran, which meant that he had to stay up there – and wait. 'I was up there for fifteen minutes, but it

Regulars on 'The Black and White Minstrel Show' were (*left to right*) Leslie Crowther, Valerie Brooks, Stan Stennett and George Chisholm.

'deplorable'. It was concerned that the series would increase people's worries about their own health. The BMA concluded: 'We hope that in its search for realism, the BBC will not find itself telecasting a death on the table. But even if it is not provided with this sensation, the viewing public should be in for a real blood-curdling treat.' And a Harley Street psychiatrist called it 'a psychologically dangerous experiment that could turn people into hypochondriacs'.

Yet the series was made with the full co-operation of the staff in the hospitals that were visited and the vast majority of doctors fully supported the programme, saying it provided a valuable service in dispelling fears about surgery.

In some respects it was quite a morbid year on television. For during the live transmission of 'Underground', a play in the popular 'Armchair Theatre' series, actor Gareth Jones collapsed and died. The rest of the cast were told when out of camera shot that he had been taken ill and they ad-libbed to cover up for his absence.

Wives everywhere threw up their hands in horror in 1958 as Saturday afternoons came to be dominated by sport – and **'Grandstand'**. Conversations, and tea, were postponed until the teleprinter had churned out the all-important football results. In the very first edition, presented by Peter Dimmock, some of the scores didn't come through at all. 'Grandstand' couldn't stay for the late soccer results as 'The Lone Ranger' was waiting. The results were read then as now by Australian Len Martin.

seemed like four days. The wire harness was horrendous – I nearly ended up as a boy soprano. But it was one of those things you suffered in the cause of art!'

Before 1958, television's view of hospitals had been confined to the romantic tales of 'Emergency – Ward 10' where the only red gory sight would be when a nurse had overdone the lipstick. But in February the BBC took the revolutionary step of transporting their cameras into a real operating-theatre to witness surgeons at work. The result was a series called **'Your Life in Their Hands'** and it divided the medical profession and the nation as a whole.

'Your Life in Their Hands' ran for six years and enthralled up to 10 million viewers; but for others it was too frightening, and it was reported that the programme was partially to blame for the suicides of three women as well as many injuries. One woman gassed herself after watching a heart operation. She was facing a similar operation. Two more gassed themselves after seeing an episode on cancer. Both thought they had cancer and were said by their husbands to have been disturbed by the programme. In fact neither had the disease. In spite of the fact that the BBC always put out a warning to prevent the squeamish from watching, when the heart operation was screened many viewers suffered shock in their own homes. A Cardiff man fainted and gashed his head as he fell off his chair; an elderly Birmingham woman was so shaken that she dropped a pot of tea over her hands and legs and was severely scalded; and a Yardley housewife bit her lip so badly that she needed seven stitches.

The British Medical Association strongly attacked 'Your Life in Their Hands'. In an article in the *British Medical Journal*, it accused the BBC of 'pandering to the morbid' and called the first programme, which showed six polio patients being kept alive by artificial breathing-pumps,

Didn't Bruce Forsyth do well in 1958 when he took over Beat the Clock on 'Sunday Night at the London Palladium'? Well, the Shadows thought so.

'Grandstand' once confused pools hopefuls when it gave the half-time scores as final results. And before modern technology artists used to climb studio ladders to paint the racing results on boards.

Two of the best-known 'Grandstand' personalities were presenter David Coleman and the Rugby League commentator *extraordinaire*, the late Eddie Waring.

Coleman was the champion miler of Cheshire at the age of twenty-three and he also boasts footballing experience. He was once recruited by Stockport County Reserves to make up their numbers for a match he was there to cover for a local paper. When in charge of the good old teleprinter, Coleman always armed himself with reams of trivia. He would know if it was the fourth time that season that Stenhousemuir had lost 4–0 to a side beginning with an 'A' and that it was now twenty-eight matches since they had last drawn 2–2 at home! He is famous for his unintentional contributions (not financial) to *Private Eye* and their 'Colemanballs' column. One classic was 'And for those of you watching who haven't got television sets, live commentary is on Radio 2.'

Yorkshireman Eddie Waring did much to encourage the popularity of Rugby League with colourful comments like an 'up and under', 'an early bath' (when a player was sent off) and 'I don't know whether that's the ball or his head. We'll know if it stands up.' An Eddie Waring Society was formed, but he didn't endear himself to the sport's hard-core supporters. Ten thousand fans signed a petition and delivered it to the BBC, demanding that Waring be relieved of his duties as they considered that his commentaries were an insult and were turning the game into a music-hall joke.

Since the demise of 'The Grove Family', the BBC had lacked a twice-weekly serial. Envious of the ratings success of ITV's 'Emergency – Ward 10', the BBC unleashed **'Starr and Company'** in March. Based around a small family buoy-making firm (original if nothing else), 'Starr and Company' was transmitted live on Mondays and Thursdays. Set in the fictional town of Sullbridge, fifty miles south of London, it starred Philip Ray, Nancy Nevinson, Patricia Mort and Brian McDermott, but didn't stay buoyant for long, lasting only four months.

Africa was the setting for two so-so series and one superb one. The lesser lights were **'African Patrol'** and **'White Hunter'**. The former had John Bentley as Patrol Inspector Paul Derek whose beat was the African jungle. Bentley went on to play Hugh Mortimer in 'Crossroads', which must have made the jungle seem positively inviting by comparison. 'White Hunter' was a tale of goodies and baddies in the African bush. Starring Rhodes Reason, it was based on the true exploits of John A. Hunter, 'the surest and fastest shot in Africa.'

These contrived programmes paled in comparison with the natural splendour of **'On Safari'** with Armand and Michaela Denis. 'On Safari' spanned eleven years and 105

By far the best of an otherwise indifferent batch of new comedies was 'The Larkins'. Peggy Mount played battle-axe Ada Larkin with David Kossoff as her timid husband Alf, a cockney couple running a country pub.

half-hour films and was sold all over the world. Michaela reflects: 'We had no idea it would be so successful. We used to work a seven-day week when we were on expedition, and Christmas, New Year, public holidays and birthdays were completely out. But the constant wonder of exploring the diversity of the earth and the spur of recording it before it disappeared or was assimilated mitigated fatigue. There was so much to film then but less sophisticated equipment. Now there is superb equipment but much less to film!' Although British television was only black and white at the time, Armand recorded everything in colour.

On 16 October a former beauty queen and a former Army officer sat down to introduce the first edition of a programme that for over thirty years has been compulsive viewing for any child wanting to learn about life in other countries, about caring for pets or how to make a fully operational Centurion tank out of detergent-bottles, toilet-rolls and sticky-backed plastic. She was twenty-one-year-old Leila Williams, the previous year's Miss Great Britain, and he was twenty-five-year-old actor Christopher Trace. The show was **'Blue Peter'**.

The programme was created by John Hunter Blair, who later died from multiple sclerosis while watching an edition of his brainchild. Originally just a seven-week experiment, it began as a fifteen-minute programme for toddlers with items on trains and dolls but it soon grew into the show we know and love today. Over the years, there have been seventeen presenters: Leila Williams, Christopher Trace, Valerie Singleton, John Noakes, Peter Purves, Lesley Judd, Sarah Greene, Simon Groom, Christopher Wenner,

Tina Heath, Michael Sundin, Janet Ellis, Peter Duncan, Caron Keating, Mark Curry, Yvette Fielding and John Leslie. Under the ever vigilant eye of the show's recently retired editor, Biddy Baxter, they have encouraged viewers to raise millions of pounds in the famous 'Blue Peter' appeals. Instead of sending in money, children are urged to volunteer old clothes, used stamps, paperback books or milk-bottle tops and by 1971 it was estimated that 7½ tons of silver paper had been sent to 'Blue Peter'. Some 3,000 letters pour into the production office each week, and when the programme held a competition to design a train of the future there were no fewer than 110,000 entrants ranging in age from two to seventy-two.

Christopher Trace got the job of presenter as a result of his expertise at building model railways. 'It was while constructing the layouts that I invented the phrase "Here's one I made earlier" because we didn't have instant glue in those days.' Chris's layouts were a feature of the show – and a source of entertainment for others, as he once discovered to his cost.

I remember a particularly complicated layout that I had gone through in great detail with the director at a dress run before we went for a tea-break. It was planned down to the last detail – all the points were set and so on. But when we did the show trains were coming from

Commercial Break

The year's commercials were enlivened by Joe, the tongue-tied Esso Blue paraffin salesman who called himself the 'Esso Blee Dooler'. We heard that Mackeson 'looks good, tastes good and, by golly, it does you good' and first realised that a chocolate bar could be even remotely sensuous. The Fry's Turkish Delight commercial (jingle by Cliff Adams) showed a male slave unrolling a carpet containing a glamorous female captive in front of an Eastern ruler. The woman, instantly submissive, ran to the prince's feet and started feeding him lumps of Turkish Delight which was said to be full of Eastern promise. Even then the way to a man's heart was through his stomach.

It is perhaps typically British that for the next eighteen years we should be captivated by a couple whose main interests seemed to be casseroles and gravy. For in 1958 married bliss Oxo-style appeared as Katie (Mary Holland) and Philip (Richard Clarke, followed by Peter Moynihan) starred in advertising's first soap opera. Everything revolved around dinner as Katie informed Philip that Oxo has nine good ingredients and 'gives a meal man appeal'. As a reward for slaving over a hot stove, she was presented with a son, David, even though neither parent had mentioned the forthcoming event and Katie had shown no signs of pregnancy. To complete this remarkable entry into the world, David aged from nought to three in the course of one summer. All that meaty goodness obviously made the lad grow. Viewers certainly took them to their hearts. When Philip spoke sharply to her once, girls in an electronics factory came out on strike. And there was uproar when Katie arrived home with her shopping-

basket and started making gravy without first washing her hands. Even the Independent Television Authority's Council on Advertising objected about the display of bad manners when Philip mopped up his gravy with bread. Mary Holland was recognised wherever she went. 'I was constantly stopped in the streets, supermarkets, anywhere and asked for advice and suggestions for cooking. I was interviewed many times as Katie since Oxo thought it was a good idea for the public to believe that Katie, Philip and David were a real family. And they did.' Katie carried on cooking until 1976 when the pair were dropped because Oxo wanted a fresher image. Ironically, a new Oxo family was created in the eighties.

everywhere except the places I was expecting. It was chaos. I just couldn't understand what had happened. Then I discovered that during the tea-break someone had sneaked in from the next studio and had been playing with all the trains. There was a big enquiry. The culprit was . . . Richard Dimbleby.

Such is the esteem in which 'Blue Peter' has always been held that in 1971 Princess Anne took part in a 'Blue Peter' Royal Safari to Kenya with Valerie Singleton. Ah, Val – the mere mention of her name conjures up days of an innocent childhood.

The other presenter everyone remembers is daredevil John Noakes. For all his parachuting and abseiling, one of his most painful experiences came from a five-pound imitation marrow. He was knocked out by it during an exhibition of marrow-dangling and was taken to hospital for X-ray. The things some people will do for a 'Blue Peter' badge.

John's constant companion was dog Shep ('Get down, Shep'), one of a long line of 'Blue Peter' pets. The most famous was Petra, who arrived as a mongrel puppy in 1962. Unfortunately, she died a few days after her début and the show had to get a replacement from a pet shop in Lewisham, South London. So there have been two Petras. Petra II was actually a bad-tempered dog with bad eyesight and not many teeth, but as Christopher Trace remarked: 'She would gum you to death if she got half a chance.' In spite of her ferocious tendencies, Peter Purves was visibly shaken when he had to announce her death in 1977, and a specially sculpted bronze head of Petra was placed at the entrance of the BBC. Other pets included Patch, one of Petra's puppies, Jason the Siamese cat, Joey the parrot, who steadfastly refused to say 'Blue Peter' or anything else, and Fred the tortoise who two years after he first appeared was found to be a girl. A 100-year-old tortoise that had 'fought' at Gallipoli was also shell-shocked when Mark Curry marked his début on the show by treading on it.

Then there was the infamous 'Blue Peter' elephant, the clip of film is still constantly requested and was without doubt one of the funniest things ever to appear on television. Lulu, a young Sri Lankan elephant from Chessington Zoo, came to the studio with her keeper Alec and had already left her deposit on the studio floor before weeing rather too close to Val's foot. This turned the floor into a skating-rink and, hard though poor Alec tried, he was unable to prevent Lulu dragging him backwards and forwards across the studio until he eventually slid ignominiously through the lot. This was too much for the presenters, who had tried desperately to keep a straight face. As John Noakes cheerfully said goodbye, he stepped back unaware of what his foot was about to land in. His parting words were, 'Oh dear, I've trodden right in it,' a marvellous piece of restraint.

Also Shown in 1958

'Monitor', introduced by Huw Wheldon, was the first regular arts programme on television and provided an opportunity for emerging talents like Ken Russell and John Schlesinger. 'The Verdict Is Yours' was a series of fictional trials with written plots but in which actors improvised their lines and the outcome was left to a jury of viewers; and a popular new crime series was 'Dial 999', in which Robert Beatty played a tough Canadian Mountie, Mike Maguire, attached to Scotland Yard.

A number of adult Westerns were on in 1958, including Clint Walker in 'Cheyenne', playing a wanderer in the years after the American Civil War, and 'Wagon Train', starring Robert Horton as the Scout and Ward Bond as Seth Adams. Another popular Western featured Dale Robertson as Jim Hardie in 'Tales of Wells Fargo', stories about the famous stagecoach line during California's gold-rush days; while 'Boots and Saddles' starred Jack Pickard and Pat McVey in a story of life in the Fifth Cavalry in the 1870s.

Other shows of 1958 included André Morell as the Professor in 'Quatermass and the Pit', in which half of London was wiped out; 'People in Trouble' where Anglo-American Daniel Farson interviewed alcoholics and other tormented souls; the play 'John Gabriel Borkman' which marked the television début of Laurence Olivier; and 'The Sunday Break', an attempt to liven up the God Slot by mixing religion, teenage life and music. 'Living It Up' saw Arthur Askey and Richard Murdoch endeavour to re-create their radio show 'Band Waggon'; Bebe Daniels and Ben Lyon appeared in 'Life with the Lyons'; and Peter Brough and Archie Andrews went visual for 'Educating Archie' in which a regular guest was Dick Emery.

Pierino Roland Como, also known as Nick Perido, introduced 'The Perry Como Show', and Andy Stewart put on his best kilt for 'The White Heather Club', a series that did more harm to the Scottish image than the World Cup in Argentina.

Among the children's favourites of 1958 were Lloyd Bridges diving among the cod and haddock in 'Sea Hunt' and the 'Popeye' cartoons. And a children's newspaper was the setting for the magazine programme 'Lucky Dip', which was like a television version of Jamboree Bags.

Another children's series of 1958 heralded the arrival of an unknown model-turned-actor by the name of Roger

Moore. Based on Sir Walter Scott's novel, **'Ivanhoe'** starred Moore as the avenging knight with Robert Brown as his friend Gurth. Moore performed his own stunts. He had his hands slashed, he was struck on the head with a battle-axe which knocked him unconscious, and he cracked three ribs. Moore also managed to injure Peter Diamond, the fencing expert on the series, while filming a fight with broadswords. Although he enjoyed 'Ivanhoe' at the time, Moore said later: 'No one seemed to know what we were doing and we all stumbled about feeling like boy scouts dressed up in armour.'

'The Adventures of William Tell' was another of ITV's all-action productions which, although aimed primarily at younger audiences, built up an adult following, too. It starred Conrad Phillips in the title rôle with Jennifer Jayne as Mrs Tell and Willoughby Goddard as the evil Landburgher Gessler. Surely named after an Alpine fast-food restaurant, the Landburgher spent all thirty-nine episodes eating. He only came up for breath when interrupted by his adversary, whereupon he would splutter through his drumstick at his brainless guards: 'Get Tell!'

One episode featured Michael Caine as a prisoner, complete with ball and chain. Any hopes the future film-star had of an exotic location were dashed when he found that his scenes were to be shot at a quarry near Watford. Not that the locations were that grand anyway – all the mountain scenes were filmed in Snowdonia.

With these limitations, it is not entirely surprising to discover that the famous splitting of the apple on the head of William Tell's son Walter was achieved by trick photography. Conrad Phillips, who once played Tell from a wheelchair after breaking his ankle in a fall, reveals: 'We used a very fine taut wire through the apple and lined it up with the shot of the bolt speeding towards him. If we had tried it for real, I think we would have got through a lot of boys . . .'

1959

Harold Macmillan won the general election, the first to be covered fully by television. He told electors: 'You've never had it so good.' ☐ The first stretch of the M1 was opened. ☐ The hovercraft made its first cross-Channel trip. ☐ Footballer Billy Wright gained his hundredth England cap. ☐ Castro seized power in Cuba. ☐ Russia and America began training astronauts. ☐ BOAC's Comet 4 began the first jet airliner service from London to Sydney. ☐ Buddy Holly was killed in a plane crash. ☐ The Mini Minor was born, its price £350 plus purchase tax of £146 19s 2d (£146.96). ☐ A new fridge cost £63 3s 8d (£63.19). ☐ The average male teenager took home £8 a week, the average girl £6. ☐ Cliff Richard earned £30,000 a year and reached number one with 'Living Doll'. ☐ Russ Conway also topped the charts with 'Side Saddle'. ☐ And Britain's Eurovision Song Contest entry was 'Sing Little Birdie' by Teddy Johnson and Pearl Carr.

As if saving themselves for the wave of innovative television that was to mark the Swinging Sixties, both BBC and ITV ensured that on screen the fifties went out with a whimper rather than with a bang. The programmes of 1959 were a particularly unimpressive collection, an indication of their mediocrity being that probably the most popular new show was **'Juke Box Jury'**.

Chaired by David Jacobs, 'Juke Box Jury' began in June in an early Tuesday-evening slot. The first clean-cut panel were singers Alma Cogan and Gary Miller, Pete Murray (then Britain's number one disc jockey) and Susan Stranks, described in *Radio Times* as 'a typical teenager'. She was so typical that nine years later she hosted her own television series, 'Magpie' – just like everyone else!

'Juke Box Jury' quickly became so successful that it was switched to Saturday peak-time to challenge ITV's rival pop show **'Boy Meets Girls'**, the latest offering from Jack Good. The 'boy' was Marty Wilde.

Whereas its predecessor, 'Six-Five Special', had been defeated by Good and ITV, 'Juke Box Jury' was to prove far more durable and became an integral part of the flourishing pop music industry. Record-pluggers would go to any lengths to get a disc played. Even the dreaded sound of the klaxon, registering a 'miss' vote from the jury, still boosted sales enormously. The show managed to attract all four Beatles on to the jury in 1963 and later even the Rolling Stones – the first time that five seats were needed on the panel.

It was, to put it mildly, a fairly sedate programme. However, Pete Murray enlivened matters somewhat when he strongly criticised a record – only to find that the singer was lurking behind the screen as that week's mystery studio guest; and there was a running argument on one show between two panellists, composer Bunny Lewis and show-writer Wolf Mankowitz, who verbally attacked the records then each other, prompting angry protests from viewers. The public also took issue with actress Lisa Gastoni and her off-the-shoulder dress. At the end of the programme, David Jacobs asked her to stand up and show it off, but the camera only showed her bare shoulders. The BBC were bombarded with calls from people complaining that her dress was so low-cut that on screen she appeared to be naked.

Still, 'Juke Box Jury' survived these minor hiccups and continued until 1967. The final panel was Pete Murray and Susan Stranks from the very first show, Lulu, and Eric Sykes who was virtually deaf in his right ear – an ideal qualification for the programme. In 1979 the show briefly returned with Noel Edmonds in the chair, but even with credible panellists like Bob Geldof it looked well past its prime.

ITV's best new series of 1959, if 'new' is the right word, was **'No Hiding Place'**, son of 'Crime Sheet' and grandson of 'Murder Bag'. Raymond Francis as Superin-

David Jacobs, trendy host of 'Juke Box Jury', asked Chris Denning, Penny Valentine, Mel Torme and Janette Scott to vote discs hits or misses.

tendent Lockhart was still the central character, but Sergeant Harry Baxter (Eric Lander) built up such a strong female following that he was promoted to his own series, 'Echo Four Two', in 1961. Unfortunately, an Equity strike meant that only seven out of the intended thirteen programmes were recorded and 'Echo Four Two' died a quick death.

At first 'No Hiding Place' was live, which meant that even car chases were done in the studio. As the series progressed, Lockhart was joined by two more detectives, played by Michael McStay and Johnny Briggs. The latter, who went on to find fame as Mike Baldwin in 'Coronation Street', joined the force in 1964 as Detective Sergeant Russell; but he nearly didn't measure up to the part. Briggs is relatively short, and Raymond Francis advised him that he stood a better chance of getting the part if he wore lifts in his shoes. 'Give yourself an extra inch, because you're a bit small,' said Francis. So Briggs did just that. Later director Ian Fordyce suggested: 'Johnny, why don't you put a pair of lifts in your shoes to give yourself a couple of inches?' He agreed, duly took the screen test and, now growing steadily, was standing at the bar with Michael McStay. Briggs says: 'I heard Raymond Francis saying to producer Peter Willes and Ian Fordyce that he wanted to give me the part. Ian said: "Yes, but Michael is six feet one inch and Johnny is much shorter." To which Peter Willes replied: "Well, that's not a problem. We can give him some lifts!"' Once he had got the part, Briggs had a pair of shoes specially made to make him three inches taller. Francis called them his orthopaedic boots.

Michael McStay suffered a far worse experience. While filming on the Embankment in London, McStay (in plain clothes) was leading two uniformed policemen in a chase for an unseen villain. A passer-by saw this, thought McStay was trying to escape from two policemen and decided to have a go. He whacked the actor over the head with a silver-knobbed cane, and McStay had to be taken to hospital. 'No Hiding Place' never lost its appeal, and when in 1965 it was announced that the series was to be dropped both the public and the police protested. So it was brought back for two more years before Lockhart finally laid his snuffbox to rest.

One of the brightest new stars to emerge that year was buck-toothed Liverpudlian comic Ken Dodd, the man who put the suburb of Knotty Ash on the world map. Dodd made his début at the age of eight as a ventriloquist at an orphanage, and **'The Ken Dodd Show'**, tickling-stick, Diddymen and all, established him as one of our top comedians and as a singer of slushy sentimental songs that mums and grandmas loved. His distinctive teeth, the result of a schoolboy cycling accident, are reportedly insured for over £10,000. It is said the insurance firm laid down certain conditions: he must not eat seaside rock, or ride a motorbike, or play rugby, and he must brush his teeth at least three times a day. It is not clear how they check the last point. His Knotty Ash home contains over 10,000 books on showbusiness, and in 1974 he entered the *Guinness Book of Records* by telling jokes non-stop for three hours six minutes. Unfortunately, his catchphrase 'How're you diddling?' acquired a new meaning in 1988 when he was charged with tax evasion.

Another entertainer who had earned his own show in 1959 was Stanley Baxter, star of **'On the Bright Side'**. This transformed him from a Scottish pantomime comic into a national favourite. He appeared with Betty Marsden in send-ups of Hollywood movies and television programmes – a format that would stand him in good stead for years to come.

A controversial production that stood apart from the lightweight offerings of 1959 was **'Face to Face'**. Conducted by John Freeman, a journalist on 'Panorama', it was the first programme to attempt to peel away the mask of public figures and to show what lay beneath. Only the back of Freeman's head was ever seen as he sat just a few yards away from the subject. The lighting was harsh and unflattering, there were no comforting pot-plants and the cameras intruded extraordinarily, putting the guest under the closest scrutiny. Freeman says: 'The subject had the whole of the screen, the whole of the time. The camera was used almost as a secondary interrogator, capturing every flicker of an eyelid, every bead of sweat.'

Critics called it 'torture by television' and complained of guests being brainwashed and fried alive by the lights. *The Times* said the 'attraction of the programme was seeing how the next man stood up to the rack'. Other detractors described Freeman as cold and unfeeling and likened his manner of questioning to being interviewed by a computer.

There were thirty-five programmes in all (only two subjects were women) spread over a period of three years and each one opened with artist Feliks Topolski's line drawings of that week's guest. Among those who agreed to face Freeman were Bertrand Russell, Henry Moore, Evelyn Waugh, Edith Sitwell, Adam Faith, John Osborne, Carl Gustav Jung, Tony Hancock and Gilbert Harding.

The biggest coup was probably that of Swiss psychologist Carl Gustav Jung. Freeman admits to being surprised that Jung was so willing to do a television show at all, let alone in a foreign country. 'I asked him why he agreed,' says Freeman, 'and he told me that shortly before he was invited he dreamed of himself in a market place surrounded by thousands and standing on a podium teaching the people. He hadn't been able to relate the dream to anything particular in his life, but when the BBC asked him to appear on "Face to Face" he considered he'd been given the OK from on high to do it!' 'Face to Face' was revived as part of 'The Late Show' in 1989 with Jeremy Isaacs as interrogator. Early guests were Anthony Burgess and Merce Cunningham.

'Wagon Train' became a British political issue in 1959 as the Labour Party fretted about the general election being held on the same day as the series in case it kept

Tony Hancock, one of the later guests on 'Face to Face'. It was a particularly moving programme and, possibly surprising to those who witnessed the severe interrogation, Freeman and Hancock became great friends afterwards.

their supporters away from the polling stations. The result of the election showed that their fears were not unfounded. For more junior viewers, the possibility of missing **'Huckleberry Hound'** would have been an equally serious issue. 'Huckleberry Hound' was the first major cartoon show to come from the prolific stable of William Hanna and Joseph Barbera, the pair later responsible for 'The Flintstones'. Hanna originally created the 'Tom and Jerry' cartoons for MGM, while Barbera was a former New York banker whose hobby was drawing. They joined forces to introduce a constant flow of new characters like Hokey Wolf, the accident-prone Snagglepuss (with catchphrases 'Heavens to Murgatroyd' and 'Exit stage left'), Augie Doggie and Doggie Daddy, Quick Draw McGraw (a dopey horse trying to maintain law and order with his Mexican sidekick Baba Looie) as well as the other stars of the 'Huckleberry Hound' show, Pixie and Dixie with Mr Jinks the cat ('I hate those meeces to pieces') and, best-known of all, the pride of the Jellystone National Park, Yogi Bear, with his little pal Boo Boo. Hanna and Barbera were definitely smarter than the average animator.

From cartoons to puppets, and the children's series **'Small Time'** greeted a new arrival in Pussy Cat Willum. 'Small Time' boasted such gems as Sarah and Hoppity, magician Larry Parker with Theodore the rabbit, and

Gerry Anderson's first two creations, Torchy and Twizzle. Torchy was a dim battery-operated boy, while Twizzle was able to twist himself to great heights watched by his fat feline companion Footso. But none became as popular as Pussy Cat Willum. Accompanied by Wally Whyton and Muriel Young, Willum, who was a proper little know-all, built up quite a following, receiving some 400 letters a week. He reigned supreme for six years before being ruthlessly axed – a cruel deed that warranted a half-page story in the *Daily Express*. A television company spokesman said coldly: 'We just thought it was time for a change.' In those days Wally and Muriel had to ad-lib in the continuity suites between programmes if there weren't sufficient commercials. This could be for anything up to eight minutes. Whyton remembers one such occasion, a New Year's Day: 'My character, Ollie Beak, came in with a balloon and announced: "I've been to the Chelsea Owls' Ball." To which Muriel replied innocently: "I didn't know owls had balls." I don't know how we carried on without cracking up completely.'

The most bizarre sight of the year was **'The Invisible Man'**, who wore a hat, overcoat and sunglasses, whatever the weather, and whose head was entirely swathed in bandages. As a mode of fashion, it never really caught on, but the series did. The Invisible Man was scientist Dr

Thankfully first aid has improved considerably since 'The Invisible Man' called into the surgery with a sprained wrist.

Peter Brady, 'A man who can investigate crimes without being seen. A man who can go where no ordinary man could hope to enter. A man searching for the answer to his invisibility.' The identity of the actor playing the unseen hero was never revealed, although it was rumoured to be Jim Turner who was Brady's voice. We do know that Lisa Daniely took the part of his sister Diane. The series was attacked for being anti-communist, and Frank Allaun, MP, called for it to be banned because it 'created enmity towards other nations'. Yet, curiously, it was sold to Yugoslavia.

By the very nature of the programme, filming was often eventful. One day, two men saw a motorbike and sidecar cruise past without a rider. They thought it had run away, so one jumped into the saddle, the other wrenched the handlebars and they managed to steer the bike safely into some railings. Their courage was not appreciated, however, by the stunt man curled up within the sidecar who was driving the vehicle at the time. He boomed: 'You've just gone and ruined a film shot.' Exit two heroes, shame-faced.

Commercial Break

On the commercial front, a devout display of patriotism prompted the managing director of Sutherland's Paste to withdraw £4,600 worth of advertising from Granada Television because the company didn't play the national anthem at the end of the evening's programmes. The soappowder war began to hot up as the White Tide Man faced Mrs Bradshaw. The former was actor Ronnie Blythe in an immaculate white suit. He claimed that White Tide 'gets your clothes clean. Not only clean but deep-down clean. Tide clean.' Meanwhile Mrs Bradshaw was the unseen inspiration behind the Surf campaign. The only person in vision during the commercial was Mrs Bradshaw's lodger, played by John Warren, who would extol the virtues of a pile of washing Mrs B had brought in. Still in awe, he would take an item over to the window and declare: 'Hold it up to the light. Not a stain and shining bright.'

Domestos was busy 'killing all known germs in one hour', and after cleaning the loo you could either 'have a break, have a Kit-Kat' or try on your new Silhouette U Bra. The makers promoted it as 'the bra for you'. They added, 'A bra should hold you, mould you ... but it should do no more' – like make a cup of tea, presumably. When all is said and done, the burning question of 1959 for both sexes and every political party was: 'Can *you* tell Stork from butter?'

Among a number of drama series to hit the small screen in 1959 was 'The Third Man' with Michael Rennie as smooth international operator Harry Lime. He always had a soft spot for the ladies – he was one operator you could get through to.

Also Shown in 1959

'Probation Officer' was a drama series that made a star of John Paul; 'Sword of Freedom' featured Edmund Purdom as fifteenth-century Italian painter and swashbuckler Marco del Monte; 'Knight Errant' starred John Turner as Adam Knight a modern crusader and early Equalizer (but without the violence); and international quartet Vittorio de Sica, Jack Hawkins, Dan Dailey and Richard Conte were the 'Four Just Men', committed to fighting injustice throughout the world. If there was any crime left, it could be solved by Inspector Paul Duval, played by Charles Korvin, in the crime caper 'Interpol Calling'.

Westerns of the year included the witty 'Maverick' with James Garner and Jack Kelly as poker-playing Bret and Bart Maverick, the first cowboys to be portrayed as cowards and lousy shots; 'Laramie', set in a Wyoming trading station during the American Civil War and starring John Smith as Slim Sherman; and 'Have Gun – Will Travel' in which Richard Boone played Paladin, a hired gunslinger.

Among other series of 1959 were 'Cannonball' with Paul Birch as Canadian truck-driver Mike Malone; 'Concentration', a game show hosted by David Gell in which contestants had to locate the other half of an identical pair of prizes on a giant board (this was revived in 1988 with Nick Jackson); 'Let's Go', an ITV Saturday-afternoon sports magazine presented by Bernard Braden and Huw Thomas; and 'Land of Song' with Ivor Emmanuel, assorted Welsh choirs and plenty of hearty singing.

For older children, the year brought 'The Adventures of Garry Halliday' whose sworn enemy was 'The Voice', with Terence Longdon and Terence Alexander (more recently to be seen as Charlie Hungerford in 'Bergerac') and also 'Whirlybirds', a series of endless helicopter-chases involving two freelance pilots, Chuck and PT.

'Flicka' was yet another tale with an equine flavour, and 'Jungle Boy' was a wildlife conservation series filmed entirely in Africa. Written by naturalist Michael Carr Hartley who owned a 30,000-acre reserve in Kenya, it starred his fourteen-year-old son Michael Junior in the title rôle.

Television was never more exciting than it was in the 1950s, that optimistic decade when it changed itself and the habits of millions of British households like nothing before.

At the start of the fifties, television was a lark, if sometimes a slog for that small gang who worked long hours producing it. Colleagues in the tried and trusted medium of radio thought the people closeted in Alexandra Palace were 'fools on the Hill', idiots whose ideas for home entertainment would fizzle out to nothing. One top man in radio said loftily that the only way he could tolerate television was to listen with the picture turned off.

Today the early fifties style of big microphones and of announcers in evening dress talking clipped genteel English may seem staid, starchy, faintly funny, but there were no complaints from customers – those privileged people who could afford to buy a magic box for around £80 (when the average wage was about £12) – only about the numbers of neighbours who clogged up the sitting-room scrounging free entertainment.

Sylvia Peters, one of those 'fools', the BBC's prettiest, most adored announcer, remembers the enthusiasm. 'We all knew we were in at the start of something that would become terribly important in people's lives. Everything was changing week by week. I was involved in colour tests, too, quite early in the fifties, and I can't tell you how exciting it was seeing myself with a red face. It was clear what a boost that would give. Everyone was so full of hope for the future. On the other hand, my parents nearly went mad. We'd had a set – obviously because they were interested in my work – and half the street used to visit most evenings. And of course they had to be given drinks and snacks!'

By 1953 Sylvia and her equally keen pals at the BBC – Mary Malcolm, McDonald Hobley, Richard Baker, Kenneth Kendall, Richard Dimbleby among them – began to be taken seriously.

The single most important event in the rise of the medium was the coronation of Elizabeth II, a spectacle which drew a record British television audience of 20 million. People huddled ten deep around receivers to view the magic pictures, and radio was relegated to a supporting rôle – a position in which it has remained ever since. The BBC's coverage of the coronation showed that television was not only exciting; it could also be trusted. Fears that the presence of cameras would spoil the great day proved to be totally unfounded. It was the Queen's decision to screen the coronation, partly to please her grandmother Queen Mary who was too ill to attend in person, and against the advice of the Prime Minister, Winston Churchill. Afterwards, the Queen became a seasoned television performer and made her first Christmas broadcast in 1957, but Churchill continued to dislike television. He hated the glare and,

Just the name struck terror – 'No Hiding Place' with Raymond Francis and Eric Lander.

although he came to appreciate its importance to the extent of having a private screen test, he was never comfortable enough to allow himself to be interviewed. He believed television had no part to play in the coverage of politics.

The other small-screen landmark of the fifties was the coming of commercial television in

1955. Churchill dismissed it as 'a tuppenny Punch and Judy show' and people felt guilty about watching it as though they were being disloyal to the BBC who had served the country so well during the war. Going over from the BBC to work for ITV was treated as 'a crime', said Sylvia Peters. McDonald Hobley, who did it, 'had a black mark against his name'.

ITV's presentation was far more relaxed than the BBC's. A couple who appeared on both sides in 1955 were cooks Fanny and Johnny Cradock. In 'Kitchen Magic' on the BBC, they were introduced as 'Phyllis and John Cradock, the Bon Viveur husband and wife cookery team' but when they switched to ITV, they were simply known as 'Fanny and Johnny'. Nowhere was the gulf between the two channels better illustrated than in their news policy of the period. The BBC affirmed: 'The object is to state the news of the day accurately, fairly, soberly and impersonally. It is no part of the aim to induce either optimism or pessimism or to attract listeners by colourful and sensational reports.' Independent Television News countered: 'News is human and alive and we intend to present it in that manner.'

Sylvia and her colleagues were jolted by ITV. 'We had to begin programmes on time – I had a clock beside the camera for the first time.' But the BBC stole a march on the upstart rival by finally agreeing to show newsreaders in vision eighteen days before the start of ITN. Richard Baker and Kenneth Kendall were the first to be seen but, still attempting to retain a level of dignity, the Corporation did not identify them to viewers. The first newsreader with a name was former Olympic athlete Christopher Chataway. And he was a news*caster*.

ITV brought us game shows – 'Double Your Money', 'Take Your Pick', 'Criss Cross Quiz' and many more – which offered cash prizes, so different from the BBC's cosy parlour games like 'What's My Line?' and 'Animal, Vegetable, Mineral?' Then, of course, ITV had commercials. With their catchy jingles, many commercials became more popular than the actual programmes; but, in those dicey days of live television, commercials weren't always popular with programme-makers. In 1956 Paul Scofield's closing speech in a television production of *Hamlet* was cut short to make way for a bunch of animated Kia Ora oranges jumping around on screen. Furious ATV boss Lew Grade rang up. 'What happened?' he boomed. The young transmission controller replied: 'Oh, they all died in the end.'

Throughout the fifties, the BBC really was Aunty, a stern guardian of morality. Programme chief Cecil McGivern was her watchdog. He had issued a directive to variety producers headed 'Vulgarity' which warned: 'There is an absolute ban upon the following: jokes about lavatories, effeminacy in men and immorality of any kind, suggestive references to honeymoon couples, chambermaids, fig leaves, prostitution, ladies' underwear, animal habits (e.g. rabbits), lodgers and commercial travellers.' 'Winter draws on' was definitely out! In 1951 he wrote to his staff: 'The amount of shoulder and chest displayed by Renée Houston in "Charivari" was definitely embarrassing and the dress as it appeared should not have been passed. Also did she wear a brassière? She is the type who needs one. Please let me have a report on this.' Sylvia Peters wore a fashionable strapless gown one evening only to receive a McGivern reprimand: 'You looked as if you were appearing in the bath. Would you please wear a stole in future.' By 1959, McGivern had begun to despair, particularly after seeing the play 'The Torrents of Spring' which featured an erotic seduction. He complained: 'The shooting of the nymphomaniac left no room for doubt as to the shape of her body, her character and her intentions. Licence is becoming licentiousness.' He was determined that the BBC should not move with the times.

It is hard to see why he was worried. Fifties television was very keen on good triumphing over evil. The Sheriff of Nottingham and Landburgher Gessler never got their man, and violence was very much at a premium. Jack Webb, mentor and star of the American police series 'Dragnet', would permit only one shot to be fired every four episodes, while George Dixon was more likely to be spraying his tomatoes than spraying bullets. George's rôle was that of the friendly local bobby – an important one against the background of teenage unrest in the latter part of the decade. Crime series preached the virtues of law and order – the very title of 'No Hiding Place' was enough to deter any would-be criminal.

Drama series became viewers' favourites then as now. Boyd QC and Harry Lime were popular heroes, but viewers were gripped as one by that futuristic masterpiece 'The Quatermass Experiment'. Sylvia Peters recalls that all rehearsals stopped for BBC staff to watch it. Its high shock factor was in marked contrast to most fifties drama, which was about as daring as the potter's wheel. That included the first British soap operas, 'The Grove Family' in 1954 and, three years later, 'Emergency – Ward 10'.

Probably the greatest revolution took place for children who had previously had to rely mainly on Muffin the Mule. The fifties introduced such classics as Andy Pandy, Bill and Ben, Billy Bunter, Sooty and 'Blue Peter'. From 1957, programmes like 'Ivanhoe' and 'William Tell' were inserted into the slot between 6 p.m. and 7 p.m. which had been known as the Toddlers' Truce. Until then, neither channel had screened any programmes for that hour in order to allow mums to tuck young children into bed and let older ones do their homework without distraction.

Youngsters, but not their parents, also greeted the wave of new pop music shows like 'Cool for Cats', 'Six-Five Special', 'Juke Box Jury' and 'Oh Boy!' in which a young singer by the name of Cliff Richard was pilloried for being 'too sexy'. These were a breath of fresh air for teenagers whose choice of music on television had hitherto been limited to little more than Eric Robinson's 'Music for You' or the old-time section on 'Come Dancing'.

The decade saw the birth of the situation comedy with the 1954 production 'Fast and Loose' starring Bob Monkhouse and Denis Goodwin. This was followed by 'Whack-O', 'The Army Game' and 'Hancock's Half-Hour', one of many shows to transfer from radio where almost every comic learned his trade.

Many fifties faces are still on our screens – a little more wrinkled but just as popular. Benny Hill, Michael Aspel and Bob Monkhouse are among our highest paid performers. When they first faced the cameras, most programmes were technically poor, unsophisticated, and the acting left much to be desired. But the energy was staggering, the commitment total. Television had been on trial in the fifties and it had won its case.

THE
SIXTIES

1960

The start of the Swinging Sixties. □ John F. Kennedy was elected President of the United States of America. □ Courts allowed Lady Chatterley's Lover *to be published. □ The Twist dance craze swept across America. □ Traffic wardens made their first appearance in London. □ Prince Andrew was born. □ Lonnie Donegan sang 'My Old Man's a Dustman'. □ A Channel tunnel was mooted. □ Britain's first nuclear submarine,* Dreadnought, *was launched at Barrow. □ Telephone answering machines were introduced. □ So were tights. □ The* News Chronicle *ceased publication, along with its London evening paper, the* Star. *□ The first motorway restaurant was opened, at Newport Pagnell. □ Hitchcock's* Psycho *was released. □ Cassius Clay won a boxing gold medal at the Rome Olympics. □ Teenagers spent an average 12s 3d (62p) a week on clothes. □ And it was the year of the 'Itsy Bitsy Teeny Weeny Yellow Polka Dot Bikini'.*

While Kennedy acknowledged the part that American television had played in his victory over Richard Nixon – 'it was television more than anything else that turned the tide' – in Britain it was the year of the most remarkable success-story in the history of the small screen. For 1960 saw the birth of Britain's longest-running and best-loved soap opera, **'Coronation Street'**.

It was born humbly, unheralded, with a cast of elderly unknowns, many in the twilight of obscure careers in repertory, in the unfashionable, unglamorous North-West of England. The first episode was transmitted live at 7 p.m. on Friday, 9 December. Yet it was not nationally networked until the following spring when the transmission days were changed from Wednesdays and Fridays to Mondays and Wednesdays where it has remained ever since. And a critic who viewed the first episode looked forward to its demise: 'The programme is doomed ... with its dreary signature tune and grim scene of a row of terraced houses and smoking chimneys.'

It was the brainchild of Tony Warren, an unhappy twenty-three-year-old actor and writer who was being paid £30 a week by Granada Television to adapt scripts. He was working on Biggles adventures (which he loathed) when he had the idea for a Northern serial. 'In 1960, the Northern Resurgence was happening in the theatre and in films. I wanted to bring it to television. I wanted to see something written from the heart, acted by genuine Northerners.'

Warren wrote the first episode overnight, and Granada loved it, but he had to alter the title of 'Florizel Street'. 'Agnes the tea lady said Florizel sounded like a disinfectant so we changed it. It would have been Jubilee but there was already a series with that in the title so Coronation it was.'

That historic first episode featured such stalwarts as Ken Barlow, Albert Tatlock, Ena Sharples, Annie Walker and Elsie Tanner and her son Dennis as well as long-forgotten characters like Elsie Lappin, who sold the corner shop to Florrie Lindley, Elsie Tanner's daughter Linda Cheveski and Susan Cunningham, young Ken Barlow's posh girlfriend. William Roache (Ken Barlow) now reveals: 'If I had known it would run for twenty-nine years, I would have run a mile. I didn't even want to sign up for thirteen weeks in 1960.' Violet Carson was sixty-one when she went for the part of Ena. She thought it was just a one-off play and didn't bother much. When the producer hinted that Ena might be difficult to play, she retorted: 'Don't be ridiculous. I have lived with this woman all my life. There is one in every street in the north of England.'

'Coronation Street' took off to such an extent that by the time Elsie Tanner got married to American army sergeant Steve Tanner in 1967 some 20 million viewers joined the celebrations, the sort of audience normally reserved for royal weddings.

In 'Coronation Street' thrusting Elsie Tanner (Pat Phoenix) told Ena Sharples (Violet Carson) to keep her hairnet on as son Dennis (Philip Lowrie) tried to drag her back t' Rover's Return.

The cast became household names, and the public treated them accordingly. Pat Phoenix and Philip Lowrie (Elsie and Dennis Tanner) were mobbed when they made a personal appearance at a Leeds store and had to be rescued by mounted police. Soon Pat was receiving an average of four marriage proposals a week and many more indecent suggestions. Lynne Carol went 'incognito' to the Ideal Home Exhibition, but hundreds recognised her as Martha Longhurst and she was advised by the police to leave for her own safety. Thousands thronged the sea-front at Blackpool when leading members of the cast, posing like film stars, switched on the resort's illuminations. And when Pat Phoenix, Doris Speed (Annie Walker) and Arthur Leslie (Jack Walker) toured Australia a crowd of 20,000 fans was waiting to greet them in Adelaide.

Harold Wilson gave the cast a sherry party at 10 Downing Street, and Jim Callaghan dubbed Pat Phoenix 'the sexiest woman on TV'. Other famous fans ranged from Lord Olivier to Sir John Betjeman, the Poet Laureate, who likened the series to Dickens's *Pickwick Papers* and declared: 'At 7.30 p.m. on Mondays and Wednesdays, I am in heaven.' And Russell Harty wrote: 'There was life before "Coronation Street" – but it didn't add up to much.' Betjeman, Harty, Michael Parkinson and playwright Willis Hall later formed the British League for Hilda Ogden.

Nobody even minded when, according to the design of the street, it was discovered that anyone going to the gents toilet at the Rover's really ended up in Albert Tatlock's kitchen. But the millions of fans did have long memories. In an early episode, Ena Sharples said she didn't like chocolate eclairs. Eight years later, she ate two on the show and the letters poured in!

'Coronation Street' has been sold all over the world – even to the Polynesian island of Oahu where 'Hawaii Five-O' was made. Apparently, the locals preferred Elsie and Ena to Steve McGarrett. The 'Street' was bought by Australia in 1963 and shown five times a week, but it has never really caught on in the United States.

The runaway success of the 'Street' was in stark contrast to the fate of its creator. Tony Warren fell out with Granada and turned to drink and drugs. He snubbed the soap's 500th-episode party and told reporters that he had burned all his scripts and disowned the series, and said it bore no relation to his original idea. Finally, after nearly dying three times from alcohol, he stopped drinking and hasn't touched a drop for over ten years. He made his peace with Granada and is now the show's consultant.

Although still immensely popular, the series was undoubtedly at its peak in that first decade. Tony Warren agrees. 'Yes, the stories were harder, grittier then because life was harder. "Coronation Street" didn't go soft – life did.'

'Coronation Street' was by no means the only quality drama to appear in 1960, for there were some other excellent series, too. One of these was **'Danger Man'** with the enigmatic Patrick McGoohan as John Drake.

A freelance spy working for the British secret service, Drake's trademark was his clipped voice. He also used numerous gadgets: tiepins that were cameras, cherries containing tiny microphones, and electric shavers which cunningly doubled as tape-recorders. He turned McGoohan into a star – whether the actor liked it or not. McGoohan was once a chicken farmer and might have stayed a chicken farmer had an illness not forced him to give it up. He turned to acting, and 'Danger Man' made him the highest-paid actor in Britain, earning £2,000 a week. But McGoohan was, and still is, a man of uncompromising principles. And he makes Garbo seem like a publicity-seeker. In a rare sixties interview, he pronounced: 'I abhor the word "star". It makes the hair on the back of my neck curl up. There are too many so-called stars today.'

He was not the easiest of people to work with. First, he wanted to direct 'Danger Man', then produce it, then write it. He even insisted on rewriting the music for one episode. And he took a firm moral stand on the show, stating in mid-series: 'When we started "Danger Man", the producers wanted me to carry a gun and have an affair with a different girl each week. I refused. I am not against romance on TV but sex is the antithesis of romance. It is phoney, promiscuous sex I am against. Television is a gargantuan monster that all sorts of people watch at all sorts of times and it has a moral obligation to its audience.'

Danger Man (Patrick McGoohan) only arsked Bernard Bresslaw what he thought of the hat.

Drake's apparent aloofness made him all the more attractive to women, and by the time 'Danger Man' finished seventy one episodes later in 1966 he was adored but untouched by millions. He was the original virgin of the secret service.

An actor who was to become even more closely associated with the character he was playing was the late Rupert Davies alias **'Maigret'**. In his trilby hat and belted mac, Maigret used to light his pipe and light up Monday nights. Davies achieved celebrity status, and at the height of the fifty-two episodes he was able to command £10,000 to make a Dubonnet commercial. When the French detective's creator, Georges Simenon, first met him he was amazed at how like Maigret he was. For a start, Davies himself was an inveterate pipe-smoker, possessing some forty pipes and a dozen kinds of tobacco. Simenon's only complaint was that Davies's hair was too long.

On the subject of complaints, both Maigret and that other wastrel George Dixon were accused of drinking too much on screen by the Reverend George Boffin from Cleckheaton, Yorkshire. 'Maigret drinks such a lot it's surprising he doesn't fall flat on his face in the middle of every programme. It amazes me he can stay sober enough to arrest anyone. And Dixon spends too much of his off-duty time in the local. I see no reason why Dixon and Maigret shouldn't drink tea and ginger pop instead of pints of ale and bottles of wine.' Can you imagine Regan and Carter from 'The Sweeney' drinking ginger pop?

It was a vintage year for comedy, bringing veritable classics such as 'Sykes', 'Here's Harry' and **'It's a Square World'**. The last-named was the glorious invention of former Goon Michael Bentine and was clearly more

acceptable to the BBC than the Goons had been. Indeed, a BBC executive had once told Bentine that he didn't care much for 'the Go On show', as he called it. As well as reports from the four corners of the world, the speciality of 'It's a Square World' was models that came to life. Famous routines included a flea circus and the reconstruction of the sinking of the Woolwich Ferry. When asked about the authenticity of the capsizing, Bentine admitted that the Woolwich Ferry had never really sunk but said: 'If it ever does, we will be the first with a documentary reconstruction.' But he did once run into trouble over a sketch showing a Chinese junk attacking the House of Commons and sinking it in the Thames. The BBC banned its screening until after an approaching general election. With commendable logic, Bentine stated: 'Apparently, there is a BBC edict that you must show parity to the parties at election time. I would have imagined that if you sank the Commons you were showing parity to everybody!'

Assisted by Clive Dunn, Frank Thornton, Benny Lee and Len Lowe, Bentine was always creating brilliant madcap comedy. One sequence had a great white whale going home to his mum in the Natural History Museum. The 'whale' was forty feet long and fifteen feet high with twenty-five scene-hands walking inside it and a man squirting water on its back. The producer had been notified that because of roadworks the streets would be

Michael Bentine led the bowler brigade across Westminster Bridge for 'It's a Square World' closely followed by Ronnie Barker.

clear early in the morning. To the dismay of hundreds of motorists, his information was wrong as the whale literally caused a tail-back.

Bentine regularly caused chaos at the BBC. He says: 'We blew it up once, and another time we sent it into orbit. But everyone was used to our behaviour. However, not long after I'd departed to ITV, there was a genuine robbery at Television Centre and as these men rushed out with stockings over their heads the commissionaire said: "Nice to see you back at the BBC, Mr Bentine . . ."'

Shortly after the war, Eric Sykes was sacked by Oldham rep for demanding a pay rise from £3 to £4 a week. Well, Oldham's loss was to be the rest of the country's gain as 1960 saw the début of one of the best-ever examples of domestic comedy, **'Sykes'**. Supported by Hattie Jacques as his sister, Richard Wattis as interfering neighbour Mr Brown and Deryck Guyler as Corky, the friendly neighbourhood policeman, Sykes constantly strove to better himself in his little neck of suburbia. Originally, the relationship between Eric and Hatt was husband and wife, but Sykes decided that it was too restricting and altered it. From the very first show, 'Sykes And A Telephone', it remained a bastion of good clean comedy, totally unaffected by the changing values of society. The partnership only ended with the death of Hattie Jacques in 1980.

The year also saw the first televising of **'The Royal Variety Performance'**, an event which has subsequently diminished in importance and, many believe, quality. Then the Royal Variety was the most prestigious showbusiness occasion on the calendar, and in 1960 attracted such stars as the Crazy Gang, Max Bygraves, Ronnie Carroll, Nat 'King' Cole, Sammy Davis, Jnr, Ronnie Hilton, Liberace, Dennis Lotis, Cliff Richard, Joan Regan, Anne Shelton, Dickie Valentine and Yana. Yet the show was stolen by a virtually unknown comedian called Harry Worth; and his series, **'Here's Harry'**, was to delight audiences for years with a similar type of gentle family humour to 'Sykes'.

The youngest of a family of eleven from Barnsley, Harry worked down the pit as a teenager before starting out on the showbiz circuit of local church-halls armed with his bicycle, a book about ventriloquism from the library, a borrowed dummy with half its head missing and a script of jokes pinched from everybody he had ever heard. Harry dropped his real surname of Illingsworth because it was too long to get on the bills. He went on to appear with artists of the calibre of Laurel and Hardy, and it was Stan Laurel who suggested he ditch the dummy and become a solo comic – no great wrench for Harry, who was not the world's greatest ventriloquist. He followed the advice, with moderate success, until on a traumatic date at the Newcastle Empire his nerves got the better of him and he discovered by chance his distinctive bumbling act. He said, 'The character is not difficult for me to play because it is

Commercial Break

One 1960 advertising campaign which flopped disastrously was the long-gone but never forgotten Strand commercial. Based on a Frank Sinatra film, it showed actor Terence Brook as the mysterious man lighting up a Strand cigarette on a street-corner and promised 'You're never alone with a Strand'. It was hugely popular. Brook became a celebrity overnight, and 'The Lonely Man Theme' reached number 39 in the charts. Yet, much as people loved it, they didn't buy the product, and the campaign was soon discontinued. The theory was that viewers believed that if they smoked Strand they would end up as lonely as the chap in the commercial. For the record, Strand cost 3s 2d (16p) for a packet of twenty.

As usual, there was plenty of debate as to which soap powder washed whiter. We were introduced to two little girls in identical dresses, one dress white, the other off-white, and told: 'Someone's mum isn't using Persil.' And the Daz Brand X commercials were so successful that a Lancashire shop-owner actually attempted to put a powder named Brand X on the market. In the year that brought us 'Coronation Street', the men of Weatherfield could discover that 'a Double Diamond works wonders', while the women could 'look a little lovelier each day with fabulous pink Camay'. If Ena Sharples used Camay, it certainly did not work.

just an exaggeration of myself. I'm clumsy and indecisive. When people used to ask my wife what I was like at home, she would just raise her eyes to heaven.' The initial idea for the television series was for Harry to be a dithering detective but it became a comedy of suburban chaos. At 52 Acacia Avenue he would ramble on about his beloved Aunty and cat Tiddles. Children, parents and grandparents were all wild about Harry – but teenagers scoffed. In an interview of the day, he reflected ruefully: 'I believe it is because I have nothing in common with Adam Faith.' That could qualify as the understatement of the sixties.

The most dramatic event of the year occurred on **'Face to Face'** where John Freeman grilled Gilbert Harding. The usually irascible Harding, remembering the passing of his mother, broke down and wept when asked whether he had ever been in the presence of death. For once, Harding attracted public sympathy. Freeman later expressed regret at his lack of sensitivity on that occasion. 'I was unaware at the time of Harding's recent bereavement and,

Among the better imported shows was '77 Sunset Strip' (click, click) about a team of private eyes operating in the nightclub quarter of Hollywood. The star was Efrem Zimbalist, Jnr, but the girls' favourite was Ed Byrnes as Kookie who was forever combing his hair.

Also Shown in 1960

'The Adventures of Hiram Holliday' was a vastly underrated comedy with Wally Cox as the meek little reporter who continually found himself in dangerous situations.

Meanwhile, after being demobbed from 'The Army Game', Alfie Bass and Bill Fraser tasted life in civvy street in 'Bootsie and Snudge'. Bootsie was an odd-job man and Snudge the pompous doorman at an old-fashioned London club. Roddy McMillan and Duncan MacRae starred in 'Para Handy', a gentle comedy about the crew of a small Clyde steamer. There was 'The Somerset Maugham Hour', a series of adapted short stories which, incredibly, won considerable critical acclaim. History became fashionable with 'An Age of Kings', a praiseworthy fifteen-part serial presenting Shakespeare's history plays (young Sean Connery played Hotspur), and 'All Our Yesterdays', a succession of newsreel clips to remind us how grim life was twenty-five years ago that week with Brian Inglis, possibly television's worst ever presenter. (It lasted thirteen years and 638 programmes before the series and the viewers were put out of their misery.)

Series that didn't survive as long were 'The Strange World of Gurney Slade', a fantasy in which Anthony Newley spoke to trees; the Fleet Street caper 'Deadline Midnight' with Peter Vaughan and Glyn Houston; 'Kipps', a Victorian saga featuring Brian Murray; 'The World of Tim Frazer', a tense thriller by Francis Durbridge starring Jack Hedley; and 'The Cheaters' which had John Ireland as John Hunter, a claims investigator for an insurance company – a scenario about as compelling as the adventures of a chartered surveyor.

'Whiplash' was an Australian Western with Peter Graves; 'Bronco' was an American Western starring Ty Hardin as Bronco Lane; and 'Bonanza' was the first cowboy soap opera – a sort of Annie Walker, Get Your Gun.

quite unknown to me, the question did touch on a sensitive point. It went beyond the bounds of civilised conversation. Had I known, I would never have asked that question.' In the same interview, Harding admitted that 'my bad manners and bad temper are quite indefensible ... I'm almost unfit to live with ... I'm profoundly lonely ... I should be very glad to be dead'. And two months later, he was. Rumoured to be a drinker, a homosexual, his Madame Tussaud's waxwork had been labelled 'the most famous man in Britain'. In a few years it was melted down to make Christine Keeler.

Unlikely comedy was a February edition of 'Gardening Club' when the face of the usually unflappable Percy Thrower went the colour of one of his prize tomatoes. He said: 'I had been warned that our programme would probably be interrupted to announce the engagement of Princess Margaret. It duly came at a moment when I was showing viewers how to plant a gooseberry bush. When we came back on air, I congratulated the Princess on her engagement but I think I rather spoiled it by adding, "And now back to the gooseberries".'

The superstar of children's television was Tex Tucker, sheriff of 'Four Feather Falls', even though he was only 20 inches tall in his cowboy boots. Tex had special powers, the result of four feathers given to him by an Indian. One feather gave the power of speech to Dusty, Tex's dog, another did the same for Rocky, his horse, and the remaining two made his guns automatically fire whenever his life was in danger. The set for this puppet Western was over 30 feet of pretend prairie on which Tex bravely fought his enemies Pedro the Bandit and Big 'Bad' Ben. Tex's voice was that of Nicholas Parsons but, mercifully, when he sang Michael Holliday took over.

One other children's series worthy of mention was the enchanting **'Tales of the Riverbank'** with such critters as Hammy Hamster, Roderick the Rat and Mr Guinea Pig. Narrated by Johnny Morris, 'Tales of the Riverbank' was filmed in Canada and ran until 1971. It used real animals, all of which had stand-ins. What's more, the animals never 'worked' for more than ten minutes at a time and were never made to do anything unnatural. Very militant, these rodents.

During the sixties, if you saw a tree tip-toeing along the pavement, the chances were that it was either Special Branch or **'Candid Camera'**. With pranksters like Arthur Atkins and the notorious Jonathan Routh, and with Bob Monkhouse as the first host, 'Candid Camera' preyed on the gullible for seven years, setting up some 6,400 hoaxes. (It briefly returned in 1974 with Peter Dulay at the helm.)

Viewers sent in a thousand ideas a week, the vast majority of which were taken by the victims in good spirit. But Jonathan Routh had a couple of scrapes. A former heavyweight boxer, Sid Richardson, gave him a black eye, adding 'I think it's a rotten programme', and another aggrieved soul chased Routh with a crowbar. On one occasion the show proved expensive for Bob when he tried selling five-pound notes for £4 10s (£4.50) in Blackpool. 'I thought no one would buy them – they'd think the money was counterfeit. The only way I could persuade "Candid Camera" to try the idea was by offering to use my own money. Unfortunately, I did a roaring trade. In half an hour I was sold out – and fifty pounds out of pocket.'

Classic hoaxes included running a car downhill into a garage forecourt and filming the face of the mechanic when he found there was no engine in it, and the cake-factory woman who tried valiantly, but unsuccessfully, to cope when the conveyor belt was run at double and then treble speed.

The show became a favourite for criminals, who posed as 'Candid Camera' workers to cover up suspicious behaviour while carrying out burglaries. Jonathan Routh and his team were looking suitably furtive one day when a police car suddenly roared up ready to arrest them; unknown to them, they had been filming near a bank and had been reported by an alert citizen. Thereafter, the police demanded to be told where the 'Candid Camera' team were filming their practical jokes. One escapade that badly backfired followed Peter Dulay appearing to eat a goldfish (it was really a slice of carrot) from a tank in a dry-cleaner's shop in front of horrified customers. A woman telephoned to say that after watching the programme her small son had gone in the next room and eaten their goldfish . . .

1961

That Was the Year When...

Russian Yuri Gagarin became the first man in space. □ The Berlin Wall was built. □ Castro's Cuba routed an American-backed invasion army at the Bay of Pigs. □ Britain applied to join the Common Market. □ Identikits were introduced at Scotland Yard. □ In the Portland spy case, Gordon Lonsdale, George Blake and Peter and Helen Kroger were gaoled for spying for Russia. □ South Africa became a republic. □ A young girl called Helen Shapiro leaped to pop fame. □ The Pill went on sale in Britain for the first time. □ Minicabs appeared. □ As did self-service petrol stations. □ Films of the year included West Side Story *and* The Guns of Navarone. *□ Tottenham Hotspur completed the League and Cup double, the first team to do so for seventy-two years. □ And Angela Mortimer defeated Christine Truman in an all-British women's singles final at Wimbledon.*

A lady who could have dealt with Angela Mortimer and Christine Truman at the same time, though not within the rules of tennis, was the redoubtable Cathy Gale, soon to become the heroine of the year's major new drama series, **'The Avengers'**.

When 'The Avengers' began in March 1961 it bore little resemblance to the flippant show we came to know and love. It emanated from a series called 'Police Surgeon' starring Ian Hendry, but when Patrick Macnee was brought in the programme was revamped and the title changed to 'The Avengers'. In the first episode, Hendry's character Dr David Keel swore to avenge the death of his fiancée who had been gunned down in a London street by a syndicate of drug barons. He met undercover agent John Steed and together they set out to track down the killers.

The £150-a-week rôle came at just the right time for Old Etonian Macnee. He had played a number of cowboys in Hollywood Westerns but was on the point of giving up acting to concentrate on producing. However, he was broke and couldn't afford to turn down work. So he jumped at the chance of Steed.

'The Avengers' quickly became a success, but the two male leads looked dowdy in their raincoats. Macnee decided the show lacked elegance and adopted his now familiar style of conservative suits, umbrella and bowler hat. When Ian Hendry left after the 1962 Equity strike, the show faced an uncertain future until producer Sydney Newman decided that the new sidekick should be a woman. Enter Honor Blackman as judo expert Mrs Catherine Gale, dressed in black leather combat-gear,

Avenger John Steed (Patrick Macnee) and Cathy Gale (Honor Blackman) mapped out the next episode.

right down to her high boots. Macnee revealed that the idea for the leather attire came from a kinky camp earl he met at a house-party, but the trousers were added purely because in fights Honor had found it difficult *not* to show her stocking-tops. There was a lot of Honor Blackman in Cathy Gale. Honor took judo lessons every week to keep fit for the part, she could use a gun and could knock men flying. She could also ride a motorbike and had been trained by the police as a motor-cycle dispatch rider during the war. She struck a blow for women everywhere and received letters of praise from downtrodden females who were tired of slaving over a hot stove. She says candidly: 'Cathy Gale touched off the secret longing of almost every woman to beat up a man once in a while.' Ouch! Honor even succeeded, albeit inadvertently, in knocking out wrestler Jackie Pallo during rehearsals for a graveyard battle. As they fought with a spade, Pallo toppled into the grave, banged his head and was rendered unconscious for ten minutes.

Macho men breathed a sigh of relief when Honor Blackman left in 1964, but there was to be no respite as her successor was Diana Rigg playing Emma Peel. At least Mrs Peel wasn't a judo expert – she did kung fu instead. It was quite a change for Diana Rigg, who had come from the Royal Shakespeare Company where her place was taken by an unknown actress called Glenda Jackson. Diana was mystified to find that she received a lot of fan mail from schoolboys. She said in an interview at the time: 'Whereas Honor Blackman got shoals of letters from grown-ups, including some from dubious gentlemen in Surbiton, I seem to appeal to the fourth form and under. I see myself as a sort of pre-puberty sex symbol.' Shops started selling Emma Peel's clothes as part of an Avengers Pack. You could also buy Steed's brown bowler by Pierre Cardin. Diana Rigg left after a row about wages and was replaced by twenty-year-old Linda Thorson as Tara King and twenty-stone Patrick Newell as Steed's boss, 'Mother'. Finally, in 1969, after 8 years, 5 series, 83 episodes, 19 gallons of champagne, 192 karate chops and 30 bowler hats, Tara King accidentally pressed the lift-off button on a rocket and she, Steed and 'Mother' soared into space theoretically never to be seen again. Steed managed to return for 'The New Avengers' seven years later.

The world-wide triumph of 'The Avengers' is easy to understand. Its tongue-in-cheek style meant that nobody ever bled or really suffered, no matter how dastardly they behaved. It was played very much for laughs – indeed, one of the show's creators, Brian Clemens, likened the relationship between Steed and his women to that of Morecambe and Wise.

The genuine Morecambe and Wise also began an illustrious career in 1961. Born Eric Bartholomew and Ernest Wiseman, both in 1926, they first appeared together in 1941 before spending years polishing their act and learning from masters like Laurel and Hardy and

The tall one with the glasses and the one with the short, fat, hairy legs brought us sunshine for over twenty years as Morecambe and Wise.

Abbott and Costello. After surviving a disastrous fifties series called 'Running Wild', they were ready for the big time in **'The Morecambe and Wise Show'** on ITV. Although their sixties days have tended to be overshadowed by the enormous success they had with the BBC after 1968, they firmly established Eric and Ernie as arguably the finest double-act Britain has ever produced. Their scriptwriters then were Sid Green and Dick Hills, who regularly used to appear on the show – as in the hilarious 'Boom Oo Ya-Ta-Ta-Ta' song. Eric and Ernie's screen characters steadily evolved during this time: Ernie was the pompous one, while Eric, often with his glasses turned sideways, tried to drag him down to his level. As was the custom with Morecambe and Wise, they had a number of running gags. One was to try to leave the stage by a door that was too small, while another was for Eric to try in vain to tell a risqué joke about two old men sitting in deckchairs. We never did hear the punch-line.

Patrick Macnee was involved in setting up the production unit of another popular series of 1961, **'The Valiant Years'**. Produced by John Schlesinger, 'The Valiant Years' was Churchill's own story of the Second World War, taken from his memoirs. The original choice for narrator was Laurence Olivier, but in the end they settled for Richard Burton because he was cheaper. Everyone interviewed for background material was paid £75, which pleased some military gentlemen but not others. Viscount Montgomery flatly refused to be interviewed for under £500, but Field Marshal Lord Alanbrooke was delighted with the sum; it meant he could thatch his cottage!

Commercial Break

Like the Strand cigarettes campaign of the previous year, the commercial for the Mark Vardy range of men's toiletries was far more popular than the actual product. Beecham's named the merchandise after one of their own directors and stipulated that the actor to play Mark Vardy should be tall, have a strong profile and be able to walk with the hint of a limp to indicate an earlier sporting accident. The actor's face was never seen in the commercial (it was that of Steve Hudson who later did the voiceover for Old Spice), but his rugged good-looks captured women's imagination. In a manner as mysterious as the commercial itself, Mark Vardy limped off the market within a year.

Bernard Miles urged us to 'go to work on an egg'; kids counting their Smarties said 'Wotalotigot', adding strangely 'Buy some for Lulu', who wasn't even famous then; and comedy husband-and-wife team Joan and Leslie Randall picked because they looked ideally happy (they later separated) reminded us that Fairy Snow 'forces grey out, forces white in'.

The man who set women's pulses racing in 1961 was **Dr Kildare**, played by Richard Chamberlain. The young intern at Blair Hospital attracted a legion of female fans only too keen to experience his bedside manner. Previously only a bit-part actor, the series changed Chamberlain's life. He received an incredible 35,000 letters a month, and ardent admirers used to grab his clothes and hair. Before Kildare, he had only been in a hospital once – and that was as a visitor – but suddenly he was expected to be an expert on medical matters. He later said: 'People really believed I was a doctor. They used to come and tell me their symptoms, expecting a diagnosis.' With its dramatic freeze frame titles, the show took off spectacularly, building up to an audience of 15 million within a year. In total, 190 episodes were shown, focusing on the professional conflict between the idealistic Kildare and his stern superior, Dr Gillespie (Raymond Massey). James Kildare was not simply clean; he seemed permanently sterilised – and the publicity people tried to promote Chamberlain in the same way. When the series had ended, he admitted: 'It was put out by the studio that I didn't smoke, drink or swear, but I do all three in moderation. Now I can finally say so.' That didn't exactly make him a hell-raiser – after all, when he graduated from high school in 1952, he was voted Most Courteous Boy in class.

Some British workers adopted a new mood of militancy in 1961, all because of a comedy series. **'The Rag Trade'** featured Peter Jones as Mr Fenner, harassed boss of Fenner Fashions, Reg Varney as his foreman Reg, and Miriam Karlin as shop steward Paddy who, with a blast on her whistle, was only too happy to declare, 'Everybody out!' After fifteen girls had been sacked at a Derbyshire electronics firm, the stewards ordered an all-out strike. The firm's boss lamented: 'I think this is a case of the girls watching too much "Rag Trade".' Other fashion bosses complained that the series gave a poor impression of the industry and working conditions. 'Rag Trade' regulars were Barbara Windsor, Esma Cannon as little Lilly, who used to be good at button-holes but wasn't the same once zips came in, and Sheila Hancock. In her book *Ramblings of an Actress*, Sheila Hancock recalls how she used to suffer badly from nerves before performances. She said that she and Miriam Karlin would 'take one of those lovely purple heart-shaped pills a nice doctor gave us' with a bath and a glass of champagne to help the nerves. It subsequently took Sheila months to shake off her addiction.

The diminutive Charlie Drake is no stranger to accidents, but his narrowest escape was in the first of a new series entitled **'Bingo Madness'**. The plot called for Drake to be hurled through a bookcase by two villains, feign unconsciousness, fall to the floor and then be picked up and thrown out of a window. The stunt nearly ended in tragedy as Drake really was knocked unconscious when he came through the bookcase. 'Had the actors realised this,' he says, 'they would have stopped, I would have come to and all would have been well. But it was a live show, so they carried on, picked me up and bundled me through the window where my head crashed against a stage weight.'

'Everybody out!' cried Miriam Karlin (left) to Esmé Cannon and Sheila Hancock (right), much to the dismay of 'Rag Trade' boss Peter Jones (centre) and foreman Reg Varney.

After the initial applause, there was a hush as everyone realised something was wrong. Drake continues: 'The director blacked out the screens as millions of people witnessed what could have been the death of me.' Drake lay in a coma for days, and the rest of the series was cancelled. 'Even today, people still come up and ask me if I'm feeling better.'

November brought the start of a ten-week trial run by the BBC's presentation department of **'Points of View'**. With the sardonic but sensible Robert Robinson in the chair, 'Points of View', made to fill a five-minute gap before the news, turned into an entertaining if ineffectual little show, drawing a mailbag of 2,000 letters a week. Robert was followed by the equally witty Kenneth Robinson, the amusing Barry Took and the sympathetic Anne Robinson. Clearly, if you want to host 'Points of View', it helps if your surname is Robinson.

Throughout the sixties, two names were to dominate children's puppet series: Gerry and Sylvia Anderson. The Andersons had started up in 1958 with only £500 capital in an old warehouse that was converted into a soundproof studio by having 1,500 empty egg-boxes nailed to its walls. The first of their remarkable futuristic series was **'Supercar'**, whose test pilot was Mike Mercury. Supercar could travel on land, underwater or in the air, and Mike was assisted by Professor Popkiss, Dr Beaker and young Jimmy Gibson who had a pet monkey called Mitch. Like many of the Anderson characters, Mike Mercury's bland countenance and mechanical personality suggested he was a prototype for today's double-glazing salesman.

The Flintstones, the cartoon Stone Age residents of Bedrock, were popular with children and adults alike. Fred and Wilma Flintstone and their neighbours Barney and Betty Rubble could have taught Terry and June a few things about domestic comedy.

How the defendants in the 1961 Portland spy trial must have wished they had appointed **Perry Mason** to represent them, for in 271 episodes, covering six years, the American defence lawyer never lost a case. Each week we knew that the safest person in the courtroom was the accused. Anyone else was liable to be found guilty

Also Shown in 1961

The year's better home-grown productions included **'First World War'**, a widely acclaimed series of lectures delivered by historian A. J. P. Taylor without referring to maps or notes; **'"A" for Andromeda'**, a science fiction serial which transformed Julie Christie from an unknown drama student into a star; **'Ghost Squad'** with Michael Quinn as American agent Nick Craig and Sir Donald Wolfit as the boss of a Scotland Yard undercover unit; **'The Rat Catchers'**, about a group of government spymasters, with Gerald Flood and Glyn Owen; and **'Top Secret'** starring William Franklyn as Peter Dallas, a British agent in Buenos Aires who joins forces with Argentine 'businessman' Miguel Garetta (Patrick Cargill) in a fight against crime. They were helped by Garetta's nephew Mike, played by Alan Rothwell, and the title-song, 'Sucu Sucu', became a world-wide hit.

In **'Coronation Street'**, a fractured gas main caused everyone to be evacuated to the Glad Tidings Mission Hall for the night; on **'Panorama'**, Richard Dimbleby questioned the Duke of Edin-burgh – the first television interview given by a member of the royal family; and director Yvonne Littlewood shocked the nation at the start of an edition of **'This Is Your Life'** when, after a sound breakdown, she was heard on air to blaspheme: 'Oh Christ, not again.'

In January, ITV screened a fifteen-minute piece about the wildlife of London, but from those humble beginnings developed **'Survival'**, Anglia's award-winning natural history series. Keith Fordyce, later succeeded by Brian Matthew, presented a new pop series, **'Thank Your Lucky Stars'**. In reply to 'Monitor', ITV produced their own arts programme, **'Tempo'**, among the editors of which was Kenneth Tynan; and **'Songs of Praise'** was introduced. Meanwhile Granada prepared a documentary about censorship, including television censorship. The programme was banned!

As for children's shows, Fred Barker joined Ollie Beak and company as 'Lucky Dip' became **'Tuesday Rendezvous'**, and down in the south-west **Gus Honeybun** did his first bunny hop to greet a birthday.

---

instead, whether it was a member of the jury, the usher or even the judge. Played by Raymond Burr, Mason was aided in his quest for justice by loyal secretary Della Street and assistant Paul Drake. His long-suffering opponent was District Attorney Hamilton Burger (or Ham Burger to his friends). Certainly, Mason attacked him with relish.

In 1963 Raymond Burr did lose a court-case off-screen when, presumably believing himself to be as invincible as Perry Mason, he conducted his own defence. A court in Phoenix, Arizona, ordered him to pay £402 to a creditor who claimed that Burr had owed him the money since 1949. The judge said he would have dismissed the case because the debt was too old but, instead of answering the summons through a lawyer as Arizona law required, Burr had followed the improper procedure of pleading his own case. This, remarked the judge, was not good law. Sometimes it simply doesn't pay an actor to identify too closely with a part.

1962

The Cuban missile crisis brought the threat of nuclear war. □ The drug thalidomide was withdrawn after causing deformities in babies. □ Britain and France agreed to build a supersonic airliner, Concorde. □ Admiralty clerk William John Vassall was gaoled for passing secrets to the Russians. □ Television was hit by an actors strike. □ The first Bond film, Dr No, *was released. □ Other new films included* Lolita *and* Summer Holiday. *□ A suburban three-bedroomed semi cost around £3,800. □ The satellite Telstar was launched and was the title of a hit record by the Tornados. □ Denis Law became the first £100,000 footballer. □ And the body of Marilyn Monroe was found in circumstances that remain suspicious to this day.*

Without doubt, this was one of the great years of television – twelve months that introduced such classics as 'Steptoe and Son', 'Z Cars', 'Dr Finlay's Casebook', 'The Saint' and 'That Was The Week That Was'.

Devised by former 'Tonight' men including Donald Baverstock, Ned Sherrin, Alasdair Milne and Antony Jay, **'That Was The Week That Was'** (or 'TW3' as it soon became known) reflected the new permissive image of the BBC under the director-generalship of Sir Hugh Carleton Greene. It was deliberately made by the Current Affairs department, and not by Light Entertainment, in case the latter played too safe. Producer Sherrin intended that it should 'discuss anything that people might talk about on a Saturday night'. They certainly talked about 'TW3' as it rapidly drew an audience of 10 million, way above the expected figure. The show was fronted by the hitherto unknown David Frost, a minister's son from Beccles, with resident accomplices William Rushton (famed for his impersonation of Macmillan), Bernard Levin (he of the acidic interview), Lance Percival, Roy Kinnear, Kenneth Cope, John Bird, John Wells, Eleanor Bron, Al Mancini, David Kernan and Roy Hudd. And Millicent Martin sang the theme song, which never scanned, incorporating the week's events. It always began: 'That Was The Week That Was. It's over. Let it go.'

Much of the show was written by journalists rather than by scriptwriters, and among regular contributors were Dennis Potter and Kenneth Tynan. It covered such previously taboo comic subjects as the three Rs – racism, religion and royalty – as well as fearlessly lampooning politicians, particularly the Home Secretary of the time, Henry Brooke.

It provoked enormous public outcry – all concerned with the programme would have been disappointed if it hadn't. In one instance, a Conservative MP wanted to have the BBC impeached on a charge of holding MPs to ridicule, but since the item in question had mocked only the Tories the Labour Party didn't back him. In his parish magazine, a Cheshire vicar described the studio audience as a 'rabble' and, with a certain lack of Christian spirit, called Levin a 'thick-lipped Jewboy'. Levin, who was once pushed off his stool by an irate member of the audience, also infuriated a dozen farmers in the studio by his opening greeting of 'Good evening, peasants'. One critic attacked Frost and Sherrin for being 'pedlars of filth and smut and destroyers of all that Britain holds dear', while there were endless complaints about Rushton's scruffiness, Frost's front teeth and Kinnear's stomach.

Frost took the format to America in 1963, but it failed to flourish; and, the following year being election year in Britain, 'TW3' was taken off for fear of influencing voters. It never returned – much to the relief of certain sections of the BBC who were horrified at the monster that had been created.

In January, ten months before the birth of 'TW3', the BBC had unveiled another controversial trailblazer, **'Z Cars'**. It arose when writer Troy Kennedy Martin,

confined to bed with mumps, passed the time by monitoring police messages. From these, he got a vastly different impression of the police from that portrayed in 'Dixon of Dock Green'. He set his series in fictionalised Liverpool: Seaforth became Seaport and Kirkby New Town became Newtown. Among the early officers at Newtown were Inspector Charlie Barlow (Stratford Johns), Sergeant John Watt (Frank Windsor), Constable Bert Lynch (James Ellis), Constable David Graham (Colin Welland), Constable Jock Weir (Joseph Brady), Constable 'Fancy' Smith (Brian Blessed), Constable Bob Steele (Jeremy Kemp), Constable Sweet (Terence Edmond) and Desk Sergeant Twentyman, played by actor Leonard Williams who died of a heart-attack a few months into the series. He was replaced by Robert Keegan as Sergeant Blackett. These men were tough. Whereas the police at Dock Green would have been hard-pressed to cope with a disturbance at the Women's Institute, the boys from Newtown had to handle the violent low-life of Liverpool.

'Z Cars' was the first series to show the police as human beings, warts and all. Lynch's début as a young constable (he later made sergeant) was to poke his head through a car window and ask the result of a horse race. Steele was seen arguing with his wife. She had bruises from an earlier row, and a stain on the wall marked the spot where he had thrown the previous night's dinner. Inevitably it sparked off controversy. Viewers rang up in droves to complain after the very first programme, and the chairman of the Police Federation claimed that it harmed the status of the police to depict them as wife-beaters and gamblers. Even George Dixon put the boot in. Speaking of the rivalry between the two series, Jack Warner said: 'When "Z Cars" have worn out as many tyres as I have worn out boots pounding the beat, they'll have something to crow about. Rough stuff? We've had our moments before "Z Cars" was thought of. I have been coshed and a boy has been murdered.' But that was in seven years, George. None of this fracas affected 'Z Cars', which went from strength to strength, lasting 667 episodes until being retired in 1978. Barlow and Watt left Newtown to tread 'Softly, Softly' in 1966, but 'Z Cars' continued to attract first-class actors as diverse as Leonard Rossiter as the abrasive Detective Inspector Bamber and Geoffrey Hayes (later of 'Rainbow') as Detective Constable Scatliff.

The eating habits of the men in 'Z Cars' were exemplary compared to those of Albert Steptoe, whose idea of *haute cuisine* was tucking into pickled onions in his tin bath. **'Steptoe and Son'** was one of the all-time comedy greats. Written by Hancock's mentors Galton and Simpson, the show started as an episode of 'Comedy Playhouse' and embodied the love–hate relationship between frustrated rag-and-bone man Harold and his 'dirty old man' of a father, Albert. The idea sprang from Ray Galton's schooldays when he used to go totting, and in the skilled

Before 1962, Shaw Taylor had been a television quizmaster, but when ATV found they had a five-minute gap in their schedules they offered the time to the Metropolitan Police as a public service. The result was 'Police 5', presented, as it has been ever since, by Taylor. At first, the police were suspicious of the venture but they now see it as a valuable aid in the fight against crime. In the seventies, there was even 'Junior Police 5', which, far from investigating burglaries into doll's houses or jellybaby snatching, sought the help of youngsters in solving bank raids and so on. Known in the underworld as 'whispering grass', Taylor always signs off with the reminder to 'keep 'em peeled'.

hands of Wilfrid Brambell and Harry H. Corbett (he added the H to distinguish himself from Sooty's handler – he said that the H stood for Hanything) it ran for twelve years, attracting an audience of no fewer than 22 million at its peak. This was despite the language which was pretty daring for the time – Lew Grade reputedly banned the show from his home.

Even Hercules, the Steptoes' horse, achieved stardom. A genuine rag-and-bone man's horse – he belonged to Shepherd's Bush brothers Arthur and Chris Arnold – he was often recognised by children on his rounds and offered carrots and sweets. Brambell, who died in 1985, three years after Corbett, went to great pains to enjoy playing Steptoe senior. For the part of the revolting Albert, he wore a special set of worn-down, blackened false teeth which he insisted were kept in a glass of his favourite drink – gin and tonic. Adapted for America with an all-black cast as 'Sanford & Son', for Holland as 'Stiefbeen En Zoon' and for Sweden as 'Albert Og Herbert', the British Steptoes still looked considerably fresher than Albert's underpants when they were repeated in 1988.

Aside from brave new productions like 'TW3' and 'Z Cars', the BBC still found a place for more traditional programmes such as A. J. Cronin's homely tales from **'Dr**

Finlay's Casebook'. Set in 1920s Scotland, this delightful series restored the dignity of the medical profession after 'Dr Kildare'. Compared to the feverish activity of 'Kildare', Tannochbrae was in a permanent state of anaesthesia. The residents of Arden House were the crusty Dr Cameron, the type of old-fashioned doctor who intimidated patients into recovery, 'young' Dr Finlay (who never looked a day under forty) and housekeeper Janet, a sort of efficient Mrs Overall. They were played by Andrew Cruickshank, Bill Simpson and Barbara Mullen respectively. The series was put together in just five weeks to fill a gap in the schedules. Andrew Cruickshank said: 'It was very rushed at first and nobody ever noticed that Dr Cameron's room at Arden House didn't have a window.' Bill Simpson was plucked from reading the news with Scottish ITV in Glasgow. Like Dr Finlay, he was an ex-farmer and hailed from the Ayrshire fishing village of Dunure, almost an exact replica of Tannochbrae. In fact the prodigal son returned to Dunure to film an episode in the series.

'Dr Finlay's Casebook' was a Sunday-evening 'must' for millions. However, one person did take exception to the odious little Dr Snoddy. When the programme finally ended at the start of the seventies, a Dr Desmond Reilly told a London conference of medical officers: 'Dr Snoddy should be in horror movies. Over the years, he has been seen to bungle cases or to be an obstructionist. The best thing to happen for the good name of public health has been the dropping of the series.'

At least Dr Snoddy did not steal hearts. The man to watch for that was the Saint, a rôle which ultimately led to

Roger Moore as the Saint comforted Gabrielle Drake. Maybe she had dreamed she would star in 'Crossroads' twenty years later.

Commercial Break

Among the commercials shown that year were three with great jingles. First Bing Crosby and later Sammy Davis, Jnr, sang: 'I'm going well, I'm going Shell, I'm going well on Shell, Shell, Shell.' A voice boomed, 'This is luxury you can afford by Cyril Lord,' and there were also the inspiring lyrics of 'Rael-Brook Toplin, the shirt you don't iron'. The commercial, accompanied by animated shirts, simply consisted of repeating the phrase over and over again.

It was also the year when a puny freckle-faced child cowboy in National Health Service glasses strode through a set of saloon doors and yelled: 'The Milky Bars are on me!'

Roger Moore playing James Bond. The part of Simon Templar was originally offered to Patrick McGoohan, but he turned it down because he didn't like the way the script called for the Saint to have an affair with a different girl each week. Based on the Leslie Charteris books, **'The Saint'** ran for seven years and was sold to some eighty countries, which was extremely beneficial to Moore as his deal gave him a share of the world-wide profits. The son of a London policeman, Moore used to be a film cartoonist and a photographic model for anything from bathing-trunks and knitting-patterns to toothpaste. As Templar, he used to brush aside Chief Inspector Claud Eustace Teal (Ivor Dean) whom he mockingly described as 'Scotland Yard's finest'. This trait of Templar's prompted Moore to declare once: 'The Saint is a bighead.' Confirming that the two had little in common, Moore momentarily let his halo slip by adding: 'I always play heroes but I am a coward – I would run miles to avoid a fight.' Many people ran miles to avoid 'The Return of the Saint' with Ian Ogilvy in 1978.

The Saint visited many exotic locations but none quite like the derelict Victorian building in Ealing which was the scene for the surprise hit of 1962, **'Bucknell's House'**. Already a television favourite with his do-it-yourself programmes, Barry Bucknell was asked by the BBC to do a series showing him renovating a neglected old house. When a likely property had been found, the BBC sent in a surveyor, who was horrified and said that under no circumstances should they buy it as the building was dilapidated and had dry rot.

'Splendid,' said producer Stanley Hyland. 'Is there any wet rot anywhere? And woodworm?'

'There's wet rot,' said the mystified surveyor. 'But happily I've found no woodworm.'

'You go back and find some,' ordered Hyland. 'We're not buying it without woodworm!'

Fortunately, the surveyor discovered woodworm.

Barry Bucknell says: 'There were birds flying in and out of the roof, and the place smelt dreadful, but being a mug who takes on anything I said OK. I had to employ a team of helpers to work on the house, and we often had to work all night to find some dry rot in a wall so that the cameras could film it the next day. Another time, we toiled away through the night so that a wall was ready to knock down for filming in the morning. But when the wall came down there was so much dust that the camera couldn't see anything. And we could hardly do a retake!' The thirty-nine-week series was a huge success, and Bucknell received half a million letters asking for pamphlets. Looking back, he concludes: 'It had the atmosphere of a serial and that feeling of one person against adversity. It was real television – if anything went wrong, you saw it.'

The house was sold at auction for £7,000, and the new owners found that even Barry Bucknell made mistakes when they uncovered a large damp patch on one of the walls. Bucknell immediately offered to put it right and pay for it himself.

In January, the same month as they introduced 'Z Cars', the BBC launched their first real soap opera since 'The Grove Family': **'Compact'**. Created by Hazel Adair as she sat waiting to deliver an article to *Woman's Own* and written with Peter Ling with whom she was to devise

Gussie (Frances Bennett), Edmund Bruce (Robert Fleming), Ian Harman (Ronald Allen) and Mark Vickers (Gareth Davies) admire the hundredth edition of 'Compact'. When the series was dropped Hazel Adair commented: 'People got us wrong. We did not set out to make a documentary about life on a woman's magazine. What we put over was the stuff the woman's magazines are selling themselves.' Perhaps it could have done with being a bit more *Cosmopolitan*, a little less *Bunty*.

Also Shown in 1962

Janice Nicholls, a sixteen-year-old Black Country lass, became a star overnight when she uttered the immortal words 'Oi'll give it foive' on **'Thank Your Lucky Stars'**.

Still feeling the effects of his accident on **'Bingo Madness'**, Charlie Drake announced his retirement. The public were horrified – some even more so when he changed his mind. **'Hugh and I'** was an inoffensive comedy in which the simple Hugh Lloyd invariably got the better of the scheming Terry Scott, and **'The Seven Ages of Jim'** featured Jimmy Edwards in seven different settings.

To combat 'TW3', ITV conceived **'On the Braden Beat'**, a mixture of entertainment and investigation into consumer complaints.

Another of the year's long-runners was the splendid **'University Challenge'**, whose questionmaster, the highly intelligent Bamber Gascoigne, has become famed for phrases like 'your starter for ten', 'no conferring' and 'well remembered, Queen's'.

In July the first transatlantic satellite transmission took place via Telstar. In the opening eighteen minutes, 200 million people in sixteen European countries witnessed such scenes as a presidential press conference from Washington, baseball from Chicago and a production of *Macbeth* in Ontario.

Nobody in **'Coronation Street'** was interested in fancy satellites; they were more concerned with the abduction of baby Christopher Hewitt, left outside Gamma Garments by his mum Lucille, and the wedding of Ken Barlow to Valerie Tatlock. Other dramas included the period adventures, **'Richard the Lionheart'** (Dermot Walsh) and **'Sir Francis Drake'** (Terence Morgan); that excellent American series **'The Defenders'** starring E. G. Marshall and Robert Reed as father-and-son lawyers Preston and Preston; **'Zero One'**, a run-of-the-mill programme about an airline detective with Nigel Patrick; and **'The Odd Man'**, a weird crime series that acquired something approaching cult status.

The junior equivalent of 'University Challenge' was **'Top of the Form'**, presented by such stalwarts as Geoffrey Wheeler, Paddy Feeny, John Edmunds and David Dimbleby. Another popular children's quiz was the crossword-puzzle formula of **'Take a Letter'** with Bob Holness. Johnny Morris put words into creatures' mouths for **'Animal Magic'**; Jean Morton appeared with **Tingha and Tucker** ('Hello, Aunty Jean'); Colin Douglas starred as the dim villain in the brilliant **'Bonehead'**; **Mister Ed** was the horse that talked, but only to his owner Wilbur Post; and Jim Backus provided the voice for the short-sighted **Mr Magoo**, the silly old fool who never knew whether he was talking to an ugly woman in a fancy hat or a moose.

'Crossroads', 'Compact' centred around 'the talented and temperamental people who worked on a topical magazine for the busy woman'. Screened on Tuesdays and Thursdays following 'Tonight', it was swiftly dismissed by the critics as 'empty-headed', 'worthless' and 'hollow', and it oozed BBC cleanliness. Characters didn't smoke or swear, and the sexiest moment was a chaste goodnight kiss (the foot of a bed was seen only once, and that was when someone had flu). When the Twist was to be featured in an episode, checks were made and, yes, a doctor somewhere had warned against sprains from the craze. So a new safe dance, the Method, was invented instead to keep 'Compact' pure and wholesome.

In the first six months alone, there were nine romances, including three marriages. Bouffant-haired editor Joanne Minster, gave way to droning heart-throb Ian Harman. Dozy Ian fell for impish secretary Sally, but she rejected his advances and left. Later she returned (Monica Evans, who played Sally, said that after earning £50 a week on 'Compact' it was hard living on 50s (£2.50) unemployment pay) and married Ian and the pair departed to America. Other popular characters were art editor Richard, warm-hearted gushing Gussie, the features editor; Mark, the mysterious fiction editor; and tubby typist Iris and her boyfriend Stan. But the ratings lagged behind ITV's 'Emergency – Ward 10', and with the understanding that journalists aren't as interesting as doctors 'Compact' was dropped in 1965.

1963

That Was the Year When...

American President John F. Kennedy was assassinated in Dallas, Texas. □ *Harold Macmillan was replaced as British Prime Minister by Sir Alec Douglas-Home.* □ *Harold Wilson became leader of the Labour Party following the death of Hugh Gaitskell.* □ *Screaming Lord Sutch formed the National Teenage Party.* □ *The nation was rocked by the Profumo affair, and by the Great Train Robbery which netted £2½ million.* □ *Dr Beeching wielded his axe on the railways.* □ *Spy Kim Philby defected to Moscow.* □ *Cassette tape-recorders came into use.* □ *The Russians put the first woman into space, Valentina Tereshkova.* □ *General de Gaulle said 'non' to Britain's Common Market entry.* □ *There were 815,000 unemployed, the highest total since 1947.* □ *Television advertising magazines were banned by Parliament.* □ *National Service was ended.* □ *And from March, with their first hit, 'Please Please Me', Britain was in the grip of Beatlemania.*

Yes, 1963 was the year that the Fab Four sent teenage girls into areas of fantasy hitherto reserved for *Bunty*, but even Hilary of the Highboard couldn't compete with John, Paul, George and Ringo. Girls screamed, boys let their hair grow and parents wondered what all the fuss was about. Anyway, what was wrong with Teddy Johnson and Pearl Carr?

Television producers were quick to book the new sensations for guest spots, but Colin Clews, producer-director of **'The Morecambe and Wise Show'**, expressed grave doubts about their future. 'We had the Beatles as guests one week,' recalls Clews, 'and they'd already had a couple of hits. After they'd done their bit, I

quietly remarked to somebody; "I know we're recording six of these shows but we'd better get the one with the Beatles out early in case they don't last!" What's more, they overheard me.'

They were also guests on the variety show **'Big Night Out'** with Mike and Bernie Winters, and Bernie couldn't believe his eyes when he and his brother arrived at the studios in Didsbury, Manchester. There were kids everywhere. We've made it, thought Bernie. This is it. Fans, autograph-books – we're going to be mobbed.

Mike continued:

So we stepped confidently from the car and we were right miffed when the kids hardly took any notice of us. I asked the doorman what it was all about. 'The Beatles are on the show today, sir,' he said, and of course we remembered the mop-heads that we had been told were big in the North. They wandered in an hour late for rehearsal, with Jane Asher carrying Paul's guitar, and John Lennon said: 'I'm sorry we're late, sir.' I said fine but please not to let it become a habit as it messed

Keith Fordyce asked the Beatles if they thought they had a future on 'Ready, Steady, Go!' Helen Shapiro looked confident.

everyone else about. In our act, Bernie did a send-up of 'She Loves You', and the lads were very appreciative. John came round with the others afterwards and said 'Thanks very much for all the plugs you've been giving us', which Bernie and I thought was rather touching.

Dance teacher Peggy Spencer was worried that the advent of the Beatles would seriously damage **'Come Dancing'**. She feared the number of girls taking up ballroom dancing would diminish, explaining: 'Girls feel it's the wrong thing to dance with a partner. They are so wound up with the image of Ringo that they can't bear to dance with someone who isn't him.' And let's face it, the chances of Ringo doing the Foxtrot were slim.

The Beatles weren't the only new pop phenomenon to arrive on the scene in 1963. For teenagers everywhere, early Friday evenings were dominated by one programme, **'Ready, Steady, Go!'**, which promised 'The weekend starts here'. The first show was presented by Keith Fordyce and David Gell, with 200 kids in the studio. That début line-up featured Pat Boone, Chris Barber, Billy Fury, Brian Poole and the Tremeloes, and Joyce Blair. Over the next three years, 'Ready, Steady, Go!' proved to be quite simply the best television pop show ever, combining its unique atmosphere and vitality with the best sounds around. It made stars of singer Donovan and a nineteen-year-old 'typical teenager' from Streatham, Cathy McGowan.

A lowly £10-a-week secretary, Cathy answered an advertisement for a teenage adviser to the show, along with 600 other hopefuls. Elkan Allan, the man behind 'Ready, Steady, Go!', remembered: 'She was awfully gauche and raw and desperately nervous but she was worth taking on because she was obviously terribly switched on in a teenage way.'

Cathy was totally unspoiled. She lived with her parents and admitted that her favourite programme was 'Danger Man' – 'he's my idea of a smashing, terrific-looking chap'. And in spite of her new-found fame, she still dusted her production office every day!

How did Cathy sum up the fashions of 1963? 'For girls, looking deliberately dowdy is the thing, dull colours and old ladies' shoes, although girls are more attractive if they've got a really marvellous, way-out pair of boots. It's the boys who have to look pretty with red and pink trousers and high-heeled boots.' She soon received 600 fan letters a week, and you could buy Cathy McGowan shirts, jeans, stockings and even a movable doll. Did it constantly flick the hair out of its eyes?

In 1965 the show decided to ban miming, a move welcomed by Beatles manager Brian Epstein. 'I think the ban's a splendid idea,' he said. Rumoured to be less happy about having to sing live were Billy Fury and Peter and Gordon. The following year saw the demise of 'Ready, Steady, Go!' and Cathy McGowan, 'Queen of the Mods'.

Created by Terry Nation, the Daleks made their début on 'Dr Who' in December 1963. Their flashing lights were the indicator lights off an old Morris car, and inside each contraption was an actor sitting on a stool with three castors. John Scott Martin, a regular Dalek, said: 'It's like a bubble-car on castors and you sit inside and trundle it along with your feet. Inside there's a bit of gadgetry to work to operate the lights, eye-stick and gun.' The Daleks achieved celebrity status and were the subject of a 1964 record, 'I'm Going to Spend My Christmas with a Dalek', which, unfortunately, was of a similar standard to most Christmas discs.

Explaining why he felt it had to come off, Elkan Allan said: 'When the Beatles got the MBE, pop music just became too respectable.'

Ever since the tragic event in Dallas on 22 November 1963, a question regularly posed throughout the world has been: 'What were you doing on the day Kennedy was shot?' In addition to providing the answer to that, millions of Britons know exactly what they were doing the day after his assassination: they were watching the first episode of the BBC's strange new science-fiction serial, **'Dr Who'**.

Previously turned down by ITV, the adventure began at an ordinary school where the Doctor's grand-daughter Susan (Carole Ann Ford) was a star pupil. Her science teacher Ian Chesterton (played by an armourless Sir Lancelot, William Russell) and history teacher Barbara Wright (Jacqueline Hill) were intrigued by Susan's vast knowledge, and their curiosity led them to the Doctor and his home – what seemed to be a police box. Of course, it turned out to be a time machine called the Tardis, which

Commercial Break

The impact of pop music was reflected in the commercials of the time. Cartoon Beatles launched Nestlé's Jellimallo bar while a live-action commercial for Quaker Puffed Wheat featured Craig Douglas, Cliff Richard, Lonnie Donegan and Acker Bilk with Brian Matthew doing the voiceover. He declared that puffed wheat was 'a swinging way to start the day'. A young Australian disc jockey was among those who auditioned for Omo with WM7. Omo were looking for a presenter with impact, so they tested a man with one arm (don't tell Richard Kimble), a chap with an eye-patch, as well as Alan Freeman. Test commercials were made and shown to a sample audience. The professionals weren't keen on Freeman, but the sample audience loved him and so jubilantly he arrived on a scooter, clutching a bottle of wine, to sign for Omo. To prove that Omo with WM7 added 'brightness to cleanness and whiteness', they embarked on a tour of Welsh valleys, offering to do people's washing. The commercial's producer did two lots himself.

Betty Driver, later to become Betty Turpin in 'Coronation Street', demonstrated the whitening power of Oxydol by claiming that Northern air was dirtier than the South's. Oxydol was finally withdrawn in 1973 after forty-two years on the market. Luxurloaf wrapped bread contained ten thick slices and fifteen thin but failed to make a crust, while 1,001 cleaned 'a big, big carpet for less than half a crown' and Pal meat for dogs Prolonged Active Life.

Housewives of 1963 gazed in awe at the Duke of Bedford's Flash-clean floor. One of the early Flash slogans was 'Flash cuts cleaning time in half', and to illustrate this they embarked on cleaning the stage at the London Palladium. To add a bit of authenticity, the director asked for three acrobats from a nearby circus. When they were asked to pose on each other's shoulders, the director was surprised to find that the man on top needed a ladder to get up there. He was even more worried when the poor fellow toppled off with a thud. In all, they did six takes, and each time the man on top crashed to the ground. It was only afterwards that the director discovered that the trio weren't acrobats at all; they were lion tamers, but they hadn't wanted to pass up the chance of £25 for a day's work!

stood for Time and Relative Dimensions in Space.

The first Doctor was played by William Hartnell with long white hair and frock-coat, but the Doctor's ability to transmute into another human form has enabled a succession of actors to play the Time Lord: Patrick Troughton, Jon Pertwee, Tom Baker, Peter Davison, Colin Baker and Sylvester McCoy. Over the years the Doctor has encountered a grisly assortment of adversaries including Cybermen, Ice Warriors, Sensorites, Voords, Krotons, Autons, Zygons, Sea Devils, Urbankans, Draconians, Silurians, Sontarans, Mara, Yeti, Terileptils, Mummies, and everyone's favourite cruet set the Daleks, with their metallic cries of 'Exterminate! Exterminate!'

William Hartnell left in 1966, partly because he was suffering from multiple sclerosis and partly following an argument with the BBC. He thought the series was becoming too evil and unsuitable for children. There were complaints about the Cybermen being too frightening, and the use of vampire bats in a 1980 episode prompted an outcry from the RSPCA and led to questions being asked in Parliament.

The most flamboyant Dr Who was Tom Baker, who reigned for six years from 1974. He was working temporarily on a building site when he was chosen for the part and later remarked that his fellow-workmen couldn't believe 'their cement mixer becoming Dr Who'. Baker was an ardent fan of the show and once launched this scathing attack on rival screen gods: 'I think the biggest bores in the hero business are James Bond, Kojak, Callan and footballers. They're non-people who do nothing but kick other people. The Doctor doesn't shoot anybody, drink, or beat up women but somehow he has heroic appeal to kids.'

Over the years, Dr Who has built up an enormous following among children and adults alike. There are even Dr Who conventions. When the then BBC programmes chief Michael Grade announced that he was axing the show in the eighties, the sheer weight of protest made him change his mind – with a couple of death threats from over-zealous fans.

Another cult series of 1963 saw a doctor relentlessly pursuing a one-armed man. It wasn't to tell him that he'd left the other arm in the operating-theatre, it was all part of the plot for **'The Fugitive'**. David Janssen starred as Dr Richard Kimble, a man on the run from an avenging policeman, Lieutenant Gerard (Barry Morse), following the murder of his wife. Over a period of 120 episodes, Kimble tried to track down the real culprit, the one-armed man. Prisoners wrote to Janssen saying they had been framed, too; convicts on a chain-gang in the Deep South threatened to riot when a warden said he'd stop them watching 'The Fugitive'; and old ladies reported sightings of suspicious one-armed men. When Granada suddenly stopped showing the series halfway through, 600 Liverpool factory-girls formed an action committee to persuade the company to change its mind. Shortly afterwards, it returned. Barry Morse was once dining in a London restaurant when a waiter brought him a note which read: 'Kimble is in the kitchen.'

The final episode, a two-parter in August 1967, caused uproar because so many viewers were on holiday. To keep everyone happy and the outcome secret, the second segment was televised all over the world on the same day: everyone was able to see Gerard shoot the one-armed bandit as he wrestled with Kimble in what is known in natural history films as a life-and-death struggle.

One of the better home-grown dramas was ATV's **'The Plane Makers'**, which told of the life-and-death struggle in an aircraft factory. Created by Wilfred Greatorex, the series was built around the late Patrick Wymark as John Wilder, the company's bullying managing director. Wymark was a gentle man in real life. His wife once said that 'far from being a dynamic tycoon, he was the most inefficient, dreamy muddler in the world'. Wymark himself confessed: 'I don't like Wilder. He is a bastard.' His daughter Jane, who was twelve at the time, wasn't too impressed with Wilder, either. 'The series is just totally boring,' she said. 'I'd rather listen to the Beatles.' The plane in the programme was the Sovereign. Viewers wanted to buy it, but inside the 5½-ton aircraft was just scaffolding – no engines, no controls and no room for seats. The only time it 'flew' was when it was once towed across Hendon aerodrome in a high wind. It got three feet off the ground and nearly landed on the jeep that was pulling it.

Eccles and Bluebottle, who in company with the likes of Moriarty, Neddy Seagoon, Major Dennis Bloodnok, Grytpype-Thynne and Min and Henry, brought the Goons to television on late Saturday afternoons in that wonderful animated series 'The Telegoons'.

After fifty episodes about management-and-union disputes, ATV boss Lew Grade agreed with Jane Wymark that 'The Plane Makers' was boring. 'Who wants machinery and the noise of a factory when they get home at night? Move out of there, I said.' So the action switched entirely to the boardroom where it improved further as **'The Power Game'** in 1965.

For more than twenty-five years, the hardest-hitting current-affairs programme on television has been Granada's **'World in Action'**, a series which has set a consistently high standard in investigative journalism. The first edition, in January, highlighted the atomic arms race and showed Khrushchev and Kennedy in conflict. Later in the year, 'World in Action' ran into trouble over an exposé of the appalling living conditions of black people in South Africa and Angola. The ambassadors of those countries

Richard Briers and Prunella Scales as a young married couple in 'Marriage Lines'.

Also Shown in 1963

The popular anthology series **'Love Story'** was shown on ATV, as were the enthralling tales of a London Victorian detective, **'Sergeant Cork'**. Patrick Allen played **Crane**, a Briton who gave up his job to run a café, a boat and a smuggling business in Morocco, while psychiatrist Dr Roger Corder (Herbert Lom) opened his casebook in **'The Human Jungle'**.

The major play of the year was the award-winning version of Tolstoy's *War and Peace* and in **'Coronation Street'** Dennis Tanner launched window-cleaner Walter Potts on a career as pop star Brett Falcon; The clerical comedy **'Our Man at St Mark's'** featured first Leslie Phillips and then Donald Sinden as a youthful vicar and Joan Hickson as the housekeeper. Two comedians who had their own series in 1963 were Dickie Henderson and Dick Emery. In **'The Dickie Henderson Show'** the star played a song-and-dance man with a penchant for falling over at least once an episode; **'The Dick Emery Show'** was for years one of the backbones of BBC light entertainment, and Emery's collection of oddball characters (the toothy vicar, old Lampwick, the bovver boy and the gentlemanly tramp) made him a national favourite. His best-known creation was the buxom Mandy who, when asked a question loaded with innuendo, would thrustingly declare, 'Ooh, you are awful – but I like you,' and send the street interviewer flying.

Free cigarettes lured customers to the pub in **'Stars and Garters'**. Regular guests were gravel-voiced Tommy Bruce, Clinton Ford, Kathy Kirby, big brassy redhead Kim Cordell and host Ray Martine's own mynah bird, which was paid the Equity rate of £5 per show.

From America came **'The Dick Van Dyke Show'**, one of the more acceptable comic offerings from across the Atlantic; and **'That Was The Week That Was'** won unaccustomed praise for its Kennedy tribute – widow Jackie even asked for a special showing.

World leaders of the twentieth century were the subject of **'Men Of Our Time'** while one who would have made a superb world leader but instead had to content himself with ruling a grubby New York alley was TC, star of the cartoon series **'Boss Cat'**. Another courageous protector of society was **Deputy Dawg**, someone who just didn't know the meaning of the word 'cowardice'. Come to think of it, there were a lot of words the dim deputy didn't know the meaning of.

Steve Zodiac was the rocket commander in Gerry and Sylvia Anderson's **'Fireball XL5'**, and the children's magazine programme 'Tuesday Rendezvous' was succeeded by **'The Five O'Clock Club'**.

---

protested, and the ruling body of Independent Television, the ITA, decided that the programme was not impartial and decreed that the authority should vet future editions. The first producer was Australian Tim Hewat who, on arriving in Switzerland to film a story about a typhoid outbreak at the height of the winter season, so incensed the normally mild-mannered locals with the prospect of adverse publicity that they pelted him with rocks.

'World in Action' has continued to upset those in high places, particularly with programmes about Northern Ireland. Even a 1964 edition about the poor facilities available to British athletes training for the Tokyo Olympics was banned; and when a film on defence spending was vetoed in the sixties part of it was broadcast instead on the rival 'Panorama', to the acute embarrassment of the ITA.

1964

Mods and rockers rioted at seaside resorts. □ In America, Congress gave the go-ahead for thousands of troops to be sent to Vietnam. □ Argentinian corned-beef stocks were destroyed after 400 cases of typhoid had been reported in Britain. □ Washing-machine millionaire John Bloom's business empire crashed. □ The Sun newspaper was launched. □ So was the Sindy doll. □ And the first topless swimsuit. □ Magistrates ordered seizure of copies of the book Fanny Hill. *□ Midlands schoolteacher Mary White-house and vicar's wife Norah Buckland founded the Clean-up TV Campaign. □ The face of the year belonged to model Jean Shrimpton. □ BBC2 started. □ Prince Edward was born. □ Lynn Davies and Mary Rand won long-jump golds at the Tokyo Olympics. □ And Ann Packer triumphed in the 800 metres. □ Among new film releases were* Mary Poppins *and the Beatles'* A Hard Day's Night. *□ Pirate radio ships, notably Radio Caroline, stole listeners from the BBC. □ The Rolling Stones shocked all but the blind; Cilla Black horrified all but the deaf. □ And the Labour Party gained power with Harold Wilson as Prime Minister.*

Wilson's victory was due in no small way to two scruffy rag-and-bone men from Shepherd's Bush. **'Steptoe and Son'** was due to be screened on election day, one and a half hours before the polls closed. Wilson spoke to BBC chief Sir Hugh Greene expressing his 'very real worry about "Steptoe and Son"' and how he feared it might keep Labour voters away from the polling-booths. So Hugh Greene decided to postpone transmission until 9 p.m., whereupon Wilson is reported to have said: 'Well, Hugh,

thank you very much. That might be worth a dozen seats to me.' Labour won the election by just four seats.

Wilson also came across on television as being far more charismatic than his opponent, Sir Alec Douglas-Home, who had a poor television image and was given a particularly rough ride by the BBC's successor to 'TW3', **'Not So Much a Programme, More a Way of Life'**.

Bernard Levin, never one to sit on the fence, called Sir Alec an 'imbecile' and a 'cretin', and the Tory leader confessed at the time: 'Nothing would induce me to appear on that show. I wish TV had never been invented – except for sport. But I suppose politicians must adapt themselves to it.'

If it's of any consolation to Sir Alec, the series didn't even last six months. First shown on Friday, 13 November (an omen in itself), it was soon dubbed 'Not So Much a Programme, More a Waste of Time'. Despite the skill of anchorman David Frost, it attracted only half the audience of 'TW3'. Willie Rushton soon became disenchanted and left after a few weeks as the show proved controversial but not very funny. Kenya's High Commissioner protested at John Bird's lampooning of their leader, Jomo Kenyatta, and there was an unholy row over a contraceptives sketch with Roy Hudd as a Catholic priest. MPs demanded that Frost should publicly apologise, but he didn't. Eventually, in April 1965, the series was sacrificed as part of a new BBC shake-up. Sir Alec's reaction to the axing? 'And not before time.'

That retort was echoed by millions in 1988 when, after twenty-four years of being one of Britain's favourite jokes, **'Crossroads'** was finally killed off. The idea for a Midlands soap had been around since 1958 when ATV's Reg Watson told Lew Grade how impressed he'd been by the live daily serials he'd seen in America. Lew said nothing – for six years. Then he asked Watson to produce a British daily serial, to be called 'The Midland Road', written by Hazel Adair and Peter Ling and centred on widow Meg Richardson and her two children who had turned the family home into a motel. Nobody at ATV liked the title, so a local newspaper ran a competition to think up

Spot the splinters as Meg (Noele Gordon) and the gang began twenty-four years of hard labour at the Crossroads Motel.

a new one – and 'Crossroads' was born, the Midlands rival to 'Coronation Street'.

Originally scheduled to run for just six weeks, 'Crossroads' went on to become as much a part of British life as wet summers or waiting to be served at Woolworth's. The immortal first words, which now rank alongside 'To be or not to be' in terms of literary importance, were 'Crossroads Motel. Can I help you?' They were spoken by Meg's daughter, Jill Richardson, and were just about the only sensible things she ever said. The sole survivor from first to last episode, Jill was married three times (once bigamously), had two miscarriages, had a child by her stepbrother, became a drug addict, an alcoholic and, for good measure, suffered a couple of nervous breakdowns. Not that Meg fared much better. Her first husband, Malcolm Ryder, tried to poison her, she was imprisoned for dangerous driving, suffered amnesia, and when she thought she'd found happiness by marrying businessman Hugh Mortimer he was kidnapped by a gang of international terrorists, with whom her partner's son was involved, and died of a heart-attack. Meg decided the safest thing was to sail off in *QE2*. And who could blame her!

In addition to Meg (Noele Gordon) and Jill (Jane Rossington), the early episodes also featured Sandy Richardson (Roger Tonge), Brian Jarvis (David Fennell), Brian's wife Janice (Carolyn Lyster), his dad Dick (Brian Kent), mum Kitty (Beryl Johnstone), Brummie waitress Marilyn Gates (Sue Nicholls) and temperamental Spanish chef Carlos Raphael (Anthony Morton). Morton was actually born and bred in Birmingham and couldn't speak a word of Spanish. In some areas, 'Crossroads' was

screened at 4.35 p.m. bringing complaints from worried parents about showing an adult serial during what was traditionally children's hour. Adult? They'd obviously never seen it. 'Crossroads' was soon mocked by the critics, and comedians started cracking jokes about 'Crossroads' actors who were sacked for remembering their lines. ATV production chief Bill Ward wanted to take it off, but Lew said no.

The quality of the acting improved, but the plots – if that's not too strong a word for them – didn't. In 1979 the Independent Broadcasting Authority criticised the standard of the show and cut the number of episodes from four a week to three, and Radio Rentals brought out an advertisement for their video-recorder which promised: 'It can take 16 episodes of "Crossroads" (if you can!).'

For all its faults, most people looked upon 'Crossroads' with great affection. And it did tackle such controversial issues as Down's Syndrome, abortion, rape, racism and test-tube pregnancy. 'Crossroads' also proudly presented the first-ever eleven-month pregnancy. It happened when Jane Rossington and her character, Jill, both became pregnant at the same time. Sadly, Jane had a miscarriage, but producer Jack Barton said to her: 'We're getting such a good viewer response that we'd like to keep you pregnant in the show. Would you mind being padded up?' Jane agreed, and two months later she herself got pregnant again. So Jill's pregnancy had to continue and, in all, it lasted eleven months. Jane said: 'Strangely, hardly anyone noticed!' But that was 'Crossroads'.

The best American comedy was 'The Beverly Hillbillies', the story of the rustic Clampett family who struck oil and moved to Beverly Hills.

Commercial Break

For years, the king of the voiceovers has been actor Patrick Allen, and they have provided him with sufficient income now to own three businesses, including a stake in the St John's Wood Studios in London where a large percentage of eighties commercials are made. 'At one point, I was doing twenty-five per cent of all the commercials on air. The worst one I did was back in 1964 where I did the voice, and appeared in an ad for cigarettes set to come out straight after the Budget. Because we didn't know what the tax would be, we had to do it twenty different ways, raising the price by a halfpenny each time. I kept forgetting what price we were up to. That was an all-day job, saying the same words over and over again. I nearly gave up commercials there and then!'

Also that year, National Benzole was the petrol for getaway people, Mai Zetterling directed the Persil 'What is a mum?' commercials, and Katie Boyle promoted Camay – after much agonising. When Katie first tested the soap, she found that her face was allergic to it. 'My face just erupted,' she said. She told Camay she couldn't possibly recommend it, so they changed the formula and not only did Katie do the ad but she's also been using the soap ever since. Katie's principles are to be admired. Some years later she was asked to publicise a hair product, but it made her hair fall out so she flatly refused.

Animals have always possessed good selling power as Dulux discovered when they introduced their famous Old English Sheepdogs. The first Dulux dog was Dash, who carried on for eight years before Digby won a competition to find his successor. Of all the Dulux dogs, Digby was the best-known; but he was not very bright, and so for

special tasks three other identical dogs were trained by Barbara Woodhouse. They were Digby's stunt dogs. He was picked up by chauffeur-driven car and treated like a star. He even had a stand-in for lining up camera angles – a specially made large stuffed dog. Digby made a celebrity of his owner, Cynthia Harrison – they even met the Queen and Prince Philip. Digby died in 1978; and Cynthia, believing her fame to be over, committed suicide the following year.

In spite of catering for a minority audience, BBC2, which was blacked out by a power cut on its opening night, screened some notable programmes in its inaugural year, none more so than the intelligent talk-show **'Late Night Line-Up'**. Among the interviewers were Denis Tuohy, Michael Dean and Joan Bakewell who, in her four-year stint from 1965, earned Frank Muir's accolade, 'the thinking man's crumpet'.

In his book *The Sky at Night*, Patrick Moore recalls one of the lighter episodes of 'Late Night Line-Up': 'A viewer once phoned me in the "Sky at Night" studio saying: "Last night on BBC2's 'Late Night Line-Up' there was a most wicked and unkind impression of you by someone who looked a little like you, dressed in a space-suit and a fishbowl helmet, claiming to be a Martian who had come down to prove that there is no intelligent life on Earth. Do you know who it was?" I did – I thought I had disguised myself just sufficiently . . .'

BBC2 also gave the first showing to that formidable series **'The Great War'** (it was repeated later in the year on BBC1). This superb twenty-six-part history of the First World War was the result of painstaking historical research, encompassing the reminiscences of over 50,000 people. The longest letter submitted was an incredible 165 pages, the shortest two lines. Thousands of photographs were used, and original film was taken from the archives of twenty different countries and put through a new technical process which made it run at normal speed instead of what looked like 100 m.p.h. The narration was by Sir Michael Redgrave.

For the first two years of its illustrious career, **'Match of the Day'** was on BBC2, and the kick-off game saw Liverpool defeat Arsenal 3–2. Commentators have included Kenneth Wolstenholme (the best ever), Alan Weeks, Wally Barnes, David Coleman, Idwal Robling (on the rare occasions that a Welsh team were featured), John Motson, Barry Davies, Tony Gubba and Alan Parry. Although 'Match of the Day' has reflected the changing face of soccer, it took the BBC a while to adjust to the trend of the club's sponsors being advertised on their shirts. In 1981, Everton goalkeeper Jim McDonagh mistakenly wore his jersey with the name of the club's sponsors, Hafnia, emblazoned across it for the second half of the televised game with Crystal Palace; so when it was shown on 'Match of the Day' viewers saw the goalkeeper from a side-angle only. The ban on shirt advertising on television has since been lifted. As a result of television's ridiculous obsession with showing only live football, 'Match of the Day' is no longer the force it was, but when it does grace our screens you can be sure of informed comment from its best-known anchorman, Jimmy 'The Chin' Hill. But even Jimmy was lost for words after a gaffe he made on one edition. It was late on Saturday night and British Summer Time was due to end the following day. Jimmy Hill's closing words were: 'Good night. And don't forget tonight to put your cocks back.'

'The Likely Lads' has deservedly gone down in the annals of television as not only one of the cleverest comedy series but also one with which millions could identify. Dick Clement was a BBC producer and Ian La Frenais an out of work salesman when the pair, who had met previously on holiday, renewed acquaintance in a London pub. Their original idea was for a sketch, but the BBC were so impressed that they asked them to turn it into a series. Set in the North-East, 'The Likely Lads' concerned Terry Collier (James Bolam), an aggressive Jack-the-lad, and his drinking partner Bob Ferris (Rodney Bewes). Either for authenticity or for sheer joy, the lads drank real beer on the show – in one episode Bewes estimated that he got through nine pints of bitter – but they staggered along manfully until 1969 and then returned with an even better series, 'Whatever Happened to the Likely Lads?' (see 1973).

It was a traumatic year for **'Blue Peter'**, which twice fell foul of viewers. Valerie Singleton slipped up when giving instructions on how to bathe the eyes of Jason, the show's Siamese cat: 'Wash your cat's eyes every two days with boracic acid,' suggested Val. They were inundated with calls saying that acid could blind the animal, so just before the six o'clock news an announcer said that Val had made a mistake – she should have said 'boracic powder'. And there was a minor furore over a ginger-pop recipe given out on 'Blue Peter'. The Temperance Union claimed it was more than half as alcoholic as beer and described it as a 'dangerously alcoholic brew'. Poor 'Blue Peter' – it's a wonder they haven't been accused of encouraging sticky-backed-plastic-sniffing.

On New Year's Day 1964 the now familiar words, 'Yes! It's Number One – it's **"Top of the Pops"**', rang out for the first time from a converted church in Manchester. That historic edition was introduced by Jimmy Savile and the featured artists were the Dave Clark Five, the Rolling Stones, the Hollies, Dusty Springfield and the Swinging Blue Jeans. Denise Sampey spun the records for the first few programmes before being replaced by model Samantha Juste. In 1967, at the age of twenty-two, Samantha left for California to be near her husband, Monkee Mickey Dolenz. The show remained in its Manchester church until 1966 and, besides Jimmy Savile, the early pool of disc jockeys comprised Alan Freeman, Pete Murray and

How's about that, then, guys and gals? Jimmy Savile's eyes popped out as the Beatles took over the Top Twenty on 'Top of the Pops'. (They're still out.)

Also Shown in 1964

One of the least successful series of the year was **'The Eamonn Andrews Show'** in which a collection of late-night guests, some daring, some downright boring, had Eamonn's forehead in an even greater lather than usual – one critic likened it to Barbirolli conducting 'Top of the Pops'.

Sitcoms included Roy Kinnear in **'A World of His Own'**; **'A Little Big Business'** starring David Kossoff and Francis Matthews, in which a young man was taught the furniture business by his father; **'Fire Crackers'**, the antics of Cropper's End Fire Brigade and their ancient engine, with Alfred Marks, Joe Baker, Cardew Robinson, and Sydney Bromley as Wearie Willie; and **'Meet the Wife'** with Thora Hird and the late Freddie Frinton, whose trademark in the series was arriving home as intoxicated as a newt.

As Jean Shrimpton was named the face of the year, **'World in Action'** followed her on modelling assignments in London and New York; and, reflecting the growing concern at the increasing number of road accidents, **'This Week'** reporter Desmond Wilcox spoke to motorists as they left public houses. The long-running scientific series **'Horizon'** began, as did **'Cinema'** which previewed films for eleven years in the capable hands of such presenters as Bamber Gascoigne, Derek Granger, Mike Scott, Michael Parkinson, Brian Trueman and Clive James; and Sir Kenneth Clark looked at **'Great Temples of the World'**.

A new Western series was **'The Virginian'** with James Drury as the polite ranch-foreman, Doug McClure as his pal Trampas, and Charles Bickford (succeeded by Lee J. Cobb) as the judge. It attracted some impressive guests, including George C. Scott, Bette Davis, Ryan O'Neal, Robert Redford, Lee Marvin and Charles Bronson. Also from the States came **'Burke's Law'** with Gene Barry as Amos Burke, an eligible police chief in Beverly Hills. He had a little more style than Jed Clampett.

Two totally contrasting British policemen were portrayed by John Thaw and Leslie Sands. Thaw was the tough John Mann in **'Redcap'**, a series about the Military Police, while Sands played a dour dogged detective from Yorkshire in **'Cluff'**.

A few miles away, the Ogdens moved in to **'Coronation Street'**, Emily Nugent jilted Leonard Swindley at the altar, and Martha Longhurst died of a heart-attack in the snug bar of the Rover's.

Presented by Robert Dougall, **'News Review'** on BBC2 was the world's first news programme for deaf people; the children's counterpart, which started in the same year, was **'Vision On'**, introduced by Tony Hart; and **'Play School'** began in 1964.

David Jacobs. P. J. Proby (of split-pants fame) performed 'Somewhere' with one arm in plaster after being bitten by his dog; Alan Freeman introduced 'Cast Your Fate to the Wind' as 'Cast Your Wind to the Fate'; and when the wrong track was put on Jimi Hendrix found himself miming to an Alan Price hit. Hendrix said: 'I like the voice, man, but I don't know the words . . .' And Dexy's Midnight Runners played their soul tribute 'Jackie Wilson Said' in front of a huge blow-up of darts-player Jocky Wilson.

The arrival of resident dancers Pan's People in 1967 outraged Mary Whitehouse, who objected to their scanty clothing. The BBC beat her to it two years later by banning the heavy-breathing 'Je t'aime' by British actress Jane Birkin and her French boyfriend Serge Gainsbourg which, although it reached number one, was never played on the show. A similar fate befell Frankie Goes to Hollywood and their eighties chart-topper 'Relax'.

'Top of the Pops' has clocked up well over a thousand editions and has just about managed to keep in touch with the younger end of the record-buying public. Back in 1964, producer Cecil Korer certainly did his bit to maintain the show's youthful image. He was horrified to see a bald head bobbing about on screen, and was even more appalled to discover that the dome was his own and that he had accidentally appeared in front of the cameras. To ensure there was no repetition, thirty-nine-year-old Korer got the BBC wardrobe department to fit him with a teenage wig. Basking in his new growth, he said: 'Now I'll look like one of the dancers.' He really was toupee the pops.

1965

Two great Britons died: Sir Winston Churchill and Richard Dimbleby. □ *Ian Smith announced a Unilateral Declaration of Independence for Northern Rhodesia.* □ *Edward Heath succeeded Sir Alec Douglas-Home as Conservative leader.* □ *The death penalty was abolished.* □ *Great Train Robber Ronald Biggs escaped from gaol.* □ *And Goldie the eagle escaped from London Zoo.* □ *Russian Alexei Leonov went on the first space walk.* □ *The 70 m.p.h speed-limit was introduced.* □ *So were Panda cars.* □ *ITV banned cigarette commercials.* □ *Tom Jones topped the charts with 'It's Not Unusual'.* □ *The film* The Sound of Music *was released.* □ *Michael Crawford and Ray Brooks starred in* The Knack. □ *And hemlines and men's blood-pressure rose in unison as the mini skirt hit town.*

Television caused two major controversies in 1965, the principal one occurring on the late-night sequel to 'TW3' and 'Not So Much a Programme': **'BBC3'**. The series was pretty forgettable apart from providing the answer to the Trivial Pursuit question: 'Who was the first person to use a four-letter word on television?' The culprit was Kenneth Tynan in a discussion about stage censorship on 13 November. As literary manager of the National Theatre, Tynan was asked by Robert Robinson whether he would permit sexual intercourse to be staged there. Tynan replied: 'Certainly. I think there are very few rational people in this world to whom the word "fuck" is particularly diabolical or revolting or totally forbidden. I think that anything that can be printed or said can also be seen.' Permissive society or not, his vocabulary led to a storm of protest and ensured that 'BBC3' earned a place in history.

This furore followed hot on the heels of the BBC's Wednesday Play, **'Up the Junction'**, shown just ten days earlier. Written by Nell Dunn, daughter of wealthy industrialist Sir Philip Dunn, and based on her own observations of life in the Clapham Junction area of South London, the play prompted numerous irate phone-calls, particularly about the scene in which a girl had a backstreet abortion. The co-founder of the newly formed Clean-up TV Campaign, Mrs Mary Whitehouse, wrote to the then Minister of Health, Kenneth Robinson, accusing the BBC of 'presenting promiscuity as being normal'.

The year of 1965 was a delight for soap-opera lovers, with no fewer than three new serials emerging, among them **'Peyton Place'**, the first major American soap and the first to travel to Britain. It made complicated love-affairs with breathless sex its main ingredient, and every episode ended with a corny cliffhanger. Thus 8 million British viewers became convinced that through the leafy backwaters of New England strutted a race of glamorous but guilt-ridden women with cupboards full of skeletons and with children fathered by the wrong men. The seed from which this huge international success grew was in fact 'Coronation Street'. American gambler-turned-television-producer Paul Monash heard of the grip the 'Street' had on British audiences, considered buying that series but decided the Americans would not understand Lancashire life or the accents. Instead, he bought the rights to Grace Metalious's salacious bestselling novel, which other producers had rejected on the grounds that it was too sin-soaked and shocking for family audiences. The gamble paid off. The 514 episodes of 'Peyton Place' made a fortune for all concerned and launched young newcomers Mia Farrow and Ryan O'Neal on glittering film careers. ITV bought the first batch of 104 episodes for just £30,000.

Conveniently, most of the seductions and murders had happened in the past, but the series was still tagged television's first 'sex opera' and 'that situation orgy'. Today it seems tame, with Allison Mackenzie (Mia Farrow) staying a virgin for 200 episodes. The link between two interweaving sagas was the town's handsome Dr Michael Rossi (Ed Nelson). One was the pregnancy, miscarriage and loveless marriage of Betty Anderson (Barbara Parkins) to rich Rodney Harrington (Ryan O'Neal) who really loved the chaste Allison. The other was the love of full-time bookshop-owner and part-time emotional wreck Constance Mackenzie (Dorothy Malone) for Rossi, the only man who knew that Elliot Carson (Tim O'Connor), the father of Constance's illegitimate daughter Allison, was serving eighteen years in gaol!

In the course of her affair with Frank Sinatra, Mia Farrow's hair was suddenly chopped off, leaving the writers to explain why Allison now looked like Joan of Arc. The haircut started a trend (Sinatra later told friends that he'd cut it), but Farrow continued to upset the producers by skipping recordings to be with Ol' Blue Eyes and eventually left 'Peyton Place'. Allison was written out accordingly, first falling into a coma and then mysteriously disappearing, maybe to search for a decent hairdresser.

The show went on. Betty, stunning but certifiable, married Steven Cord, who had defended Rodney on a murder charge, then two years later remarried Rodney. Connie married Elliot, who had become the town's newspaperman, before, in the face of dwindling ratings, 'Peyton Place' came to an end with Dr Rossi arrested for murder and Rodney in a wheelchair.

'Peyton Place': In contrast to the womanising Dr Rossi, Ed Nelson was a devoted family man and was named America's Father of the Year in 1968. But Dorothy Malone found it easy to identify with her character, Constance Mackenzie. 'People say the series was overdone, but after all that has happened to me in my life it reflected a great deal of reality.'

Following the closure of 'Compact', October saw the birth of two new BBC soaps, **'United!'** and 'The Newcomers'. The tepid tale of a fictional Midlands football club, 'United!' kicked-off on Mondays and Wednesdays and appeared thoroughly authentic – except to anybody who had ever been to a real match. The genuine action from Stoke City (where games were filmed) was fine; but when the actors took control it became farcical, with crucial penalties being taken by the club's big-money signing with all the muscular power of Larry Grayson. The actors were said to be keen amateur players but, although Jimmy Hill, then boss of Coventry City, was hired to vet the scripts, distinguished former footballer Danny Blanchflower summed it up when he described 'United!' as wholly unrealistic.

The United in question were Brentwich United, supposedly languishing near the foot of the Second Division when new manager Gerry Barford (David Lodge) took over. Barford had to handle a tycoon chairman with snooty wife, an ingratiating club secretary, his own anxious wife and desperately keen footballing son, a prickly team captain (Bryan Marshall) and a womanising goalkeeper (Stephen Yardley, later to leer at ladies in 'Howards' Way'). The chairman of the supporters' club was played by another soap favourite, Arthur Pentelow from 'Emmerdale Farm'. What with Ken Masters in goal and being cheered on by Mr Wilks, it was hardly surprising that Brentwich were struggling. At the time, Wolverhampton Wanderers were also faltering, and they complained that the plots of 'United!' were too close for comfort to their own plight. The BBC assured them it was pure coincidence.

By February 1966 seven of the cast were dropped and new writers were brought in to make it 'sweatier' and less cosy. The team's woman physiotherapist was dispatched, but the BBC insisted that bathing-trunks were still worn in the after-match shower scenes. In March, Barford was sacked (David Lodge asked to leave), and later that year 'Compact' pinup Ronald Allen was chosen as Brentwich's new manager. This doubtless won more women supporters, but prompted cynics to wonder if 'United!' would become 'Compact' in boots with Gussie as the next goalkeeper. In March 1967, with audiences stuck at around 6 million in the ratings league, 'United!' was finally put on the transfer-list.

'The Newcomers' was marginally more successful, thanks mainly to the strength of Australian leading lady Maggie Fitzgibbon as Vivienne Cooper. Set in a fictional East Anglian overspill town, Angleton (really Haverhill, Suffolk), it centred around the newly moved Cooper family: Viv, husband Ellis (Alan Browning) and their children Phillip (Jeremy Bulloch), sixteen-year-old Maria (played by Judy Geeson before she became a film star) and long-haired Lance (Raymond Hunt). There was also a glum gran who seemed riveted to the settee; and Wendy Richard of 'EastEnders' fame was the Coopers' neighbour,

The 'United' football team were relegated to bottom of the soap opera league, but Brentwich's strikers George Layton (*centre*) and Bryan Marshall (*right*) went on to other fixtures.

twenty-year-old cockney Joyce Harker.

Ellis Cooper was the shop superintendent of Eden Bros, a computer-components firm, but industrialists complained that the chairman was a crook, the managing director an ass and the image of British industry was sullied. However, Mary Whitehouse and company gave 'The Newcomers' an 'honorary mention' in their annual awards for morally sound shows.

Ellis died of a heart-attack in December 1967 (because Alan Browning was bored), and the widowed Viv was due to have a ratings-pulling wedding to new character Charles Turner. When the story-line was changed to a whirlwind romance and an unseen wedding in New Zealand, former singer Maggie Fitzgibbon decided the producers had hit a bum note and quit. Her stand provoked rival Pat Phoenix, star of 'Coronation Street', to say bluntly: 'If they asked me as Elsie Tanner to go and cut somebody's throat in Stoke Poges ... well, it might not be according to my usual character, but I'd do it just the same. An actress is paid to do a job, like anyone else.' Some years later, Pat Phoenix left the 'Street' because she was fed up with Elsie doing little more than sitting in the Rover's asking for gin and tonics!

Another product of 1965 which is still with us today is that showcase for scientific invention **'Tomorrow's World'**. There are two main reasons why so many viewers have tuned in to 'Tomorrow's World': one is in the hope that one of the live experiments will go wrong (they frequently do), and the other was because for many years it was on immediately before 'Top of the Pops'. Youngsters would plough through Raymond Baxter just to get at

Gary Glitter. Baxter, a former Second World War pilot, was the mainstay of the show for twelve years, but in 1977 he left, having fallen foul of new editor Michael Blakstad, who had described him as 'the last of the dinosaurs'. Other presenters have included James Burke, Su Ingle, Michael Rodd, Maggie Philbin, Judith Hann, Kieran Prendiville, Peter Macann, Howard Stableford and Anna Ford. The last-named joined in 1977, but less than six months later, after stating that she had 'no wish to be a public figure', she departed to ITN and fame as their first woman newsreader. One of the most awkward situations on 'Tomorrow's World' occurred when a lady was demonstrating a new portable bath. In the best BBC tradition, she was suitably concealed with bubbles – until the heat from the studio lights began to melt the foam ...

The year also saw the start of the documentary series **'Man Alive'** and the end of 'Tonight', which was replaced by the nightly current affairs show **'24 Hours'**, among whose anchormen were Cliff Michelmore, Kenneth Allsop and Ludovic Kennedy; and 1965 witnessed the death of probably the greatest anchorman of all, Richard Dimbleby. His last major state occasion was in January when Churchill's was the first state funeral of a politician to be televised. Dimbleby was as masterly as ever in his commentary for the BBC on an occasion which was watched by some 350 million via Eurovision (ITV's commentator was Brian Connell with narration from Sir Laurence Olivier and Paul Scofield); but in December, after five years fighting the disease, Richard Dimbleby died from cancer at the age of fifty-two.

A strong Churchillian figure dominating British drama in 1965 was managing director Brian Stead (Geoffrey Keen), the power behind the Mogul oil company. Stead was aided by gentle financial wizard Willy Izzard (Philip Latham); but the company's young go-getters, Alec Stewart (Robert Hardy) and Peter Thornton (Ray Barrett), became the centre of attention and the title **'Mogul'** soon changed to 'The Troubleshooters' (see 1966).

The setting was infinitely less glamorous for Frank Marker in **'Public Eye'**. Whereas the boys from Mogul thrived on overseas travel and luxury hotels, poor old Marker never got further than Birmingham or Brighton. Sympathetically portrayed by Alfred Burke, Marker struggled to earn a living as a private eye. This was the realistic side of detective work, far removed from '77 Sunset Strip'. Dressed in a shabby raincoat, Marker never carried a gun and usually operated from a tatty office where the rent was cheap. His idea of a glamorous case was one where he made enough money to pay the electricity bill, and to him a beautiful woman was one who didn't take her teeth out at night. It was rumoured that Marker only smiled at coronations, and his misery was compounded when he was imprisoned after being framed and caught in possession of stolen jewellery. Then fortune smiled on him as worried viewers made him cakes and sent socks and

Mattingly). Hedley, in particular, was an astonishing character – so wooden that he blended in perfectly with the trees and with an upper lip so stiff he looked as if he had swallowed a packet of starch.

Four years after 'Z Cars' had started, Charlie Barlow (Stratford Johns) and John Watt (Frank Windsor) left Liverpool and turned up in the South-West Midlands for the spin-off police series 'Softly, Softly'. Barlow, who became a Detective Chief Superintendent, and Watt, a Detective Chief Inspector, were joined in time by Norman Bowler as West Country pinup Inspector Harry Hawkins,

and by Terence Rigby as dour dog-handler PC Snow, a man who seemed to think that smiling was liable to get him drummed out of the force. One of his Alsatians was Inky, which had been sacked as a real police dog when it went AWOL over a wall. When Inky was shot in the programme, angry letters poured into the BBC so the dog had to appear on 'Blue Peter' to show that it was only acting. The series title changed to 'Softly, Softly, Task Force' before sprouting another spin-off, 'Barlow at Large', where Barlow was promoted to the Home Office. After some eleven years in all, even an excellent character like Barlow

Also Shown in 1966

Mickey Dolenz, Peter Tork, Mike Nesmith and Davy Jones caused mayhem as the **Monkees**, the first pop group to be formed especially for a television series; the manic Michael Bentine switched to ITV for **'All Square'**; the **Addams Family** appeared as grisly rivals to the Munsters; and Sidney James and Peggy Mount played a handyman and housekeeper at a stately home in the situation comedy **'George and the Dragon'**. A more gentle comedy was the splendid **'All Gas and Gaiters'**, one of the first to allow laughs at the expense of the Church. Gerald Harper starred in **'Adam Adamant Lives!'** as the Edwardian hero let out of the deep freeze in the 1960s to tackle modern evils. Also combating crime was Carlos Thompson as an import–export agent in **'Sentimental Agent'**. And in **'The Baron'** Steve Forrest played John Mannering, on the face of it an antiques dealer but behind the grandfather clocks an undercover agent.

A new slant on a police series came in **'The Informer'**, which cast Ian Hendry as a disbarred barrister turned police informant. **'The Rat Catchers'** featured Gerald Flood, Glyn Owen and Philip Stone as a group of government spymasters, while **'Talking to a Stranger'** was a collection of four moving plays by John Hopkins looking at the break-up of a family as seen in turn by the various members. From America, came two lightweight Westerns: **'A Man Called Shenandoah'** with Robert Horton as an amnesia victim seeking his true identity after the Civil War and **'The Big Valley'** starring Barbara Stanwyck as a widow running a ranch in 1870s California. An enthralling factual series came from Hans Hass, who left the oceans and took to dry land for **'Man'**, in which he studied

the sexplay and general behaviour of humans all over the world.

It is not known whether he studied the staff at the **Crossroads** Motel where waitress Marilyn Gates left to become a singer. Meanwhile Bet Lynch made her début in **'Coronation Street'**, Ena Sharples was fined for shoplifting and Stan Ogden celebrated eight draws on the pools – only to find that Hilda hadn't filled in the coupon properly.

At the other end of the age-scale, toddlers enjoyed **'Camberwick Green'**, while their older brothers were hooked on the dolphin **Flipper** or the adventure series **'Orlando'** with Sam Kydd as smuggler Orlando O'Connor, a character first introduced in the adult drama 'Crane'. Schoolchildren could even learn French with **'Suivez La Piste'** where they could discover 'Ou est la plume de ma tante?' But best of all was the superlative spoof **'Batman'**, based on the old comic strip. Adam West was Bruce Wayne alias the Caped Crusader, with Burt Ward as Dick Grayson otherwise known as Robin, the Boy Wonder. In protecting Gotham City, they zapped, bammed and kerpowed such arch-villains as the Riddler (Frank Gorshin) Penguin (Burgess Meredith), Catwoman (Julie Newmar), Joker (Cesar Romero) and Egg-Head (Vincent Price).

For two days nobody knew the whereabouts of **'Double Your Money'** hostess Monica Rose. Viewers complained about her low-cut dress on the show and the distraught Monica fled and only re-appeared after an appeal by her mum. Hughie Green said: 'Monica was most upset by the letters about her dress, particularly by one from 174 members of the Mothers' Union in Morecambe which accused her of wearing a dress like an under-skirt and having her breasts exposed.'

'Mrs Thursday' starred Kathleen Harrison and Hugh Manning before he took the Sunday job as vicar of 'Emmerdale Farm'.

series 'Mogul' notched up an astonishing list of coincidences. When BP struck oil in Alaska, three days later in an episode of 'The Troubleshooters' viewers saw Mogul also strike oil in Alaska – except that the programme had been recorded four months earlier. In one edition Mogul took over a chemical firm; four days later BP did the same. The show predicted that men would live in underwater houses to probe the seabed for oil. By 1969 that was happening. There was a huge explosion in an episode called 'The Day the Sea Caught Fire'; no sooner had it been recorded than there was a real explosion in the North Sea and the RAF had to set fire to the sea as a warning to shipping. A real earthquake happened the night that 'The Troubleshooters' recorded one, and another occurred the night before that episode was transmitted. And the programme predicted to 0.1 of a penny the price that oil companies would charge the Gas Council for North Sea gas. Small wonder that a Shell executive commented: '"The Troubleshooters" is extremely good. I am staggered how accurate they are in technical matters. Of course in real life we don't have blondes lying about on beds. We miss this facility.'

The name of Mogul spread thoughout the oil industry. Enterprising Yorkshire garage-owner Harold Baker registered the name with the Board of Trade. When one of the show's producers was driving past Baker's petrol station at Featherstone, he was so delighted to see the Mogul sign that he filled the tank up. And Baker found that business boomed. Geoffrey Keen was so convincing as Mogul boss Brian Stead that he was invited to the Oil Industries Club dinner. 'Everyone nodded to me or shook my hand as though they recognised me as an oil man but nobody could quite remember to which company I belonged!'

was beginning to wear a bit thin (though not around the waist) and it was a relief when the BBC didn't try to promote him yet again. Besides, there wasn't much further he could go as a crime-fighter short of becoming Fatman.

A person who hit the jackpot that year was **Mrs Thursday**, star of a gentle comedy about a charlady who inherited £10 million and a controlling interest in a huge company. The show was an instant, if somewhat surprising, success, knocking 'Coronation Street' off the top of the ratings in its very first week. Created by Ted Willis, who claims to have sold the idea to ATV boss Lew Grade in a mere twenty seconds, 'Mrs Thursday' starred sixty-seven-year-old Kathleen Harrison, veteran of radio shows like 'Meet the Huggets'. She took the part to heart, purchasing all the character's wardrobe herself, in the process horrifying shop assistants by deliberately buying gaudy clothes – the sort that Mrs Thursday would wear. Kathleen was as shocked as anyone by her sudden success. 'With all those sex and violence plays on TV, I didn't think there would be parts for people like me.' One drawback to her new-found fame was the fan mail. Nearly all were begging letters from people who thought she really had inherited £10 million.

Television drama is often accused of being far removed from reality, but nobody could accuse **'The Troubleshooters'** of that. This slick follow-up to the oil-company

Geoffrey Keen and Philip Latham in 'The Troubleshooters'.

waited for the ending like everyone else. I knew there'd be an ending because Pat *told* me there would. Then one day, near the seventeenth episode, Pat came up to me and said: "I cannot find an ending – I've become too confused with the project."' McGoohan denies he ever intended an ending as such.

In the last episode, Number One's face changed from that of an ape to McGoohan's and the village control-centre was sent skywards in a rocket. Viewers were more confused than ever and phoned ATV to register their fury at the inconclusive finale. McGoohan was besieged in his Mill Hill home and physically attacked in the streets. He claimed: 'I wanted to have controversy, arguments, fights, discussions, people in anger waving fists in my face.' Nevertheless, he was soon to depart these shores and now lives in Los Angeles, but the spirit of 'The Prisoner' is very much alive. A 'Prisoner' appreciation society (called the Six of One Club) was formed in the mid-seventies and now boasts over 2,500 members who all wear the white-piped black blazer and straw hat associated with the series. They regularly converge on the private village of Portmeirion in North Wales where the programme was filmed. The series was revived in 1976 and shown again on Channel 4 in 1983 when the fans were furious because one episode was shown out of sequence. Not many people would have been able to spot the error.

It was very much the year of the secret agent. The Bond film *You Only Live Twice* was doing the rounds at cinemas, while on television, in addition to 'The Prisoner', were **'Man in a Suitcase'** (with Richard Bradford as bounty-hunter McGill who lived out of a suitcase containing only a change of clothes and a gun) and the callous **Callan**. The idea for a cold discredited agent about whom nobody cared stemmed from an Armchair Theatre play, 'A Magnum for Schneider'. Created by James Mitchell, Callan was the complete opposite to James Bond. He was constantly on edge and talked in cryptic phrases; he was ruthlessly efficient and, if necessary, brutal; and whereas Bond was surrounded by a string of leggy lovelies Callan's only acquaintance was an unwashed petty burglar named Lonely who, when nervous, 'stank like a skunk'. Russell Hunter, who played Lonely, conceded that the unclean jokes got to him. He said then: 'I take more baths than I might playing other parts. And when Lonely is in the public eye I use only the very best of toilet water and a hell of a lot of aftershave.' The fifty-two episodes made a star of Edward Woodward in the title rôle. At the end of the 1969 series when Callan slumped to the floor, Thames TV were flooded with calls asking whether he was dead. Viewers had to wait a year to find out, but then Callan returned with Patrick Mower as his mean partner Cross. Woodward and Hunter came back for a one-off, 'Wet Job', in 1981. In this, Lonely ran a company called Fresh and Fragrant Bathroom Installations, which was about as likely as Cilla Black running elocution classes.

Callan (Edward Woodward) could keep Lonely (Russell Hunter) quiet but not sweet-smelling.

The major new game show of 1967 was **'The Golden Shot'**, a programme inspired by the legend of William Tell. It originated from Switzerland and involved competitive crossbow-shooting, the jackpot being won if the bolt cut a thread holding a bag of money. It was a great hit abroad where celebrities used to queue up to play (contestants included Gina Lollobrigida and Princess Grace of Monaco), but in Britain it was slow to take off. The first compère in this country was genial Canadian singer Jackie Rae with hostesses Andrea Lloyd, Anita Richardson and Carol Dilworth; but soon ATV boss Lew Grade asked Bob Monkhouse, who had been a guest on one of the shows, to take over. Bob says: 'Jackie was relieved – he hated the show. He was a lovely man, but it was all live and Jackie was the sort of guy who couldn't ad-lib a belch after eating a Hungarian goulash!'

'The Golden Shot' really hit the jackpot in 1968 when the show was switched from Saturdays to Sunday tea-time and attracted 17 million viewers. 'We did it live fifty-two weeks a year,' says Monkhouse, 'and something went wrong on every show. Everything that could go wrong did and everything that couldn't possibly go wrong did. I remember when we lost two contestants from the previous week's show. They just vanished in the studio – they were nowhere to be found. So we got two complete strangers from the audience who looked nothing like them and continued to call them by the same names. Nobody noticed. I believe the original couple were later found in the canteen.' Another contestant disappeared from the contest when she went to the lavatory just as she was about to go on. While there she suddenly heard her name shouted, jumped to her feet and knocked herself out on the loo door.

Accompanied by such stalwarts as Anne Aston, the dizzy blonde who thought one and one made eleven, and Bernie the Bolt, Monkhouse stayed with 'The Golden Shot' until 1971. Norman Vaughan then took over before being succeeded by Charlie Williams, who looked as comfortable as a hedgehog crossing the M1. It wrecked Williams's career, and Monkhouse was asked back in 1974 to give 'The Golden Shot' a final boost.

Monkhouse's favourite 'Golden Shot' story concerns Father Deed, a preacher who had complained vigorously about the show using weapons of the devil on a Sunday afternoon. He was invited along to the Birmingham studios to see the safety procedures and sit in the audience. 'It so happened that the contestant who had qualified from home the previous week (and who we had therefore not seen) was a woman with a glass eye and a violent twitch like Jack Douglas's Alf Ippititimus. She fired, the bolt flew heavenwards, struck two studio lamps and landed in the audience on the head of the priest. It knocked him out cold and he just lay there for the rest of the show. Ironically he had

been praying for us at the time – until then, I had never believed in the power of prayer . . .'

The year of 1967 saw a revolution in news presentation with the July arrival of ITN's **'News at Ten'**. For a start, there were two newscasters, which meant that late items could be handed to the man off-camera. There were the distinctive chimes of Big Ben opening each edition, although they were only included by default: a sound engineer should have faded them out but failed to do so, and the chimes have stayed ever since. And there was the individualistic sign-off from reporters, introduced to show how international 'News at Ten' was. For the inaugural programme, they had teams as far afield as South Vietnam and Alabama, and the then Deputy Editor of ITN, David Nicholas, said: 'We thought: We'll start this off in a way they'll never forget. Then the Ford-strike story broke, and our first sign-off line was "Richard Dixon, News at Ten, Dagenham".'

Viewers loved the new look, and it became the first news programme to get into the top ten television ratings. But those early days were pretty uncomfortable, crammed in a tiny studio in Kingsway House with poor air conditioning. There was a particularly hot summer in 1967 and it became so warm under the studio lights that the newscasters had buckets and trays of ice packed round their feet. Andrew Gardner, who read the first bulletin with Alastair Burnet, says: 'It was so hot we even took our shoes and socks off.'

Among other newsreaders have been Sandy Gall, Gordon Honeycombe, Anna Ford, Leonard Parkin, Selina

Tim Brooke-Taylor joined John Cleese, Graham Chapman, Marty Feldman and the lovely Aimi Macdonald in the excellent 'At Last the 1948 Show'.

Jackson, Moira Anderson and Cliff Michelmore – before the series finally ended in 1979.

There was a glut of dramas for 1969 as colour came to BBC1 and ITV. The number of colour sets increased in the course of the year from 100,000 to 270,000 as viewers were able to see which of their favourites had just returned from holiday and which looked in need of one. Among the colourful new drama productions was the twenty-six-part **'Paul Temple'**, which cost £630,000 to make, over twice the cost of the black-and-white 'Forsyte Saga'. And this was at a time when the BBC were faced with a £5 million overdraft. Paul Temple was played on television by the elegant Francis Matthews, but the private investigator was created by writer Francis Durbridge as far back as 1937. Temple certainly wore well. In 1969 he was officially thirty-five, but he'd been the same age for thirty years.

Aged sixty-six, the distinguished art historian and critic Kenneth Clark created, wrote and presented a thirteen-part BBC series called **'Civilisation'** which was a true television landmark. Clark was the first-ever chairman of the Independent Television Authority, from 1954 to 1957, and his cultural masterpiece examined the ideas and values which make up the term 'Western Civilisation'. The series cost £200,000 and took two years to make. In that time, Clark and his crew travelled 80,000 miles, went to 117 different locations in 11 countries, visited 118 museums and 18 libraries. And it wasn't all because the lady loved Milk Tray! They shot 200,000 feet of film – enough to make six full-length movies. Clark became an unlikely celebrity. His smart suits contrasted with what so many were wearing in 1969. He took viewers back to splendid cathedrals and palaces and he showed them beautiful

'Special Branch' was the first programme to show policemen as trendy dressers.

tapestries and paintings whereas they had been used to Vietnam, race riots, protest demonstrations and pop festivals. His popularity grew to the extent that at Washington's National Gallery he was mobbed by a huge crowd. How uncivilised!

His story began in the Dark Ages following the fall of Rome and continued through history to the sixties. Clark feared we were sinking into a new barbarism, and this frequently affected his appraisal of a magnificent historical building. In Chartres Cathedral he said: 'Even the tourists have not spoiled its atmosphere, as they have in so many temples of the human spirit.' From Greenwich Observatory and its seventeenth-century science he looked out across factories and high-rise flats, 'the squalid disorder of industrial society'. Clark didn't conceal his distaste for the way civilisation had turned out. He talked about the 'hellish traffic' and 'all those forces which threaten to impair our humanity – lies, tanks, tear gas, ideologies, opinion polls, mechanisation, planners and computers'. In spite of everything, he decided that the sixties were quite civilised but personally, he would have liked to have lived just before the First World War. 'Almost everything that has happened in the arts and indeed in science had pretty well happened by then. If the bloody war hadn't taken place, we should really have got somewhere.'

Patrick Moore has always been civilised and only too willing to listen to people even more eccentric than himself. His 1969 series **'One Pair of Eyes'** contained interviews with people who were sometimes classed as cranks. One edition took him to Stoughton Vicarage near Chichester and a meeting with the Reverend P. H. Francis, a man who was convinced that the sun was cold. Alas, the vicar didn't turn out to be the world's greatest

Also Shown in 1969

As usual, police series had got viewers surrounded. Patrick O'Connell and Joanna Van Gyseghem starred in 'Fraud Squad', Peter Vaughan tracked down bullion thieves in 'The Gold Robbers' and 'Hawaii Five-O' ran for 220 episodes and starred Jack Lord as Steve McGarrett with James MacArthur as his sidekick Danny Williams and assorted assistants like Kam Fong as Chin Ho. Meanwhile, John Neville, Susan Hampshire and James Villiers headed the cast for a thirteen-part period saga of the Marlborough family, 'The First Churchills', and Susan Jameson, Lisa Goddard and Angela Down starred in 'Take Three Girls', the tale of three young wenches who shared a London flat. The 1982 sequel, 'Take Three Women', revisited the trio thirteen years on. 'The Doctors' was the BBC's first twice-weekly serial to be made in colour. Justine Lord was soon tagged the 'sexiest woman on TV' for her portrayal of the efficient Dr Liz McNeal. Betty Turpin arrived in 'Coronation Street' with policeman husband Cyril, and Albert Tatlock broke an arm in a coach accident. That was nothing to the gloom and doom in 'Crossroads'. Kitty Jarvis died from a heart-attack, Carlos Raphael was killed in a fire in Spain, and Meg married Malcolm Ryder who promptly tried to poison her.

The hero of 'The Mind of Mr J. G. Reeder' would have had a field-day in 'Crossroads'. The series re-created Edgar Wallace's stories from the 1920s with Hugh Burden as Reeder, the mild-mannered clerk in the office of the Director of Public Prosecutions who unravelled mysteries in his quiet unassuming way. The behaviour of Mr Reeder was also in total contrast to that of the young London gangster played by Peter Egan in 'Big Breadwinner Hog', the first British programme to be axed in mid-series owing to its violence.

Also that year, 'The Life and Times of Lord Mountbatten' was a thirteen-part filmed autobiography, a style chosen by him in preference to a written story of his life; Cliff Michelmore introduced 'Holiday 69', the start of the longest-running holiday programme on television; in 'Entertaining with Kerr: The Galloping Gourmet', Graham Kerr raced around the kitchen like a man high on senna pods; and 'Pot Black' introduced snooker to television.

Comedies of the year included Spike Milligan in 'Q5', Ronnie Barker as the ancient Lord Rustless in 'Hark at Barker', Les Dawson in 'Sez Les' and Rodney Bewes in 'Dear Mother ... Love Albert', centred around the letters a young man sent home to his mum. 'The Dustbinmen' starred Bryan Pringle, Trevor Bannister and Brian Wilde as refuse-collectors with names like Heavy Breathing and Cheese and Egg. Their dustcart was called Thunderbird Three. Unbelievably, all six episodes were number one in the ratings. Richard Gordon's 'Doctor' books were adapted successfully for television, beginning with 'Doctor in the House' which paraded an excellent cast led by Barry Evans, Robin Nedwell and Martin Shaw.

Frankie Howerd, who had enjoyed a West End hit with A Funny Thing Happened on the Way to the Forum, carried the Roman theme to television for 'Up Pompeii'.

After the demise of 'Take Your Pick', Michael Miles resurfaced with the game show 'Wheel of Fortune'. And women tore off their clothes over 'This Is Tom Jones' and tore up their pension-books over Derek Batey, host of the geriatric quiz 'Mr and Mrs'.

For children, Dick Dastardly and his hound Mutley drove their rivals to distraction and, if possible, over the edge of a cliff in 'Wacky Races'; Oliver Postgate, the man behind Ivor the Engine and Noggin the Nog, came up with 'The Clangers'; and Bernard Cribbins was the voice of The Wombles, who went on to bombard the charts with eight records, including four Top Ten hits, all composed and sung by Mike Batt.

---

expert on heat. Patrick Moore says: 'It was winter and we wanted a cosy scene. So Mr Francis suggested that we might liven up the drawing-room fire by pouring a little paraffin on to it. Unfortunately, we were rather over-generous and while the cameras were running we became conscious of a dull roaring, followed by clouds of black smoke billowing from the hearth. I am glad to say the local fire brigade dealt with the situation very promptly.'

Of course, believing the sun was cold was quite illogical, and that was totally alien to Mr Spock, the half-earthling, half-Vulcan first officer of the starship Enterprise in the cult series 'Star Trek'. Made by NBC, 'Star Trek' was first screened in America in 1966 but proved far from successful. Even in Britain, it was originally scheduled for children's consumption, but when the hippies of the early seventies lapped it up the show was switched to peak-time and has never looked back.

The mission of the futuristic spaceship was 'to boldly go'

1971

Britain's pounds shillings and pence were replaced by new decimal currency. □ The Angry Brigade bombed the home of Employment Secretary Robert Carr. □ Californian hippy Charles Manson and three others were convicted of the Sharon Tate murders. □ A barrier collapsed at Glasgow's Ibrox Park stadium, killing sixty-six football fans and injuring 200. □ Rolls-Royce and Upper Clyde Shipbuilders went into liquidation. □ The Daily Sketch folded. □ Women's Liberationists marched to Downing Street. □ Hot pants replaced the mini-skirt. □ The Secretary of State for Education abolished free milk for schoolchildren and became known as 'Margaret Thatcher, Milk Snatcher'. □ Bangladesh was born after wholesale slaughter in Pakistan. □ Apollo XV astronauts David Scott and James Irwin not only walked on the moon; they drove on it in a moon-buggy. □ Princess Anne won the European Three-Day Event championship on Doublet and became Sports Personality of the Year. □ Films included A Clockwork Orange and Straw Dogs. □ The Open University began on BBC2. □ And 'Chirpy Chirpy Cheep Cheep' topped the charts.

'Upstairs Downstairs' butler Mr Hudson (Gordon Jackson) complimented cook Mrs Bridges (a padded Angela Baddeley) on her puddings.

It was the year ITV showed it could make quality goods, too. In a time of contrasts in Britain – prosperous business as usual in the South, rumblings of hard times to come from the North – London Weekend Television came up with a series for all ages and all classes about age and class, which became a hit around the world.

'**Upstairs Downstairs**', life in an English aristocratic household early this century, was steeped in real upstairs and downstairs experience. The idea for it came to Eileen Atkins and Jean Marsh, two actress friends, whose parents had been in domestic service. The drama, which was to run for sixty-eight episodes, was script-edited by Alfred Shaughnessy, whose stepfather was the son of a lord, and who grew up with the Prince of Wales and other royalty dropping in for dinner. Producer John Hawkesworth had enjoyed a similarly glamorous upper-class childhood in Belgravia and knew how people stepped through the minefield of Edwardian manners. Together they were free to re-create some of the sexual and social scandals Victorian writers had discreetly glossed over. Between them all they developed an elegant entertain-

ment – 'history without tears' – about the family and staff of Lord Bellamy, set in a world about to be changed for ever by the First World War.

Jean Marsh's mother was a Hackney housemaid, and Jean, who'd played many smooth rich ladies, longed to explore the trapped regimented lives of servants so little of which had been seen on television. She created for herself head parlourmaid Rose, no longer young, who'd missed her chances of marriage and who earned a miserable £30 a year yet ironically took more pride in the aristocracy than either pampered Lady Marjorie or young Miss Elizabeth, the women she waited on upstairs.

The rôle for Eileen, daughter of an under-butler, was to have been Sarah, the under-parlourmaid who arrived at the Bellamys' grand Eaton Square home and caused upsets on all floors. Unfortunately Eileen made too much of a success playing a woman further up the social scale, Elizabeth I, on stage in *Vivat Regina* and wasn't free for television, so the rôle went to Pauline Collins.

But it was perhaps the older servants who appealed the more strongly when the series began in October 1971. Scots actor Gordon Jackson made an immediate impact as the butler Hudson, playing him, as the *Daily Mirror*

Glenda Jackson shaved her forehead and laced her corsets to play the Virgin Queen aged fifteen to seventy in the six-part £200,000 BBC2 series 'Elizabeth R'. Each day she and other actresses in the cast – they included Daphne Slater as her half-sister Mary Tudor and Rachel Kempson as her governess – spent three hours being made up and climbing into some of the 380 elaborate costumes, costing £14,000. Trouble was taken to make the settings authentic, too. When Elizabeth entered the Tower through Traitors' Gate it was the real thing – the producer arranged for it to be raised for the first time in a hundred years.

commented, 'with an air of a man who'd been a preacher in some joyless kirk'. Gordon had never met a butler in his life and said Hudson stood for everything he disliked, but his starchy stiffness was partly due to an accident which almost robbed him of the rôle. After a car crash on the day before the first day of recording, he'd broken bones in one hand and received five stitches over an eye. It meant he had to turn his left profile to the camera and do everything left-handed.

Angela Baddeley's fat huffing-puffing cook Mrs Bridges was another favourite, especially with American audiences who garlanded her with awards. The sixty-six-year-old actress weighed 7½ stone, so was padded out for the part. She died only months after the series ended in February 1976. Much enjoyed, too, were Christopher Beeny's inept young footman Edward and Jenny Tomasin's hopeless kitchen-maid Ruby. Her pathetic defeated face deserved an award of its own.

Upstairs characters – David Langton's suave Lord B and Rachel Gurney's fragrant Lady Marjorie – stayed this side of caricature. When a second series was rushed to the screen in January 1972, and Lady M had an affair with a dashing captain (played by David Kernan) but returned dutifully to her family ('They need me, Charles') viewers must have sympathised entirely. The actress wanted to leave the following year, so the writers had her sink with *Titanic* when the fourth series began in October 1973. Mourning followed. One family in a Worcestershire village draped their front-door knocker with black crêpe. After a decent interval Lord B was allowed to remarry. Viewers' pet Hannah Gordon came in as the lucky girl, Scots widow Virginia Hamilton.

The younger nobs – Simon Williams's dissolute Captain James who ended his own life, Nicola Pagett's pouting Miss Elizabeth and Lesley-Anne Down's flapper-turned-war-heroine Georgina, Lord B's ward – came to the fore later in the series. By then the plots had become more melodramatic, and critics couldn't fail to notice that despite a time-lapse of nearly thirty years no one looked a day older. But life at 165 Eaton Square was still highly watchable with a charming cameo performance from Robert Hardy as a homosexual house-guest and the arrival of Anthony Andrews as the Marquis of Stockbridge whose lavish wedding to Georgina ended the phenomenally successful show.

Exported to America and thirty other countries, 'Upstairs Downstairs' was television's biggest earner so far. The Americans, whose National Academy of Television Arts twice voted it Best Series, produced their own copy called 'Beacon Hill' about a rich Boston family, then another, 'The Adams Chronicles', following four generations over 150 years. Oddly they had to wait until 1988 to see all of 'Upstairs Downstairs'. The censors rejected thirteen episodes, some in black and white, because they dealt with suicide, homosexuality and adultery, subjects thought too daring for family audiences in the seventies.

ITV's other successful dramas to start that year were aggressively contemporary. Thames TV supplied a modern hero with Kenneth Haigh's Joe Lampton, the ambitious womanising Northern clerk-turned-businessman in **'Room at the Top'**, based on John Braine's novel. Raw language and sexual biplay upset some viewers, and the businessmen's pressure group Aims of Industry objected to the 'myth' the show perpetuated that men could get to the top 'on waves of wine, women and marrying the boss's daughter'. Zena Walker, who played Joe's long-suffering

wife Susan said men like Joe made her sick; but by 1972, 20 million viewers had made the series ITV's top show, and Kenneth Haigh was to top viewers' polls as Best Actor.

Meanwhile Sir Lew Grade at ATV gave Roger Moore, then forty-three and as yet un-Bonded, the go-ahead to try to repeat his success in 'The Saint' with a lark about two wealthy adventure-seekers, **'The Persuaders'**. The series, to be made at Pinewood, had a £2½ million budget, making it the most expensive series yet. (Sir Lew shrewdly presold it to an American network for over £3 million.) Roger was to play Lord Brett Sinclair, rich, bored but brilliant; and they needed an American to play Danny Wilde, the self-made streetwise oilman with whom Lord Brett teamed up. Rock Hudson was approached and unavailable, but Tony Curtis agreed and moved to London from Hollywood with his family. Despite a few problems – Roger had to give up cigarette-smoking because Tony was a fervent campaigner for the American Cancer Society, and Tony was arrested for possessing marijuana when he arrived here – the two egos didn't clash, and as relaxing hokum 'The Persuaders' did tolerably well. Its sales around the world demonstrate that it has been shown somewhere since at almost any time, but it flopped in America – the network dropped it before all episodes had been shown. And no one could persuade Roger Moore, its producer and star, to make more than the allotted twenty-four. It had already made him the first actor to become a millionaire from a television series.

Over at the BBC the most enduring period drama launched that year was **'The Onedin Line'**, a salty tale of Captain James Onedin's driving ambition to run a shipping line, stay solvent, win some of the arguments with his more prosperous brother and beautiful sister, and put an occasional smile on the faces of his two unlucky wives. It dealt with ruthless deals in precarious times, and for almost nine years it had the simple but unfailing appeal of an old schooner pictured in full sail on a blue sea – the seventy-year-old *Charlotte Rhodes* was the star. Peter Gilmore and Howard Lang grew side-whiskers to play the gruff hero and his faithful Captain Baines, but few of the cast were sea-dogs off-set. Working on the ocean waves off the Devon and Cornwall coast unnerved some of them. New arrivals were told not to worry – *someone* knew how to drive the boat; and not to be embarrassed if they felt seasick. While they couldn't afford to stop filming each time an actor or actress felt queasy, the pep-talk went, there was always a bucket nearby.

The BBC's great comic finds of the year were two comedians of differing height and girth who shared the forename Ronald. **The Two Ronnies**, Barker and Corbett had appeared together in 'The Frost Report' and, although each was to have a successful career on his own – Corbett did cabaret comedy and later starred in the sitcom 'Sorry!', Barker was the shining star of 'Porridge' and

LWT's 'Budgie', made in black and white, was Keith Waterhouse and Willis Hall's creation of a chirpy cockney fresh out of gaol who couldn't seem to do anything right. Adam Faith, the small but nicely marked 'Worr' Do Yer Wonn' pop-singer made a change in his career to play the likeable villain. Lynn Dalby and Georgina Hale played his wife and girlfriend, and Iain Cuthbertson played the Mr Big, the tough Scot Charlie Endell. Mrs Whitehouse attacked 'Budgie' for its bad language, but the audience loved it. When Adam Faith left after twenty-six episodes, television lost its 'colour'.

'Open All Hours', two of the BBC's very best comedies (we won't mention 'The Magnificent Evans') – their partnership in this joke-and-sketch show was a television triumph until Barker's retirement in 1988. After this the repeated compilations of their work still drew audiences of more than 14 million. Over the years the format of the shows changed little; there were always sketches involv-

ing dressing up as women (though Ronnie B hated drag – he said it made his wife Joy feel sick to watch him) and there was always a grand musical number near the close. They usually appeared as old codgers somewhere in the show and as rock singers or punks, looking particularly gruesome. The centrepieces were sometimes brilliant adventure-serials such as 'The Phantom Raspberry Blower of Old London Town' and 'The Worm That Turned', a funny futuristic saga of life with rôle-reversal – women were in charge, Gestapo-style, and the late Diana Dors was an excellent commandant. The humour was seaside-postcard rude, which made it irresistible to children, but adults loved the cleverness of much of the writing, often the work of Ronnie B whose pen-name for many years was Gerald Wiley. Here's a sample: Ronnie B in bank manager suit. 'I am squeaking to you tonight as secretary of the Loyal Society For The Prevencenation of Crispenunciation. Our patrons include Her Majesty the Queeg, Prince Phyllis, the Grime Minister Mr Grim Calorgas.' To open the pair usually sat at a news-desk in fluorescent jackets (the sort golfers might wear), and one would announce, 'In a packed programme tonight . . .' followed by some of the 150 or more joke news items the writers had submitted each week, delivered very fast. The number was whittled down to a final eighteen often only minutes before the start of the show. The show would close in a similar way with 'And it's good night from him . . .' to finish.

Not such a laughing matter was Sir Harold Wilson's rage at the BBC that year. As the anniversary of Labour's defeat in the 1970 election approached, '24 Hours' prepared a special programme, 'Yesterday's Men' – the title being the phrase the Labour Party had itself used in its campaign to describe the Conservatives. David Dimbleby interviewed the former Prime Minister in his House of Commons room, asking him cheekily halfway through about the book of memoirs he had just written. 'Many of your colleagues have told us they are suffering financially from being in opposition, but you are said to have earned between £100,000 and £250,000 from writing your book. Has that been a consolation to you over this time?' Sir Harold, angry that he seemed to be being accused of profiteering, replied that Dimbleby should ask how people (meaning Edward Heath) buy yachts. Then he said the question had been disgraceful and must be edited out. At that he stopped the interview and later threatened an injunction to stop the programme being screened if this cut and others were not made and the title were not changed. An anonymous caller leaked the question and answer to the newspapers, and the BBC governors were shown the programme (this was the first time they had been given a preview in a dispute). It was screened as planned with just the one cut, but it angered several Labour politicians with its Gerald Scarfe cartoons and satirical songs from the group Scaffold. Anger turned to fury the following night when the same programme

Ma Sugden (Sheila Mercier) in the pinny saw trouble brewing at Emmerdale Farm.

Peggy, wife of Matt, mother of twins, decided to leave. Her death was arranged, and not long afterwards the two toddlers also met with fatal accidents. Andrew Burt, who played the original Jack Sugden, the artistic elder son, wanted to do other things, so the writers dispatched him to Rome. Andrew went on to take the lead rôle in the BBC drama series 'Warship', which began in 1973. As soon as he began appearing in his commander's kit on the bridge, 'Emmerdale'-watchers began writing to Annie Sugden informing her that her boy was not in Rome but in Portsmouth. There! But he seemed to have done well for himself.

The series continued to meet the challenge of rowdier soaps – mind you, amid its scenes of pastoral peace it packed in a fair few murders, betrayals, adulterous affairs, shock arrivals of illegitimate offspring, even the threat of having a nuclear-waste plant among sheep on t' moors. Les Dawson called it '"Dallas" with dung', which seemed about right.

'General Hospital' was the other home-made soap opera to start as the afternoon restrictions went. Made by ATV, it was strikingly similar to their 'Emergency – Ward 10', which wasn't surprising in view of the fact that Sir Lew Grade had mournfully declared that dropping 'Emergency – Ward 10' five years earlier had been a mistake.

Surgery, romance and problem-solving among the doctors, nurses and surprisingly perky patients began at lunchtimes for half-hour sessions twice a week using a set so small you would have thought the NHS cuts happened in the Midlands fifteen years before the rest of the country. By 1975 ATV had built a bigger set at Elstree and changed viewers' treatment to one weekly hour-long dose at suppertime. Although some of the best-loved nurses two were played by Lynda Bellingham and Judy Buxton – had moved on, women viewers could still dream about being under Dr Baxter (James Kerry) or Dr Bywaters (Tony Adams before his 'Crossroads' fame) and enjoy the power-conflicts of Dr Armstrong (David Garth) and prickly Dr Parker-Brown (Lewis Jones). Carmen Munroe's sensible West Indian Sister Washington was a great favourite. But the scripts rarely sent pulses racing. The show was diagnosed terminally dull and put out of its misery in January 1979.

Worse than the real thing? Appearing in 'Colditz', Robert Wagner (*second left*) and David McCallum with the BBC's Third Reich in Colditz.

War could be wickedly funny with Hawkeye (Alan Alda), Hotlips (Loretta Swit) and Trapper John (Wayne Rogers) in the comedy that became a cult, 'M*A*S*H'.

long-range hearing and the ability to appear a split second before being called. 'M*A*S*H' the series was born. Later Jamie Farr came in as Klinger, the hairiest, ugliest crossdresser on television.

At first the show was only a moderate success there and here where it was shown in a late slot; but the song based on the 'M*A*S*H' theme, 'Suicide Is Painless', became a hit, though the BBC's Director-General Charles Curran banned it from BBC radio because he thought it too morbid. The American network had insisted on fewer serious stories and more skirt-chasing, and censored out such words as 'breasts' and 'virgin' (though writer Larry Gelbart got that in the following week, inventing a soldier from the Virgin Islands). A great improvement came after Larry interviewed a bunch of real M*A*S*H doctors and

he and Gene Reynolds went to Korea. (Several true stories couldn't be included because they were too bizarre – one whole unit dyeing hair red for a party, for example, or deliberately getting frostbite to get demobbed.) Its jokes were brilliant. Frank Burns: 'Why do people take an instant dislike to me?' Trapper John: 'It saves time, Frank.' It never forgot it was about saving lives. In one episode, the Colonel remarked that Radar looked dead beat. Radar replied that he had given blood twice: 'I fell asleep in the mess and two guys syphoned me.' And it always put people above causes: 'This man has a chest wound, he should be in surgery.' 'But he's Chinese.' 'OK, we'll operate with chopsticks.' And: 'Anyway, Klinger's not a pervert.' 'How do you know?' 'I'm a pervert. We have meetings. He's never there.'

Eventually, after 251 episodes, 'M*A*S*H' had run out of anecdotes to turn into plots. Alan Alda tired of putting boot polish on his hair to hide the grey. The show had collected fourteen Emmies, had had ninety-nine nominations, and Alan Alda had won awards as one of its writers and directors as well as its leading actor. The final extra-long episode, shown in 1983, attracted a record 125 million viewers in America.

A British television series about war – a documentary, not a comedy – also won awards here and in America in 1973. Thames Television's **'The World at War'**, produced by Jeremy Isaacs, narrated by Laurence Olivier, took four years to make, cost £1 million and deserved its success for its skilful use of archive news-film with new interviews – including one with Traudl Junge, Hitler's personal secretary, U-boat commander Admiral Doenitz and James Stewart, the Hollywood film actor who became a brigadier-general in the United States Air Force. A book of the series sold half a million copies and was translated into fourteen languages.

Compared with 'M*A*S*H' our comedy hits that year were unashamedly childish. **'Some Mothers Do 'Ave 'Em'** might have been appreciated only by children had the hero in the mac, the too-small tank-top and the beret, with the idiot voice and the slack face, Frank Spencer, not been played with the consummate skill of a little-known young actor called Michael Crawford (real name Michael Dumble Smith). Michael was to prove to writer Raymond Allen, who said he was the real Frank Spencer – someone for whom everything always went wrong, who thought of himself as a total failure – that luck could change. At first the BBC weren't so confident. When Raymond asked them if he should risk giving up his job cleaning in a cinema, they said he should keep it on for a while to see how things went. But Michael's Frank, with his sweetly forgiving girlfriend, then wife Betty (Michele Dotrice) and his disastrous effect on machinery, was a success from the start. He looked funny because of Raymond Allen's own admitted lack of style.

'I've always lived on the Isle of Wight where fashions

are way behind,' Raymond Allen says. 'I'd never earned more than £4 a week, so I rarely bought clothes. When the BBC asked me to come to London to the rehearsals, I went out and bought this long mac I thought was really smart. Michael Crawford saw it. I'd told him that I thought Frank should look really quaint, but I was horrified when he turned up in one just like it for the recording the next week and it became his trademark. I couldn't wear my mac in London again – but it went on for years in the Isle of Wight.' When Frank was to become a father, bachelor Allen researched babies at a fathers' class. A midwife handed him the demonstration doll. As he touched it the arm fell off. Happily the Spencers' baby, Jessica, survived.

Michael took quite staggering risks to do his own stunts. They certainly wouldn't be allowed today; and Michael, now our most successful stage star, wouldn't do them. They included being whisked fifty feet into the air by a helicopter; driving over the edge of a cliff in a car, balancing on the brink; hanging by the fingertips outside an office window 150 feet up; roller-skating along a road underneath a passing lorry; jumping a thirty-foot wall on a motorbike; and having an old factory chimney crash to the ground, missing him by inches. Michael once said, sounding like Frank: 'I'm not really all that keen on heights.'

The heroes of **'Last of the Summer Wine'** have over the years made Frank Spencer seem quite mature. Writer Roy Clarke, a former policeman from Doncaster, based his adventures of a trio of Yorkshire codgers on the notion that men over sixty-five can be as reckless, anti-social and silly as any juvenile. You don't need your own teeth to be a delinquent.

Large and loyal audiences slowly built up for the series with its mellow witty dialogue ('How are you to know when you're dead?' 'Well, you're supposed to take the hint when they bury you') and its pretty pictures of the threesome flying kites on the moors or sailing on the reservoir or mooching around the cobbled streets and stone cottages of Holmfirth, near Huddersfield, population 19,000. And there was always an especially male mischievousness about Compo, Clegg and company as they and the other old boys in the series annoyed the womenfolk who, in their turn, saw it as their duty to fold their arms and disapprove of the men. Jane Freeman's Ivy ran the café with Sid, played by the late John Comer. Later Thora Hird arrived as Edie, Seymour's tut-tutting sister. But most dogged of the women was Kathy Staff's dragon-like Nora Batty whose wrinkled lisle stockings, curlers and pinafore inspired insatiable lust in Compo, forever drawn to her front steps but savaged by her carefully aimed broom.

There were problems with the third man. First with Peter Sallis's chirpy Clegg, widower and redundant manager of a Co-op furniture department, and Bill Owen's Compo, smelly National Assistance tramp, there was

Ummm! Frank (Michael Crawford) and Betty (Michele Dotrice) in 'Some Mothers Do 'Ave 'Em' made a train take the strain.

Michael Bates's Blamire, a retired bachelor Royal Signals sergeant. When Michael was injured in pantomime in 1976, Brian Wilde's Foggy Dewhurst, an ex-army signwriter with ideas above his rank wandered in and joined the pranks. In 1985, when the actor wanted to leave, Foggy departed for Bridlington, having inherited his uncle's painted-egg business, and Michael Aldridge's pompous Seymour Utterthwaite, retired from teaching, made up the trio. The characters squabbled and giggled like life-long friends but ironically Peter Sallis, Bill Owen and Brian Wilde barely exchanged words with each other off-set and Brian got on so badly with Bill that he declined to appear in a stage version of the series in Eastbourne in 1983.

The eleven-year success of **'Are You Being Served?'**, the BBC's series set in the clothing department of Grace Brothers store, is more difficult to explain. This was slapstick comedy, laden with double meanings and vulgarity, once nicknamed 'Are You Being Stereotyped?' It was most famous for its mincing homosexual men's-wear assistant, Mr Humphries, played by John Inman, who was bitterly criticised by the newly militant Gay Rights groups. Probably as popular as Mr Humphries was Mollie Sugden's blowzy overbearing Mrs Slocombe, in ladies' lingerie, an all-the-year-round pantomime dame with piled-up mauve hair and an unseen much-fussed-about cat. Her pussy (nudge, nudge) had existed but suffered stage fright and was sacked. Wendy Richard, now put-upon Pauline in 'EastEnders', put the glamour in the show, bursting her blouse buttons as flighty Miss Brahms who worked with Mrs Slocombe. And perhaps the best joke in the show was Harold Bennett as Young Mr Grace. He was young with Queen Victoria.

By contrast **'Whatever Happened to the Likely Lads?'** was a British comedy with serious points to make about the class system, the sex war and the problems of young men in the North trying to improve their lives as the Swinging Sixties turned into the sober and soon-to-be-unemployed seventies. Dick Clement and Ian La Frenais brought their Terry (James Bolam) and Bob (Rodney Bewes) together again after four years of growing-up and had the cocky cynical Terry comment on his shyer but more ambitious pal's new middle-class lifestyle and affectations. (Saturday night at the Trattoria, winter sports in Austria, don't you know?) They also turned the twosome into a triangle. While Terry had joined the Army, played the field with girls and got himself lumbered with a distant wife he was keen to dump, Bob was only just learning with fiancée Thelma (the brilliant Brigit Forsyth) that women sometimes like to change men and control them. The Likely Lads proved that some sequels can be better than the originals. Fittingly it won the Best Situation Comedy award for the year.

The most praised documentary series was **'The Ascent of Man'**, a thirteen-part scientific and philosophical treatise by Dr Jacob Bronowski which explained how man came to be drawn, step by step, from one field of scientific discovery to the next. The doctor's confident and careful words were heard as his hunched figure bestrode the deserts or climbed the monuments and exciting pictures unfurled. His face reflected in a bubble of mercury was one of these. The air waves as a spear cut its high-speed path was another. Hours of experiment had gone into perfecting the technical effects, of course. The prop for one sequence, filmed in Holkham, Norfolk, explaining the early methods of X-ray photography and radar, gave the producers headaches and the locals something of a scare. It was a large human head, made from canvas over a chicken-wire base; and it appeared, apparently from nowhere, on the beach one day, staring eerily out to sea. 'The Ascent of Man' took four years to reach the screen and when it did Jacob Bronowski was in hospital suffering from the fatigue of it all. He died the following year.

There was some ascent for woman in television drama. Three years after Germaine Greer published *The Female Eunuch* Britain had a feminist magazine, *Spare Rib*, and Richard Bates, son of H. E. Bates, finally persuaded LWT to make **'Helen – a Woman of Today'** – a serial featuring a none-too-glamorous woman in her thirties choosing to end a marriage – after all the other television companies had rejected it.

Richard Bates's idea was a follow-up to **'A Man of Our Times'**, the 1968 series starring George Cole as a man at a crisis point in his life. Here, in thirteen parts directed by Jim Goddard, Alison Fiske played Helen, a conventional middle-class wife and mother who decided to divorce her husband Frank after he had an affair, to study and become self-reliant after years of dependency. Many male viewers, including several critics, thought Helen an obstinate baggage. Did not her husband, played by Martin Shaw, pre-'Professionals' perm and with a droopy moustache, regret the affair (with Sharon Duce), love her and the two young children? Parents and neighbours advised her to swallow her pride and carry on as before. But Helen went on irritating them but inspiring millions of women, looking realistically fed up and, later, turning down the proposal of a rich new man.

When the first modern feminist drama ended its Friday-night run, Alison Fiske should have been a star. She wasn't. Martin Shaw who'd played weak Frank was. But, then, Germaine Greer hadn't said it would be easy.

This was the year television producers began believing that what sportsmen and women *said*, we wanted to hear. In **'UK Superstars'**, shown on BBC1 at peak times, vast numbers of sportspersons unknown to most normal viewers competed in programmes of gruelling events. Watching the sports wasn't so nerve-racking. The killer was the knowledge that the moment they'd finished running a hundred metres or doing eighty press-ups David Vine would shove a microphone under the nose of one of the participants and ask: 'How does it feel?'

The talent show returned with ATV's **'New Faces'**, much to the distaste of Hughie 'Opportunity Knocks' Green: 'I strongly disagree with the idea of artists having to stand up in public and be criticised by a panel of judges; it's too unkind,' he said. Equity, the artists' union, agreed, branding the panels too cruel. Several of the judges, who included 'Housewives' Choice' presenter George Elrick, comic Ted Ray, record producer Mickey Most and nightclub-act booking agent John Smith (possibly the least charismatic panellist in the history of television), Clifford

(Mr Nasty) Davis and Tony Hatch (the hatchet man), were easy as pie to please. Arthur Askey liked every act ('I thought they were great,' he always said). But it was the more savage (truthful?) verdicts viewers enjoyed. Tony Hatch gave comedian Harry Dickman 'two points for his nerve', and the switchboard was jammed with complaints. Both Lonnie Donegan and journalist Clifford Davis awarded acts no marks. Clifford gave nil for 'star quality' to

In 'Sam' we were in trooble-at-t'-mill territory with John Finch's thirty-nine-part story for Granada of how a boy grew up in an impoverished Pennine mining town in the thirties. Written and acted with conviction, it made glum viewing, especially when the action shifted from the adult Sam, played by Mark McManus (later to become Taggart), and Barbara Ewing and Ray Smith as his parents to the grim-faced stoical grandfather played by Michael Goodliffe.

STAR QUALITY 80

GRAND TOTAL 00

NEW FACES

The 'New Faces' panel scored two out of ten for 'star quality'.

ventriloquist Ken Graham and was booed by the studio audience one member of which later slapped his face. He left the studio under escort.

She doesn't boast about it now but 'Emmerdale Farm' star Malandra Burrows (she plays Kathy Sugden) using a stage name of Malandra Newman won one show in 1974 as an eight-year-old singer. Tony Hatch, one of the judges that week said she didn't need the break for another ten years. Some viewers called in to say she sang out of tune.

Of course there were discoveries of real talent. Lenny Henry then sixteen emerged in 1974. (He appeared with his back to the camera doing an impersonation of Frank Spencer. When he turned round, the audience howled at seeing a black Frank.) Others included Victoria Wood, Jim Davidson, Gary Wilmot, Showaddywaddy and Marti Caine (who replaced Derek Hobson as the show's host when it

came back after an eight year absence, from 1986 to 1988).

A rumpus usually followed the discovery that an act had appeared on television before (strictly against the rules); there were arguments between panellists, punch-ups between losing musicians and sound technicians blamed for poor performances. A singer tipped a bowl of sugar over the head of record producer Alan A. Freeman who'd called him 'too camp'. It was all great fun in the worst possible taste.

The most important new face of 1973 was Esther Rantzen's. Her giant gnashers became *the* teeth of television, and as the consumer watchdog for millions she needed their bite and used it more and more on tricksters and charlatans. What came out of her mouth over sixteen years of **'That's Life'** was a great deal of sound sense and sincere concern, if you could stand the schmaltz and poor puns. Esther presided over a succession of lap-dog males who sat behind desks on the stage and brightly reported back to Big Sister on their investigations. The shows were recorded so close to transmission that there was no time to edit out any but the most serious mistakes, which added a near-'live' edge of excitement.

'That's Life' loved animals – and not only dogs who could say 'sausages'. Esther once tried to investigate Scent-Off pellets, claimed by the manufacturers to dispatch any hound which sniffed them. A viewer had reported that her dog, far from being repelled, had liked the pellets so much he'd eaten them all. Esther arranged for a dozen assorted dogs with their owners to come into the studio to test them. There was chaos. A large Airedale took passionate interest in a Yorkshire terrier and pursued it round the studio. Two others fought, while another decided to cock its leg up by the pot-plant next to Esther's chair. The scent on the plant encouraged others to follow suit. Esther had to get help to remove the dogs so that she could carry on with the show.

As Esther produced three children and became a famous working mother, she championed more children's causes. Ben Hardwicke, a toddler with liver disease, became the focus for Esther's campaign for child organ-donors. In 1986 she began publicising a help-line for children suffering sexual and other abuse. Strangely, viewers responded to such life-and-death heart-breaking subjects, wedged as they often were between tax inspectors gargling to music and racing bunny rabbits. 'That's Life' was always in the BBC's Top Ten, and by the late eighties its peculiar mix of pranks and preaching had made Esther Rantzen (the surname translates as 'old bag') the most authoritative woman in British broadcasting.

Also Shown in 1973

'Beryl's Lot', with Carmel McSharry as a milk-man's wife trying to go up in the world, and 'Spring and Autumn', about the generation clash, with Jimmy Jewel, were weak ITV comedies of the year. The strongest on that channel was 'Man about the House', milksop knockabout with standard well-signposted jokes which had the benefit of three pleasant young stars: Richard O'Sullivan as student chef Robin Tripp sharing a flat with Chrissy, played by Paula Wilcox, and Jo, played by toothsome Sally Thomsett.

The most praised light-entertainment series of the year – winning the Society of Film and Television Arts awards for both 1973 and 1974 – was 'The Stanley Baxter Big Picture Show', elaborate variety made by LWT with plenty of over-long Hollywood spoofs usually featuring the Scottish comedian in drag.

Harlech Television managed to get Richard Burton (one of its directors) and Elizabeth Taylor (one of its major shareholders) to hold to their promise to put the little ITV company on the map by appearing together in 'Divorce His, Divorce Hers', a two-part play about a marriage under stress written by John Hopkins. A dotty story, poorly played, it wasn't a success and proved to be the most expensive television play so far produced.

Other drama series that year stayed on familiar ground. 'Shabby Tiger' had John Nolan and Prunella Gee in a seven-part adaptation of a novel about a wild Irish girl and her love for an artist. 'Hunter's Walk' was ITV's plodding police drama to begin that year. Created by Ted Willis, there was a 'Dixon of Dock Green' feeling to crime-detection in fictional Broadstone. The BBC did better with 'Warship', a drama which ran for five series until 1978, about life in a Royal Navy frigate, HMS *Hero*.

The Americans sent us the odd few heroes that year, none odder than David Carradine's Caine, the shaven-headed Chinese-American Buddhist monk who suffered bouts of slow-motion flashback in 'Kung Fu'.

The outside broadcast of the year was the wedding in Westminster Abbey of Princess Anne and Captain Mark Phillips – the first major royal wedding in colour. It boosted sales of colour sets – only a quarter of the sets until then had been colour receivers – and 28 million in Britain, 530 million world-wide, tuned in to enjoy a good cry.

It wasn't a vintage year at the **Crossroads** Motel and not a jolly one for Miss Diane whose son Nicky was kidnapped by his father, taken to America and never seen or mentioned again. In 'Coronation Street' Len Fairclough bought a shop in Rosamund Street, called it The Kabin and installed Rita as manageress. She hired Mavis as her assistant. Poor Bet was mugged, and Elsie Tanner (Elsie Howard at the time) unwisely went to t' Smoke and was knocked unconscious by a taxi.

Commercial Break

The hero of the television commercials that year was Ben, the freckled consumer of Bird's Eye beefburgers. Leeds boy Darren Cockerill was directed by Alan Parker in a series of tiny stories dealing with his interest in the beefburgers and his friend Mary's interest in him.

Probably the best deep voice in television began telling us that Carlsberg was 'probably the best lager in the world; Molly Weir, Jill Gascoine and Jean Rogers joined forces to amaze us with the cleaning powers of Flash (it prepared Jean, as 'Emmerdale Farm''s Dolly, for the times husband Matt trailed his sheep across her kitchen floor); and English actress Jennifer Clulow and French actor Christian Toma began making eyes at each other over a couple of glasses of Cointreau. It took them fifteen more years to reach the engagement-ring stage, by which time sales had soared to a million litres a year in Britain alone.

Kenneth More began drinking Mellow Birds instant coffee in commercials – but it wasn't as easy as it looked, he said. The set kitchen was so full of people, you'd think they were filming *Gone with the Wind*. There was a coffee-making person, a person to make sure the steam wafted up properly from the cup, and a person in charge of the number of bubbles in the cup. After about thirty takes, the steam and bubble quotients were still not right, so the bubble lady had to whip up bubbles in a spoon and drop them in the cup at the last moment. If they hadn't been paying him handsomely – enough to allow him to pick and choose his rôles for the rest of the year – he might have stuck to tea.

1974

That Was the Year When...

The three-day week meant the television year began with a 10.30 p.m. curfew. □ Labour was returned to power in two general elections: the first in February gave them no overall majority, the second in November gave them a majority of three. □ Princess Anne was shot at but unhurt after a kidnap attempt in the Mall. □ At the Flixborough chemical plant an explosion killed twenty-nine. □ Labour MP John Stonehouse, thought to have died off Miami Beach, turned up in Australia. □ The cost of living went up 20 per cent in one year. □ In the wake of Watergate, Richard Nixon became the first American president to resign. □ Lord Lucan disappeared and was sought by the police after his children's nanny was found murdered. □ Video-cassette recorders became available for home use. □ Abba won the Eurovision Song Contest with 'Waterloo'. □ Five young Scotsmen created Rollermania – the Bay City Rollers. □ The Wombles were the most successful chart act. □ Selfridges, Harrods and Edward Heath's home were bombed in an IRA Christmas campaign.

As if the year wasn't punishing enough, television went to gaol. We at home did time eagerly and wanted no parole. When we weren't cheeking the screws with Fletch and Godber and the other crusty crims in **'Porridge'**, we were chuckling at **'Thick as Thieves'**; and if stretches inside Stone Park Women's prison, the setting for the LWT drama series **'Within These Walls'** had been voluntary viewers would have queued at the gates.

Our cult prison show was to be 'Porridge', but before Ronnie Barker was sent down for his term in Slade Prison two other old lags began making us laugh. Writers Dick Clement and Ian La Frenais, who were to create that

much repeated series, first wrote 'Thick as Thieves' for LWT, about Dobbs (Bob Hoskins), a small-time crook who came out of gaol to discover his best mate Stan (John Thaw), another villain, had moved in with Annie (Pat Ashton), his wife. The six-part series was highly praised, and the writers wanted to develop it, sending both men back inside; but two things happened: LWT bosses dithered – they thought the writing was too clever and could go over people's heads; and John Thaw appeared in an Armchair Cinema film, 'Regan', which led to his being offered the lead rôle in 'The Sweeney'.

Clement and La Frenais took the idea to the BBC instead. Ronnie Barker, the roly-poly actor-writer who'd played a constant offender in 'Prisoner and Escort', one of seven short comedies in a series he'd made, dyed his silver hair rat-brown and put his large talent into Norman Stanley Fletcher, his greatest comic achievement. Fletch was smarmy, sneaky, cynical, stupid and marvellous. To his naïve cellmate Godber, played sleepily by the late Richard Beckinsale, he was protector and pest. To Chief Warden Mackay – a wonderfully stiff Fulton Mackay – and Brian Wilde's stuttering Barraclough, the soft screw, he was a perfect pain.

Because there were proper relationships between these carefully drawn characters, and the actors were so skilled, 'Porridge' was an instant success. Cons at Maidstone gaol loved it – a warder there phoned the BBC to tell them. In gaols all over the country, the punishment for bad behaviour became not being allowed to watch 'Porridge'. In their few short visits inside prison allowed by the Home Office, the writers had absorbed the atmosphere, the slang, and had spotted the tensions they could joke about. On hand to advise was former thief Jonathan Marshall. Prisoners, ex-prisoners and prison officers all agreed that they got it right. Ronnie Barker found himself a much in-demand guest at police balls, and Christmas brought cards from 'The Boys in B Block' and similar addresses. Fletch, whose spirit never sagged, was a hero.

Another Fletcher household was introduced to viewers in 1974, and its inmates took longer to go away. **'Happy**

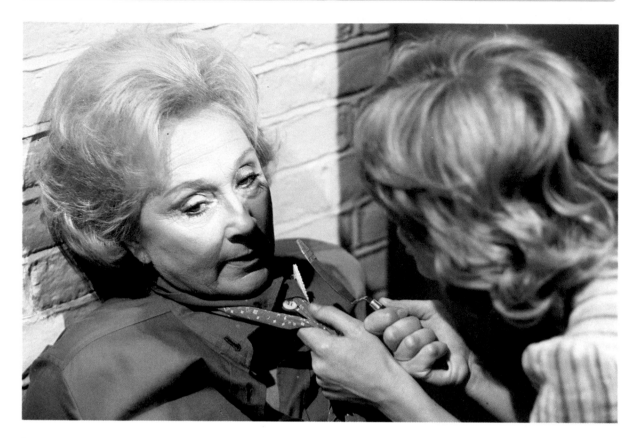

Ever After' was the series in which Terry Scott first took up with June Whitfield (though they'd met, five years earlier, when she was on top of a wedding cake featured in a bit of nonsense called 'Scott on Marriage'). The series which grew into 'Terry and June' was twee domestic slapstick – middle-aged, middle-class and middle-of-the-road comedy featuring Terry as a clumsy child crazily allowed a job and a mortgage. With him were June his long-suffering wife, Aunt Lucy (Beryl Cooke) and their two daughters Debbie and Susan (Caroline Whitaker and Pippa Page) who had just left home. There was also a mynah bird in the house. The original bird was dumb, and it was June's voice that viewers heard. Later they hired a new one which jabbered away as soon as the studio lights went on so that the actors could barely be heard.

The show had a certain warmth, despite its narcotic effect, and was a smash hit. But writers Eric Merriman and Christopher Bond were soon involved in a copyright row and Happy Ever After they weren't. Viewers hadn't forgotten the cuddly couple, and five years later Terry and June returned, alone. Neither the mynah bird nor their daughters were ever again mentioned. Hundreds of episodes followed. In the summer of 1987 the silly old stuff reached number three in the ratings, behind 'EastEnders' and 'Coronation Street'.

Life 'Within These Walls' may not have been a laugh a minute but it was firm and fair – rather like the hairstyle of its governor, Faye Boswell, played by Googie Withers. Among the scowling unhappy inmates in their drab clothes and the big butch wardens bellowing 'Yes, Mum', 'No, Mum', Faye looked like the winner of a glamorous granny competition, on whom the Avon Lady had just called, something critics chose to mock. Googie (real name Georgina) argued back that she had visited Holloway and other institutions for her research and had found the governors to be extremely well groomed. Viewers loved the idea of a *nice* prison boss and in what turned out to be a two-year stretch for the Australian actress she became a national symbol of law and order. The show inspired their soap, 'Prisoner, Cell Block H', cult viewing (for giggles) here in the 1980s.

The BBC's other comedy hit of 1974 was unashamedly a lark. **'It Ain't Half Hot Mum'** by David Croft and Jimmy Perry was about a platoon of British soldiers organising a concert-party in India during the war. Fake palm-trees and a polystyrene crocodile were additions to a 'jungle' in Norfolk where the immensely popular series was made. But it wasn't half cold there for the cast, who included Windsor Davies as Sergeant-Major Williams, Michael Bates blacked up as Rangi Ram, and Melvyn Hayes as

Gunner Beaumont. They shivered with glycerine 'sweat' on their foreheads and to make the 'swamp's' mist, dry ice was dunked in mud and stirred. The desert was a Sussex coast sandpit.

Leonard Rossiter, till his thirties an insurance claims inspector, began to make millions of people laugh in 1974 as Rigsby, the sneering, leering, lip-curling landlord of a run-down house in **'Rising Damp'**. Almost as smelly and ignorant as Steptoe senior, Rigsby insulted two of his tenants – black Philip, son of an African tribal chief (Don Warrington), and hopeless medical student Alan (a second new series for Richard Beckinsale – here under hippy-length hair) – while lusting for his third tenant, slightly dotty spinster Miss Jones (splendid Frances De La Tour). For some the real star was Rigsby's cat, a mournful moggy called Vienna. If Leonard hadn't made them laugh with his stream of jokes, his nodding and funny face-pulling, Eric Chappell's deadbeat characters who'd first appeared in his play 'The Banana Box' might have made them cry. Labour MP Tom Pendry did cry – with fury when Rigsby made disparaging remarks about a fictional election candidate called Pendry, calling him homosexual, hypocritical and dishonest. Yorkshire Television cried, too, when they had to pay up in damages for the defamation.

America sent us three new series, each of which broke a television tradition, and a fourth, **'The Waltons'**, a superior soap, which was as old-fashioned as could be. 'The Waltons' was a series of sentimental stories, created and narrated by Earl Hamner, Jnr, about a family of backwoods pioneers in the Blue Ridge Mountains of Virginia during the Depression. Mom, Pop, seven kids, Grandpaw, Grandmaw and a dawg ran a lumber mill and were excessively keen on moralising. The series, a huge hit with Middle America, had earned six Emmy awards before the BBC cleverly slotted it into Sunday evenings and it took hold here. The action was seen through the warm and usually moist eyes of John Boy (played by fresh-faced actor Richard Thomas) who wanted to be a novelist, began publishing his own newspaper and, when Thomas decided to leave, moved off to New York. Thomas became a sort of Sunday-school pinup but, like so many soap stars, when he quit his success in movies was modest.

If 'The Waltons' was for and about hicks, **'Rhoda'**, the new series about Mary's friend in 'The Mary Tyler Moore Show', was sharp American humour for city folk. Rhoda was a window-dresser who anguished about the width of her hips, a Jewish girl surviving alone in New York. Her

Officer Mackay (Fulton Mackay) spelled it out to crafty crims Fletch (Ronnie Barker) and Godber (Richard Beckinsale) in 'Porridge' – winner of the BAFTA Best Situation Comedy award.

Jewishness was in itself a breakthrough – though Valerie Harper, who played her, was not Jewish nor was Nancy Walker who played her emotional mother Ida Morgenstern. It was also unusual for an American network to allow a heroine to want more than a fitted kitchen, husband and kids. In fact the writers gave in to convention, had Rhoda marry Joe Gerard (David Groh), but soon decided that this was a mistake and had the couple separate. Making jokes about a failed marriage was another first for American comedy; but the best jokes were often saved for Rhoda's sister Brenda (Julie Kavner) and Carlton, the unseen doorman with the doomy voice on the entryphone in Rhoda's apartment. It belonged to Lorenzo Music.

By the seventies, television detectives had to have obvious handicaps. We'd had the blind detective Longstreet; the wheelchair-bound detective, Ironside; the snuff-taking detective, Lockhart in 'No Hiding Place'; and in the distance were the ex-convict, Rockford; the ex-drunk, Bergerac; several sleuths hampered by their wealth or their poverty; the Chinese Detective, hampered by the prejudice of his colleagues against his background; and, spectacularly, the one covered in scabs, the Singing Detective.

The three most popular American crime-fighters in those mid-seventies years were middle-aged and far from pretty. Columbo had one eye and a shabby mac; Cannon was obese and balding; and Kojak was completely bald with a squashed nose. Bing Crosby was first choice for Columbo. He turned it down: it would have eaten into his golf time. The role went to the excellent Peter Falk who first played the character he modelled on Petrovitch, the detective in Dostoevsky's Crime and Punishment, in the television film 'Prescription: Murder' in 1968 before filming the television series of **'Columbo'** between 1971 and 1977. He made television history by earning the record fee of $320,000 for each of four ninety-minute episodes.

ITV screened the series – in which the humble underpaid Los Angeles police lieutenant would always infuriate the people involved in the crimes by prattling on about his dragon-like wife and by turning back from the door to ask one last, crucial (and of course brilliant) thing. In 1988 the BBC repeated the series in a peak Saturday-night slot. A new series is now in production.

But the major ITV series that year, costing half a million pounds, was Thames Television's **'Jennie, Lady Randolph Churchill'**, made to tie in with the centenary of Winston's birth and starring beautiful American Lee Remick in the title rôle of Churchill's mother, corseted into more than a hundred 1870s gowns. Ronald Pickup played her husband Lord Randolph Churchill, Barbara Parkins of 'Peyton Place' fame was Aunt Leonie, and Christopher Cazenove came in as George Cornwallis West, the man twenty years her junior with whom she had an affair. The casting of Warren Clarke, star of the controversial film *A*

Had Kenneth More not agreed to play Father Brown, in an adaptation of G. K. Chesterton's stories, he might have gone on receiving early-morning telephone calls from Lew Grade, now Lord Grade, addressing him as 'Father'. Kenneth was not sure he was the right man for the rôle of an elderly priest turned detective, but after three years of Lew's hints agreed. Lew knew he'd got his man when he greeted Kenneth with the customary 'Morning, Father' and heard the reply, 'God bless you, my son.' The quaint stories, in which Kenneth's wife Angela Douglas also starred, were much enjoyed, though not by some Muslim viewers. In one episode Muhammad was referred to as a 'dirty old humbug', which led 2,000 Muslims in Bradford to march in protest at the defamation.

Clockwork Orange, as Winston from sixteen to forty-seven, caused a few Tory faithfuls to worry that the series might be less than flattering to their hero.

They needn't have worried. Writer Julian Mitchell had been allowed to study the Churchill family files on condition that Sir Winston's widow, Lady Spencer Churchill, approved his scripts. She did. Cameras went into the family homes at Blenheim Palace, Salisbury Hall and the Isle of Wight, and the viewing public came to learn that Winnie's mum was a daring pace-setter, a romantic and a flirt, that she was ambitious for both her husband and her son, and that she died after a fall wearing high heels quite unsuitable for an old lady.

The year also launched the first popular science series, **'Don't Ask Me'**, in which experts answered such crucial questions as why do jellies wobble, why are fleas good jumpers and do crocodiles really shed tears? It launched the career of a pretty young doctor, Miriam Stoppard; a botanist with a funny face and a worse voice, Dr David Bellamy; and an eccentric birdlike nutritionist who talked very fast, Dr Magnus Pike. Magnus was keen on demonstrations. Ask him to mix 4 hundredweight of custard in a cement-mixer and you'd have a happy man. Some experiments went wrong, though. He worked out the speed truck-driver John England should use to 'fly' a minibus across the River Avon. It was too slow. The bus sank, trapping John for 40 seconds. 'By Jove, you are wet,' said Magnus.

Derek Griffiths was replaced as the host by Adrienne Posta, but she lasted only one show. Don't ask me, she was told when she asked why she'd been sacked. Her too modern clothes seemed to have been her crime. Brian Glover took over, but it eventually became Miriam's job to ask the questions, with Dr Rob Buckman – also part of a cabaret comedy act and a future partner with Miriam on 'Where There's Life' – joining in 1977 as one of the experts. The unstoppable Stoppard was halted only once when labour pains caused her to break off in mid-sentence.

The Wilkinses, the family in 'The Family', were indisputably the television stars of the year. As Labour came back into power, the BBC decided to make one working-class family in Reading the subject of an important twelve-part documentary series distilled from filming hour upon hour of life with the Wilkinses over a period of three months. The Wednesday-night screening attracted 6–9 million viewers, many of whom watched slack-jawed with amazement. This was no modern-day Walton family. These people were – how shall we put it? – *common*. 'We are not a problem family, we are a family with problems,' said Margaret Wilkins, the large loud mother with more fighting spirit than all the soap heroines rolled into one. The problems included those of her daughter Marion, aged nineteen, whose loping live in boyfriend Tom was rarely seen without a pint of beer in his hand and seemed comically reluctant to fix the wedding; those of her younger daughter Heather, aged fifteen, who wanted to be a hairdresser, sulked at having to stay on at school and had an uninhibited manner with Melvyn, her half-caste boyfriend. (When the lad whispered affectionately to her during their holiday in Majorca, she replied: 'Get lost, yer stinking smelly pig.') Margaret's son Gary, eighteen, had married his girlfriend Karen when they were sixteen because she was pregnant, and the series coincided with the couple's move to a council flat in which Karen proceeded to mope. Her second son Christopher, then nine, was the love-child of an affair, she revealed in one episode. Her bus-driver husband Terry, aged thirty-nine like her, had accepted the boy as his own and sat patiently in the scruffy kitchen of their crowded maisonette over a greengrocer's for most of the series, ignoring the peeling paint, smiling through the rows and quietly munching meals of mash and beans.

Paul Watson admitted it had been a mistake to screen episodes while still recording others. The pressures of ordinary family life, which the series had set out to reflect, had become pressures of coping with extraordinary

Also Shown in 1974

Bernard Manning was resident compère at 'The Wheeltappers and Shunters Social Club', ITV's raucous variety series set in what was supposed to be a typical working-men's club. The 'turns' included the Bachelors, Matt Monro, Mrs Mills, Tessie O'Shea, David Whitfield, Johnny Ray and other old-timers, and the series was so successful that after a few weeks coachloads of people arrived at Granada Television in Manchester asking if the mythical club was open to non-members.

The little-noticed 'Squirrels' starred Bernard Hepton and Ken Jones as office-workers (Phil Redmond of 'Brookside' fame wrote scripts for early episodes of this). 'Get Some In', an ITV comedy about RAF recruits doing their national service in the fifties was a moderate success. And ITV produced two other light comedies: 'Moody and Pegg', in which spinster Pegg (Judy Cornwell) and formerly married Moody (Derek Waring) shared the apartment they both wanted to rent; and 'No, Honestly', in which John Alderton played a patient husband to a scatty wife played by his real wife Pauline Collins. Later the title was changed to 'Yes, Honestly' and Liza Goddard shared the jokes with Donal Donnelly as her husband. Perhaps the most under-rated comedy of 1974 was 'The Top Secret Life of Edgar Briggs', in which David Jason played a bumbling British spy, a post to which he'd been transferred by mistake.

Dramas that year included 'The Zoo Gang', which starred Lilli Palmer, Sir John Mills, Brian Keith and Barry Morse as members of a wartime Resistance group who meet again thirty years on to use their special skills in combating modern crime. 'South Riding' was Yorkshire Television's splendid adaptation of Winifred Holtby's novel of a progressive schoolmistress in Yorkshire in the thirties. Dorothy Tutin glowed in the rôle, Hermione Baddeley and Nigel Davenport supported her, and the serial was repeated at peak time on Channel 4 in 1987.

In 'Crossroads' that year Wilf Harvey married Myrtle Cavendish, played by Gretchen Franklin (later Ethel in 'EastEnders'), before he died of pneumonia. In 'Coronation Street' Annie Walker played Lady Bracknell in the dramatic society's production of *The Importance of Being Earnest*, and Bet Lynch's long-lost son turned up at the Rover's Return and was so appalled at his mother's vulgarity that he left without telling her who he was.

Glamorous they weren't, but Marion and her reluctant bridegroom Tom, members of 'The Family', put peep-show television on the map.

by the sackful after Margaret spoke of the affair with a dustman which led to Christopher's birth. They had to change their phone number. But none of this upset Margaret for long.

Paul Watson went back with his cameramen to the family three years later and again in 1988 to find them much changed – but not by their three months of living dangerously in 1974. Margaret, the leading lady, and Terry, the hen-pecked husband, had parted after twenty-four years, and each had remarried. Gary and Marion had divorced their partners and remarried (Marion was on her third husband). Heather the rebel had four children but had not married; Christopher had an illegitimate son; and Tom, the lodger who had cursed and belched and downed his pints with such glee for the cameras, was still a family friend. Margaret, still chain-smoking, still opinionated, regretted nothing.

American television had made a similar series the year before with the Louds family in which the mother discovered her eldest son was gay and told her husband she was divorcing him. Nothing the Wilkinses revealed was anywhere near as shocking, but in those distant days before 'EastEnders' shocked we were. Perhaps it was the peeling paint.

Commercial Break

Favourite television commercials in 1974 included two for Cadbury's: in one Jeremy Hawk, the 'Criss Cross Quiz' host, sang 'Nuts! Whoo-ole ha-a-zelnuts! Cadbury's take them and they cover them in choc-late'; in the other Frank Muir informed us that 'Everyone's a fwoot and nutcase'.

Yellow Pages began to insist you should 'let your fingers do the walking', and the Milk Marketing Board warned us about 'Humphreys' with their 'Watch out – there's a Humphrey about' campaign. These were invisible creatures who sucked milk from bottles left on doorsteps through red-striped straws. But perhaps the most poetic was the new commercial for Pepsi Cola which, the singer told us, was 'the lipsmackin', thirst-quenchin', ace-tastin', motivatin', goodbuzzin', cooltalkin', highwalkin', fastlivin', evergivin', coolfizzin' Pepsi'. So there.

publicity. Terry Wilkins's workmates believed he was doing it for money, but it turned out the whole family received only £1,500 after tax for putting themselves on show (with no right of veto), not to mention putting up with Paul Watson as a lodger for almost three months and stepping over four cameramen around the flat (they'd taken rooms in the pub opposite). Poison-pen letters came

1975

The war in Vietnam ended as North Vietnamese tanks rolled into Saigon. □ *Margaret Thatcher beat four male rivals to become leader of the Conservative Party.* □ *International Women's Year brought laws on equal pay and sex discrimination.* □ *The number of people unemployed in Britain rose to 1 million.* □ *The first oil came ashore from the North Sea.* □ *In a record year for financial failures more people went bankrupt than ever before.* □ *Inflation soared to 27 per cent.* □ *Electricity prices rose by a third.* □ *In the first-ever referendum in Britain electors voted by more than two to one to remain in the EEC under renegotiated terms. Arthur Ashe became the first black singles champion at Wimbledon.* □ *The Moorgate Tube crash killed forty-three.* □ *Snow fell in June in London for the first time since records began.* □ *Hit records included 'Sailing' and 'Bohemian Rhapsody', and Bruce Springsteen arrived in America as the 'boss' of blue collar rock. His* Born to Run *album stayed in the charts for forty weeks.* □ *Film successes were* One Flew Over the Cuckoo's Nest *and* Jaws.

One in the eye for King Harold in 'Churchill's People'. Dennis Waterman, who played the part, fought a personal setback when he really did get something smack in the eye in a field near Hastings – nothing to do with the longbow, it was the lace of his cloak. Dennis, who needed to survive the Norman Conquest in good nick to start to thump thugs in 'The Sweeney' the following week, required medical treatment, rest and new make-up – all of which delayed the recording of the battle. Still, the episode ended on the eve of the King's clash with William The Conqueror, so at least he didn't have to keep and eye out for anything else.

I t is hard to know what recommends itself the more strongly about the golden year of 1975. Was it the splendid varied crop of quality television programmes? Or was it the rare opportunity people had to invite another grown-up to share the bath in order to win praise as a public-spirited conserver of energy rather than scorn as a pervert? Certainly the Save It campaign seemed to make people careful not only with water and fuel but also with many drama and comedy series which were made with thought and feeling and made to last. We may now know off by heart every joke in 'Fawlty Towers' and every car chase and kicking in 'The Sweeney', but we don't tire of the repeats.

But before the high-flyers, a thought for a turkey, *the* turkey of the year: **'Churchill's People'**. Those who wish to be charitable might say that Gerard ('Six Wives of Henry VIII') Savory's eight-years-in-the-making twenty-six-part series based on Churchill's *History of the English-Speaking Peoples* was dogged with bad luck. An industrial dispute caused a postponement: the series effectively missed the 1974 Churchill centenary year. It began – and so did the critical slings and arrows – on New Year's Eve with the first part, life in AD 43, which included the Roman invasion – by an army of two people.

But by then BBC bosses had already surrendered. They'd barely trailed anything of the £1¼ million series and refused to show previews to critics (a sure sign they know a series will flop). They scheduled it after the nine o'clock news and opposite ITV's ratings-topper **'Public Eye'**.

Still, on and on, down the centuries 'Churchill's People' battled, the 800 leading actors, 1,000 extras and 20 directors bravely ignoring the audience's non-Churchillian V-sign and dismissing claims that their efforts resembled a Women's Institute pageant in a slightly tatty town hall. When BBC1's new controller, Brian Cowgill, slotted 'Kojak' in front of it some British viewers stayed tuned, perhaps gaining a little history with a giggle, but American viewers couldn't switch off fast enough.

BBC bosses had little time to lick their wounds. They were ducking more missiles when **'Days of Hope'**, four plays about events in the Great War and life in the Labour movement up to the crunch of the General Strike, began one of the most bitter rounds in the sporadic war between conservative viewers (spearheaded by sensitive Tory MPs) and the allegedly subversive Reds Under BBC Beds. Written by Jim Allen, as an antidote to sentimental period dramas such as 'Upstairs Downstairs', produced by Tony Garnet, directed by Ken Loach, the series starred Nikolas Simmonds and Pamela Brighton as Phillip and Sarah the young Christian, pacifist and socialist lovers, whose lives were touched by the events. The plays were praised by critics for their visual beauty and emotional power. The Broadcasting Press Guild awarded them Best Drama of the Year prize. But the *Daily Telegraph* had declared them 'a party political broadcast for the Communist Party'. Equity, the actors' union, was upset, too. The chap hired to play the young Ernest Bevin, Melvin Thomas, was not one of their members. One scene in which a conscientious objector was tied to a post within range of enemy fire set off an explosion of anger and claims of historical inaccuracy and bias.

Granada's drama series **'The Stars Look Down'** about a Northern mining community in the thirties was no bundle of laughs, either. At one point the seven months' pregnant wife of the miners' leader was seen preparing breakfast: a cup of hot water.

Twenties and thirties hard times seemed inescapable; but a catchy theme tune and the irrepressible self-interest of jaunty Jack Ford, played by James Bolam, made the BBC's **'When the Boat Comes In'** less punishing and more entertaining. Setting his story in his native South Shields, writer James Mitchell (the 'Callan' creator) kept the boat coming in for years as viewers south of the Tyne learned about 'bonnie lads' and took 0-level colloquial Geordie (so useful later for understanding the jokes in 'Auf Wiedersehen Pet'). They also enjoyed good solid stories with vintage cars and cobbled streets, and the relationship between the roguish Ford and Jessie Seaton, the passionate but upright (till Ford had his way) heroine played by Susan Jameson (Bolam's partner off-camera, too).

But it was with two other period dramas that the BBC wooed its women viewers that year: **'Poldark'**, which left no swash unbuckled, and **'The Pallisers'**, a sort of 'Son of the Forsyte Saga'.

Both Pauline Collins and Hayley Mills declined when asked to play the lead rôle of Lady Glencora in 'The Pallisers'; the former apparently wanted more money (this was no lavish production – all twenty-six parts were made for under half a million pounds) and the latter felt weak at the idea of a long series. Well, she *had* just starred in the birth of a son.

Susan Hampshire took up the challenge and was loved for it, playing opposite Philip Latham's snooty Plantagenet Palliser. Serious students of Anthony Trollope's novels accused Simon Raven of taking liberties with the dialogue in his adaptation, but those were nothing compared with the liberties a commercial radio station took when a BBC strike halted the recording of the final two episodes. They cashed in by broadcasting excerpts from the novels covering the passing of Lady Glencora. Still, viewers eventually enjoyed Susan Hampshire's last gasps – though she'd lain on her deathbed for two months.

In October, a man wearing a flowing cloak, a Dick Turpin hat and the sort of look that was to turn his enemies to stone and about 12 million women viewers to jelly, rode his horse along a Cornish cliff. Ross Poldark, hero of the Winston Graham saga about skulduggery, smuggling, tin-mining and of course sex in eighteenth-century Cornwall, had come home from the wars to conquer Sunday evenings for the BBC.

For mild-mannered Robin Ellis, an actor who wouldn't dream of ripping a bodice in this International Women's Year, if ever, becoming a 1975 version of Don Johnson was an embarrassment. When his underwear was pinched from his neighbourhood launderette he wanted to believe it was simple theft, but we *knew*.

There were other instant favourites in this workmanlike hokum, not least the scenery around Charleston, Cornwall. Clive Francis played the embittered Francis Poldark, mostly with a sore backside. He'd lied at the auditions about his horse-riding skills (he had none), then went off to learn fast and painfully – only to find that his character was required to sit on a horse once during two long series, and even then the beast was stationary.

Another was the fiery nit-ridden urchin Demelza, one of the none-too-trustworthy servants, who clawed her way up to become Ross's wife, though he loved the beautiful, elusive (and clean) Elizabeth, played by Jill Townsend. The rags, dirt and nits well became actress Angharad Rees. Ross's main enemy was scowling vicious Warleggan played by Ralph Bates, later to immortalise the mid-eighties wimp hero of 'Dear John'. It may have been tin in them thar Cornish mines, but the BBC were digging up gold. Unlike 'Churchill's People' (backed by an American co-producer, Universal Television) 'Poldark' was a hit in America and understandably mourned when it ended here. Cornish women petitioned for the return of the series in 1984. The BBC relented by screening afternoon repeats in 1987 and nudging Winston Graham to write three more Poldark books for a new series the following year.

The major ITV triumph was ATV's **'Edward the Seventh'**, the first royal soap. The Queen approved the scripts (by David Butler – once loved as dishy doctor Nick Williams in 'Emergency – Ward 10'). She allowed cameras into Sandringham, Osborne House and St George's Chapel, Windsor, to film sequences for the £2 million series.

Perhaps Her Majesty judged that Queen Victoria would have been amused by Timothy West's performance as her womanising son, Robert Hardy's Albert, Sir John Gielgud's Disraeli, Helen Ryan's Alexandra and, in particular, by Annette Crosbie as herself. Playing Victoria from a young girl to the aged disgruntled pudding in black turned Annette into a firm fan. Queen Victoria, she concluded, was 'emotional, hysterical, obstinate, possessive and jealous. In fact, perfectly normal.'

Fittingly, Annette won BAFTA's best actress prize for her efforts, which during the death scene were not helped by the dog hired to play the old Queen's darling. The white Pomeranian fell sick so the make-up department had to dye the fur of a substitute brown dog. It ended up with sticky unpleasant-looking tufts. Worse, each time Annette stretched out her hand to touch it and it was required to lie still and give a last baleful glance at its dying mistress, it playfully rolled on its back exposing its belly to the camera.

The series ended with around 16 million viewers as number one in the ratings (five of the thirteen episodes had been in the top spot). Lew Grade had sold it to CBS in America in less than an hour before Britain had seen it, and it was a hit there.

Queen Victoria had a rival in 1975, a woman almost as regal, certainly as sharp-tongued, possibly more refined. Whether there was a connection between the nation's delight in Margo Leadbetter, the snooty fearsome Empress of Suburbia in **'The Good Life'** and that other event of International Women's Year, Margaret Thatcher's becoming leader of the Conservative Party, we cannot be sure; but beaky striking Penelope Keith with her oxyacetylene voice became a small-screen superstar with this portrayal. Co-stars Paul Eddington, Richard Briers and Felicity Kendal didn't fare too badly, either.

The Goods' comic problems with self-sufficiency – Percy Edwards played the 'voice' of their pig – inspired thousands to try to grow their own. Lawns everywhere were dug up, vegetables pushed out flowers, and goat-keeping was on the up. By 1980 the pursuit of the good life had resulted in a record number of 51,000 smallholdings in Britain. When the Queen was asked in 1978 to help raise money for British athletes competing in the following year's Commonwealth Games by picking a television programme she'd like to see being made with a specially invited audience, it surprised no one that she chose 'The Good Life'. Margo, it was guessed, had a very high class of fan. Four series cropped up over ten years, then the stars decided to throw in the trowel.

Margo's exasperation with her hen-pecked husband Jerry and with the Goods was nothing compared with the volcanic eruptions of the year's greatest television tyrant, Basil Fawlty, thwarted and luckless proprietor of Fawlty Towers.

By 1975 many of the daring sixties swingers of television had mellowed, their ideas had been distilled and enriched. **'Fawlty Towers'**, which was witty, visual and universal, written by John Cleese and his then wife Connie Booth, had been born during a 'Monty Python' location filming session near Torquay. The 'Python' team had stayed in a hotel where the punctilious proprietor Donald Sinclair had, among other things, thrown Eric Idle's briefcase into the street in case it contained a bomb, and complained that American Terry Gilliam's table manners were too American. Mr Sinclair was small, his wife large, and John Cleese wrote them into one of the scripts for the 'Doctor' series on LWT, prompting the producer Humphrey Barclay to say: 'There's a series in those two.' He was right. The Sinclairs' husband-and-wife sizes were reversed when lanky John Cleese played the manic moustached Fawlty, the failed Führer, and Prunella Scales piled her hair into an elaborate meringue to contradict him as the immortal Sybil, she of the refayned voice and ever-so-nayce manners. Connie Booth played sane chambermaid Polly, and little Andrew Sachs became Manuel, the Spanish ('I ham from Barthelona') waiter, a one-man dining-room disaster. Fawlty developed waiter-abuse to a violently funny level. It is hard to forget Cleese, dragging Manuel by the ear, spitting: 'That's Sybil, me Basil, this is a slap round the ear.' Luckily Andrew survived the batterings, which included a whack over the head with a frying-pan, which all but knocked him cold (the studio audience chorused 'Ouch!'), and a scene in which he had to emerge from a blazing kitchen, his jacket smoking.

Basil Fawlty found a new use for Manuel as a battering ram for the Fawlty Towers fire exit.

illiterate men in prisons and borstals the producers were told in short angry words that their lives were already a nightmare and they didn't need smart-alicks from the BBC to show them another one. This left the series budget in big trouble – they were bound to pay six contracted actors for fifty episodes. Happily most of the actors agreed to smaller fees for bit parts in the replacement serial, written by Barry Took, involving removal men Alf (Bob Hoskins) and Bert (Donald Gee) travelling the country and commenting on the illogicalities of the English language.

The most widely and wildly popular programme which began in that year was **'The Sweeney'**, a police drama. The title – Sweeney as in Sweeney Todd – was cockney rhyming slang for the Flying Squad, that arm of the Metropolitan police force that was supposed not to beat about the bush in catching criminals. For fifteen years

John Hurt won a BAFTA best actor award for Thames Television's 'The Naked Civil Servant', a ninety-minute play based on the autobiography of sixty-seven-year-old Quentin Crisp. It was not only enthralling and deliciously shocking; it was also a breakthrough in television's treatment of the effeminate homosexual. At last one was presented as seeing the funny side of the conundrum and being brave, too. Crisp, one-time model at art school (a government employee, hence the civil servant of the title), prostitute and graphic artist, wore make-up, dyed his hair and lived by his own rules in his dirty Soho flat. He was a martyr for homosexual freedom, often beaten up but never shut up.
Some time later it was revealed that both the BBC and the IBA had had jitters about it. The BBC had been offered Philip Mackie's witty script of Crisp's story first yet turned it down. More amusingly, the IBA had censored a line of Mackie's script. Out went 'Sexual intercourse is a poor substitute for masturbation'. In its place went 'Wasn't it fun in the bath tonight?'

When the cameras stopped he discovered that the prickly heat he'd felt was the smoke-inducing chemicals seeping through to his skin. He needed hospital treatment and burns on an arm dressed daily for three weeks.

Only thirteen episodes were made – six in 1975, then seven more in 1979 when Cleese and Connie Booth had divorced – but they were repeated regularly throughout the eighties until we knew all the words. (Each episode took about four months and ten drafts to write.) The great moments – the gourmet evening, the German guests, the corpse in the cupboard – live on as classics. And who could ever forget the world's most tolerant guest, Ballard Berkeley's deaf and senile Major Gowan?

Perhaps the most praiseworthy effort of 1975 was the ten-minute BBC series **'On the Move'**, which every week encouraged thousands of the country's estimated 3 million illiterates to take the first steps to conquer their problem. The original idea was a fifty-part science-fiction serial in which a group of slaves turned against the ruling class of 'Wordmen' who kept their knowledge of reading and writing a secret; but when it was tested on groups of television had been presenting policemen as heroes, but the world of the police in 'The Sweeney' was to become more complex. The cops themselves were more brutalised by their work, more harassed by their superiors, and when they were loose on the streets swooping on villains the action was more exciting than ever before.

'The Sweeney' was made by Euston Films, a group of like-minded producers, directors and writers allowed to do their own thing by Thames Television – so long as it didn't cost much. They worked out of Colet Court, an old school in Hammersmith, using the phone in the pub across the road, often buying the props they needed for the next scene with whatever 'readies' the producer happened to have in his back pocket.

In the first series each episode was completed in only ten days and on a budget of around £40,000. Today it would cost ten times that amount. Shown early in 1975, it wasn't an instant success, but after four series and two cinema films it had overtaken 'Starsky and Hutch' and 'Kojak', seen off the BBC's pale imitation, 'Target', and become a much loved model for the next generation of series-makers. Viewers, both male and female, would go on adoring its heroes for about fifteen years, when their kipper ties and flared trousers made them almost a joke.

The main character was Detective Inspector Jack Regan, played by John Thaw, a young actor with a lived-in face, already known from 'Redcap', a drama about military police, and from 'Regan', which introduced the character as a hard-working, hard-drinking, impatient and often frustrated policeman. His wife (played by Janet Key) had left him after years of coming second to villains. Dennis Waterman, an actor Ted Childs had used in 'Special Branch', came in as Regan's sidekick, Detective Sergeant George Carter, a sharp cockney from Bermondsey. Like Regan, he thought like a crook, was great in a fight and fast on the draw – although Dennis admitted that he was so short-sighted that he'd never have made a bobby on the beat let alone a sharpshooter. Later Carter, too, was to become wife-less (his wife, played by Stephanie Turner, later the star of 'Juliet Bravo', was to die), so the two cops could spend off-duty hours together, supporting each other's doomed entanglements with a series of women.

A former Flying Squad officer, Jack Quarrie, advised the writers on police procedures, but inevitably the big boys in blue objected to this convincing image of detectives whose idea of questioning suspects was to hold them up against walls and pummel them. Less easy to dismiss were the objections to the show's scenes of violent action. Mrs Whitehouse hated the sex and bad language as well as the violence, not surprisingly; and the series came under attack after Dr William Belson's 1977 survey with London boys was taken to suggest that boys exposed to high levels of television violence are more likely to commit serious violence than others. Ted Childs points out that half the series' audience was over sixty. 'If our critics had

Commercial Break

Actor John Slater died of a heart-attack after recording a series of commercials for Kellogg's Special K for healthy eating. British Rail plugged Intercity, which 'makes the going easy'. The voice of James Hayter began assuring us that 'Mr Kipling does make exceedingly good cakes'. Brian Glover told us about the little perforations counted by the Tetley tea-folk, and the Hovis commercial, where a bike was pushed up a cobbled street, was greatly admired.

been right, shopping precincts would have been full of marauding OAPs beating the rest of us over the head with pension books.'

There were funny moments. There was a scene with a girl whom Regan had persuaded to sleep with him while she wore nothing except a German helmet (the actress made Ted promise he'd never release the stills). There was the appearance of Morecambe and Wise, playing themselves caught up as innocent bystanders in a story about a missing professor in the final episode (John and Dennis had appeared in 'The Morecambe and Wise Christmas Show' in 1976, and this was the 'return bout'). And there were the special lines of Sweeney dialogue every writer would try to include. The favourite was: 'Get yer trousers on; you're nicked.'

Also Shown in 1975

People didn't care that much for **'I Didn't Know You Cared'**, Peter Tinniswood's black comedy series about a dour and peculiar Yorkshire family, which was a shame because it was witty and well acted. Also above average that year was the comedy **'Sadie It's Cold Outside'**, in which Rosemary Leach and Bernard Hepton played a couple frustrated by dull routine. **'My Brother's Keeper'**, with George Layton and Jonathan Lynn as a policeman and his layabout brother, won the weak-comedy-of-the-year award.

Weak, too, was the American input that year. Two series, not *that* different from 'Kojak', were **'The Streets of San Francisco'**, starring Karl Malden and his magnificent nose with the young Michael Douglas as his assistant, and **'Police Woman'**, starring Angie Dickinson as Sergeant Pepper Anderson.

The other blond bombshell of 1975 smoked a cigar. Spindly peroxided James Savile, DJ, now OBE and national monument, marathon-runner, part-time hospital porter, and millionaire, began that children's delight, **'Jim'll Fix It'**. Over the years the huge mailbag has meant even lucky ones must wait. One eight-year-old who asked to do a funny walk with Max Wall was twelve before it was 'fixed'. But a 103-year-old was granted his wish within months. It was to drive a Formula One racing car.

Two million little horrors also lapped up **'Tiswas'** – the letters stood for 'Today Is Saturday Wear A Smile'. Kiddies got chaos, slapstick, pop and Lenny Henry and Chris Tarrant being noisy, while daddies began their weekends by considering the finer features of co-host Sally James's tight T-shirts. And didn't she know it.

In **'Coronation Street'** Bet loved and lost Len Fairclough, Deirdre loved and married Ray Langton, and Albert Tatlock was a mere eighty. In **'Crossroads'** Benny Hawkins (Paul Henry) and woolly hat arrived to work on a poor unsuspecting farm and Meg married Hugh – half of Birmingham turned out to watch the couple's arrival at church. But Hugh was to die a few years later: kidnapped by terrorists, as soap stars can so easily be, his heart gave out.

This was not a vintage year for documentaries. David Attenborough fronted **'The Explorers'**, a series which unexcitingly reconstructed the lives of famous explorers. Yorkshire Television's two-part documentary **'Johnny Go Home'**, about the plight of homeless teenage boys in London, caused a bigger rumpus. Halfway through it turned into a murder story and led to at least one prosecution. It won the year's factual film award.

People who thought Bob Monkhouse was just a smiling face and a fast mouth changed their mind when **'Celebrity Squares'** became the game of the year. It included an interlude in which general knowledge questions were fired at the host, and Bob, widely read, with a brilliant memory, was able to answer most correctly, crack jokes if he couldn't and win money for charities.

Other dramas of the year included **'The Survivors'**, which imagined life after a virus epidemic had wiped out most of the human race. Chaucer inspired **'Trinity Tales'**, six tall stories told by supporters on their way to a cup final, starring Francis Matthews and Bill Maynard. Michael Jayston was a spy shaken and stirred in **'Quiller'**, and the late Colin Blakely was very watchable (when wasn't he?) as a building-industry boss who faked his death in order to track down his enemies in **'The Hanged Man'**. The BBC made a version of **'Robin Hood'** and probably wished they hadn't. Martin Potter looked fetching in Lincoln green and Diane Keen played a spirited Maid Marian, but both got arrows in the back from Mary Whitehouse who was less than merry about the violence.

1976

That Was the Year When...

Prime Minister Harold Wilson suddenly stood down.
□ *James Callaghan beat Michael Foot to take over
the job.* □ *Supersonic travel began when two
Concordes took off from London and Paris.* □
Israelis freed 100 hostages at Entebbe airport. □
*Liberal leader Jeremy Thorpe resigned after allega-
tions about a homosexual affair with former male
model Norman Scott. David Steel took over.* □ *South
African police opened fire on rioters in Soweto; more
than a hundred died and a thousand were injured.* □
*Britain enjoyed a long hot summer – temperatures
reached 95° at times in June – but it came with the
worst drought for 250 years.* □ *China's Mao
Tse-tung, leader of a quarter of the world's population, died at the age of eighty-two.* □ *Jimmy Carter
was elected as America's new President.* □ *Rocky
and* All the President's Men *were top films that year,
'Save Your Kisses for Me' won the Eurovision Song
Contest, and the safety-pin became a fashion acces-
sory as the punk era began.*

It helped to be a bit odd on television in 1976. Eccentric
was even better. Heroes who played by the rules didn't
make the ratings. In domestic dramas, a chap had to fancy
his own daughter; if you were a policeman, you had to
wear a cardigan and jump over a couple of cars before
catching your crook; and when in Rome your emperors
had to decline and fall every five minutes while one goodie
was stuttering his way weakly to the top.

The most engaging traditional heroes we saw that year
were the 2,500 men in **'Sailor'**, which celebrated life on
the ocean waves aboard the aircraft-carrier HMS *Ark
Royal*. A BBC film team worked among the crew for ten
weeks and introduced us to a navy which returned to ship
with black eyes and cracked heads and even, in one sorry
case, without trousers. Once at sea, the lads drank,
cursed, dressed up in drag and mocked their superiors.
And viewers loved it. They cheered pilot Alan Gibson,
who took seven attempts to land his fighter plane and
survived the ribbing of his mates. They didn't mind when
Chaplain Bernard Marshall used four-letter words:
'Swearing is not so bad as blasphemy,' he said, adding that
most of these once-shocking words were common parl-
ance and 'a term of endearment in *Ark Royal*'. And they
loved the adventure when a sailor with acute appendicitis
had to be airlifted off an American submarine by helicopter
and transferred to *Ark Royal*. When he was halfway
between the two vessels, hanging on the end of a rope, a
huge wave swept him and the winchman who clung to him
into the sea. Eventually they were rescued to the lilting
theme tune of Rod Stewart's ballad 'Sailing'. When the
series was rerun in 1984 with a postscript that showed all
that was then left of *Ark Royal* was a rusting hull in a
breakers' dock, the tough master-at-arms, Tom Wilkinson, was seen to be moved to tears.

The other trad types were the chaps in the sheepskin
jackets in **'Wings'**, the BBC's drama about First World
War flying aces. Hard as Tim Woodward, Nicholas Jones
and Michael Cochrane tried, this wasn't a dashed good
show, although the planes – models of Blériot Ex-
perimentals and other historic flying machines doing studio
simulated aerobatics – were pretty enough. Tim's Alan
Farmer (all short back and sides and Pam Ayres accent)
didn't endear himself to the producers when he spent his
first 'Wings' cheques on a pair of motorbikes, crashed
driving one and broke a leg. He was ordered not to ride
again, and the injury had to be written in – blamed on the
Hun, he was shot in the leg in action over France, old
bean!

The BBC did better with **'The Duchess of Duke
Street'**, the fictionalised rags-to-riches story of Rosa
Lewis, maid-turned-caterer to the rich, who eventually
ran the Cavendish Hotel in Jermyn Street. She was

Eccentric, utterly original and a wee bit weird, too, was 'Rock Follies', Thames Television's musical serial about the tatty batty world of rock music, which won the BAFTA Best Drama Series award (and a clutch of craft awards) that year. Howard Schuman's satirical, often savagely funny script told how 'Q', Anna and Dee (Rula Lenska, Charlotte Cornwell and Julie Covington) were formed into the Little Ladies by a composer who thought it was time for women's rock. The girls went through the mill of clubs, pubs and porn, meeting rats and rip-off merchants and belting out – not always very well – a total of about fifty songs composed by Andy Mackay of Roxy Music. Schuman said the series was about the failure of bright women to stop themselves being dominated by much more stupid men. Three actresses who sang together as the group Rock Bottom said it was about them and won half a million pounds in a court case for it.

nicknamed 'Duchess' by her regular clients who included Edward VII, Kaiser Wilhelm and 'Upstairs Downstairs' producer John Hawkesworth, then a young Grenadier Guards officer, whose idea the series was. Admittedly this drama was slotted between Bruce Forsyth and 'The Two Ronnies' on Saturday nights, and the lavish food prepared by Michael Smith was mouthwatering, but the real reason it attracted 12 million viewers a week was Gemma Jones's portrayal of the bustling heroine Louisa Trotter, all throaty exasperation with her staff, especially the pretty Welsh maid (Victoria Plunkett) and Starr, the hall porter (John Cater), and his faithful fox terrier Jumbo. When the Honourable Charles Tyrrell (Christopher Cazenove) arrived, romance was on the menu, too. It took Charles some time, of course, to spot that cockney Louisa was a better bet than his refined society ladies, but he got there. In the second series, Lalla Ward came in as the Duchess's illegitimate daughter and there were sturdy cameo performances from Robert Hardy and Angharad Rees among others.

The lovableness of Louisa was roughly matched by the loathableness of Livia, Sian Phillips's evil empress in **'I, Claudius'**, the BBC's thirteen-part adaptation of Robert Graves's bloodthirsty black comedy, told from the point of view of the one sane soul in the Senate – making it a sort of Ancient Roman 'Secret Diary of Adrian Mole'. A snake slithering over the mosaic in the opening titles immediately set the tone. Derek Jacobi won the BAFTA Best Actor award for his Claudius, the ridiculed runt with a speech impediment, but Sian deserved a medal for bravery above and beneath the monstrous make-up she endured as his mother. Often she was seven hours having it done. She had to have her hair soaked flat, then a bald cap fitted with holes cut for the ears, foam rubber glued on to her cheeks, then make-up and a wig. By the final episodes she was made to look almost bald and hideous. She said: 'One day I took the rubber face home to show my mother. I wanted sympathy. I left it on the window sill, not thinking about the heatwave. When I picked it up next day the paint on the sill had blistered. I fled in panic to the make-up girl and asked what she was trying to do to my face.' Sian's husband at the time was Peter O'Toole, who was making the feature film *Caligula*. Sian recalled: 'When I visited him on the *Caligula* set, I was shocked by their armour – it was all plastic and foil, cheap imitation. All the good stuff was at the BBC.' And not just the props. In 'I, Claudius' John Hurt played Caligula brilliantly, ending up covered in blood. Brian Blessed was Augustus and Stratford Johns the head of the guards. The series was repeated in 1986 and adored over again.

Over on LWT they were having a huge success with what they called a modern Greek tragedy, **'A Bouquet of Barbed Wire'** (or 'Bucket of Barmy Whiners', as it should have been called). Thanks to novelist Andrea Newman, television had discovered incest – among the middle classes, too – and 20 million viewers were tuning in to see how miserable it made all concerned. Frank Finlay played Peter Manson, a wealthy publisher living in ticketyboo Surrey, stricken with jealous passion when pouting Prue, his daughter (played by Susan Penhaligon), married. American James Aubrey who played Gavin, the girl's husband, recalled: 'I was introduced to the actress who plays my wife. About thirty seconds later I was in bed with her. Then I was beating her senseless and within a flash I was at her funeral.' You could barely believe it – in Surrey!

Susan's all-purpose tease Prue was soon tagged television's 'right little bitch', but unlike soap opera proper she died at the end of the first series (of a pulmonary embolism after childbirth) and the producers could find no way of bringing her back the following year. But they didn't do badly, considering. In 'Another Bouquet' in 1977, Sheila Allen, who played Manson's wife and was about the only decent person in the cast, promptly took the grieving young Gavin as her lover and Peter then had a fraught affair with Gavin's new girlfriend played by Elizabeth Romilly.

'The Fosters': an all-black comedy which starred Lenny Henry, then seventeen, as Sonny, one of the kids. Norman Beaton, who played his father, felt that a show featuring black families was long overdue, but some West Indian community leaders attacked this one for offering nothing but cheap stereotypes.

A monstrous hit that year was **'Rich Man, Poor Man'**, ITV's marathon to challenge the 130 hours of Olympics coverage by the BBC during three weeks in the summer. The twelve-hour television treatment of Irwin Shaw's novel had already been a spectacular winner in America, and British viewers – especially sport-hating women – lapped up the story of the divergent careers of two brothers between 1945 and 1960. Although the cast was peppered with famous Hollywood faces, unknowns Peter Strauss and Nick Nolte played the brothers and both became rich men from it. Peter was rich Rudy Jordache, who triumphed over his impoverished immigrant beginning to become a business and political success, and Nick was poor Tom, who turned boxer and was eventually murdered by vicious Falconetti in the last episode. The show began the vogue for imported mini-series wedged either side of 'News at Ten'.

Moses 1976-style, in the form of Burt Lancaster with a big beard, was a freedom fighter struggling against tyranny and oppression (Burt's son Bill played Moses as a young man). **'Moses the Lawgiver'** even overcame the biblical strife three years earlier during filming in 1973

Two men who came to the front in 1976 and stayed there for four years were Starsky and Hutch, the preposterous police pals of Los Angeles. Starsky was the junk-food-eating streetwise one with dark curly hair played by former daytime-soap star Paul Michael Glaser. Hutch was the quieter health-food-preferring blond one played by David Soul, an actor who wanted to be a singer, too. Together they brought the tradition of the 'buddy' film, violent action and sentimentality into television. Each episode included scenes of police cars crashing through piles of cardboard boxes and the fearless detectives diving on to the roofs and bonnets of at least a couple of cars. Unfortunately they started trends. Ken Oxford, head of Merseyside police, complained: 'When the Starsky and Hutch series was showing police on patrol duty were adopting sunglasses and wearing their gloves with the cuffs turned down.' A council in South London had to lower a wall after young fans used it as a launchpad to jump on to parked vehicles. Worse still, the series spawned a fad for dreadful chunky belted cardigans for men, worn also by women. British Homes Stores did a roaring trade.

when the Egyptians rose up to smite the Israelites in the Yom Kippur War. The film unit was caught in the battle zone and found their Israeli actors and technicians disappearing into the Army, the trucks confiscated and

some of the extras wandering dangerously on to minefields. Producer Vincenzo Labella tried to keep on filming with a camera strapped to the back of a donkey, but had to give up for twenty days until the fighting was over. Lord Grade, as he'd then become, was always confident. Asked at a press conference how production on 'Moses' was going, he replied: 'It looks good in the rushes.' And this time he wasn't exaggerating. When it was finally screened over six Sundays, slotted between 'Stars on Sunday' and 'Doctor on the Go', the critics were stunned to find it looked spectacular. The scripts, partly by Anthony Burgess, were intelligent, and the filming of such high spots as the burning bush, Moses' festering hand and the parting of the Red Sea was handled with tact and taste.

'The Fall and Rise of Reginald Perrin', with brilliant scripts from his novel by David Nobbs, provided us with *the* rebel of 1976: middle-aged suburbanite office-worker Reggie, played by the late, fast-talking Leonard Rossiter, ground down by the awfulness of life at Sunshine Desserts. There his booming boss CJ (played by John Barron) told him what he hadn't got to where he was today without, as his two colleagues David and Tony (Bruce Bould and Trevor Adams) parroted 'Super' and 'Great'. During the first series Reggie became so dejected that he faked his suicide, leaving his clothes on a beach (David Nobbs wonders if John Stonehouse, the MP who did the same, got the idea from reading the original Perrin book). Reggie was a cult success by the second series in which he went around under an alias, remarried his wife Elizabeth (Pauline Yates) and founded Grot, a company selling rubbish at extortionate prices. Eventually CJ, the two yes-men and his son-in-law joined him in a commune dedicated to making the world a better place.

No children's show that year bore comparison with **'The Muppet Show'**, another of Lord Grade's good decisions for 1976. The madly designed Technicolor creatures varied from glove puppets to men dressed up and were all created by Americans Jim Henson and Frank Oz. The Muppets started out as characters in the American educational series 'Sesame Street', graduated through 'The Julie Andrews Show' to their own series which was bought by over a hundred countries and became the most widely seen and enjoyed television programme of the seventies.

The laconic Kermit the Frog was always the master of ceremonies at a theatre in which the puppet prima donnas vied with each other for starring parts in half-hours of chaos. It's hard to pick favourites, but top of the list would be Miss Piggy, a pink egomaniac also in love with Kermit, Rowlf the shaggy piano-playing dog, Fozzie Bear, Dr Teeth and the Electric Mayhem Band, and the small bald scientist Dr Bunsen Honeydew, modelled on Lew Grade. There were running features including 'Pigs in Space', 'Dr Strangepork' and the ballet 'Swine Lake'. What was most unusual was that top stars such as Roger Moore, Peter

Sellers, Elton John, Rudolph Nureyev, Steve Martin and Raquel Welch (and a galaxy of Americans nobody here had ever heard of) took turns to appear and be upstaged.

Meanwhile, a trio of television frontmen landed out back in 1976. One night in May, Peter Woods, the baggy-eyed anchorman of BBC2's **'Newsday'** programme, seemed to stumble and his speech was slurred. Robin Day, who'd cued him in to interview William Whitelaw, swiftly took over the interview himself. Ninety minutes later, after the switchboard had been jammed with callers who said they thought he was drunk, there was an announcement that Peter had been suffering from a sinus condition. In the same month Reginald Bosanquet was suspended from **'News at Ten'** for four weeks following newspaper interviews by his ex-wife Felicity who had taken all the goods from his Kensington home. But the frontman who lost most brownie points that year was Bill Grundy, who attempted to interview the Sex Pistols punk rock group for the Thames family programme **'Today'**. The air turned blue as Johnny Rotten and his pals effed and blinded and Bill appeared to goad them. The television station's switchboard was flooded with protest calls, some claiming that Grundy was also drunk. He was carpeted and suspended for two weeks, Thames broadcast an apology, and the 'Today' programme was scrapped five months later.

Peter Sellers, modelling the latest in Viking corsets, prepared to pillage Kermit and the Muppets.

Also Shown in 1976

In **'Oil Strike North'**, Nigel Davenport, Barbara Shelley, Angela Douglas and others tried to suggest that life on a North Sea oil-rig wasn't always crude. They failed. **'Clayhanger'** was a straightforward adaptation of the Arnold Bennett novels, so straight that it went down like . . . well, clay. At twenty-six hours it was the longest-ever ITV drama. It was made, one concluded, by mistake. Sir Lew Grade must have thought they said 'Cliffhanger'.

Even in the soap world there were movements away from the conventional. **'Angels'** was the BBC's twice-weekly story of six student nurses at St Angela's Hospital. Unlike 'Coronation Street', against which it was slotted, there was a documentary-like style and the nurses' work was shown as thankless – some way from the romance-promising world of 'Emergency – Ward 10'. Meanwhile in **'Coronation Street'** Hilda Ogden acquired her 'muriel', a large poster of the Alps supplied by lodger Eddie who'd been decorating the parlour and run out of paper. And Mavis Riley, broken-hearted over Derek, wrote a semi-bodice-ripping novel, *Song of a Scarlet Summer*. In **'Crossroads'** Glenda Brownlow ran away from home and was raped while hitch-hiking and a Malaysian girl arrived from David Hunter's wartime past.

Only one other comedy character approached Reginald Perrin pitch. Ronnie Barker was Arkwright, the Welsh hardware shopkeeper in **'Open All Hours'** – mean with money and mean in spirit. He cheated his customers, bullied Granville, his semi-legitimate nephew and assistant (David Jason), and lusted after big buxom Nurse Gladys Emmanuel (Lynda Baron) who lived opposite and on whom he spied. The series gathered viewers steadily rising up the ratings poll by the mid-eighties.

Other comedies that year included **'Yus My Dear'**, a vehicle for Arthur Mullard (some people wished it had been an on-coming train). He played a bricklayer, and Queenie Watts was his demanding wife. Funnier (but not much) was **'Oh No, It's Selwyn Froggitt!'**, starring Bill Maynard as a hopeless handyman. **'Yanks Go Home'**, a comedy set in an American air-force base in Lancashire during the Second World War, offered nothing but cheap stereotypes, but nobody seemed to care enough to complain. The gentlest comedy was Granada's **'Cuckoo Waltz'**, in which newlyweds

Fliss and Chris, played by Diane Keen and David Roper, were the young parents of twins who took in a lodger, the original medallion man Gavin, played by Lewis Collins. It lasted five years, by which time the triangle had become rather square. In **'George and Mildred'** the gruesome twosome who'd first appeared as the landlords in 'Man about the House' began making us laugh despite ourselves. Mildred (Yootha Joyce) wanted sex and a better place in society, while George (Brian Murphy) had a permanent headache and didn't fancy becoming upwardly mobile if it meant getting off his backside to look for a job.

'Just William' was a successful remake of the adventures of Richmal Crompton's horror – thanks to a splendid cast including Diana Dors and Bonnie Langford. Another event for children that year was the start of **'Multi-Coloured Swap Shop'** on Saturday mornings. Noel Edmonds hosted this mix of pop, silly features and phone-in toy-swappings.

The Avengers came back, this time backed by French money and produced by Rudolf Roffi, as **'The New Avengers'**. Patrick Macnee was the same old bowler-hatted Steed, but his rôle was reduced. Joanna Lumley was new and very fetching as Purdey with a pudding-basin haircut copied by thousands of women. New, too, was Gareth Hunt as Gambit.

The standard of serious drama was high that year. **'Laurence Olivier Presents the Best Play of . . .'** began a grand series of six important plays, starting with Harold Pinter's *The Collection* in which the great actor also appeared. Frederic Raphael's series about people who met as undergraduates at Cambridge in the fifties, **'The Glittering Prizes'**, won critical praise. Tom Conti, one of the stars, won heart-throb status, and Sarah Porter survived the longest topless scene – eight minutes – as a defiant student. The BAFTA Best Play winner was Jack Rosenthal's touching and funny **'The Barmitzvah Boy'** about a Jewish boy who opted out of his own barmitzvah, with Jeremy Steyn, Maria Charles and Bernard Spear. On ITV, Jack Shepherd became a cult figure as **Bill Brand** whose fraught life as a left-wing MP was the subject of a worthy series.

Commercial Break

New commercials that year included Kenneth Williams advising us to use Brobat's Bloo Loo and David Bailey telling us that we'd take great photos if we used an Olympus Trip. At Christmas, Ronco bombarded us with gift ideas for the person who had everything but good taste. If you wanted an electronic device for measuring the size of your ear-lobe, Ronco probably made one.

1977

That Was the Year When...

Britain celebrated Elizabeth II's Silver Jubilee with bonfires, a carriage procession to St Paul's Cathedral and street-parties all over the country. The Sex Pistols record of 'God Save the Queen' was not played at many of them. □ *Virginia Wade won at Wimbledon.* □ *Two Jumbo jets collided on the ground in Tenerife, killing 574, the worst tragedy in aviation history.* □ *Red Rum won the Grand National for the third time.* □ *Australian publisher Kerry Packer split the cricket world by signing players for his own international contests.* □ *Freddie Laker began his no-frills £59 flights to New York.* □ *Egypt's President Anwar Sadat addressed the Israeli Knesset, promising an end to the Middle East war.* □ *Elvis Presley, poisoned by tranquillisers and barbiturates went to Hamburger Heaven aged only forty-two. Bing Crosby and Maria Callas also died that year.* □ *Gay News was fined £1,000 for publishing a poem suggesting that Jesus was gay after Mary Whitehouse won the first prosecution for blasphemy in fifty-six years.* □ *Top films were* Close Encounters of the Third Kind, Star Wars *and* Saturday Night Fever, *and children on skateboards terrified pedestrians.*

At Easter in 1977, the Pope was making his usual appearance on the balcony overlooking St Peter's Square. He gave his blessings, his messages of hope and

---

As Jesus of Nazareth, Robert Powell, roped by his arms to a wooden crosspiece, was hauled five times to the top of a twenty-foot cross before the cameramen had the perfect take. As the crosspiece swung out of control, the actor cried out in panic. 'I didn't have to fake the torment,' he said later.

sympathy; then he added something extra – a plug for a British television show. Go home and watch the rest of **'Jesus of Nazareth'**, he told the crowds.

It turned out that the two-part film had been his idea. Lew Grade's wife Kathie, a Christian, had been delighted to accompany her husband to an audience with Pope Paul. As they left, the Pope told Lord Grade that he hoped one day he would do the story of Jesus. Lord Grade forgot the request, but Kathie nagged him and he agreed. Announcing his new project to the press, he stressed that this

Jesus would be for all religions. 'It doesn't matter what faith you are. I am a Jew. Jesus was a Jew. We were both born on the same day – but, believe me, I'm not doing this to celebrate my birthday.' Three years later what was nicknamed 'The Most Expensive Story Ever Told' – it had finally cost around £9 million – was screened on ITV on Palm Sunday and then on Easter Sunday. Lord Grade said then: 'I think it's the best thing I will ever do.' Most critics thought so, too.

Getting the money to back the project wasn't hard at first. Lord Grade flew to Detroit to see the head of General Motors and told him he needed £3 million. Asked when, Lord Grade replied, 'Yesterday will be fine,' and got it; but when the businessmen heard that producer Franco Zeffirelli would be portraying Jesus as man not myth and would show him as 'gentle, fragile and simple' they feared a backlash from America's Bible Belt and demanded that the name of General Motors be removed from the credits. Happily Procter & Gamble stepped in as the principal backers.

There were problems, too, with casting. Robert Powell had been chosen for the title rôle, but the first schoolboy to play the young Christ was dropped – Mr Zeffirelli hadn't been satisfied. The older stars were easier to sign; they included Laurence Olivier, Ralph Richardson, Peter Ustinov, Rod Steiger and James Mason. But there was some nervousness about the actress for the Virgin Mary. In the end Olivia Hussey, who'd earlier been Franco Zeffirelli's Juliet, was picked despite being nine years younger than her 'son'.

Tunisia became Palestine, and building a full-scale model of Herod's temple ran up a bill of £250,000. It was worth it. In America one-third of all the television sets were tuned in to 'Jesus of Nazareth', and in Britain at least half the population were reckoned to have watched it. World-wide 140 million were thought to have seen it, a number that increased to 500 million after reshowings in the eighties.

The BBC slaved to dampen the drama of 'Jesus of Nazareth' by screening over the weekend of the second part the first three parts of '**Roots**', their much-fanfared American import. They boosted it with a Parkinson interview with 'Roots' writer Alex Haley and fixed the third instalment to clash with the final part of the ITV epic. The tactic worked. America, undergoing an ethnic renaissance, had been gripped (and possibly surprised) by this story of a black man's search for his ancestors. They awarded it a batch of Emmies. Here around 19 million British viewers also became hooked on what turned out to be a decent yarn despite its comically unlikely sets of African villages – manicured lawns and dwellings straight out of an Ideal Hut exhibition. It was hardly a serious history of slave-trading, but the emotional charge of a monstrous injustice was still there and John Amos's performance as the adult Kunta Kinte, the African chief's

son transported to Virginia in 1770, and Ben Vereen's Chicken George were much enjoyed. It was also fun seeing Lorne Greene, the 'Bonanza' hero, as a heartless slave-owner and Lloyd Bridges, goodie of 'Sea Hunt', as a founder member of the Ku Klux Klan. By the time the twelve-part series was over, the claims of retired coastguard Alex Haley that he had in fact found Kunta Kinte's origins in Gambia were challenged by the international news reporters, but it didn't seem to matter to us.

Later that year the BBC imported another American drama, part fact, part fiction, which was possibly enjoyed more here than on the other side of the Atlantic, dealing as it did with their recent Watergate disgrace. '**Washington Behind Closed Doors**' was a six-part story of the Nixon régime partly based on John Erlichman's book *The Company* and starring Jason Robards as a Nixon-like President and Robert Vaughn as his devious aide. The plots and subplots seemed surprisingly close to what was known to have happened, confirming British prejudices about widespread corruption Over There. David Frost went one better that year with '**The Nixon Interviews**', which he and John Birt produced using backing from America, Australia and the BBC. David Frost had secured the rights to four ninety-minute filmed sessions by guaranteeing the former President $600,000 and 10 per cent of the profits. Trickie Dickie admitted to David Frost that he had told some lies over Watergate, denied being involved in a conspiracy and, looking contrite, confessed to letting the American people down.

David Frost said 'Hello, good evening and welcome' to another political leader that year. Having interviewed Harold and Mary Wilson 'at home' at 10 Downing Street in 1969 (and allowed Mrs Wilson to deny that she *ever* drank Wincarnis), David Frost was favoured with the former PM's views on twelve of his predecessors in Yorkshire Television's series '**A Prime Minister on Prime Ministers**'. Sir Harold was not hampered by modesty, and David found his assessments absolutely fascinating even if we didn't.

The BBC was broke in 1977, but it managed to come up with two sturdy series which lasted longer than was at first expected. The adventures of Yorkshire vets was one. For the other they'd gone back to the war. After a three-year rest since the end of 'Colditz', the British stiff upper lip was back in '**Secret Army**'. The same producer, former Spitfire pilot Gerard Glaister, used real stories about some of the 3,500 airmen shot down in occupied Europe as the basis of the sixteen-part series, starring the former Colditz Kommandant actor Bernard Hepton. Bernard played the owner of a Belgian café, the Candide, which was the headquarters for the Resistance. Angela Richards played his mistress, with Jan Francis and Juliet Hammond Hill as two brave and beautiful workers for the life-line. Looking back, the series had much in common with the BBC's later wartime comedy ''Allo 'Allo', but the Resistance girls never said 'I will say this ernly wernce' and the plots were often quite tough. The man they loved to hate in 'Secret Army' was Clifford Rose's Gestapo Major Kessler, with close-cropped hair, rimless specs and an accent which stopped short of 'Vee haf vays . . .', but only just. By the end of the three series in 1979, Kessler was a colonel. By coincidence the real Kessler, the SS chief in Brussels, Ernst Ehlers, was tracked down in 1980 and went on trial for war crimes which included the sending of 26,000 Jews to Auschwitz. In 1981, Clifford's sadistic Standartenführer returned in his own series as a successful businessman and neo-Nazi who, it slowly transpired, was a fugitive from the Israelis.

ITV drama departments had problems that year, too. Expensive mistakes were made on **'Love for Lydia'**, a thirteen-part serial based on H. E. Bates's short novel. The author had approved a television treatment before his death in 1974, and his son Richard, a freelance writer and producer who regarded it as his father's best work, had spent seven years expanding it and producing the first three episodes for London Weekend Television. But when LWT's Controller, Cyril Bennett, viewed the episodes he disliked them – there was too much misty Northamptonshire countryside, too little of the beautiful heroine – and he ordered them to be scrapped at a loss of £100,000. He sacked Richard Bates, passing the project to Tony Wharmby, LWT's Head of Drama. On top of that a director withdrew, a programme executive had a heart-attack, and writer Julian Bond had hurriedly to revise scenes forty-eight hours after a gall-bladder operation. Even the weather was against them. Snow, ice and heatwaves had to be created, and locations were rained off, blown away and once even set on fire.

But the drama finally reached the screen and the tale of a wilful beautiful heiress in the twenties who yearns for worldly experience and plays havoc with the feelings of four young men delighted critics, even if viewers found it too slow and whimsical at times. Mel Martin was a spirited Lydia, but perhaps it *was* hard to accept that she didn't want Jeremy Irons, Peter Davison, Christopher Blake *or* Ralph Arliss. Was she waiting for Tom Cruise?

The same ITV company had more success with **'The Professionals'**, which no one ever accused of being whimsical. But there were serious problems with casting the macho heroes of this secret crimebusting outfit. It seems incredible now, but Albert Fennell and Brian Clemens, partners in 'The Avengers', originally signed posh-voiced Anthony Andrews as William Bodie, the ex-soldier, with Jon Finch as Ray Doyle, the former CID policeman. Jon Finch decided he couldn't play Doyle as an ex-cop, so, to avoid rewriting, the producers went back to auditioning every tough man in town. One they liked was Martin Shaw, so they hired him – but then came a snag. In a screen test he looked remarkably similar to Anthony Andrews. The producers remembered Lewis Collins, who

Martin Shaw (*left***) back from a tough assignment at the hairdresser's with Gordon Jackson (***centre***) and Lewis Collins: 'The Professionals'.**

had worked with Martin in an episode of 'The Avengers' called 'The Obsession'. They were delighted to find that Lewis was available. So it was out with Anthony Andrews, who had to make do with starring in 'Danger UXB' and becoming an international star with 'Brideshead Revisited'. (Perhaps he looks back on it as a lucky break.)

For the rôle of George Cowley, scathing taskmaster of CI5, formerly with MI5 and troubled by an old wound which made him limp, the producers had wanted Clive Revill. Then they thought of Gordon Jackson, who was finishing in 'Upstairs Downstairs'. They actually delayed the start of filming in June to wait for him. When this began at Pinewood each hour-long episode cost as much as £115,000. Viewers, especially men, who saw it that autumn thought it worth every penny, liked the not-too-sophisticated boyos and put 'The Professionals' straight into the ratings, even though some of the thunder was stolen by the start of a BBC action series, **'Target'**. This introduced Patrick Mower as a detective with a regional police force and had strong performances from Philip Madoc and Vivien Heilbron. Both series had high body-counts and a level of bloody action television watchdogs and some viewers were beginning to complain about – by the following year both 'Target' and 'The Professionals' had been toned down to include fewer violent scenes. Two explosions an episode was the new rule on 'The Professionals' but this series filmed almost entirely on location around Wembley had even more Action Man stuff.

It wasn't enough for Lewis. Parachute-jumping in his spare time, he broke an ankle and halted production for four months. Meanwhile Martin Shaw was having self-esteem problems. The thoughtful, vegetarian, non-drinking actor wanted to leave after the first year of his four-year contract, saying he hated being a 'personality'. He was bound to stay, but later he was to describe the series as 'a prison', calling Ray Doyle a 'violent puppet'. He loathed his famous permed curls, too – 'That awful haircut – Lewis used to call me the Bionic Golly,' he said. The fourth and fifth series had to include more and more spectacular stunts to fend off the growing competition from 'Minder', 'Hart to Hart' and even LWT's 'The Gentle Touch'. Bodie and Doyle were seen hanging from the landing gear of a helicopter in flight, piloting a hovercraft down the Thames and abseiling down office-blocks. Rather less attention was paid to devising half-sensible plots, and by now both actors were bemoaning the fact that they had no say in the stories. Gordon Jackson scoffed at them, but Lewis said he was ashamed to watch some episodes.

Although the final episodes were screened in the early part of 1983 – the ending was an explosive crash between an inflatable dinghy carrying Bodie and Doyle and the launch they were chasing – there were several repeat runs and the shows were sold widely overseas. Libyan viewers clearly believed CI5 actually existed after watching the series. They besieged the British embassy in Tripoli after the People's Bureau shooting drama in London with shouts of 'Down with CI5!' But in 1988 Martin Shaw blocked further repeat screenings, which was bad news for around 500 actors who'd also taken part. His co-stars were not pleased. Gordon Jackson stood to lose £50,000 – he'd received £3,700 an episode (Lewis Collins had been paid £2,400 and Martin Shaw £2,200). Martin's reason for refusing permission was his belief that the Doyle image had led to his losing film rôles.

If it was hard being a CI5 agent, it was harder still being one of **'Charlie's Angels'**, the battling bimbos who claimed to be police-trained detectives, working for an unseen boss who relayed instructions by telephone. Most of the cases involved health spas, nightclubs or other places where the girls could appear out of uniform and out of almost everything. In its five-year life this American 'jiggle appeal' series went through more anguish than any before at Twentieth Century–Fox. Everything went wrong for every Angel. Kate Jackson, who played Sabrina the leader, and Jaclyn Smith, who played Kelly and former showgirl, were both involved in divorces. They said the pressures of the show shattered their love-lives. Farrah Fawcett-Majors, who played the sporty Jill, became the centre of a new fad, partly because she had masses of shaggy blonde hair and partly because she'd taken the trouble to have her photo taken in a swimsuit, looking sexy as can be. Farrah dolls, T-shirts and other merchandise were rushed out, and the actress also tried to rush away, believing she had a big future in films; but she landed herself in a series of lawsuits for breach of contract and

made guest appearances in the series from then on. Jill was replaced by her sister Kris, played by Cheryl Ladd (whose marriage also broke up), and then Sabrina was replaced by Julie, played by Tanya Roberts. Kate Jackson said later: 'I didn't consider it was acting. We might as well have been Barbie Dolls in some store window.' The only cast member who didn't complain was John Forsythe, then a mere lad of fifty-nine, not yet the suave Blake Carrington of 'Dynasty', who was years later revealed as the mysterious Charlie. 'I must be the only actor in Hollywood who can phone in his lines,' he said, adding that it gave him time to play golf.

The best comedy of the year was not exactly written. The BBC's first full-length improvised play was **'Abigail's Party'**, a Mike Leigh production starring Alison Steadman as Beverley, *nouveau riche* Queen Bee in a ghastly orange dress alternately stinging and sweetening her neighbours while her little worker husband buzzed himself into a heart-attack. A savage send-up of lower-middle-class manners, it was shown three times and would probably have won the BAFTA Best Play award for the year had the BBC not also produced Jack Rosenthal's **'Spend, Spend, Spend,'** based on the true story of Viv Nicholson who won £152,000 on the football pools and spent it all with the help of several disastrous husbands. Susan Littler portrayed the girl going from rags to riches to rags, making her story heart-rending. The real Viv lives alone in a modest terraced house in Castleford. After five husbands, spells of drug-taking and heavy drinking, she is now a Jehovah's Witness, preferring churches to pubs.

Reginald Bosanquet, in trouble the previous year, kept his nose clean in November 1977 by keeping his mouth straight – or straightish. Firemen had been on strike for some weeks, and on **'News at Ten'** Reggie had to read the sad-funny story of an old lady's cat which had been rescued from a tree by soldiers who'd arrived in their Green Goddess trucks. The old lady was so grateful she invited them in to tea. As they left the old lady's house their Green Goddess ran over the cat. David Nicholas, the programme editor, warned the jovial newsreader that if so much as a flicker of amusement appeared at the corners of his mouth he would personally pass 10,000 volts of electricity through his body. In the end, David recalls, Reggie read the item with a face like an Easter Island statue. Reggie must have been the only man in Britain who wasn't laughing. The programme was called 'Mews at Ten' for some time afterwards.

Meanwhile up on the Yorkshire moors some cows, pigs, sheep, dogs and cats were preparing to rival the Muppets. The BBC had made one series about vets, 'The McKinnons', which had flopped, but after the success of two feature films based on the James Herriot vet books they decided a series of **'All Creatures Great and Small'** could do well. How right they were. Finding someone to play James Herriot wasn't so easy, though. Both cinema

Commercial Break

Stars of commercials that year included Martin Fisk, who improved the image of long-distance lorry-drivers no end as well as selling Yorkie bars: John Cleese, who tried to sell us Accurist watches; Buzby, British Telecom's telephone bird (Bernard Cribbins supplied the voice); and, in the absence of Katie, who had by then been sacked, Dennis Waterman telling us about Oxo. The 'Sweeney' star was paid £10,000 for the job of wearing a red T-shirt. He must have done it well because it prompted thousands of requests for copies. The voice of Robert Powell was heard advertising Playtex bras during Jesus of Nazareth, the epic in which he played Christ. (He was paid only £20,000 for his three years on the epic. So he must have needed the voiceover fee.) On Christmas Day, Sir Peter Parker advertised British Rail for seven minutes (about the time it takes to get through to passenger enquiries) in the longest commercial yet seen.

Herriots, John Alderton and Simon Ward, declined. So, too, did Richard Beckinsale. Christopher Timothy, an actor with a bony face suddenly transformed by a boyish grin, was their answer. Robert Hardy and Peter Davison came in as Siegfried and Tristram Farnon, his partners. The countryside around Askrigg in Yorkshire was an obvious attraction, though it proved difficult to find farm animals who looked right for the thirties setting. Cows had horns then.

Right from the start the actors found out what vets' right arms are for: shoving up animals' backsides. Christopher Timothy soon learned about getting to know a cow in depth, and several unfortunate cows learned early how easy it is for a novice to take the wrong turning. But luckily viewers weren't shown the whole process until the 1987 and 1988 series (in which the actors seemed to do very little else). The sick animals seen in the stories are usually local beasts with injuries courtesy of the make-up department. (Sometimes the make-up is to hide their real blemishes. The pig who played the Pumphreys' porker Nugent was glamorised in this way.) Sometimes expensive shire horses and foals are tranquillised to look lifeless, with anxious owners looking on. But operations are genuine ones, actually performed for proper reasons by real vets with the actors being filmed doing easy bits. Eddie Straiton, a vet who is also a friend of James Herriot, was for a long time the consultant on the series. He was reported as recalling only one occasion when an animal was operated on unnecessarily. A mongrel dog had been brought into his surgery to be put down. In the series, James was to operate on a dog which had swallowed a ball. Eddie Straiton anaesthetised the dog, cut a part of its throat and inserted a squashed ball for Christopher to remove. The animal recovered completely and was found a new owner. But the scene upset some of the technicians, who claimed it was vivisection. Eddie is reported as agreeing with them and resolving: 'Never again.'

By 1978 the series had become one of the BBC's biggest successes. It survived the small scandal of Christopher Timothy's real romance with his leading lady, Carol Drinkwater, pulled viewers away from the Muppets and later helped to knock 'Bruce Forsyth's Big Night' out of the ratings. American tour companies were arranging 'Herriot Country' trips around Askrigg, and the Pekinese who played Tricki Woo, Mrs Pumphrey's pampered pooch, had to have a batch of photographs printed to send out to his growing legions of fans. But a dachshund missed a chance for an Oscar when it was supposed to have lost the use of its back legs. John McGlynn, who was playing Calum Buchanan, a new vet in the practice, had to tell the owner that the treatment had not been successful. As he broke this bad news, the dachshund stood up and walked friskily off the set.

Christopher Timothy (*left*) had a talk with pork in 'All Creatures Great and Small'.

Also Shown in 1977

Jack Hedley and Betty Arvaniti starred in 'Who Pays the Ferryman', a lavish-looking romantic adventure by Michael J. Bird about an Englishman returning to a mixed reception from his former pals in the Resistance. The BBC's lack of cash showed in 'A Horseman Riding By', a thirteen-part drama based on the R. F. Delderfield novels. Luckily there was just the one horseman most of the time – played by Nigel Havers.

They launched few notable new comedies, and at ITV the most successful, 'Robin's Nest', was only half-new, being the second spin-off from 'Man about the House'. Richard O'Sullivan's character of Robin Tripp had now become a partner in a restaurant and had moved in with air hostess Vicky, played by Tessa Wyatt. There was also a one-armed dish-washer played by David Kelly – possibly the best joke in the show. New Zealand's then Premier Muldoon didn't think a joke about his country's wine funny at all. He invited all the cast to New Zealand House and made them drink their words. Peggy Mount and Pat Coombs starred in 'You're Only Young Twice', a sitcom set in an old folks' home. It was a good argument for mercy killing. Paula Wilcox played an unmarried mother in 'Miss Jones and Son'. It was a daring subject for a comedy, but unfortunately not a very funny one. Daring, too, in its way, was a comedy about a six-man political movement, the Tooting Popular Front, which was the theme of 'Citizen Smith' on BBC1. Robert Lindsay was terrific as Wolfie Smith, South London's answer to Che Guevara, who was not taken seriously enough for his liking.

The new game show that year was 'The Krypton Factor'. Krypton was the planet whence Superman came, so this mix of assault-course sessions and quizzes set out to find a superperson.

If you were a literary type and understood the in-jokes, the BBC's 'Don't Forget to Write' was a hoot. It starred George Cole as a playwright swinging between elation and despair, Gwen Watford as his wife and Francis Matthews as a fellow-scribe. It lasted three seasons, by which time the moody writer had become dodgy Arthur Daley in 'Minder'.

Peter Barkworth won the BAFTA Best Actor award for his rôle in Tom Stoppard's 'Professional Foul'. Another outstanding play that year was 'Philby, Burgess and Maclean', Ian Curteis's drama documentary about the traitors who fled to Russia, starring Derek Jacobi, Anthony Bates, Michael Culver, Elizabeth Seal and Arthur Lowe. There was high praise, too, for 'Hard Times', Arthur Hopcraft's adaptation of Dickens's dark novel starring Timothy West, Patrick Allen and Edward Fox.

This being Elizabeth II's twenty-fifth year on the throne, the BBC waved the flag with 'Royal Heritage', a nine-part series which took the viewer inside Windsor Castle, Hampton Court Palace, Osborne House and Balmoral. Barry Norman began a sort of tribute to the royalty of Hollywood, beginning warts-and-all portraits of dead stars in 'Hollywood Greats'. In his first batch was a portrait of Clark Gable, jug ears, false teeth and a voice that could shoot up high if he wasn't careful, and he got better with Charles Laughton, Edward G. Robinson, Marilyn Monroe and many more over the following six years. Denis Norden began rubbing the gloss off television shows and films with his well-researched collections of the bits of film that had to be cut out; the fluffs and guffs of 'It'll Be Alright on the Night' became occasional, much-looked-forward-to treats on LWT.

In the year that Steve Biko died in a South African police cell the prizewinning documentary series was Anthony Thomas's 'The South African Experience', a thoughtful personal account. Other documentaries included Bamber Gascoigne's history of Christianity, 'The Christians' and 'Hospital' which recorded life in two Bolton general hospitals and began a fascination for real hospital drama. David Attenborough donned his khaki shorts again for a much appreciated series of 'Wildlife on One' and the discovery of radium was explored in 'Marie Curie' starring Jane Lapotaire and Nigel Hawthorne.

It was a hectic year in 'Crossroads'. David Hunter had become a compulsive gambler for a week and Benny's fiancée Maureen Flynn (Nell Curran) was killed on her way to their wedding. (Drastic – but it saved her the embarrassment of hearing him say 'Oi do be' instead of 'I will'.) In 'Coronation Street' Rita accepted Len's proposal and agreed to give up her singing career, and Annie Walker – who else? – played Elizabeth I on the float to celebrate the Jubilee.

1978

The world's first test-tube baby, Louise Brown, was born at Oldham District Hospital. □ The supertanker Amoco Cadiz went aground off the Brittany coast, spilling 50,000 tons of crude oil into the Channel. □ Joyce McKinney was accused of kidnapping and sexually abusing a Mormon. □ In Guyana 913 members of the People's Temple committed mass suicide by taking poison. □ Jeremy Thorpe, the former Liberal Party leader, was sent to trial for conspiracy to incite murder. □ George Davis, who was innocent OK, went back inside for fifteen years for robbery. □ Pope Paul VI died; his successor, Pope John Paul, died after thirty-three days; Wojtyla became Pope, and tarmac-kissing began. □ Anorexia was the fashionable illness. □ Blondie's Debbie Harry's face adorned teenagers' bedroom walls, and Elvis Costello in Buddy Holly specs proved weeds won, too. □ Top films were Grease, The Deer Hunter *and* Superman. *□ And as the nation was hit by strikes the Winter of Discontent began.*

This was a good year for naughty children, a surprising year for Shakespeare – celebrated on both ITV and BBC – and a great year for soap opera. It was also the year a lot of us found that to see Bruce Forsyth was not as nice as all that.

Not many people on television in 1978 felt a mission to inform about contemporary society – perhaps with bombings and strikes it was too dismal – but a children's drama serial, **'Grange Hill'**, decided to boldly go where none had gone before, to show what actually goes on inside schools and how children actually talk and behave (at least, some of the time), using cameras at their level. The twice-weekly serial, like a good soap opera, followed a group of first-year pupils at their fictional London comprehensive school (they used Kingsbury High School in North-West London for the recordings). Their lessons produced shocks for grown-ups and whoops of delight from young viewers. Shoplifting, smoking, racial taunts, truancy, child-molesting, a schoolgirl's crush on her teacher and bullying featured in the story-lines. Later came sex, drug abuse, worries about not finding a job. Teachers and parents said this was encouraging hooliganism and bad language, and how dare children call teachers by their first names! The children said at last this *was* school life.

The idea for it had come from a struggling Liverpudlian comedy-writer, Phil Redmond, himself one of the first products of the comprehensive system. To ensure authenticity, producer Anna Home and a team at the BBC visited schools all over the country (and kept visiting seven or eight of them) asking children what sort of issues they thought would be interesting. And they didn't want stories about nice kind teachers and golly-gosh fun in the playground. They liked the realistic stories, even if they were disturbing. One child wanted a story about a man who snatched children at the school gates. Another suggested they copy a true story about a school trouble-maker who organised a boat-race on benches in the swimming-pool while the teacher was seeing to a child with an injured foot. When this became a prank of 'Grange Hill' bovver boy Tucker Jenkins, the episode was criticised for being wildly unlikely and for setting a bad example – this despite the fact that Tucker was punished for it. When bully Gripper Stebson (wonderful names!) rolled a fat boy down a corridor, the producers were deluged with letters of protest. (Gripper was expelled.) Mary Whitehouse said the series encouraged bad behaviour and undermined teachers' authority. Mr Russell Knott, an official of the National Association of Schoolmasters, said in 1980: 'The teachers come out as buffoons and all we see are strikes and sit-ins, larceny and violence.' But a survey in 1981 showed it was the favourite programme of children aged between six and fourteen, and by 1987 it was still followed by 36 per cent of all children. In the past few years the number of complaints has thinned out – although the story-lines are still hard-hitting. Perhaps the penny has dropped that these are cautionary tales. The struggle of one Grange Hill pupil, Zammo, to beat heroin addiction led to the cast's record of 'Just Say No' which raised over £100,000 for an anti-drugs charity.

In the same year as 'Grange Hill', the BBC claimed a breakthrough with **'Empire Road'**, a five-part serial conceived, written, directed and acted by black people and intended to be both entertaining and serious – about racial tensions, the clashes between first- and second-generation immigrants and the conflicts between West Indians and Asians. Inevitably it was tagged a 'black "Coronation Street"', though it was never as cosy. To accentuate this, producer Peter Ansorge chose a specially run-down house in Westbourne Road, Handsworth, as the main characters' home. Unfortunately the real residents misunderstood and thought they were helping the BBC by painting it bright green; and ironically some among Westbourne Road's 15 per cent white population were upset. They didn't want their street branded 'immigrant'. Several critics praised the writing of Guyanese Michael Abbensetts and the acting of Norman Beaton as Everton Bennett, the West Indian 'Godfather'. But it was only with the second series, shown in 1979 at a better time – 8 p.m. instead of 6.50 p.m. – and now with two white women playing long-established residents in the street and Rudolph Walker (nice Bill from 'Love Thy Neighbour') as a sinister new landlord, that the series began to knit together. Even then as comedy its appeal was not wide enough (audiences were only 4–5 million), and as soap opera it had too much man-talk and too little crisis-survival by strong women. The series that had so much to live up to was granted no more time or support. After fifteen episodes the Empire was lost.

Had Shakespeare been alive in 1978, he'd have loved J. R. Ewing, the Iago of Dallas, hero of a soap opera which was to dominate the soap scene for more than a decade and to prove conclusively that Americans *are* different (they wear stetson hats without embarrassment, for one thing). **'Dallas'**, made on 35-millimetre film like a Hollywood movie, was the glossiest, most luxurious soap yet seen. It began as a saga of the oil-rich Ewing family, their feud with poor Digger Barnes who'd originally found the oil and said he'd been swindled, and the survival of Pamela, Digger's daughter who'd married Bobby, the favourite, squeaky-clean Ewing boy. Larry Hagman, an actor known for comedy rôles, particularly for the stammering astronaut in 'I Dream of Jeannie', was to turn 'Dallas' tongue-in-cheek into his *tour de force* as JR, the black-hearted baddie who gets real job satisfaction from dirty-dealing. Taking his cue from Shakespeare, Larry Hagman decided that he would 'smile, and smile, and be a villain'. His malicious glee, his corrupt chuckles as he

If there were a Nobel Prize for nastiness, J. R. Ewing (Larry Hagman), villain of 'Dallas', would walk it in his cowboy boots.

tricked the other oil barons, betrayed his wife with a stream of women (six mistresses in the first six episodes) and plotted disasters for Digger's son and daughter soon put the absurd melodrama on the world's television map.

'Dallas' had started almost by accident. Lorimar Telepictures had had the actress Linda Evans under contract for some time, and 'Untitled Linda Evans Project' was gathering dust on a shelf. It was passed to David Jacobs, a New York writer of children's books, who'd moved to Los Angeles purely to be close to his twelve-year-old daughter and needed a stop-gap scriptwriting job to pay the new bills. They wanted Big and Brash, so he gave it to them – five episodes of 'Dallas' – without ever having set foot in Texas. When he went there for the filming he found he didn't have to change a thing. Texan Larry Hagman merely commented that he hadn't made the characters corrupt and power-crazed enough. By then Linda Evans wasn't on the scene. Lorimar released her from her contract. The feeling was that she was too old to play Pam – the part went to angel-faced Victoria Principal who'd had the sense to come to the audition in a tight sweater – and too straight-looking for sultry Sue Ellen, JR's suffering vodka-loving wife, a rôle for which Linda Gray deserved an Oscar.

By 1979 the Ewing family, Jim Davis's Big Daddy Jock, Barbara Bel Geddes's wet-eyed matriarch Miss Ellie, Patrick Duffy's Bobby, Charlene Tilton's Lucy (the world's tiniest nympho), Steve Kanaly's Ray Krebbs (the cowboy who'd lose in an IQ contest with his hat) were a familiar sight, taking breakfast on the patio of Southfork Ranch in gales, marrying and remarrying in the driveway, living as one big unhappy rich family, while Ken Kercheval's Cliff Barnes, the show's perpetual patsy, and assorted other oilmen swigged Bourbon and sought revenge. The women, with their perfect make-up day and night, made other television heroines look drab, and the continuing crimes of JR made other villains look cissies – although the writers made sure he lost as often as he won. In 1985 there were 'Dallas'-style manoeuvres off-camera. In the Great Dallas Robbery as it was called, Brian Cowgill of Thames Television gazumped the BBC's price to the 'Dallas' distributors. He offered £54,500 an episode for the seven-year-old series instead of the £29,000 the BBC were paying. This infuriated BBC1 Controller Michael Grade, who pulled the remaining episodes off the air promising to run them in the autumn at the same time as the 'poached' new series. Ultimately Thames's overlords at the IBA put pressure on Cowgill to withdraw. He did so, and the BBC won the new episodes at the old price, but Thames had to pay the difference between that and the price they'd agreed. For Brian Cowgill who left Thames shortly afterwards, it was not at all like striking oil.

Also in 1985, Patrick Duffy decided not to renew his contract, the writers had him killed off and ratings in America and here fell. It seemed the show needed its saint as well as its devil, JR. In the following year Patrick discovered that for him there was no life after soap; but in soap there can be life after death as 'Dallas' producers were to prove. The actor received a pay rise, Bobby came back from the dead by suddenly materialising in Pam's shower and all the events of the past season were written off as Pam's dream. Surely viewers would not stand for this cynical manipulation, said horrified critics. They could and did. Although 'Dallas' fever never made the world giddy again, the soap bubbled on and in Britain JR always beat the 'Dynasty' bitch, Joan Collins's Alexis, in the British ratings.

Because it's a shared experience among millions, binding society together, soap opera is more important

than Shakespeare, but in 1978 for no particular reason Shakespeare was a television rage. The BBC decided to stage all thirty-seven of his plays over a six-year period. It was easier announced than done. One of the first productions, *Much Ado about Nothing* with Penelope Keith and Michael York, was scrapped at a cost of £150,000. The BBC blamed 'technical problems' but started again with a new cast. In 1980 they ran into another hitch when they had to recast *Othello*. Equity had refused to allow them to bring black actor James Earl Jones from America. Finally Anthony Hopkins took over the rôle. The style of the productions varied from play to play – some confined to a studio and formal, others shot on location and realistic. Jonathan Miller took over two years later and cast John Cleese in *The Taming of the Shrew* with Sarah Badel. Shaun Sutton took over for the final two years.

In the same year Lord Grade decided that after Moses the Man and Jesus the Man what was called for was Will Shakespeare the Man. John Mortimer was given the task of writing the bard's life to fill six hours of television, entitled **'Will Shakespeare'**. He found that the known facts could be written on one side of a postcard, so he did what all good writers do – made it up. The part of Will Shakespeare went to a newcomer to television, Tim Curry, who'd made his acting début in the stage show *Hair*, starkers, graduated to suspender belt, black corselette and high heels in *The Rocky Horror Show* and had clearly learned it paid to make Much Ado about Nothing On. Meg Wyn Owen, who'd played Captain Bellamy's wife in 'Upstairs Downstairs', played Anne Hathaway. The series worried a few scholars but was declared ye showbiz success and was sold around the world. The Russians, who'd loved 'The Forsyte Saga' bought it, too. It was the first ITV series sold there.

John Mortimer also brought Horace Rumpole – he who must be watched – to television that year in **'Rumpole of the Bailey'**. Will Shakespeare would surely have applauded the sardonic old barrister, who took only defence briefs and had to defend himself against skulduggery in his chambers, erratic and stone-hearted judges and a dragon-like wife, 'She Who Must Be Obeyed'. The wag in a wig had appeared first in a BBC 'Play for Today', but the BBC took so long deciding about a series that Thames Television snapped it up. Australian Leo McKern, then fifty-nine and – at fifteen stone – well rounded, took the rôle, complaining that Rumpole's wig was too prickly but seeming to enjoy himself. Like barrister Mortimer, Rumpole hated prison, liked cocking a snook at authority and relished such crimes as the Penge Bungalow Murders and the Great Grimsby Fish Fraud. There was a second series in 1979; but the actor refused a third, fearing being stuck in the one rôle. He relented in 1983 and again in 1987, by which time he could command £100,000 for six shows. Patricia Hodge was a great success with him as plummy barrister Phyllida Trant, and Peggy Bates boomed beautifully as his wife until 1988 when she was replaced by Marion Mathie. Viewers enjoyed the droll stories, and to those lawyers who still had a sense of humour he was a hero.

Thames Television's most stunning drama series that year – the one that went into production as 'The Sweeney' ended – was the same team's **'Out'**. The title referred to the release from prison of the hero, who was also a villain bent on revenge, in a thriller which eventually showed the villain was a policeman. The police were running their corruption-routing Operation Countryman at the time. 'Out''s powerful opening episodes revealed both a man obsessed with crime and a wife wrecked by her husband's never-admitted involvement in it (with a startling searing performance by Pam Fairbrother as the mentally ill Evie). While there was plenty of grievous bodily harm over the six weeks, writer Trevor Preston's believable, miserable criminals (inside and outside the police force) put it way above the bash-and-grab level of most cops-and-robbers stories. Tom Bell, an actor who would probably look menacing doing 'Play School', was at his most intense, wearing a deathly prison pallor and the same out-of-date

Edward Fox and Cynthia Harris as Edward and Mrs Simpson. The series didn't take sides but delivered a picture of the high and low times with pretty clothes – Wallis Simpson's costumes alone cost £20,000 – and a fine sense of the romance of a king giving up his throne for love.

suit throughout (his entire wardrobe for the series cost £70 from a secondhand-clothes shop). He deserved the year's Best Actor award; but Edward Fox came up with a performance as Edward VIII, torn between duty and 'the woman I love', climaxing in a re-enactment of the abdication speech, phrase by halting phrase like the real thing, and was so effective in stirring up the old controversy that he simply had to win.

'Edward and Mrs Simpson', a £1½ million Thames production based on Frances Donaldson's biography, covered Edward's life from 1928 to 1936 and included a short excerpt filmed in Kenya for £40,000. The Queen was said not to be amused at the timing of the series (Princess Margaret's divorce was enough scandal for one year), and the Queen Mother was said to have been upset by some scenes depicting her late husband George VI (played by Andrew Ray) so shocked by his brother's behaviour he was dumbstruck. But royal disapproval was mild compared with the bitter protest from the Duchess of Windsor – Mrs Simpson that was – by then a frail eighty-two and living in Paris. Her lawyer, Madame Suzanne Blum, issued a statement declaring that 'The Duchess of Windsor has been portrayed as a cheap adventuress' and promised to produce letters proving that she was the reluctant partner in the love-affair and that she was not Edward's mistress before they married. To counteract the early criticism Thames spent £10,000 on a thirties-style ball and special screening to which politicians, socialites and every VIP in town were invited. They and more than 13 million viewers seemed to like both Edward Fox's Edward (though people who knew the former king told him later he was nothing like him) and the Mrs Simpson portrayed by American redhead Cynthia Harris (freckles covered and in dark wigs). It was keenly watched again in 1980 and 1986 and sold world-wide, though not to France where the Duchess had it banned. On her death in 1986 it was bought by a French television company.

The British series that got people up on their hind legs ('Sheer filth, obnoxious and bordering on pornography,' said a Reverend David Williams as Mrs Whitehouse was given oxygen) was **'Pennies from Heaven'**. The BBC, having just ditched the borstal play 'Scum', at a loss of £120,000, and dropped Dennis Potter's 'Brimstone and Treacle' at a loss of £70,000, went ahead with Dennis Potter's six-part musical about the travels of Arthur Parker, a randy sheet-music salesman (Bob Hoskins) who ended up facing a murder charge, with his frigid wife, the innocent schoolmarm he seduced and a stammering epileptic accordion-player.

Dennis Potter was worried about the degree to which scenes would be censored (in the event they removed a full-frontal male nude, Gemma Craven's nipples and a four-letter word), but he had a ready excuse if the series had been banned. He stipulated that the records used

were by Al Bowlly, Harry Roy and others – *not* by Billy Cotton's Band. 'I'll put it about that the BBC1 Controller Bill Cotton who banned "Scum" was upset that I didn't use any of his dad's numbers,' he joked.

Part of the series was filmed in Potter's actual junior school in Berry Hill in the Forest of Dean with children at desks breaking into song. When the parents and teachers were shown the finished product there was uproar. The schoolmistress (Cheryl Campbell) had been made pregnant by Arthur; he'd arranged for an abortion with a pimp (Hywel Bennett) who'd then put the girl to work as a prostitute. You can see their point. But 12 million viewers followed Arthur, and the series put Al Bowlly and company back in the charts, outselling punk. The LP sold 50,000 copies in six weeks, and a second record was produced. For Bob Hoskins it was a triumph, but he hated one aspect of his own performance: his dancing. The choreographer Tudor Davies convinced him he looked like Fred Astaire, Bob said. 'When I saw the film, I was so ashamed. I looked like a little hippopotamus shaking its hoofs.'

As for game-shows – the BBC had 'The Generation Game', but ITV needed something new. Yorkshire Television's Light Entertainment boss Duncan Wood went on a golfing holiday in Spain and found himself watching 'Un Dos Tres', which he neatly turned round to make

Cheryl Campbell and Bob Hoskins in 'Pennies from Heaven'. The plays – mainly about people's dreams of romance and excitement, their longing for the Garden of Eden – included four-letter words, an abortion, a drag act, much nudity and several weird scenes where dull pictures burst into colour and the characters suddenly lip-mimed to thirties tunes. These 'most banal and drivelling pop songs' as Potter called them were often made to sound more strange by having men mime to women's voices and vice versa.

'3–2–1'. It became ITV's longest-running quiz and enjoyed ten years at the top, regularly attracting 16 million viewers. It is still wheeled out now for special occasions.

The host was comic Ted Rogers, who'd been a hit in the 1974 Royal Variety Show and had gone on to peddle his patter to audiences in America. Ted tends to say everything twice, but everything else about '3–2–1' came in threes: three couples competing for three prizes and answering questions at the rate of one every three seconds. And Ted invented a finger-sign for the show when the producer told him to say 'We'll be back on "3–2–1" after the break' and made an indeterminate hand-gesture at him. Ted replied, 'You must do it like this,' and the famous gesture was born.

But from the start he took second billing to Dusty Bin – an electronically operated dustbin with a face on the front which cost £10,500 to build – the show's mascot and (in miniature form) booby prize. Corny jokes, sketches and charades performed by a trio of comics and incomprehensible verses were meant to help the contestant couples unravel clues. Usually the audience was completely mystified. 'Mastermind' winner Chris Hughes tried to unravel the verse clues once and won the bin. The hardest thing, according to Ted, was to hold his tongue with some of the contestants. One elimination question was about a German composer famous for his 'Water Music'. 'One of the contestants answered, "Handel's 'Water Music',"' said Ted. 'And I said, "Yes, but who wrote it?" "Schubert", he replied. Then we gave it over to the others and they said, "Beethoven".'

As we said at the start, 1978 was not Bruce Forsyth's year. Since 1971 he had dominated popular television in 'The Generation Game', which he'd made a Saturday-night institution; but he made the mistake of thinking that he was bigger than the game and believed that his West End production *The Travelling Music Show* would take him triumphantly to Broadway. It folded in just four months. When Michael Grade at LWT offered Bruce £15,000 a week for two hours of peak viewing-time on Saturday nights in a show whose budgets would be a massive £250,000, he needed little persuasion.

But **'Bruce Forsyth's Big Night'** turned out to be Bruce Forsyth's Big Nightmare. Despite a decent new game, 'The Pyramid Game' hosted by Grade lookalike Steve Jones, despite the presence of Bruce's sidekick Anthea Redfern, despite the revival of Jimmy Edwards's brilliant comic family the Glums and Charlie Drake's

---

In April the BBC invited Larry Grayson to take over 'The Generation Game' with Isla St Clair, a fresh-faced folk-singer the show's producer Alan Boyd had spotted on a trip to Edinburgh. It was bad news for Bruce Forsyth. Larry and Isla were even more popular than he and Anthea had been.

Worker, and despite the fact that Cannon and Ball recorded six sketches, were billed but *didn't* appear, the big audiences shrank fast. The press attacked the formerly bumptious Bruce for the show's failure. Bruce bit back, claiming it was everyone else's fault and, anyway, the only thing you can believe in newspapers is the date. By 1980 he had learned to 'Play Your Cards Right'. He had kept his big chin up and some new ginger hair on. And he did well.

Commercial Break

It was a good year for new commercials. Glenrycks introduced their three singing pilchards; Lorraine Chase drank Campari at Luton Airport ('Nice 'ere, innit?'), and Victor Borge's voice began the wonderful stream of visual jokes to go with the puns about Heineken refreshing the parts other beers cannot reach. Woolwich Equitable Building Society began calling itself 'the safe place with the nice face', the face belonging to Sue Bryan who squeaked 'Good morning' in a way which reminded many of Soo from the Sooty show.

Also Shown in 1978

Historical controversy was stirred up when LWT re-created the war years on the German-occupied Channel Islands (partly in the naval dockyard at Gillingham, Kent) in their series **'Enemy at the Door'**.

ITV produced new popular heroes almost weekly. **Hazell**, a cockney sparrow of a detective, was the prettiest, thanks to actor Nicholas Ball (then the husband of Pamela Stephenson). James Hazell was an ex-cop, invalided out of the force and hampered by Choc Minty, a CID officer with a grudge against him. But the BBC slotted a season of Robert Redford films opposite, which did him more harm than Choc Minty.

From Yorkshire Television came **'The Sandbaggers'**, which put spies in grey suits, gave them short haircuts and short tempers, cut out the car chases, sex and swashbuckling and unexpectedly made a pinup of Roy Marsden. But they upset the Foreign Office by flashing the phone number in the opening titles – a joke by writer Ian Mackintosh, once a spy himself. And after 'The XYY Man' series in 1977, which had Stephen Yardley (later of

'Howards' Way') as a villain trying to go straight though plagued by the extra chromosome which made him aggressive, the policeman who hounded him, the bizarre, glove-wearing, Shakespeare-spouting George Bulman (Don Henderson) returned in **'Strangers'**.

There was more detective work in **'The Return of the Saint'**. In this Ian Ogilvy, who looked uncannily similar to the young Roger Moore, was persuaded to re-create Simon Templar, the Leslie Charteris sleuth in a sports-car Roger had played in the sixties. It was a mistake. Yet more sleuthing was done in **'The Wilde Alliance'**, a silly series from Yorkshire starring Julia Foster and John Stride as a couple of married good eggs who just happened upon crimes and solved them. In Granada's **'Fallen Hero'**, Del Henney was a Rugby-player forced to quit the game through injury, and his marriage to Wanda Ventham was a bit of a scrum. Married life for the Langtrys wasn't a bowl of cherries, either; but the settings, costumes, colourful scandals, and a blooming Francesca Annis made LWT's **'Lillie'** a delicious period soap. (Francesca had a baby only weeks after the series was broadcast.)

The other woman of the year was Geraldine McEwan's blinkered but passionate spinster schoolteacher in 1930s Edinburgh in **'The Prime of Miss Jean Brodie'**, and three actresses – Anna Massey, Anne Stallybrass and Janet Maw – gave an extra sparkle to the BBC's **'The Mayor of Casterbridge'**. Dennis Potter's script and Jonathan Powell's production helped, too.

'Law and Order' was a series of four plays by G. F. Newman which suggested even more bleakly than Trevor Preston had in 'Out' that in 1978 corruption was as rampant among cops as among robbers. The results were claims of bias, a ban on the BBC from filming inside gaols for a year levied by the Prison Officers' Association, and a demand by the police that the BBC give certain assurances before other police series on which they wanted co-operation.

The best documentary series that year was **'The Voyage of Charles Darwin'** made by the BBC. They built a replica of Captain Fitzroy's ship, HMS *Beagle*, and took actors – Malcolm Stoddart was Darwin, Andrew Burt was Captain Fitzroy – over the same route that Darwin took in the 1830s (only in two rather than five years). David Bellamy, sounding as though his head were inside a bucket, looking as though it should be, traced the evolution and adaptation of living things in **'Botanic Man'**, a

modest series for Thames. It made him quite a star. And **'The South Bank Show'** replaced LWT's 'Aquarius', beginning a long reign as the most thoughtful, unrushed series about art, music, the theatre, film and television, too. Melvyn Bragg, the series' editor and presenter, has sounded enthusiastic for eleven years – despite his cold.

There were few new comedies in 1978. **'The Kenny Everett Video Show'** on ITV featured technical trickery, Hot Gossip dancers, Cleo Rocos' cleavage, and sketches with Everett characters, including Sid Snot and Captain Kremmen, very few of them done in the best-possible taste. Christopher Blake, who'd looked forlorn through most of 'Love for Lydia', turned up as half of a mixed marriage in the LWT alleged comedy **'Mixed Blessings'** with Muriel Odunton. **'Life Begins at Forty'**, made by Yorkshire Television, was almost worse but it topped the ratings, thanks to the valiant acting of Derek Nimmo and Rosemary Leach, and it was sold to East Germany – not as comedy, but as part of their adult education programme to encourage people to have more babies.

Eric Idle and Neil Innes sent up the Beatles in **'The Rutles'** comedies, Ronnie Barker's Fletch came out of gaol in **'Going Straight'** and Carla Lane began **'Butterflies'** starring Wendy Craig – a whimsical situation comedy which was to mature and become a great favourite with women.

America sent us one gloriously funny show, **'Soap'**, a send-up of American day-time soap operas, featuring life with the Campbells and the Tates, incorporating homosexuality, religion, sex, the Mafia and senility – often in the same episode. They also passed on **'Battlestar Galactica'**, an expensive but poor attempt at space fantasy and **'Centennial'**. Based on James Michener's novel, this told the story of a Western town from Indian times to the present day and starred Richard Chamberlain, Raymond Burr and half of Hollywood; while it failed to be the white man's 'Roots', it ranks as one of the best maxi-series ever made. Also from America came **'Wonder Woman'** with Lynda Carter, a six-foot busty former Miss USA as the forties cartoon character – Women's Lib meets Batman.

The Americans also sent us a deadly serious seven-hour story of a Jewish family in Nazi Germany, **'Holocaust'**, which the BBC screened over four nights in September. Critics objected to the often trite dialogue, gushing music, the blunted horrors and the phoney serenity of some of the supposed victims, but people who watched expecting to find that it trivialised the greatest crime in history found themselves moved to tears. In Blackpool a Jewish widow, Mrs Fanny Godall, was so upset that she committed suicide after watching it.

Back home, in **'Crossroads'** Jill was divorced by Stan Harvey because she had an affair with her step-brother (and that's as near as any British soap got to incest). She had baby Matthew by him – but might not have noticed. The child went off with Dad and Jill forgot to mention him again. In **'Coronation Street'** Elsie divorced Alan but found a taxi-man to take her to Majorca, and Emily Bishop was widowed when shotgun-touting raiders at the warehouse fired on Ernest. Stephen Hancock who'd played him had got the bullet because he asked for a pay rise.

Esther Rantzen began to offer adults the chance to fulfil their dreams and make **'The Big Time'** in a series of fifty-minute light-hearted documentaries in 1978. A housewife cooked a banquet at a top hotel; a vicar wrote a newspaper gossip column; a Marks & Spencer shop-girl joined the circus; but what seemed Esther's most successful bit of wand-waving was her launching of Scottish teacher Sheena Easton to pop stardom.

Not so much a dream come true as a bit of British masochism was **'Living in the Past'**, BBC2's eight fifty-minute films recording how a group of volunteers made out living as Iron Age settlers, with no mod cons for twelve months. Many dropped out, unable to bear the hardships, but ten stuck it out, going without toothpaste and tea-bags, Wellingtons and watches, while developing new recipes like Pig's Head Loaf (method: remove eyes and take wax out of ears . . . .), Nettle and Garlic Soup, and Iron Age coffee made from whole wheat and barley.

1979

The Shah of Iran was driven into exile and the Ayatollah Khomeini took power. □ Rubbish piled up in Britain's streets, the dead weren't buried and ambulances were unmanned in the Winter of Discontent. □ Egypt and Israel signed a peace treaty, and Brezhnev and Carter signed the SALT peace treaty. □ Vietnamese troops entering Cambodia found the mass graves, some containing 2,000 bodies, of Pol Pot's régime. □ Margaret Thatcher became Britain's first woman prime minister. □ Earl Mountbatten was killed by an IRA bomb while fishing in County Sligo. □ Sebastian Coe set three new world records for middle-distance running. □ Anthony Blunt, the Queen's art adviser, was revealed as a Russian spy. □ The Rubik cube was manufactured. □ Herpes arrived. □ Trevor Francis became the first British £1 million footballer. □ A strike at ITV lasted eleven weeks. □ Milton Keynes was officially opened. □ And top films were Alien *and* Kramer vs Kramer.

Some of the most unlikely people tried to become television stars in 1979 – Harold Wilson had a go as a chat-show host, and the former Commissioner of the Metropolitan Police, Sir Robert Mark, turned actor-salesman in commercials. Neither did frightfully well. But an Irish disc-jockey who seemed not only to have kissed the blarney stone but also to have married it became ever so slightly wildly popular on television as well as on radio. Terry Wogan had arrived.

But first let us take a fast canter through the dramatic events in drama. If some sections of British industry were grinding to a halt, the people in television drama departments were working flat out for 1979 and the quality of their products had never been higher. Two brilliantly

original shifty so-and-sos, both manglers of the language and neither of them gentlemen you'd invite into your home in the normal way, introduced themselves that year. And both were badly affected by the long ITV strike. They were Worzel Gummidge and Arthur Daley.

Worzel Gummidge was a scarecrow who could get out of most scrapes but couldn't scare off the rotten luck this series had. Eventually it was defeat for the hugely popular character and for Jon Pertwee who played him and whose idea the show had been. Jon was desperately keen to get a series going after he stopped playing Dr Who, and as a child he had loved the books about Worzel by Barbara Euphan Todd. When Keith Waterhouse and Willis Hall adapted the stories of Worzel, who could change character by magically changing his head, of Aunt Sally the skittle Worzel lost his straw heart to, and of Saucy Nancy, the ship's figurehead, Southern Television had a hit on their hands. Jon's skill at make-up – he made Worzel's warts from Sugar Puffs cut in half and a wispy beard from carrot roots – and his talent for comedy, together with his Worzelese – expressions such as 'dang me' and 'bumswizzled' – made him a favourite with children and adults alike. Una Stubbs was perfect as the skittle-skinny Aunt Sally, and Barbara Windsor filled the part of Saucy Nancy ideally. Then the ITV blackout stopped filming. Only eight of the planned thirteen episodes were made, and the Christmas edition, made in October in Lymington, Hampshire, snowed more trouble for him. The fake snow – a white powder used for making toothpaste – blew everywhere, stickily clinging to the food in shops as well as to furniture, clothing and washing in people's homes. Restaurants had to chuck out the dish of the day and dress shops had to get rid of ruined items. But that was nothing. Southern Television then lost its franchise, and the new company, TVS, declined to continue with Worzel. A saviour appeared in the form of Harlech Television, but eleven days before they were due to begin filming more episodes the project was cancelled because of a dispute with technicians. Channel 4 repeated the series in 1986, and then Worzel and Jon remained bumswizzled until an

independent producer in New Zealand came to the rescue. 'Worzel Gummidge Down Under' was shown on Channel 4 in 1989.

Arthur Daley, the endearingly ineffectual spiv hero of **'Minder'**, and Terry McCann, his boneheaded bodyguard, might have met a similar fate but they had a fairy godmother in the form of Brian Cowgill, Thames Television's managing director at the time. The first two series were not a success. The first went out straight after the ITV strike and should perhaps have been called 'Mindless' – it couldn't make up its mind what it was. Audiences were still confused by Dennis Waterman looking and sounding like the tough cop in 'The Sweeney' but playing the thick thug Terry here. Should they laugh? And where was John Thaw? But Cowgill felt viewers would come round and backed the show. In doing so he probably saved the career and restored the health of Leon Griffiths, creator of 'Minder'. Leon, born in Sheffield, raised in Glasgow, but with an ear for London slang second to none, had originally written a tough humourless film story. His agent told him to dump it all except for two characters, a used car dealer and owner of a lock-up containing items recently fallen off the back of a lorry, and his bodyguard, who'd done time but didn't want to get in trouble with the police again (he'd say 'No, ta' to any 'easy tickle'). Euston Films wanted a

---

The Winchester, Arthur and Terry's drinking-haunt in 'Minder', has become famous. There have been two, one in a boys' school in Olympia, the other on the first floor of a converted warehouse near Wormwood Scrubs, West London. But the outside has stayed the same – it's a picture of the Eton Club in Chalk Farm, North London. The beer there is real – two brewers supply it, happy to be associated with the show; but the manufacturers of the panatella cigars Arthur smokes are not. Arthur does nothing for their brand image, they say.

---

successor to 'The Sweeney', liked Leon's cockney twosome and his idea of using the 'new exotica' of London, the cul-de-sacs, breakers' yards and railway arches in places like Fulham and Camden Town, not shots of Big Ben, as a backdrop. But after the first series Leon suffered a massive stroke, and it seemed unlikely that he would ever work again. Script executive Linda Agran had to commission new scripts quickly. In 1980 Leon won an award for 'Minder' despite not having been involved. This was said to have been a jolt to his pride. He resolved to make it his own again and slowly returned to writing.

George Cole was making *Brimstone and Treacle*, Dennis Potter's banned play, when the offer of Arthur Daley the dodgy dealer came through. He accepted, never thinking the rôle would last for six series and that Arthur, with his posh suits, expensive overcoat, trilby, cigar, unseen wife – ''er indoors' – and magnificent malapropisms such as 'the world is your lobster, my son' would pass into folklore. He also never imagined that people would worry about cashing his cheques, automatically assuming they would bounce like Arthur's. Dennis Waterman was happy to take on Terry McCann, dim though he was in always letting Arthur con him and underpay him, because he liked the comedy and the fact that the scripts were not limited by the goodies-versus-baddies constraints of police drama.

The crimes in the plots tend to be minor fiddles, thieves-against-thieves stuff with Patrick Malahide's dogged Detective Sergeant Chisholm always on the trail. The production suffered from petty crime, too. One week some 'antique' chairs (or as Arthur called them 'true treasures of the antique persuasion') were stolen from the set and new ones had to be made speedily at a cost of £1,000. At another location thieves got away with the van and load of tins labelled 'pickled walnuts' and 'pineapple chunks'. The tins actually contained sand. By 1984 the flop had become a success, the two stars had become among the highest-paid television actors in Britain and, though every series was billed as the last – George and Dennis took it in turns to claim they'd had enough – there have been sixty-nine episodes and a couple of ninety-minute Christmas specials. They also kept cockney rhyming slang from the knackers' yard. Quite what they make of 'a sky-ful of Eddies' in The Philippines or Swaziland or any of the other countries where 'Minder' is a nice little earner, is not clear. (It's a pocket full of ready cash, to you, my son.)

Euston Films also produced a less dodgy hero in a more traditional series called **'Danger UXB'** (the initials stood for 'unexploded bomb'). This traced the life of a bomb-disposal squad from the beginnings of the Blitz to the preparations for the Normandy landings. John Hawkesworth, the 'Upstairs Downstairs' producer, had borrowed Royal Engineer Major A. P. Hartley's book, *Unexploded Bomb*, from the library fourteen years earlier. He suggested a drama on the unsung heroes in wartime bomb-defusing to the BBC, who turned it down, and finally interested Euston Films. The thirteen-part series looked authentic with a converted Clapham school doubling as the army HQ for 97 Bomb Disposal Company and demolition work in nearby Wimbledon proving handy for scenes where houses were bombed flat. Making a bomb crater turned out to be a problem. They ended up having to build one, a thirty-foot hole, thirty feet deep. Some viewers found the characters less dynamic than the bombs, but when a romance developed between the nervous subaltern Brian Ash, played by Anthony Andrews, and the daughter (Judy Geeson) of the bomb-dismantling boffin the serial improved. Debbie Watling's man-mad Naughty Norma and Maurice Roeves's dour sergeant assisting our Brian helped. We could have watched more – but Brian ended up blasted off a seaside pier.

In quite a different vein, Alec Guinness as ageing, self-effacing George Smiley was the hero of **'Tinker Tailor Soldier Spy'**, the serial that changed for ever our image of spies, not to mention circuses, cousins and plumbers. Women didn't swoon. John le Carré's thriller depicting the plots and counterplots of the faceless grey men who work for British Intelligence came to the screen after several plots and counterplots of its own. LWT first obtained the rights in 1975, sounded the trumpets about it and set Julian Bond to write a screenplay for a ninety-minute film, but it was never made. KGB skulduggery? It's not clear. All that is known is that two men met in a remote corner of Hampstead Heath, possibly after having left messages in dead-letter boxes. They were the author and Jonathan Powell, then a producer at the BBC. They talked about a £1 million project, a co-production with Paramount, for a seven-part serialisation starring Guinness (for the first time on television) and discussed how a cameraman should be sent to the no man's land on the Austrian-Czech border to film the real thing in secret so they could make sure their location filming (in Lisbon, Scotland, London and Wiltshire, as it turned out) looked right. Alec Guinness then had a meeting with a former diplomat at the Foreign Office, almost certainly having signed the Official Secrets Act first.

Mass audiences were baffled, but Guinness's weary old George, polishing his specs on his tie – pained at having been betrayed by his wife (Sian Phillips), Beryl Reid's decrepit Connie Sachs, Ian Richardson's treacherous Bill Haydon among many other fine performances – drew a tense devoted following and critical praise. Mole-spotting became a national pastime but when the serial was finished le Carré wrote a mischievous letter to the *Guardian* in

Alec Guinness was the unsmiling George Smiley in 'Tinker Tailor Soldier Spy', here with Ian Bannen.

which he said there was no mole, never had been a mole, it was all an evil scheme of Control's. Smiley had been making a fool of himself again.

The comedy everybody thought was terrific that year was **'To the Manor Born'**. It worked because Penelope Keith has a special talent and because in 1979 we still loved snobs. Also, like the best comedy, it contained the germ of truth. In Cricket St Thomas, Somerset, the widow of the owner of a thousand-acre estate actually moved into the small estate lodge and watched a businessman transform the place. Gag-writer Peter Spence, who used to supply Roy Hudd and Kenneth Williams with jokes, lived in the village and wrote his comedy about Audrey Fforbes-Hamilton (Penelope Keith), a grand-mannered lady saddled with death duties and forced to move out of her stately home into a poky lodge. She took her aged butler Brabinger (John Rudling) and beagle with her. Peter Bowles played Richard De Vere, the self-made millionaire grocer with a down-to-earth Czech mother who bought Grantleigh Manor and proceeded to make small but significant social gaffes. Angela Thorne's character, mousey Marjorie, Audrey's best friend, was allowed to put the monstrous woman down once per episode. The show topped the ratings, drawing audiences of 24 million, and was the most popular show at Christmas.

Another comedy success that year was LWT's **'Agony'**, also based on a true story (well, truish). Anna Raeburn was the young, attractive and relatively out-spoken problem-page writer of a woman's magazine. Skilled at guiding others out of their muddles, her own domestic life was often a shambles. With Len Richmond she devised a sitcom about Jane Lucas – played engagingly by Maureen Lipman – with a worrying Jewish mother, friends who were homosexuals and a psychiatrist husband who understood nothing about people. These gave her more problems than all her letter-writers. Further series, written by Stan Hey and Andrew Nickolds, had better jokes.

Few would have predicted that **'The Antiques Road-show'** would draw bigger audiences in some regions than 'Coronation Street'. The BBC's Sunday-teatime show in which silver-haired Arthur Negus was the main expert looking at ordinary people's treasures was a slow but steady hit, and Arthur became a favourite uncle until he retired from the show in 1983. He once dropped someone's treasure, a clock. The 500-strong audience and crew froze in shock as it shattered on the floor. The owner forgave Arthur instantly: 'Never mind, Mr Negus,' he said. 'It'll give me something to do in the evenings putting it together.' There have been spectacular finds, including a Ming-dynasty temple-bell worth £30,000 and a Victorian painting dumped in a garden shed but valued at £100,000. In 1988 an old teapot brought on the show by a Merseyside grandmother ended up fetching £14,300 at auction and buying its owner a council house. But all the experts were stumped by one wooden object which was finally identified as a wooden leg made for a bull. There has been one unfortunate mistake. In 1987 resident expert David Mason told a Cambridge couple that their painting was by Swedish artist Bruno Liljefors and worth £50,000. Sotheby's confirmed it, but then realised that the genuine article was in a collection in Sweden and this was a fake.

One new and highly popular game-show was Thames Television's **'Give Us a Clue'**, a cheap and easy-to-produce charades game played between two teams with Una Stubbs as the captain of the women's team and Lionel Blair as the men's team captain. Michael Aspel was the relaxed first host. Later Michael Parkinson, no longer the king of chat, took over, presiding rather like a headmaster over unruly fourth-formers. Problems have arisen in finding new titles and phrases for miming which don't have double-entendres. The producers have had some anxious moments with such choices as 'Cockney Rebel', and when Faith Brown had to mime the song-title 'Like a Virgin' there were worrying minutes.

The BBC was far more embarrassed by **'Blankety Blank'**, which was loved by 20 million viewers but was not the BBC's sort of thing. The Annual Report graciously accepted that it was 'harmless fun handled skilfully by Terry Wogan', then added: 'yet the prominence of its success in the schedules led to suggestions that the whole network had become trivialised'.

Terry Wogan had to agree: 'It's a bit noisy, all those bells ringing and lights flashing, the sort of thing ITV usually do.' But, given this chance to ad-lib, waggle his strange stick-like microphone and send up the proceedings, he was soon a household name. The value of the prizes was never more than £250 at the start, and Terry was able to scoff at them. 'I don't want them to be any good,' he said. 'That would mean us all having to concentrate.' Terry had some influence over the panellists. The seating arrangement went like this. Front row: a strong character in the middle flanked on his right by a pretty actress and on his left in the 'idiot seat' usually a dumb blonde. Back row: a comedienne in the middle, and on her right a witty but less dominant funny man and on the left a personality such as Patrick Moore. Many celebrities found the show more difficult than it looks. Tracey Ullman hated being on – she was expected to be funny but was terrified – and Paul Daniels was accused of hogging the show. Wogan believed Lorraine Chase, Freddie Starr and Kenny Everett, who once produced a packet of Spanish peanuts called Bum in the middle of a question, helped the show take off.

Terry had won the best prize going in British television during his five years there. He never looked back. Les Dawson took over in 1984, began kissing the women contestants and stepped up the jokes about the prizes. Many deserved it. The door of a dishwasher fell off in front of the audience during the recording of one show. 'Some prizes are so bad they're left in the foyer,' he said. A seventy-two-year-old woman won a body-building kit, and the BBC refused to let her swap.

The BBC replaced 'Target', their violent cop-show, with their first private eye – or private ear, in this case. Shoestring was no smooth operator but a scruffbag of a computer expert who had had a breakdown, did a phone-in problem-solving service at Radio West, drove a secondhand Ford Cortina around Bristol, and rented a room from a woman lawyer who gave him legal advice and a cuddle when needed. He was played by newcomer to television Trevor Eve, and the general consensus among women viewers was that he looked divine. The series became a Sunday-evening institution, with viewing figures reaching 23 million at times, stylishly produced by Robert Banks Stewart and with polished performances from Michael Medwin as Radio West's slick boss, Doran Godwin as the lawyer-landlady and Liz Crowther, daughter of Leslie, as the radio station secretary.

The sketch-show which began to make headlines that year was 'Not the Nine O'Clock News'. In a sense the daring aggressive humour of newcomers Mel Smith, Rowan Atkinson, Pamela Stephenson and Chris Langham (replaced later by Griff Rhys Jones) was comedy for the punk age. It was also the first sign of an alternative to the BBC's traditional comedy. Like many BBC2 series, the first run slipped by almost unnoticed, but by the second series a cult following had built up. Griff Rhys Jones's brilliant impression of a hand-wringing Donald Sinden discovering churches, Pamela Stephenson's Angela Rippon impression and the hilarious lorry-driver-and-hedgehog-squashing sketch became classics.

Also in 1979

The heroes for LWT's drama were two fifteen-year-old lovers who ran away from home in **'Two People'**. The touching and timely series was almost sunk by the censors, but happily we were allowed the brilliant performances by Gerry Cowper and Stephen Garlick.

'The Mallens' should have been drowned at birth, not made into two long series by Granada starting that summer. Based on Catherine Cookson's bodice-ripper, this poor man's *Wuthering Heights* portrayed life in High Banks Hall where an oversexed Victorian tyrant (John Hallam) raped people. Juliet Stevenson and Gerry Sundquist strove hard as doomed lovers meeting on the moors, but they should have stayed at home.

'The Racing Game' provided us with a more wholesome, horsey hero, a jockey (played by Michael Gwilym) forced off the track and into sleuthing by injury. But Yorkshire's series, based loosely on Dick Francis's thrillers, proved only that when you've seen one set of hoofs you've seen them all. Alan Dobie's bowler-hatted Victorian detective sergeant **'Cribb'** was in the running for longer, deservedly so. Based on Peter Lovesey's thriller novels, this Granada series lovingly re-created the period not only with aspidistras and sidewhiskers but also with plots about real Victorian pastimes.

At the other, very noisy extreme was **'The Dukes of Hazzard'**, a sort of 'Beverly Hillbillies' with car crashes, violence, scantily clad girls and no jokes unless you counted the local corrupt politician, Boss Hogg, fat and always in a white suit.

Much more civilised was **'Telford's Change'**, which, depending on your point of view, was either a serial about the menopausal mid-life muddle of a moping bank manager or a ten-week campaign to prove that bankers aren't as boring as we thought. Either way Peter Barkworth had a hit on his hands. Middle-class ladies revelled in it and Mrs Whitehouse found it 'very sexy' but (and this must be a record) 'liked it'.

In the excellently creepy **'Malice Aforethought'**, a BBC serial set in the thirties, Hywel Bennett played a country doctor who plotted to murder the wife who stood between him and an affair. Equally good was **'Rebecca'**, the BBC's sepia-tinted serialisation of the Daphne du Maurier romantic classic. This starred Joanna David as the primly dressed heroine and sparked off a fashion for pageboy haircuts and lace collars. Jeremy Brett was a sinister De Winter and Anna Massey a brilliantly severe Mrs Danvers.

'Prince Regent' was the BBC's eight-parter on the Prince of Wales who became George IV. The co-production (with a West German company) cost £1 million, most of it seeming to have been spent on fake stomachs and latex rubber chins to make skinny Peter Egan look like the bloated over-indulged royal. It wasn't very good. Nor was **'Penmarric'**, a sort of 'Son of Poldark', set in Cornwall. Nor was ATV's **'Sapphire and Steel'**, featuring ghostly do-gooders and capitalising on Joanna Lumley, who'd been so popular in the short-lived 'New Avengers', as Sapphire. Steel was played by the still boyish-looking David McCallum with David Collings as Silver.

'Testament of Youth' was the drama series which inspired women that year. Elaine Morgan's sensitive adaptation of Vera Brittain's book brought back the pain of the First World War using clips of archive film and a stirring musical score from Geoffrey Burgon (who was later asked to write for 'Brideshead Revisited'). Cheryl Campbell won the Best Actress award for the rôle of Vera.

'Tales of the Unexpected', Anglia's series of half-hour plays with a sting in the tale and usually featuring well-known stars, many of them American, began. When the tales were based on Roald Dahl stories they had a special edge, but by the mid-eighties, the fund of good stories seemed to have run out and the series became Tales of the Totally Predictable.

It was a great year for plays. A favourite was **'The Knowledge'** by Jack Rosenthal starring Mick Ford as a would-be cab-driver learning the names and peculiarities of London streets by moped, with Nigel Hawthorne hilarious as the sadistic examiner. **'Charlie Muffin'** was a comedy thriller adapted from the Brian Freemantle novel by Keith Waterhouse, a tale of a three-way espionage deal involving defecting top agents. Sadly, viewers whose brains were just recovering from the torments of 'Tinker Tailor' didn't seem to take it as the gentle send-up that was intended.

Professor **Quatermass** came back in 1979 in the form of Sir John Mills and discovered that frightening people wasn't all it had been cracked up to be in the fifties. Audiences used to *Star Wars* and *Close Encounters of the Third Kind* weren't impressed, but one scene shot at Wembley showing the future of football – a gladiatorial conquest with players fighting on the pitch while supporters battled on the terraces – lingered in the mind.

The BAFTA award-winning play that year was Dennis Potter's **'Blue Remembered Hills'** for BBC1 which was a stunningly effective portrayal of children, not as innocents, but as small versions of the adults they are to become. It also showed adults as nothing more than large children. Seven-year-olds were played by actors and actresses well past the age of consent and, in the case of porky Colin Welland, far from small. (Can we ever forget those thighs in short trousers?) Helen Mirren, Michael Elphick, Colin Jeavons and John Bird, among many, were comically horrific.

Yorkshire Television began their comedy about three patients spending an eternity in a hospital ward. **'Only When I Laugh'** (which wasn't often) starred James Bolam, Peter Bowles and Christopher Strauli, with Richard Wilson as the pompous doctor. **'Metal Mickey'** was a children's comedy series about a household in which the most intelligent resident was a robot. It starred the incomparable Irene Handl, so we wouldn't dream of suggesting MM should have been melted down. **'In Loving Memory'** was Yorkshire's comedy about a woman undertaker and her idiotic nephew assistant set in the late 1920s. As a vehicle for talented Thora Hird, it was a bit of a hearse, but Christopher Beeny, boyishly beaming as the nephew, won many fans. **'Rings on Their Fingers'** was a Richard Waring comedy for the BBC starring Diane Keen and Martin Jarvis as a couple who lived together and eventually married. Guess what? She wanted to, he didn't. Needless to say it went top of feminists' hiss-lists. **'Pig in the Middle'** was wittier but sillier. Terence Brady wrote it for LWT with Liza Goddard playing a mistress and Joanna Van Gyseghem a wife. Dinsdale Landen was the dotty ditherer they both wanted, but few could see why. Later Terence Brady himself played the part. Ditto.

'Turtle's Progress' was ATV's under-rated quirky comedy drama about two crooks (John Landry and Michael Attwell) who unwittingly stole a hoard of safety-deposit boxes. They opened one per episode. Better was **'Ripping Yarns'**, Michael Palin's comic dramas for the BBC, sending up *Boy's Own* stories.

'Question Time' began in 1979. Sir Robin Day was asked to do for BBC television what 'Any Questions' had been doing for radio for years: put a foursome of politicians, serious journalists, trade unionists and other presentable experts on a platform and let an audience quiz them. He was told it would last six months but ten years on he is still barking at panellists and 'the lady at the back in blue'.

Sir Harold Wilson seemed to have forgiven the BBC for 'Yesterday's Men' by 1979. He agreed to be the host of a late informal discussion-show, **'Friday Night Saturday Morning'**, for two weeks. His main guest was Tony Benn. Parkinson and Harty were not eating their hearts out.

It was a sad year for **'Crossroads'** fans. The IBA ordered the number of episodes a week to be cut from four to three the following year on the grounds that it would give the producers more time to improve the standards. It just gave the writers time to squeeze in such everyday events as Lynda Welch's murder, for which Benny was charged but later found innocent, and Hugh Mortimer's kidnapping by a gang of international terrorists led by David Hunter's son Chris who had just married Diane to inherit his grandmother's money. Hugh died in captivity (from disbelief). In **'Coronation Street'** little Tracey Langton, only one year old was feared killed when a lorry-driver had a heart-attack at the wheel and ploughed into the pub. Had she known how rarely she'd be seen over the next ten years, she might have volunteered. As it was, Deirdre found her at a friend's house. Gail made the mistake of marrying Brian Tilsley, but Elsie came back from her long absence in time for Christmas.

The spectacular documentary series that year was Sir David Attenborough's thirteen-part BBC series **'Life on Earth'** about the arrival of living species. The series was made with 1.25 *million* feet of film shot in thirty countries, and the team travelled 1½ million miles over three years. The hard work paid off. The series was rightly hailed as a television masterpiece. Thames Television's thirteen-part series **'Hollywood'** by Kevin Brownlow earned similar praise from film buffs. For the BBC, Magnus Magnusson's history of **'The Vikings'** and architect Alec Clifton-Taylor's **'Six English Towns'** (which became another six the following year) were much enjoyed. **'Fred Dibnah, Steeplejack'**, showed life from a set of tall chimneys, and a whimsical seven-part series followed in 1982.

While Kenneth Kendall was reading the early-evening news one day in June, one of his front teeth dropped unceremoniously on to his script. He carried on. But Reggie Bosanquet quit 'News at Ten'. Co-presenter Anna Ford wished him 'Good luck, old bean'.

The hour-long obituary film for Earl Mountbatten shown by the BBC twice on the anniversary of his death, 27 August, made history. It included his own thoughts about his death which, with a sad irony, he had recorded earlier that year. He told Ludovic Kennedy how he wished for a peaceful end (he was killed by an IRA bomb) and mentioned the hymns he'd chosen for his funeral and the guests who would be asked.

Commercial Break

Sir Robert Mark, the newly retired Commissioner of the Metropolitan Police, made commercials that year. How many more Goodyear tyres were sold because he said they made a major contribution to road safety is unclear, but agents weren't hammering on his door. The fee for the first one, £135,000, he gave to charity; but his fees for a new series, of about £50,000, he reportedly kept. 'The time has come to think of my own needs,' he said. 'It is not often a policeman can be a philanthropist.' Much jollier was the Hamlet cigar commercial showing a golfer in a bunker discovering happiness in a smoke. People were ordered to Get the Abbey Habit and invest with Abbey National Building Society. Harry Secombe extolled the joys of Woolworth's ('what what what!'). Barbara Murray was seen in a supermarket (with a caption to say who she was) buying Fairy Liquid, and a series of people started telling us not to leave home without an American Express card. Marie Helvin, photographed by her then husband David Bailey, looked fetching in Goggles sunglasses, and we were given forty-five seconds' worth of poetry on behalf of Foster Grant sunglasses: 'Foster Grants, Foster Grants, frosty glance, Foster Grants, Fist of Prince, flustered faints, lost gendarme. Foster Grants, boss of France, imposter aunts, lotsadents, twisty gents, greased her palm, pots of plants, foster grunts, Foster Grants, tasty tarts, takes a bath, sits on path, busts her front, fussed we aren't. Foster Grants, forced a grin, Foster Grants.'

I f the sixties were television's age of awkward adolescence – at times impishly outrageous, at others painfully serious – the seventies saw television reap its rewards in talent, get its act together and grow up.

It was the decade in which ITV became respectable, competing with the BBC in producing high-quality costume drama and creating British biff-bash buddies, Regan and Carter, Bodie and Doyle, Arthur and Terry, heroes we watched and watched with such intense enjoyment it almost melted the screen.

At the BBC the job was to pretend not to care that Aunty's shows were low in the ratings, to forge ahead in factual series, to maintain the decent standards of middle-brow drama such as 'The Duchess of Duke Street' and 'Shoestring' and to indulge in those favourite pastimes of middle age: moaning about money and slapping down the young by banning their work now and then. Probably their greatest achievement in that decade was to encourage and foster exceptionally good humour in situation comedies, 'Porridge' and 'The Good Life' probably topping the list, so that these series written and acted with such commitment became golden oldies, regularly reshown over the next fifteen years.

Bill Cotton, son of bandleader Billy, born and raised in a television-studio trunk, worked with Val Doonican, Cilla Black and Kathy Kirby in the days when producing live television was 'like being a Spitfire pilot, everyone thinking one was terribly in the front line, in the trenches and all that lark'. He rose to become the BBC's Head of Light Entertainment Group during the seventies and became Controller of BBC1 in 1977. Not everyone at Television Centre approved of his sometimes brash tactics, and he puts his rapid promotion down to the fact that ITV, which early on grabbed over 70 per cent of the viewing audience in some regions, had shattered the BBC's confidence in its more orthodox methods.

His style worked, and coups such as stealing Morecambe and Wise from the enemy were almost as satisfying as getting back in a Spitfire. He hadn't hung about after Michael Grade, then a boss of London Artists, the comedians' agents, rang him to say he felt they were being 'taken for granted' at ATV. 'I'd watched a few of their shows and I thought they were quite good, very good, but no one was trying to improve them. Eric Morecambe needed more time to expand,' Bill recalls. 'So I saw them and made them an offer they couldn't refuse. It was a three-year contract. I forget how much, but it frightened the life out of the BBC. I explained to them that we'd be paying through the nose for the first year, by the second year it would be about right and by the third we'd have the biggest bargain ever. I was right, because by the

Barbara and Tom (Felicity Kendal and Richard Briers) tried to be self-sufficient in 'The Good Life' but needed Margo (Penelope Keith) and Jerry (Paul Eddington), possibly hiding at the golf-club, to stay funny.

third year Morecambe and Wise were so big they could have asked five times the fees.'

Eric and Ernie left the BBC for Thames for more money and – it is generally accepted – worse shows when Bill became Controller. 'Eric was reported as saying, "Well, Bill Cotton has looked after himself; I think we should take the money and run," and it was awful – like a divorce,' said Bill. 'We got on all right after that, but it was never the same.'

Probably his best day's work was bringing Ronnie Barker and Ronnie Corbett back to the BBC and keeping them some of the time together, some of the time apart. The two comedians had gone from the BBC with David Frost to support him on his 'Frost on Friday', 'Frost on Saturday', 'Frost on Sunday' shows for LWT. Bill watched them at a BAFTA awards ceremony. 'All the machinery had broken down, and they just came forward and did something together off the cuff,' Bill remembers. 'Paul Fox, who was running BBC1 then, was sitting next to me, and I said, "How would you like them on your network for the next three years?" Naturally he said he would. So I spoke to David Frost and then made Ronnie Corbett and Ronnie Barker the offer of a show together and a situation comedy each, both of which would be repeated for three years – something we could do because we had two channels. ITV couldn't match that. The boys agreed, and it worked out very well.'

The Ronnies were perhaps *the* comedy discovery of the seventies, inventive, intelligent, bouncy and bawdy; and 'Porridge', starring Ronnie Barker, was perhaps *the* sitcom of all time.

A Dutch housewife devised 'Een Van de Acht', which became *the* game-show of all time, 'The Generation Game', and begat Brucie of the jutting chin, *the* host we hate to love. But 1971 also promoted another long-distance runner. Cilla Black, buck-toothed songstress, chatter-box and professional Scouser, starred in live Saturday-night variety shows, at one point turning up with a camera crew to knock on someone's front door. The scenes she disturbed sometimes resembled Benny Hill sketches: a chap came out blinking on to his balcony in shirt-tails, followed by someone else's wife wrapped in a sheet; one of her most famous 'Come on, luv, it's Cilla 'ere' intrusions brought her into a room where a number of embarrassed men sat on rows of chairs and gave terse replies to her jolly questions. They were customers at the local brothel.

The BBC took risks knowingly, too. Michael Crawford in 'Some Mothers Do 'Ave 'Em' dangled over cliffs, jumped on moving trains and did other stunts which would today give insurance men a cardiac arrest. A top BBC official loathed John Inman's mincing Mr 'I'm free!' Humphries and told 'Are You Being Served?' producer David Croft: 'Get rid of the poof!' Croft is alleged to have replied: 'If the poof goes, *I* go.' The poof stayed, and 'Are You Being Served?' was a slapstick success for eleven years.

Some classics were nearly dumped. Bill Cotton remembers his doubts about John Cleese's plan to write a comedy about a hotel based on the one the 'Monty Python' team used in Torquay, 'Fawlty Towers'. Some were funny peculiar. 'The Fall and Rise of Reginald Perrin' kept office workers sane and may have inspired politician John Stonehouse to fake his suicide by drowning. Another, 'The Good Life', changed Britain. It killed off herbaceous borders for self-sufficiency spuds and chicken-coops in back gardens everywhere.

In drama ITV took centre stage – it had the cash. The BBC could do its duty shaving Glenda Jackson's front hair for a gutsy 'Elizabeth R', stiffening the upper lips of David McCallum, Jack Hedley and many others as they kept wartime peckers up in 'Colditz'. Later 'Secret Army' kept the war dramatically if not spectacularly alive. They also prepared us for full-strength biological soap opera by delivering regular doses of 'The Brothers', their feuding families and Jean Hammond's dragon mother who dominated them. I wonder if Mrs Thatcher was a fan? Anyway, it was no wonder we fell for 'Dallas' in 1978.

But dominating the first half of the decade was 'Upstairs Downstairs', the beautifully set soapy saga of Edwardian nobs and their salt-of-the-earth servants in Belgravia. 'Edward the Seventh' and the far-better-than anyone-expected 'Jesus of Nazareth' proved that Sir Lew at ATV understood about quality, too. When he added the Muppets to his list in 1976 he really made the grade.

There were celebrated controversies. Former Prime Minister Sir Harold Wilson decided the BBC's current-affairs department was biased after David Dimbleby in a '24 Hours' report entitled 'Yesterday's Men' asked him about the money he had received for writing his memoirs. Sir Harold replied that Dimbleby should ask how some people (meaning his successor, Edward Heath) afforded yachts. The question was edited out after a row which was greatly enjoyed by the press, as were the banning of two plays a few years later. In 1976 the BBC's managing director Alasdair Milne found the scene in Dennis Potter's 'Brimstone and Treacle' of a devil-man raping a brain-damaged girl 'repugnant' and stopped transmission. Two years later Bill Cotton refused to screen Roy Minton's 'Play for Today' about boys in a corruptly run borstal, 'Scum'. He thought it horribly violent and worried about one scene in particular where a boy places three snooker balls in a sock and cold-bloodedly hits another with it before running away.

The best rumpus accompanied the showing of 'The Family', the BBC's fly-on-the-wall series about a Reading bus-driver's crowded home. Never could a casting director have found a gutsier leading lady than Margaret Wilkins, who was Peggy Mount, Mildred Roper and Lou Beale rolled together. Her liberal attitudes to her sexually active daughters, her confession that her younger son was the product of an affair with a dustman and many other 'secrets' disgusted middle-class viewers. How *could* the Corporation make stars of people who were so . . . so . . . *common*?

Abroad the BBC's reputation was high. Alistair Cooke's 'America' did better than at home, as did the stunning documentary series 'The Ascent of Man' which drained its writer-presenter, the colossus of 'The Brain's Trust', Jacob Bronowski. But the traffic was heavier the other way across the Atlantic in the seventies, a trend deplored by some. Detectives of all shapes and hairiness wore out car tyres and took pot-shots at criminals, and most of us cheered. Starsky and Hutch, Kojak, Cannon, Columbo, Rockford – Bill Cotton makes no apology for it. 'There is a certain type of show the Americans do magnificently, and there were loads of them then,' he said. 'We knew if they'd done well in America and we bought them we could rope them down for twenty-six weeks and build a schedule of programmes for the evening round them. It's very mealy-mouthed of people always to talk about American rubbish.' They also imported the best-ever comedy about the craziness of war, 'M*A*S*H', from 1973. No one dared call that rubbish.

In the seventies there was more of everything. Restrictions were lifted so that the lunchtimes and afternoons could be filled with programmes to amuse the ladies. 'Pebble Mill at One' became an institution, cosy, newsy, dull, but better than a Cup-a-Soup alone. Yorkshire Television's 'Emmerdale Farm' amused women so well it has remained the most cultured twice-weekly soap opera on the screen, followed faithfully despite being moved from slot to slot day to day.

Through it all, as Bill Cotton saw it, the ITV companies made programmes to get money and the BBC got money to make programmes. It was never enough money, and Fleet Street (then perhaps the most inefficient and extravagant industry in Britain) repeatedly attacked the BBC for misspending. 'I always used to say we did a damn sight better than most people trying to make television throughout the world,' he said. 'There was always the feeling that if you had money you could do it better. But that's as it should be. The worst thing anyone could say to a producer was "Have all the money and resources you want". He usually ended up in the funny farm.'

THE
EIGHTIES

1980

Soviet forces invaded Afghanistan. □ War broke out between Iran and Iraq. □ Greenham Common and Molesworth were named as storage sites for nuclear missiles, and the long protests of the Greenham Common women began. □ The offshore platform Alexander Keilland *collapsed to cause the first North Sea oil disaster: 147 workers died. □ Special Air Services men rescued nineteen hostages held in the Iranian embassy after two hostages were executed. □ The Moscow Olympics were boycotted by forty-five nations because of Afghanistan. □ Ronald Reagan became President of the United States of America. □ Poland's striking shipyard workers formed Solidarity with Lech Walesa as leader. □ John Lennon was shot dead by Mark Chapman in New York. □ A simulated homosexual rape scene in the play* The Romans in Britain *at the National Theatre caused outrage. □ Peter Sellers, Steve McQueen and Alfred Hitchcock died. □ Sixpences went out, Sony Walkmans came in. □ Unemployment topped 2 million, and Mrs Thatcher vowed: 'The lady's not for turning.'*

If the bloody and depressing events in the world in 1980 had merely been on video-tape, it would have made sense to record on top. The same could be said for much of the output on television. Drama gave art a miss, laughing seemed to be on ration, and the one new star to emerge was over seventy, wagged her finger at us, sounded like Margaret Rutherford, trained dogs and brought people to heel.

What Britain didn't need was a big public row with Saudi Arabia; but to everyone's surprise **'Death of a Princess'**, an ATV dramatised documentary film by Anthony Thomas about the public execution of a princess who'd adopted some Western ideas and thereby questioned the strict traditional Islamic way of life, brought the worst one yet. No television programme had ever caused a stink like it. The two-hour film was shown in April. It had actors and actresses playing witnesses describing life under Islam (Saudi Arabia was never mentioned). Egyptian actress Suzanne Abou Taleb played Princess Misha'al as a Joan of Arc who went to the stake for women's rights, Judy Parfitt played a German nanny telling how women were cooped up in palaces all day watching foreign videos ('We must have seen *The Sound of Music* twelve times,' she said), Paul Freeman played the film-maker (called Ryder) asking questions about how and why such reactionary régimes were supported and something as barbaric as this happened.

It turned out that ATV had refused the Saudis' request for the film to be withdrawn or a sequence – believed to be the one in which veiled women in chauffeur-driven cars cruised around picking up men – cut out. It led to the British ambassador in Jeddah being sent home, King Khaled cancelling his plan to visit Britain that summer and £200 million in exports being lost. Diplomatic relations were restored at the end of July after Foreign Secretary Lord Carrington condemned the film and did what was generally seen as a bit of 'grovelling' to the Arabs.

But the story of the princess's death in 1977 (allegedly for taking a young student lover who was also shot) had not been new. A British carpenter had witnessed it, and his photographs appeared in British newspapers. Anthony Thomas, a film-maker with a reputation for passionate concern (his 'The South African Experience' was widely praised), heard the story from a minister of an Arab state and began four months of research, interviewing the carpenter, the German nanny who had known the princess and people at the university in Beirut where she had studied. He also travelled extensively in Saudi Arabia, noting the extremes of poverty and wealth, never pretending to understand this culture, and aware that he was becoming obsessed with a dead girl who had become a folk-hero.

As if the political rumpus was not enough, a controversy raged in the letters columns of *The Times* and the *New Statesman* between Thomas and novelist Penelope Mortimer who had been involved early in the making of the film but had disagreed with some of Thomas's decisions and dropped out. She wrote saying the interviews in the film were 'fabrications' and later, when challenged, wrote that she had not meant they were 'invented' but simply that they should have made a feature film so that the evidence wouldn't have to be defended. Her original remarks were reprinted in American newspaper advertisements placed by Mobil urging the Public Broadcasting Service there not to show the film. Looking back recently, Anthony Thomas said: 'It was all slightly farcical. These drastic things were happening yet a number of Arabs were telephoning me to apologise. I was assured there was a lot of play-acting going on.'

And was 'Death of a Princess' a good film? Was it 'unforgivable' as the Saudi spokesman said? More confused than controversial, critics seemed to agree, and not even the *Sunday Telegraph*, that most right-wing of newspapers, could detect malice towards the Saudis. We would suggest that it is still essential viewing for any Western woman planning to live under Islam.

Around September people began reporting nightmares about a weird bespectacled man in long shorts carrying a golf umbrella on a beach in Sri Lanka spouting in convoluted sentences about such phenomena as Big Foot the Abominable Snowman, showers of frogs and why prehistoric man bothered to build Stonehenge. It was Arthur C. Clarke, science-fiction writer and Thinker, with a large supporting cast of loonies in his thirteen-part ITV series 'Arthur C. Clarke's Mysterious World'. His message almost always turned out to be that there is a logical explanation to the unexplained, but the main response from viewers was 'Uh?'

The execution scene in 'Death of a Princess' cut off diplomatic relations with Saudi Arabia.

There were breakthroughs that year. Two programmes explored the myths, problems and concerns of homosexuals. London Weekend ran **'Gay Life'**, an eleven-part series which investigated touchy subjects such as the attitude of security services towards homosexuals; and a few months later BBC2 showed **'Coming Out'**, about five gay men who were seen kissing. The programme was followed by a *vox pop* in which an Alf Garnett type denounced homosexuals as filthy abominable beings in league with the devil.

There was also a brave and disturbing account of life in an overcrowded Victorian prison in Britain, shown in the best documentary series of 1980, Rex Bloomstein's **'Strangeways'**. As the rows over the BBC2 1978 series 'Law and Order' subsided, the Home Office gave Bloomstein and his team permission to go inside for three months, film interviews in cells and capture all the noises, frustrations, miseries and – almost – the rancid smells. The eight-part fly-on-the-wall series was shown as prison officers began a dispute about their working conditions and should have dispelled for ever the notion that prison is a sort of Butlin's with bars. One episode followed an illiterate suicidal young housebreaker who complained he had been assaulted by a warder for taking too much bread. He was charged for making false allegations and sent to the punishment-block. The camera caught him, stripped naked in a padded cell banging his plastic bedpan against the wall. No commentary was needed. Bloomstein had said at the start: 'If you don't feel that what you've seen is so bad and so disgusting, I shall be bitterly sad.' Nine million viewers agreed prisons like these were hopeless places, but little has changed.

Another closed institution, a boys' boarding school, was examined that year in a BBC2 documentary series, **'Public School'**. The school chosen was Radley College near Oxford, and the series tackled such sensitive subjects as homosexuality and alcoholism and made a star of the warden Dennis Silk. While a good proportion of viewers raged against Radley, this bastion of privilege, the number of enquiries for entries to the school tripled.

Deliberate mystification, a weapon used by civil servants to bring politicians to heel, was the main joke of the year's best new comedy, **'Yes, Minister'**. The witty and cynical version of how we get governed was written by Anthony Jay and Jonathan Lynn. Jay had worked on the 'Tonight' programme and chatted to politicians after the programmes. He picked up much of the jargon (such phrases as 'going native', used when a minister had become indistinguishable from civil servants) and learned of the battle tactics. For instance, it seems that civil servants see that ministers get too much work so that they can then take it off their hands for them and craftily take control. But ministers can fight back, giving the kiss of death to a civil servant's scheme by publicly calling it either 'controversial' or 'courageous'. The pair also drew on the Crossman diaries and used several 'moles' in Whitehall and the Commons to keep the scripts remarkably topical.

Paul Eddington, as James Hacker, MP, newly appointed Minister of Administrative Affairs, should have been top dog, but Permanent Under-Secretary Sir Humphrey Appleby – he of the sixty-six-word sentences – played deliciously by Nigel Hawthorne, was far more devious. Flitting nervously between them was Derek Fowlds as private secretary Bernard. The BBC2 series shown in February was repeated in October, having become a great success with viewers and won several awards as the year's best sitcom. Politicians and civil servants were flattered by it, and it was soon tagged 'Mrs Thatcher's favourite programme'. After three series, Jim Hacker was elevated to Prime Minister – it was a shock as much to him as to the electorate – and **'Yes, Prime Minister'** was even more accurate. The show had the good luck to screen an episode in which Hacker fell out with his defence secretary the same day that Michael Heseltine resigned from that post in the Government. Honours rained on it. At the awards ceremony in 1984 of the National Association of Listeners and Viewers, Mrs Thatcher 'starred' in a scene with Paul Eddington (the script was written by her press secretary), and by 1985 the series had been sold to forty-five countries, including China. Everyone involved was delighted when Paul and Nigel were each awarded CBEs in the 1986 New Year's Honours (although some felt the writers deserved more of the credit) but the fifth series in 1987 was the last. The actors and the writers wanted to resign from office before they lost the viewers' votes.

Meanwhile the phone-lines were hot between Michael Grade, then LWT's Head of Light Entertainment, and ATV's Programme Controller, Francis Essex. Grade had acquired the rights to the American show 'Card Sharks' – to become 'Play Your Cards Right' – and knew Essex had the rights to a much better game, 'Family Feud' – to become **'Family Fortunes'**. Grade told Essex how well he thought Bob Monkhouse would get on with 'Card Sharks'. Bob recalls: 'He added: "By the way, I'm stuck with Bruce Forsyth and I've got to find something for him. He thinks he can do something with 'Family Feud'. He's a crab if you ask me, but I'll swap."' Essex laughed and told Grade it was just the sort of trick his father Leslie would have tried and he wouldn't have got away with it, either.

Both game-shows began in 1980 and did well – 'Family Fortunes' did very well with over 14 million regular viewers. Here two family teams answered questions about the answers other people would give, as calculated on a computer called Mr Babbage (after the inventor of the first computer in 1837). Viewers and contestants were baffled at first, but soon cottoned on, although some of the answers given ended up on the cutting-room floor. Two of those were: 'What do little children miss most on holiday?'

– 'The toilet', and 'Apart from the Grand Prix, name a dangerous race' – 'Arabs'. One show pitted members of the two aristocratic families of Lords Bath and Montagu against each other. It taught viewers a few things about how the other half lives. Question: 'Name a high-street store.' Answer: 'Harrods.' Question: 'What kind of birds do you see in your garden?' Answer: 'Peacocks.' Max Bygraves took over from Bob in 1983. He found all that explaining somewhat taxing but enjoyed reminding contestants that they could win 'Big Money'. One contestant won a cassette-recorder. Max proudly gave her a *Singalonga-max* LP and said: 'Here's some music to play on it!' Perhaps she's still trying to slot it in. In 1987, Les Dennis took over the job.

'Play Your Cards Right' turned up trumps for Bruce Forsyth. There was no shortage of the sort of contestants happy to behave on television as they might on the last night of a Club 18–30 holiday, and apparently there were 13 million viewers who could stand the 'higher' and 'lower' shouting from Rent-a-mob audiences as contestants had to say if a card was greater or smaller than the previous one. The game relied upon market research which discovered the answer to such vital questions as 'How many people out of one hundred think Bo Derek is flat-chested?', but they stirred up trouble with the 'Crossroads' producers when the correct answer to how many actresses out of one hundred would accept a part in the much-mocked soap turned out to be only slightly more than half. It seemed that 43 per cent said they wouldn't go near it. By 1987 the game's audience had dropped to 8 million and Bruce decided to quit.

There were several television 'events' in 1980. The ITV companies had to reapply for their franchises. Southern and Westward lost out to TVS and TSW, and the following Year Lord Grade's ATV acquired a new board and Central took over in the Midlands. Thames Television held the first telethon, ten hours of fund-raising live programmes which netted £1.25 million for charity. Australia wanted Michael Parkinson and got him for £3.5 million. And **'Dallas'** 'fever' erupted on both sides of the Atlantic. Who shot J. R. Ewing was an issue kept hot for six months by newspapers and bookies who gave odds on the guilt of the six or more possible suspects. It had started when the producers of the two-year-old soap wanted another two episodes and devised a cliffhanger which nearly hung the show. The fever among viewers peaked in November when the episode revealing who it was (Kristen, Sue Ellen's sister, for the record) was watched by 27.3 million in Britain (3.3 million more than had watched the original shooting episode). Around the world an estimated 500 million saw it. The culprit was even named as a main item in the BBC's 'Nine O'Clock News'. But in the mean time Larry Hagman, who played JR, had seen the story-line as a chance to play the wheeler-dealer for real. He wanted four times his then salary and a percentage of the merchandis-

ing profits. He flew to Britain for interviews and was not present when the rest of the cast gathered to film new episodes. The angry producers leaked rumours that a new actor might take over the rôle (Robert Culp's name was mentioned) or that they may let JR die, but they quickly backtracked and paid their incomparable star most of what he asked.

In 1980 people came to believe that Barbara Woodhouse in her woolly tartan kilt and sensible shoes, who at seventy seemed to have the sparky energy and high spirits of a puppy, could do almost anything. She endeared herself to dogs and to Englishmen – particularly those who yearned for Nanny's firm hand.

Barbara Woodhouse made sure she got what she asked for and became a huge star in the process. When she began her **'Training Dogs the Woodhouse Way'** series on BBC1 she was described as the 'best entertainment since Morecambe and Wise', and what was meant as a further educational series became a cult hit. She received 300 fan letters a day and believed that even dogs watched her shows, drawn to the screen by telepathy and the tone of her voice – which was Joyce Grenfell crossed with Lady Bracknell. To prove it she gave commands over a radio link to Australia, and apparently 6,000 miles away they obeyed her instructions to 'Sit!' and 'Wait!' Her BBC LP sold in thousands.

A doctor's wife who began by training horses, went to agricultural college and had written seventeen books, she had made a comfortable living from her star Great Danes Juno and Junia, who'd worked with David Niven, Clark Gable, Douglas Fairbanks, Jnr, and Roger Moore among many. Her 1980s dog Junior could open windows, ring the gong, vacuum the carpet, strip the beds of dirty linen and put it in a basket, water the garden with a hosepipe and answer the phone by taking off the receiver and fetching its mistress. She had no time for bad owners who were so much slower at picking things up at training sessions than their pets. But dog fights broke out between her and other trainers who said she was barking up the wrong tree by using a choke-chain. The RSPCA also claimed such chains could be cruel. This hardly seemed to affect her popularity. A few dogs didn't rate her at first – Ted Willis's Labrador Lucky bit her hand, and she once needed sixty-two stitches after trying to prise a bulldog off her arm. But most dogs fell under her spell. She was their supreme champion until she died in 1988. As she told Michael Parkinson, who asked what we should do if we saw a dog fouling a public place: 'Take the nearest heavy object, like a book or a rolled-up newspaper and give the culprit a hefty smack on the head,' she said. 'Hit the dog?' asked the surprised Parkie. 'No, silly boy, the owner,' she said.

Commercial Break

It was a good year for commercials. Leonard Rossiter poured Cinzano over Joan Collins; David Niven drank Maxwell House coffee; Twiggy told us that 'You meet the nicest people on a Honda'; Ronnie Barker relied on his Sekonda watch; Singapore Airlines were a 'great way to fly', they said; and various men asked each other if a pretty girl was or was not wearing Harmony hair-spray. PG Tips went to work with a troupe of Italian circus chimps in Italy and introduced a chimp with the voice of Michael Jayston saying: 'My name is Bond, Brooke Bond.' And we heard that the Midland was the 'listening' bank, the credibility of which was lost after a twenty-year-old student was arrested when she went to see her bank manager about an overdraft. In another commercial we learned that if we were kept waiting ages to be served it was probably because the cashier was having a 'Condor moment'. That year Guinness ran a series of commercials with a toucan, but a commercial for toilet paper being made in the Hebrides was wrecked when the star, Hercules the 54-stone grizzly bear, went missing and played hide and seek with thirty-three soldiers and two helicopters for several days until caught by a marksman with a tranquilliser dart.

Also Shown in 1980

Actor-writer Peter Tilbury created **'Shelley'**, a comedy almost in the Hancockian style, featuring the wit and wisdom of a university dropout (Hywel Bennett) who lived mostly on social security and other people's good nature. Thames Television's other new comedy that year was the soppy **'Keep It in the Family'**, starring Robert Gillespie as a cartoonist working from home with Pauline Yates as his standard good-egg wife and Stacy Dorning and Jenny Quayle (later Sabina Franklyn) as standard sitcom bubbly teenage children. **'Holding the Fort'** wasted the talents of Peter Davison and Patricia Hodge in a comedy about an executive who stayed home to run his brewery and mind the kids while the wife went back to army work. **'Young at Heart'** by ATV was an even more tragic waste of Sir John Mills as an ever so 'umble pottery worker facing retirement with Megs Jenkins as his wife. Far more rewarding was Arthur Lowe's pensioner **Potter** in a short-lived series written by Roy Clarke for the BBC. Potter was cantankerous, pompous, bossy with his wife (played by Noel Dyson) and more of a pest than a pal to John Barron as the local vicar.

Other ITV comedies that year – **'Cowboys'** with Roy Kinnear, **'Just Liz'** with Rodney Bewes, **'Rushton's Illustrated'** and **'Grundy'** – are best forgotten. In **'Nobody's Perfect'**, Elaine Stritch introduced Richard Griffiths as her fat frumpy GP husband. Richard, at thirty-three, was far too young for her, and the series far too soft; but it was Oscar Wilde compared with ATV's **'Doctors' Daughters'**, almost certainly the worst comedy series ever made.

'Girl Talk' should have helped people accept the idea of women as comedians, but this six-part sketch series starring straight actresses including Carol Royle and Frances Cuka, making fun of men and reversing sexist jokes, was only moderately entertaining.

There was nothing shocking about the **Royal Variety Show** except the energy of some of the performers. The combined ages of the thirteen hoofers for Flanagan and Allen's 'Strollin'', in front of the Queen Mother (80) totalled 891 years. Making up the oldest chorus-line ever were Billy Dainty (53), Chesney Allen (86), Stanley Holloway (90), Sandy Powell (80), Arthur Askey (80), Richard Murdoch (72), Tommy Trinder (71), Cyril Fletcher (66), Ben Warriss (69), Charlie Chester (66), Arthur English (61), Charlie Drake (54) and the baby, Roy Hudd (43).

The comedian of 1980 was the lanky loon with the nice smile, Russ Abbot. He was one of the few good things to come out of **'Bruce Forsyth's Big Night'**, and LWT had the sense to sign him for **'Variety Madhouse'** with Freddie Starr. The title was soon changed to **'Russ Abbot's Madhouse'**, and his characters – the weakling superman Cooperman, the Tyrolean Fritz Crackers, bungling flyer Boggles, Jimmy the incomprehensible Scot, and teddy boy Vince Prince among many – became firm favourites.

In 1980, Geoffrey Wheeler devised **'Winner Takes All'**, a gambling quiz which Jimmy Tarbuck kept successful until 1987. Geoffrey himself took it over after that.

It was the year of the woman police officer. The BBC's drama series appeared to be about someone called **Juliet Bravo**, but this, we learned, was a call-sign. Jean Darblay (Stephanie Turner) was the heroine, a police inspector in a small Lancashire town called Hartley, a place where most crimes seemed to be solved with a nice cup of tea. By 1983 she had been promoted, and Inspector Kate Longdon (Anna Carteret) took over and had to fight prejudice against women all over again. A policewoman's lot was not a happy one in Hartley or in Seven Dials, the beat of Detective Inspector Maggie Forbes in LWT's **'The Gentle Touch'**, otherwise known as 'The Feeble Touch'. The series attempted to show more of the home life of its heroine (it seemed there wasn't the budget for exciting cops-and-robbers action), but the thing about Maggie (played by Jill Gascoine) was that she was always in a bad mood. There was also the problem that Jill couldn't drive, so she was always seen at the wheel of a stationary car. In 1985 Maggie moved to TVS's 'CATS Eyes'.

The serial which picked up a BAFTA award for the BBC was **'To Serve Them All My Days'**, about a First World War shattered idealist who took a job in a private school and became a kind of left-wing Mr Chips. But the serial everyone was talking about that year was **'Mackenzie'**, based on a sex-and-guilt novel by Andrea Newman, which starred Jack Galloway as a small Scottish builder with over-active hormones. The production was said to be something of a breakthrough in terms of censorship – and managed to carry on panting even though Jack's false moustache came unstuck at a crucial moment between BBC sheets.

'**Thérèse Raquin**', which starred Kate Nelligan in long white drawers, was actually far more sexy. Thanks to Terry Wogan's comments on radio, the BBC2 four-parter became a cult and helped to win Kate a Best Actress award. '**The Martian Chronicles**', a three-part co-production with American and German companies, won the BBC no praise but a row with Equity that the BBC's £300,000 cut could have been better spent on home-made drama. It was interesting nevertheless to watch Rock Hudson, then fifty-four, in a fetching tight-fitting two-piece as a spacecraft commander of 1999.

Malta played Mars, although gales kept blowing away the sets, and bald, earless Martians probably did nothing for America's Space programme that year. The series did wonders for Hudson's bank balance though. Despite his 60 films he had been practically broke before it.

The best Thames serial that year was '**Fox**', the story of a South London Godfather's large family who disintegrate on his death and then gradually come together again. The thirteen-part story starring Peter Vaughan and Elizabeth Spriggs never made the top twenty despite being given the Monday 9 p.m. slot but it was compelling drama all the same.

No warm reception, either, for Thames Television's '**Love in a Cold Climate**', an attempt to re-create Nancy Mitford's books about her eccentric family in the twenties. Not even the skills of Judi Dench and Michael Williams could save this arch and empty effort. The other family saga that year was '**Funny Man**' in which Jimmy Jewel starred in a thirteen-part series about a music-hall family act based on his own father's company in the twenties and thirties. Similarly unsuccessful was '**Flickers**', ATV's drama series written by Roy Clarke, tracing the life of a brash movie pioneer in the silent film days before the First World War. '**Bulman**' began as a series that year with Don Henderson as the glove-wearing, nasal-inhaler-using, plastic-bag-carrying copper first seen in '**The XYY Man**'. One of his gimmicks, his scarf, hid the burns from throat cancer treatment. The fact that Bulman sometimes talked only in a whisper, put down in the script to a cold, was also due to the disease. Luckily it's cured.

Outstanding among the plays was Stephen Poliakoff's stylishly made '**Caught on a Train**' for the BBC. Michael Kitchen was an arrogant young businessman and Peggy Ashcroft a haughty Viennese widow travelling between Ostend and Vienna. '**The Sailor's Return**' starred Tom Bell as a sea-captain who returned from Africa in 1858 with an African princess as his bride with whom he planned to run a country inn. Nigerian Shope Shoedeinde was the beautiful Princess Tulip. As a tale of period prejudice and cruelty it was well done but deeply depressing. '**Bloody Kids**', a Sunday-night special from ATV was even more depressing. It had rock star Gary Holton (later of 'Auf Wiedersehen Pet' fame) as Ken, a drug-crazed thief and vandal leading two eleven-year-old runaway boys through a night of madness. Holton said at the time that his life had been like Ken's until he stopped taken drugs. His freedom from them was short-lived, though. He died from them in 1985.

'**Knots Landing**', the American series David Jacobs sketched out before '**Dallas**', arrived in Britain in 1980. It was a saga of five neighbouring families – one of them Ewing poor relations who live in a cul-de-sac in the hills in California.

In '**Coronation Street**' that year Emily married Arnold Swain, who was later unmasked as a bigamist, and Gail and Brian Tilsley had their first son, Nicky. In '**Crossroads**' David Hunter was shot and wounded by his mad ex-wife Rosemary, who was jealous of his engagement to Barbara.

1981

That Was the Year When...

Prince Charles married Lady Diana Spencer as 700 million people watched on television. □ Pope John Paul II was shot four times in the stomach by Turkish assassin Mehmet Ali Agca while driving in his open car through St Peter's Square. □ Ronald Reagan was shot in the chest by disc jockey John Hinckley as he left a Washington hotel. □ Egypt's leader Anwar Sadat was shot by Islamic extremists at a military parade in Cairo. □ The Pope and the President survived; Sadat was killed. □ Race riots erupted in Brixton, Toxteth and other parts of Britain. □ The fifty-two hostages in the American embassy in Tehran were released. □ Peter Sutcliffe, the Yorkshire Ripper, confessed to killing thirteen women and was gaoled for life. □ John McEnroe ended Bjorn Borg's reign at Wimbledon. □ The Gang of Four Labour MPs, Shirley Williams, Roy Jenkins, David Owen and William Rodgers, founded the Social Democratic Party. □ Bob Marley, who brought reggae out of the Jamaican slums, died of cancer. □ Hunger-striker Bobby Sands won the Fermanagh and South Tyrone by-election but died three weeks later. □ Adam Ant was Britain's pop sensation. □ Hit films were Chariots of Fire *and* The French Lieutenant's Woman.

Forget for a moment the baleful beauties of 'Brideshead Revisited', the beasts of 'The Borgias', breezy 'Bergerac', barmy 'Bullseye' and boring 'That's My Boy'. There was an unseen heroine of British television in 1981: Nipper, a ferret.

Nipper assisted in the coverage of the wedding of Charles and Diana in July. Her rôle was to pull a camera cable through an underground duct between Buckingham Palace and a television commentary-box on Victoria Monument. This allowed viewers to see Charles and Di from an additional vantage-point. The cable was attached to nylon cord tied to her tail, and a piece of streaky bacon dangled in front of her face was the bait. While commentator Angela Rippon vied with Tom Fleming for purple phrases – and was reportedly paid a five-figure sum for her stint – the ferret's fee was the bacon, at last.

The wedding led to a doubling of the sales of video-recorders. Around 3 million videos were busily taping the scenes of the royal couple at St Paul's. About 39 million people enjoyed a good cry in Britain, and the spectacle was beamed to seventy-four countries. American networks paid up to £2,000 to place their cameras in desirable windows in the streets along the route to the cathedral. CBS paid £8,000 to use someone's balcony.

Even more daring and more difficult than Nipper's task was the work of three women on palantype machines (the phonetically operated ones usually used to record court proceedings) creating instant subtitles for the deaf. This was the first time the technique had been tried for a long broadcast, and the operators' royal wedding day nerves caused a few giggles and some grievous bodily harm to the English language; 'Lady Dja na foamed out of the glass coach wearing hundreds of jarts of veil, a tiny bodies and a gate big skirt,' the wording went, while Princess Anne was 'wearing an amasing outfit. Very sump. Shs flat a big firll down the sid.' Good for her.

In other ways on television, 1981 was a year for women. From a gravel pit in Dorset came **'Tenko'**, an all-expense-spared series about mean Japanese men in Malaya with ragged women in shabby prison-camps and every problem under the burning sun. To everyone's surprise, especially the BBC's, their group of actresses – hair matted with fuller's earth and Brilliantine, bodies sprayed with dirt and covered in cosmetic sores and wearing costumes that were never washed – proved wonderfully popular. The idea had come from producer Lavinia Warner, who had researched wartime Malaysian

Stephanie Beacham managed to look tantalising as rape victim Rose in 'Tenko' despite losing far too much weight for the rôle.

prison-camps for 'This Is Your Life'. 'Tenko' was about the sufferings, class clashes and ways of survival of European women herded on long marches and into camps after the invasion of Singapore in 1942. Suddenly cut off from their menfolk, and largely forgotten by the British War Office, they included the weak and the strong, old and young, the officer's wife, the woman doctor, the old blue-stocking, a nun, a ridiculous Dutch woman, shopgirls, housewives and whores. Some viewers felt the known cruelties of the Japanese soldiers had been played down, but around 11 million followed the ten episodes and the numbers swelled to 14 million for the second ten in 1982 when the show topped the ratings. By then in the script the war was over, so the BBC decided to demolish the set, but as soon as they did they were hounded by viewers wanting more.

In 1984 the BBC gave in to the fans and spent £2 million flying the seventeen-strong cast and a large crew to Singapore to film ten new episodes (in suffocating humidity and 95° heat) depicting the women's struggle in 1945 to adjust to life with relatives who could never understand. There was a final roll-call in 1985, set in 1950 when the women gathered for a reunion and a murder tale.

Almost as popular as those 'Tenko' scruffbags and the shoulder-padded painted dolls of 'Dallas' was a scrubbed, starched, not-so-young children's nurse called Barbara Gray – heroine of **'Nanny'**.

'Nanny' was the brainwave of actress Wendy Craig after she flipped through the pages of *The Lady* magazine which has columns of advertisements for children's nurses. She sent the BBC her idea under the name of Jonathan Marr, believing that they'd take more notice of an unknown writer who was male. It worked. Terence Brady and Charlotte Bingham wrote splendid scripts for the ten-part

drama, and Wendy took the leading rôle of enlightened Nanny Gray caring for the children of the ruling classes of the 1930s. The proprietors of colleges for nannies, already delighted that Prince Charles had married a former 'nanny', reported a boom in girls wanting to train for the job. More episodes, equally popular, followed in 1983.

Two serials of the year provoked strong reactions. News that the BBC were making 'Blood Royal', Arden Winch's thriller about a ten-year-old earl, seventeenth in line to the throne, who is kidnapped and held to a £1 million ransom, brought a swift intervention from Buckingham Palace. It was feared children of members of the royal family would be put at risk as targets for fanatics. To the dismay of Winch, who said terrorists hardly needed him to give them ideas, the title became **'Blood Money'**, the story was changed, £10,000 of extra filming was undertaken and the boy was demoted to the ranks of a peer's son and then of the son of United Nations official – someone just important enough to warrant the help of the SAS. A book prepared to accompany the original series had to be pulped. After a year's delay the six-part serial was shown in September with enjoyable performances from Michael Denison as an intelligence officer, Bernard Hepton as a police chief, and Juliet Hammond Hill (Bernard's co-star from 'Secret Army') as a German terrorist. A couple of months later a third 'Secret Army' star, Clifford Rose's crafty kraut, returned in his own series **'Kessler'**.

But poking fun at the BBC's £2.4 million ten-part serial **'The Borgias'** proved the best pastime for the long winter evenings. This fifteenth-century Vatican Behind Closed Doors might have looked like another 'I, Claudius' on paper (in fact the BBC presented it as a high-minded history lesson) but on screen it was simply a sick farce made in a mish-mash of styles. Centre stage was pasta mountain Adolfo Celi, playing Rodrigo Borgia, Pope Alexander VI, and speaking English like most real popes (badly), who planted podgy hands on assorted virgins and knives through assorted cassocks. Oliver Cotton was supposed to scare the wits out of us as Cesare, his son, but unhappily resembled Basil Fawlty in full fury, so his already over-the-top performance became a total joke. Lucretia, his sister (Anne-Louise Lambert), turned out not quite the fiendish poisoner and murderer of history, more a fool, involved incestuously with her brother and father. At one point Cesare arrived to tell her how he'd spent the day raping children and splitting the bellies of pregnant women just after Dad, red-nosed Rodrigo, had forced her into a third arranged marriage, removed her children and fixed an orgy at which women scrambled on the floor like dogs picking up chestnuts in their mouths as men lolloped all over them. (The scene was apparently so embarrassing to film that no amount of wine drunk by the cast seemed to help.) When the serial was shown in Italy the following year, the Vatican joined British critics in

He may have looked like Chico Marx but this was Adolfo Celi as the fiendish Pope of 'The Borgias' holding what was possibly his lunch.

giving the show the thumbs-down. Perhaps if they hadn't been quite so ugly . . . .

Over on ITV there was also cause for embarrassment when **'The Flame Trees of Thika'**, a Euston Films series from Elspeth Huxley's autobiography, almost didn't flame. The seven-part series was shot in Kenya during the dry season, but late in the day they found out that flaming flame trees flower suddenly and for short spells only after the brief rains in October and November. When scenes of a thunderstorm were needed for episode 4, most of Nairobi's fire brigade had to open hoses on the dry plains as a crew scuttled off to film some flame trees which researchers had found miraculously flowering some miles away. More problems cropped up over scenes where big game was supposed to be killed. Luckily stuffed animals from the Nairobi Natural History Museum could be borrowed, but the Kenyan government refused to allow Kikuyu women, who built a house for the Grant family in the story, to be filmed bare-breasted. They were conscious of Western racist portrayals of Africans in traditional dress as primitive savages. In the end the Grants, nice-as-pie coffee-growers (Hayley Mills and David Robb), scolding servants for their own good, cut little ice with black people in Britain in the year of its worst-ever race riots. Still, this was quality drama compared with **'Diamonds'**, ATV's attempt to make a sparkling series about boardroom and bedroom shenanigans in a jewellery dynasty. Originally the family was to be Jewish, but the actors and the script kept forgetting. John Stride and Hildegard Neil braved it out. Happily these Diamonds weren't for ever.

But with the ridiculous came the sublime: **'Brideshead Revisited'**, the series that cost Granada more than twice what was planned, drew more viewers than anyone dared hope and gathered more awards and praise than could ever have been prayed for. Adapted into eleven parts by John Mortimer from Evelyn Waugh's book, this was a lazily told lavish tale of decay and despair in the interwar years. Jeremy Irons was the devastatingly stylish painter hero and narrator Charles Ryder who became inextricably bound up with fellow Oxford student Sebastian Flyte (Anthony Andrews) and his strange aristocratic Catholic family. The young blades became lovers, but later, while crossing the Atlantic, Charles met and fell for Julia, Sebastian's sister, played by Diana Quick. Their scenes together were perhaps the most passionate on television that year (even though Jeremy apparently pinned his underpants to the sheets for the filming) and they helped to make the homosexuality something viewers could accept – part of the English process of growing up.

Before it was screened, 'Brideshead' looked set to become the costliest mistake in ITV's history. The ITV strike in 1979 held production up, and the sixty-man crew was disbanded. When the strike ended the director Michael Lindsay-Hogg had to leave, and young Charles Sturridge, a junior director at Granada, found himself in the job, giving orders to Laurence Olivier (who played Lord Marchmain, Sebastian's absent father) as well as to John Gielgud, Claire Bloom, Stephane Audran and many other glittering stars. In 1980, Jeremy Irons – part of almost every scene – had to leave to work on the film *The French Lieutenant's Woman* for three months. Filming finished late and editing took for ever. But producer Derek Granger, who had beavered since 1972 to televise the novel he so admired, was never disheartened. When his and Sturridge's creation began to be seen in October around 9 million viewers adjusted to the pace (the actors were all told to speak slowly) and were hooked. If only for the care they took, the producers deserved the accolades. To make the Atlantic sequences, for instance, deck scenes were shot aboard QE2 in the Atlantic. Scenes supposed to be inside the liner, were shot in the panelled dining-room of the Adelphi Hotel, Liverpool, and in the Rainbow Room above a Kensington store, in the corridors of a Manchester office building and in the thirties-style ballroom foyer of the Park Lane Hotel. The cabins were built in Granada studios.

We have left comedy until last because . . . well, there wasn't much of it that was any good in 1981. **'Hi-de-Hi'**, the BBC's pantomime-styled lark about staff in a fifties holiday camp, had had a slow start in 1980 but caught on wildly in 1981 to the dismay of Butlin's and other camp-owners who'd been trying to bury just this sort of old-fashioned image for the past twenty years. Writer Jimmy Perry had been a redcoat at Butlin's years before and had the full measure of the tatty batty business and of his characters who included spivvy comic Ted (played superbly by Paul Shane), his snooty ballroom dancers

Anthony Andrews won the BAFTA best actor award for his performance as the dissolute drunken Sebastian Flyte in 'Brideshead Revisited' – though he was originally auditioned for the rôle of Charles Ryder and Jeremy Irons for Sebastian.

Barry and Yvonne (the brilliant Barry Howard and Diane Holland) and the vague upper-class entertainments manager Jeffery Fairbrother (played with just the right amount of pomp and dither by Simon Cadell). But the darlings of the show were the women. Ruth Madoc's bossy chief yellowcoat Gladys, the voice of Radio Maplin, desperately romantic but locked in cast-iron knickers, was based on her childhood memories of the women in her Welsh village competing fiercely for the few eligible men not sent off to war. Her accent was modelled on an aunty whose reaction to everything was 'Ooooaaawer!' When first Fairbrother then his replacement Squadron Leader Clive Dempster (David Griffin) broke her heart, around 10 million fans could have killed them. Similarly the skill of Su Pollard made chambermaid Peggy the sort of dope who could leave you with a lump in your throat each time her hopes were brutally dashed. She dreamed of becoming a yellowcoat, if only in heaven. The series, made at a real camp in Clacton, became a family favourite. And the real joke was that the series underplayed the crumminess of real holiday camps. Barry Howard, who'd worked at a Butlin's camp after leaving drama school, recalled seeing men putting plastic blossom on the trees. 'I told the "Hi-de-Hi" writers about it, but they said the viewers wouldn't believe it,' he said. By 1988, Barry had been

dropped because his heavy drinking affected his work (his place in Yvonne's tulle-wrapped arms was taken by pig-farmer Julian), the gang had appeared triumphantly in pantos and in a stage show, but the BBC felt it was hi-de-hi time to go.

Early in 1981 writer John Sullivan chatted with BBC producer Ray Butt about street-markets. Both had worked in them. They decided the market 'character' they most liked was the fly-pitcher, the wide boy who didn't have a regular stall and sold anything and everything. Sullivan went home and devised a series based on one and called it 'Readies'. For some time nothing came of it – its colourful attitudes about fiddling and tricking customers worried the BBC – but eventually they took it off the shelf, renamed it **'Only Fools and Horses'** and ran it.

John Sullivan remembers; 'I went into BBC TV Centre one day and the foyer was filled with people from their other comedies but we hadn't been asked. There had been no publicity for "Only Fools". It had sunk without a trace.

The stars of 'Only Fools and Horses', Grandad, Del Boy and Rodney, in their luridly painted, flashily furnished council flat in Peckham. Del used to brag that he had designed the décor.

Well, it had had an audience of about thirteen – all from my family.' But in that true BBC tradition of 'the right to fail' the show was given a second series.

Sullivan's idea had revolved around three ages: Grandad (Lennard Pearce) who had seen it all, Del Boy (David Jason) who was young enough to be ambitious yet was streetwise and sharp, and Rodney (Nicholas Lyndhurst) who yearned for things to be different yet was innocent and gauche. In each episode two joined forces against the third. Butt had been clever with the cast. There was a touch of the Hancocks in Nicholas's slow half-honest aspiring intellectual Rodney. And David Jason, whose family had had a fish-stall in Roman Road Market, was ideal as Del, sly but sentimental, pretentious but protec-

tive of the kid brother he called a 'right plonker'. David made him ridiculous yet lovable, waggling his head like a turkey, a camel-hair overcoat draped stagily over his shoulders, an identity-bracelet jangling on the pub bar as he ordered his Drambuie and grapefruit. The matiness of Del has had disadvantages for David. Over the years he has grown used to being seized by strangers and pulled across a shop or restaurant to meet 'the wife'. On one occasion a fan – male, luckily – followed him into the gents' and tried to shake his hand while it was otherwise engaged.

The series was rich in lovable idiots, minor characters, drawn in the round, such as Jaffa, the crook, who happened to be sterile (hence the name, meaning seedless). When the second series got into its stride, the audience woke up to the warmth of the relationships, the clever acting and the finely timed comic twists. By the third series 'Only Fools' was the BBC's most appreciated sitcom. Then, in 1984, Sullivan was telephoned by Lennard Pearce's landlady with news that the old actor had had a heart-attack. A day later he died.

'When I broke the news to David and Nick, they simply couldn't take it in. Even now it brings tears to people's eyes mentioning his name,' he said. 'I had to write two new episodes, one in which it was mentioned that Grandad was ill and in which Del thought he'd found his daughter and another one in which they buried Grandad. It was the saddest half-hour of comedy you could imagine. When Buster Merryfield came in the following year as the boys' Uncle Albert, David and Nick were quite unintentionally hostile to him. They couldn't bear the idea of anyone taking Lennard's place.'

Lennard would be tickled to know that a bumper edition of 'Only Fools and Horses' beat 'Minder' in the 1985 Christmas ratings, that the 1989 series won the Best Comedy prize at BAFTA, was widely hailed as a masterpiece (it ended with Rodney's wedding) and that the silly old sod he played is never forgotten.

Commercial Break

Among the commercials of that year was one assuring us that British Caledonian 'never forget you have a choice'. A syrupy tune accompanied the news that softness is a thing called Comfort. Norfolk turkey-farmer Bernard Matthews's commercial for his fowl should have been given the bird, but his 'bootiful' became an affectionate joke.

John Cleese starred in a series of commercials for Sony as inventive and funny as Leslie Crowther's Stork SB 'tests' in supermarkets were corny and traditional. But Leslie's work had the element of surprise. One couple he approached begged: 'No, don't film us.' It turned out Leslie had intruded on a 'dirty' weekend.

Also Shown in 1981

The BBC began several worthy workmanlike series. Bald Patrick Stewart starred as psychiatrist Eddie Roebuck in **'Maybury'**, a serial which bravely showed that shrinks can often make things better but sometimes make them worse. **'The Chinese Detective'** was an intelligent police series written by 'Sweeney' creator Ian Kennedy Martin. It starred Liverpool-born half-Chinese David Yip as Johnny Ho, a scruffy loner in Limehouse who joined the police force partly to clear his father's name and showed racist attitudes inside the police. It was fast-moving and exciting stuff. **'Bergerac'**, the BBC's other new detective for 1981, had a drink problem, a gammy leg, a broken marriage and worked for the Channel Islands Bureau des Etrangers whose peculiar cases made it more a Bureau de Strange Behaviour. John Nettles's Jersey Jim Bergerac didn't dazzle at first, but viewers warmed to him as he buzzed around the coastal roads in his vintage sports-car sneered at by the rich yet remaining philosophical about his millionaire ex-father-in-law Charlie Hungerford (Terence Alexander) who was uncannily involved in every crime Jim tried to solve. There was one unsolved mystery: the wrong leg case. John Nettles broke his right leg falling from a motorbike. It caused him to limp. Bergerac limped on the left.

Much enjoyed, too, were the serials. **'The Day of the Triffids'** starred John Duttine as John Wyndham's hero among the blind and several giant stalks of rhubarb as the slash-you-to-death triffid plants. Women especially liked **'A Chance to Sit Down'**, starring Jan Francis as a ballet dancer; and there were millions of fans of the wryly comic **'Private Schultz'** on BBC2 which cast Michael Elphick as a bemused German soldier detailed by Ian Richardson as his mad boss Neuheim to flood Britain with forged fivers as a scheme to wreck the economy. For sharper satire and some of the longest and most daring nude scenes to date, there was **'The History Man'** based on Malcolm Bradbury's novel. Anthony Sher played posturing lecturer Howard Kirk, marking his students' papers according to how left-wing they professed to be and bedding almost every female at the University of Watermouth.

In one of the excellent plays of the year, Norman Wisdom crossed the great divide from acting the goat to acting, as a man dying from cancer in the BAFTA-winner **'Going Gently'** he was superb.

Helen Mirren produced a lot of steam in a shower scene with Brad Davis in **'Mrs Reinhard'**. Robert Hardy was Winnie in **'Winston Churchill, the Wilderness Years'** a play about biding time when his advice went unheeded. Jim ('Land of Hope') Allen's **'United Kingdom'**, about a North-East council which rebelled against government spending cuts, made important political points (and disgusted yet more in Tunbridge Wells). **'Artemis 81'** was a three-hour brain-tease starring Hywel Bennett in which the forces of darkness nearly took over but pop star Sting as the Angel of Life saved us. (Did we ever find out why?) There were no such problems understanding **'The Seven Dials' Mystery'**, LWT's silly Agatha Christie blockbuster starring Cheryl Campbell as sporty sleuth Bundle and James Warwick as the dashed good chap who helps her and wins her.

There were other disappointments. **'Second Chance'**, a serial about a divorcing couple played by Ralph Bates and Susannah York, rarely rose above the second-rate despite Adele Rose's sensitive script; **'Funnyman'**, created by and starring Jimmy Jewel and based on his family's travelling music-hall act in the twenties and thirties, was anything but funny; and **'Bognor'**, Thames Television's half-hour series about a sardonic investigator from the Department of Trade (based on Tim Heald's witty books) was anything but gripping despite David Horovitch's likeable hero.

It was not a great year for factual series. Jeremy Isaac's **'Ireland: A Television History'** won the BAFTA Documentary Series award and Yorkshire Television began **'Where There's Life'**, a popular science and sentiment programme hosted by Miriam Stoppard and Rob Buckman. Newsreaders made the news – Richard Baker, Kenneth Kendall, Peter Woods and other BBC stalwarts were sacked from the 'Nine O'Clock News' to make way for younger John Humphrys and John Simpson. Angela Rippon quit the BBC newsroom as did Anna Ford at 'News at Ten' (both women were heading for TV-am), and Lady Diana lookalike Selina Scott took Anna's place at ITN. Perhaps because no one had asked her to do high kicks with Morecambe and Wise, pregnant Jan Leeming sang 'Hello, Young Lovers' on the Russell Harty show and we all pretended she'd been a wonderful sport.

Two game-shows began. **'Bullseye'**, dart-throwing hosted by Jim Bowen, should have died an early death. That was the outcome expected by Jim, whose line in chat ran from 'Smashin'' to 'Loovely' (as in, to contestant: 'Hello, Ken, and what do you do for a living?' Contestant: 'I'm unemployed, Jim.' Jim: 'Smashin', Ken, loovely').

ATV burned £100,000-worth of recorded material because it was so bad but viewers loved it and Bullseye lives today.

'Game for a Laugh' on the other hand was an instant success for LWT. Developed from American game-shows such as 'People Are Funny' and including some filmed items on 'Candid Camera' lines, beaming pranksters Sarah Kennedy, Jeremy Beadle, Matthew Kelly and Henry Kelly cajoled contestants to perform silly stunts in the studio as the audience shrieked its collective head off.

It was an important year for soap. The BBC brought us **'Flamingo Road'**, a load of over-dressed tosh set in the Deep South, and in case the decadent luxury went to our heads they also brought us **'Triangle'**, offering all the glamour of Felixstowe and the heady delights of life on a North Sea ferry. When a passenger committed suicide by jumping overboard we understood her feelings.

It wasn't a spectacular year on **'Coronation Street'**. Ken Barlow married Deirdre Langton and Jack Duckworth kicked out his wife Vera for carrying on with another man. But in **'Crossroads'** the motel burned down after a children's firework-party and viewers were supposed to worry that Meg had died in the blaze, having knocked herself out first with sleeping-pills but we knew that no pesky inferno could finish her off. Noele Gordon was sacked, but Meg was seen waving from the deck of *QE2* on her way, inexplicably, to New York. Noele died of cancer in 1984.

America was forgiven in 1981 for all the dross she'd sent in the past. **'Hill Street Blues'** arrived on ITV and became a cult favourite until it ended in 1989. Set in a run-down precinct of an unnamed city' and full of sleazy characters, several of whom were fine police officers, it brought fast fragmented story-telling and language – 'first we must interface with the perpetrators' – Dixon wouldn't have understood. Each episode began with a roll-call and ended as Captain Furillo (Daniel J. Travanti) embraced lovely lawyer Joyce Davenport (Veronica Hamel) in bed. Where *did* they get the energy?

They also sent us superior made-for-television films. **'Playing for Time'**, the true story of women in concentration-camps who survived by forming an orchestra, with a screenplay by Arthur Miller and Vanessa Redgrave shaven-headed as Jewish cabaret performer Fania Fenelon. On the down side was **'Magnum PI'**, the thumps-smiles-and-bimbos series set in Hawaii which took over from 'Hawaii Five-O'. It made Tom Selleck's muscles and moustache famous.

Two children's series launched that year became hugely popular. One was the cartoon series **'Dangermouse'**, using the voice of David Jason. The other was the animated adventures of **'Postman Pat'**, loved by kids, objected to by adults. Teachers complained it was sexist (it should have been called 'Letter-Carrier Pat', said one) and farmers were horrified when in one episode Pat allowed his cat Jess to perch on the back of a tractor. Letters pointing out how dangerous this was flooded into *Farmers' Weekly*.

Ronnie Corbett was sex-starved moped-riding librarian Timothy Lumsden tied to his mother's apron-strings in **'Sorry!'**, a sitcom which would have floundered in farce far sooner in less skilful hands, and the best ITV comedy was **'A Fine Romance'**. Written by Bob Larbey, it starred Judi Dench and her real husband Michael Williams as two middle-aged, awkward and set-in-their-ways people in love. For this, and for **'Going Gently'** in which she played a nurse, Judi won BAFTA's Best Actress award for the year.

1982

That Was the Year When...

On April Fool's Day, Argentinian troops set out to invade the Falkland Islands. ☐ On 2 April the Royal Marines guarding Port Stanley were overwhelmed and British administration of the islands was ended. ☐ Two days later a Royal Navy task force set out. ☐ On 14 June the Argentinians surrendered. The death-toll was 255 Britons and 652 Argentinians. ☐ Princess Diana gave birth to Prince William. ☐ The Queen woke to find Michael Fagan sitting on her bed. ☐ Laker Airways collapsed with debts of £270 million. ☐ Unemployment reached more than 3 million. ☐ Victoria Gillick, mother of ten, tried to stop contraceptive advice being given to people under sixteen. ☐ Channel 4 began, and its 'bad language' and 'political bias' worried politicians. ☐ Henry VIII's flagship Mary Rose *was raised from the Solent mud. ☐ There was a visit to Britain by the Pope – the first for 450 years. ☐ Top films were* Gandhi *and* ET, *and Boy George took over from Adam Ant as the teeny pop sensation.*

The big entertainment event of 1982 should have been the arrival of a cheeky upstart, Channel 4. The world of broadcasting would never be the same again, said the commentators early and often. But this historic event turned out to be a small side-show. It was upstaged by something not trailered or plugged in *Radio Times*, something that became through television almost a tragic pantomime. In the Falklands' War a glittering cast was led by Prime Minister Margaret Thatcher, playing a Churchillian leader, quoting Queen Victoria. Lord Carrington was an early heroic victim, taking blame for the invasion. The men from the ministry Ian McDonald and John Nott, were sort of comic goodies, McDonald, dour and doomladen,

Nott sparrowlike and huffy. General Galtieri was the Prince of Darkness and his Argi legions the simple villains.

We in the audience tuned into the daily news, most of us too young ever to have thought properly before about patriotism or war – real stabbing and shooting and burning on freezing muddy hillsides. With reporters such as Brian Hanrahan we tried to understand the killing and tried in his famous phrase to 'count them out and count them in'. War in fictional television drama could never be treated lightly again. It was six years before a play about fighting in the Falklands was shown – and then only after a row.

But the planned output on BBC and ITV in 1982 seemed an attempt to show that the Channel 4 chaps (due to open

'The Young Ones', a BBC2 comedy series about a festering flat shared by weird students, deranged dropouts and a brain-dead hippy, caused as much damage to older viewers' blood pressure. Suggesting the world was full of psychopaths, it became a long-lasting cult with young viewers and not surprisingly launched comic actors including Rik Mayall, Ade Edmondson and Nigel Planer and writer Ben Elton to future success.

The best drama of 1982 (and the BAFTA winner) was Alan Bleasdale's pessimistic 'Boys from the Blackstuff' about a gang of unemployed asphalt-layers in Liverpool, the city where in the early eighties landing a job was like winning the pools. Bleasdale beat us with a political pole and tickled us, too. His characters became heroic victims. Bernard Hill's Yosser, trailing his kids, robbed of his wife, his job and his self-respect, reduced to headbanging, chanting 'Gissa job' and muttering 'I can do that' at the sight of another human working, became a symbol of the depressed times.

shop in November) weren't needed and might as well pack up, go home and not bother. Documentaries were especially controversial. The year began with **'Police'**, Roger Graef's eleven-part series for the BBC showing how British coppers behaved, worked and swore – the term 'boys in blue' took on a new meaning. A BBC team had followed officers of the Thames Valley force for nine months. The first episode showed a massive dawn stake-out of the home of Mr Donald Stimpson whose wife had telephoned the police during the course of a New Year's Eve row to tell them he was about to shoot the family dog. After the police told him on loudhailers to 'Come quietly' he came, revealing himself as mild, non-violent but amazed by their presence. Eventually he sued the Thames Valley force for £500 for troubling him.

Later episodes showed a detective breaking down in tears after being demoted, a stake-out to catch a thief as he robbed a duchess, a drunk accusing the cops of beating him up in a van and an officer being reported and suspended for slapping a black youth. The scenes to have the most lasting effect, though, were those showing Detective Brian Kirk and other officers bullying a girl who claimed she'd been raped. As a direct result one year later the Home Office introduced new guidelines stressing the need for tact and understanding in such cases.

In September there was a five-part sequel, **'Operation Carter'**, delayed until after the court-trials, showing the same force's success in rounding up and putting behind bars twenty-nine criminals for a total of 411 years. It made a national hero of Detective Chief Inspector Brian Ward, who looked like John Thaw and spoke like Eddie Grundy. Security had been so tight that Graef and his co-producer Charles Stewart had had to store their films in a fridge at Reading police station.

It was the year for American imports. **'Fame'** fever developed with British children with the arrival of the series (after the film) about the New York Academy of Performing Arts ('the hot, burning centre of the galaxy' – they talked like that, truly, usually while shaking every limb, singing, dancing, playing the cello, the bongos or the piano and generally hanging loose, brilliantly). It made you sick. It worked because it was like a kids' 'Hill Street Blues', full of energy and different stories. Only there was music and sore feet in place of shooting and blood. The BBC also imported **'Cagney and Lacey'**, a series about women cops with women's woes in New York. They were soon to become cult heroines with women viewers yet were created by the same man who produced the totally unemancipated Charlie's Angels. Loretta ('Hotlips') Swit was cast first, then replaced by Meg Foster as the liberated daring Christine Cagney. Tyne Daly was Mary Beth Lacey, the worrying wife and guilt-ridden mother. Later Meg was fired for being too butch, and Sharon Gless took over the rôle. The series was a great success, but the following year came the news that the American television chiefs had dropped it, with other favourites here, including 'Fame', 'Taxi', 'Quincy' and a children's series about motorbike-riding cops, 'Chips'. But there was a reprieve after Tyne Daly won an award for her performance and the American network was deluged with letters from fans. Plots continued to explore social issues. Cagney suffered as the victim of rape and of alcoholism (Sharon Gless later confessed to just this problem), and by 1986 the actresses were probably the best female friends on television, sharing their problems often in the dingy confines of the police station ladies' lav, a closeness developed when Tyne's pregnancy was written into the plots and the enormous Mary Beth was wheeled into the delivery-ward (clutching husband Harv's bowling trophy) with Chris mopping her brow. Later John Karlen, who played the idyllically supportive Harv, blamed the stresses of the show for the break-up of his twenty-one-year marriage. The cops were finally arrested in 1988 when the series ended.

The most popular mini-series was **'Shogun'** based on James Clavell's book. There was so much Japanese in it we began to wonder, which terryvision station we were watching. It glamorised sweaty men in baggy pants and pigtails performing suicidal stabbings, head-choppings and other nastinesses, with Richard Chamberlain as the English captain who joined them remaining squeaky clean and deodorised even in the dankest dungeon.

Meanwhile in Hollywood Joan Collins was pinning on the false hair, clipping on the diamonds, slapping on the lip-gloss and getting ready to make a grand entrance as the wicked witch of **'Dynasty'**, Alexis Carrington. The series had not been a success in its first year in America; then the writers had spotted that their saga of oil tycoon Blake Carrington, his secretary-turned-wife, her former lover, his gay son and nympho daughter from a first marriage lacked a basic conflict. They decided that they needed a villainess, a female JR, and Aaron Spelling, the hugely rich mogul behind the series, had decided he needed a Name. Sophia Loren was hired to make three appearances (her husband Carlo Ponti thought it was time she played a baddie), but writer Eileen Pollock bravely bearded both Spelling and Ponti in their dens arguing that the villainess needed to be a permanent fixture. As they couldn't afford Loren at $150,000 an episode (and she didn't want to be tied down), the 'Dynasty' people began searching for someone cheaper. Joan Collins, at that stage if not over the hill then wobbling on the brow, appearing in skin-flicks such as *The Stud* and *The Bitch*, and taking bit parts in low-grade television series like 'Fantasy Island', was the someone they found.

The series producers introduced the character of Alexis at the end of their first series. Wearing a big hat with a thick veil she (actually a model whose face was never seen) appeared in court. The show was thirty-eighth in the American ratings. At the start of the second series Joan's

Alexis emerged from under the veil to testify against her ex-husband on a murder charge. Soon her style of swaggering around in thirties-movie-queen outfits, aggressively fiddling with black cigarettes, spitting out venom and playing preposterous games with a succession of men became a much-enjoyed joke. (Joan believed she inspired women to be strong.) Alexis turned the popularity of the series round. When she fired a shotgun into the air causing her rival in Blake's affections, Linda Evans's Krystle, to fall from her horse and lose her unborn child, she became the world's most famous she-devil. (Joan had actually argued with the writers against the scene and, filming it, accidentally caught the gun in her hanging scarf and shot herself in the foot.)

On 2 November, Channel 4, the station we feared would be too highbrow for any but the eggiest eggheads, arrived, and verdicts varied from 'Uh?' to 'Ouch'. First show on was **'Countdown'**, a teatime anagram game with smug Richard Whiteley as questionmaster and farmer Ted Moult moulting over his encyclopaedias. It proved a lasting success. The night's big drama, reviewed in the *Daily Mirror* as 'compulsive viewing for psychiatrists', was **'Walter'** based on David Cook's novel about a mentally subnormal man's agonies after the death of his mother. In harrowing scenes we saw him being dragged screaming from the corpse, covered in pigeon droppings, to a hospital where he was attacked by a homosexual dwarf. For the rôle Ian McKellen had spent time with intelligent handicapped people in Spastics Society day-centres and hospitals. Then one day before filming started he played Walter, lolling mouth, poor clothes and gruesome short-back-and-sides haircut, in Marks & Spencer to see how ordinary people might react. He was jostled by angry shoppers but was so convincing that nine women in succession took pity on him and tried to help. The play wasn't a bundle of laughs, but Ian was terrific.

What was a bundle of laughs was the show which ended the first night, the Comic Strip's spoof on Enid Blyton, **'Five Go Mad in Dorset'**. The Five included Dawn French and Jennifer Saunders with actor producer Peter Richardson; and, to everyone's amazement and delight, Ronald Allen, star of 'Crossroads', turned up at the end as Uncle Quentin shouting 'I'm a screaming homosexual, you little prigs', to be arrested by Raymond Francis of 'No Hiding Place' for his perverted deeds. Ronnie had been asked, said Peter Richardson, because he was famous for looking serious.

Channel 4's most highly rated series was its soap **'Brookside'**, set in a Liverpool cul-de-sac, created and produced by Phil Redmond, originator of the parent-scaring BBC serial 'Grange Hill'. Redmond bought the houses and all the equipment using a Department of Trade loan. It meant he could dispense with the plywood sets used in the other soaps and these families could be seen to use bathrooms and dustbins, drop clothes on the stairs and

take ketchup-bottles from real cupboards to the table. (It also meant good business. A few years ago the site was valued at £8.5 million.) However, his fictional residents – the Grants, the Collinses, the Crosses and others – were too real for comfort at first. They were earthy, radical; they spoke unashamedly in thick guttural Scouse accents; and they swore. Mary Whitehouse and the *Daily Express* declared themselves outraged. Viewing figures fell. Then Redmond decided to clean up the language, inject a little comedy, but retain the social issues. Unemployment was the constant backdrop. Characters debated who were the greater rogues: capitalist tax-avoiders or the jobless driven to go on the fiddle. Contraception, AIDS, loss of virginity, rape, homosexuality, drug addiction – they were all subjects discussed over family dinner-tables. The writing style was low-key and the acting excellent, especially that of Ricky Tomlinson and Sue Johnston who played Bobby and Sheila Grant. But the closeness to life brought problems. 'Brookside' was often as boring as the

Joan Collins as Alexis and John Forsythe as Blake in 'Dynasty', the soap which cost around a million dollars an episode to make. Alexis wore clothes which screamed 'My God! Is she rich!', ate real caviare and lay on satin sheets that cost $1,000 a set. She was and is wildly popular in America and remains fairly popular here on BBC; but she has never pulled the audience mousey Mavis Riley and other frumpy matrons of 'Coronation Street' could attract.

real thing. When they forgot the lofty ideals and resorted to melodrama with a siege complete with gunman and double death, the ratings shot up to 8 million. After that ratings settled for many years around 4 million, older viewers and many Southerners trying it, wishing there were subtitles and giving up.

For most young viewers Channel 4 came to mean one show: **'The Tube'**. This was an attempt to re-create 'Ready Steady Go!', the sixties pop show (only now it was called a rock show). It was screened live by Tyne Tees from Newcastle on Friday nights. Jools Holland, once a musician with Squeeze, was co-host with blonde Paula Yates, daughter of Jess and now wife of Live Aid's 'Saint' Bob Geldof. In the following year Prince Andrew's friend Koo Stark contributed filmed interviews with rock stars and Leslie Ash replaced Paula for a while. In order to upset a few adults and please teenagers, the presenters and guests sometimes swore. Paula once said, 'It's effing freezing' and received a stern warning. In 1987, just before the show was cancelled, Jools was suspended after swearing in a trailer item. The IBA reported that some of the show's material was in 'bad taste', but several of the editions, notably the shows featuring Dire Straits and the Eurythmics, were highly praised and picked up awards in television festivals in America. Paula admitted that she hadn't always been brilliant. Her worst interview was one with Duran Duran. She found out when it ended that she had been sitting on the microphone and no one heard a word. Wasn't that a shame? Well, please yourself.

Comedy took new strides in 1982. 'OTT' – the initials stood for Over The Top – was a late-night Saturday show, well below the top and somewhere near the bottom. Inspired by 'Tiswas' and featuring clumsy sketches, behind-the-bike-shed-style rude jokes, nudity and custard-pouring, it starred Lenny Henry, Alexei Sayle, Chris Tarrant and American actress Colette Hiller, who was sacked after just two minutes and three lines apparently for not fitting in with the others. (She may well have taken this as a compliment.) The first show produced complaints over a line-up of naked men clasping balloons, and a Birmingham vicar urged his congregation to pray the show was taken off. Their prayers were answered when Bob Phillis, new boss of the newly named Midlands company Central, gave it the boot. ' "OTT" was cruel and sexist,' he said. 'And I don't think tipping custard over people made particularly exciting television.'

Commercial Break

Sebastian Coe was the first British athlete to be allowed to use his own name to promote products on television. From a £500,000 campaign of twenty second commercials for Horlicks, he earned £30,000 but will not receive any of it until he retires from athletics. In 1982 Thames refused to allow Christmas greeting advertisements which the London Gay Switchboard tried to place on Channel 4. And Australian comic Paul Hogan began a series of hilarious commercials for Fosters lager.

Also Shown in 1982

Television's teach-yourself-medicine course, begun with 'Your Life in Their Hands', progressed with BBC2's **'Heart Transplant'** series – seven trips to Harefield Hospital, following the work of surgeon Magdi Yacoub. Rex Bloomstein's two-part documentary for the BBC, **'Auschwitz and the Allies'**, was an attempt to uncover why the British and Americans took so long to believe stories of mass extermination during the war. Over on ITV the most publicised documentary was **'Chicken Ranch'**, a ninety-minute visit to a Nevada brothel, supposedly a Ritz among knocking-shops but in fact a prefab in the desert to which gamblers, salesmen and truck-drivers are flown to 'party' with listless girls for $20 or more.

Of the quieter, contemplative documentaries, most enjoyed was BBC2's **'One Man and His Dog'** in which Phil Drabble, Eric Halsall and thousands of Oscar-deserving sheep were joined by a succession of talented Border Collie dogs in rolling green meadows.

The most enduring documentary series to begin that year was BBC2's **'Forty Minutes'**. Under the editorship of Roger Mills and later Edward Mirzoeff, short films on subjects as varied as lavatories and pigeons, child prostitutes and prize leeks have earned wide praise.

And there were experimental programmes. In **'The Real World'** science series from TVS a three-dimensional programme showing the uses of stereoscopy was screened. Viewers used special specs with red and green lenses supplied by *TV Times* magazine.

Comedy took new strides in 1982. **'Whoops! Apocalypse'** in which lunatic politicians brought about global nuclear war, left most viewers baffled. But an eerie backdrop of a bombed world and performances by Barry Morse, as America's actor president Johnny Cyclops, Peter Jones as Britain's crazy Prime Minister Kevin Pork, Richard Griffiths and Alexei Sayle as Russians, John Cleese as a terrorist and Bruce Montague as the Shah of Iran brought it a cult following.

Thankfully there were new-wave comedians who were keener on being funny ha-ha than funny peculiar. Victoria Wood and Julie Walters in Granada's series **'Wood and Walters'** proved a weekly highlight. Jasper Carrott had been an occasional television treat since his ITV show in 1978, but **'Carrot's Lib'** on BBC marked his emergence as a real comic find.

There were as usual a load of rotten sitcoms. **'Don't Rock the Boat'** which cast plummy Nigel Davenport as a rough diamond in the boat-hire business seemed the worst until **'Union Castle'**, in which Stratford Johns pretended to be Clive Jenkins starring in a trade-union version of 'To the Manor Born', came along.

Esther Rantzen's series 'The Big Time' spawned **'In at the Deep End'**, polished but pointless programmes which she produced and in which Chris Serle and Paul Heiney tried to prove they weren't drips by learning other people's trades at breakneck speed. Noel Edmonds began his **'Late Late Breakfast Show'** on Saturday evenings, usually a harmless breathless bundle of bits and pieces. But twenty-five-year-old Michael Lush was killed in 1986 when a Whirly Wheeler stunt went wrong, and the BBC stopped the series and banned members of the public from dangerous tricks on any BBC programme. Noel Edmonds was deeply affected by the tragedy, made worse when he later received death threats.

New chat-show hosts that year included B. A. Robertson, who proved what we'd always suspected – that rock singers can't talk – and David Soul, who turned up some days for his spot on **'Six Fifty-Five Special'** and left Sally James, thankfully, to carry the show on others. **'Blockbusters'**, the hugely successful quiz for youngsters began bringing fame for the bracelet and cufflinks of host Bob Holness. And as a Christmas treat that year ITV gave us **Chas 'n' Dave**, them bearded cockney geezers wot done the 'rabbit, rabbit, rabbit' beer commercial, in a studio supposed to be a luvverly friendly boozer with revellers from Rent-a-crowd swaying self-consciously and guzzling LWT's beer. Eamonn Andrews attempted to muscle in on Magnus Magnusson territory with an international quiz **'Top of the World'** which was good for a giggle, the poor man smiling bravely as electronic gremlins took over. (Eamonn Andrews – This Was Your Nightmare!)

Quality drama was in good supply. There was former ITN reporter Gerald Seymour's stylish and plausible **'Harry's Game'** set in Northern Ireland, with Ray Lonnen as an undercover army captain on the trail of Derek Thompson as an IRA assassin. 'Not the Nine O'Clock News' funnyman Mel Smith's lack of good looks won him the lead rôle as a devious builder and property developer in **'Muck and Brass'**, with Bullseye's Jim Bowen playing an accountant. By contrast LWT's **'We'll Meet Again'** was an old forties weepie reborn and a whopping success. It brought the overpaid, over-sexed Yanks over here once more for a series of love-affairs with Suffolk women – principally Susannah York. One B17 Flying Fortress and a couple of models served for a whole American squadron.

'Claire', starring Caroline Embling, was the BBC's serious serial about the pains of fostering a teenager. Granada gave us 'A Kind of Loving', their worthy version of Alan Sillitoe's novel, starring Clive Wood and Joanne Whalley.

The BBC came up with its quota of costume-drama series. Lisa Harrow played Nancy Astor, and 'King's Royal' was a saga of guilt, skulduggery, traumatic childbirth and other disasters in the lives of members of a whisky-blending family headed by Tom Bell. 'Fame Is the Spur', about the rise of the Labour movement in Victorian Manchester, starring Tim Pigott-Smith, was better but duller. The BBC also gave us 'The Woman in White', Wilkie Collins's classic detective story featuring young blades in funny tights and girls in bonnets and starring Ian Richardson as loony Uncle Frederick.

Easy to forget was 'I Remember Nelson' ATV's serial about the hero of history, played by Kenneth Colley. His finest hour was postponed at the last minute. David Frost defeated Nelson with an unscheduled Falklands discussion.

Alec Guinness returned to play the disillusioned intelligence chief in the excellent 'Smiley's People'. Beryl Reid won the BAFTA Best Actress award for her cameo rôle of Connie Sachs in this. Richard Griffiths was the heftiest hero in drama that year – he played Henry Jay, a quiet civil servant who uncovers a computer conspiracy, in the thrilling 'Bird of Prey'. But ITV's best series was 'Shine On Harvey Moon', a light comic saga written by Laurence Marks and Maurice Gran of the domestic trials of a demobbed RAF clerk played by Kenneth Cranham, his tough old ma (Elizabeth Spriggs), flighty fag-ash wife (Maggie Steed) and two worldly kids. The half-hour series was so popular it returned later in the year in hour-long episodes and was greatly enjoyed until 1985.

Among many excellent plays were the BBC's 'Another Flip for Dominic', a sequel to an earlier science-fiction story starring Peter Firth and Caroline Langrishe. Dennis Waterman reminded us that he is more than Arthur's thick friend in 'Minder' when he produced and starred in a Tyne Tees film, 'A Captain's Tale', about a Durham miners' football team which won the World Cup. It was a joy. So was the BBC's 'Ballroom of Romance' by William Trevor, a tale about a tatty dance-hall in Ireland where dreams of love blossom and fade. Central's 'Oi For England', a film about a skinhead band, written by Trevor Griffiths, was relevant and depressing.

A new soap arrived from across the Atlantic. 'Falcon Crest', the wine-growing saga set in a North Californian valley was made by the 'Dallas' producers Lorimar and starred Ronald Reagan's ex-wife Jane Wyman as the tough all-conquering boss of Falcon Crest Wines. At the same time in 'Coronation Street' Mavis was clinking glasses with ardent Victor Pendlebury, and Mike Baldwin tried to have the cat who spilled coffee over his sports-coat put down by the RSPCA. In 'Cross-roads' Adam Chance returned to the motel and became engaged to Jill before having a fling with Valerie Pollard.

1983

Margaret Thatcher was re-elected as Prime Minister with an overall majority of 144. ☐ *Cabinet minister Cecil Parkinson resigned in disgrace after former Tory party worker Sarah Keays stated in* The Times *that he was the father of the child she was expecting.* ☐ *CND supporters formed a fourteen-mile chain through Greenham and Aldermaston, but Cruise missiles arrived seven months later.* ☐ *A bomb in Harrods killed six.* ☐ *Dennis Nilsen was gaoled for six murders and admitted fifteen.* ☐ *One-pound coins were introduced.* ☐ *Neil Kinnock was elected leader of the Labour Party.* ☐ *Wheel-clamping of illegally parked cars began in London.* ☐ *The* Sunday Times *and historian Hugh Trevor-Roper were hoaxed over the Hitler diaries.* ☐ *President Reagan backed the Contra rebels in Nicaragua.* ☐ *Mrs Janet Walton of Liverpool gave birth to sextuplets, all healthy girls.* ☐ *Cordless telephones arrived.* ☐ *And Wham!'s George Michael and Andrew Ridgeley became pop idols.*

Never in the history of breakfast was more egg left on more famous faces in fewer weeks than with the start of breakfast television in 1983.

Helped by a £25,000 government grant for computer equipment, the BBC won the race to start first on 17 January at 6.30 a.m. An avuncular Frank Bough in a jumper and a tangled-tongued Selina Scott in a grey 'nanny' dress with a severe white collar were the anchor persons on the **'Breakfast Time'** red leather sofa, introducing items which included a horse race, cricket and pearl-fishing. During the five weekdays Nick Ross added a slightly more serious note as a co-presenter, but the bigger stars were a skinny blonde in a lurid green body-stocking, Diana Moran the Green Goddess of

'Black Adder', co-written by and starring Rowan Atkinson, was based on a little-read history-book about Prince Edmund, Duke of Edinburgh, described by producer John Lloyd as the Hitler diaries of the fifteenth century. He added that Atkinson's bald cringeing, cowardly son of York in black tights and winkle-picker boots was nothing like the present Duke of Edinburgh ('apart from the haircut'). Not many viewers enjoyed the early blood-spattered japes, and the BBC was about to drop the series when 'Black Adder' slithered 140 years ahead, lived in a house not a castle. Ben Elton came in as a writer, Miranda Richardson came in as a naughty schoolgirl version of Elizabeth I and the show was a hit. By the third series, set in Regency England with a Prince Regent (whose brain was the size of a 'weasel's wedding tackle'), Black Adder's smelly stupid servant Baldrick, played by Tony Robinson, had become the best part of the show. But for seventy-year-old Mrs Florence Blackadder of Sheffield nothing about the show was good. For years she received fun-poking telephone calls from people asking to speak to her husband, the dastardly Blackadder. She begged him to change their name by deed poll.

exercise, bubbly Russell Grant who babbled about the stars, and Francis Wilson the whimsical weatherman who told us everything we did not need to know.

Two weeks later with **'Good Morning Britain'**, TV-am began its 'mission to explain', as Peter Jay its leading light had called it when his group of celebrities (David Frost, Michael Parkinson, Robert Kee, Angela Rippon and Anna Ford – collectively the Famous Five) won the franchise amid strong competition. Starting at 6 a.m. with the price of pigs and other farming news, and running seven days a week, they promised viewers not only news and entertainment but also what David Frost called 'sexual chemistry'. This seemed to mean that, seated on their fawn-coloured sofa, he could make silly remarks when either Anna Ford or Angela Rippon was trying to link items or ask straight questions. But despite the glamour of the practised presenters, always in suits or smart dresses, despite their militaristic weatherman, Commander David Philpott, despite their answer to the Green Goddess, the even more frantic Mad Lizzie, audiences dropped to a disastrously low level and there seemed to be only about three companies willing to advertise their wares in the breaks. Within six weeks Peter Jay had been forced out. In April both Anna and Angela were sacked from their jobs (Anna's wage was £75,000, Angela's £60,000) by Timothy Aitken, one of the bosses of the ailing company. (Esther Rantzen, an original member of the gang, must have been grateful she had backed out on discovering she was pregnant and unable to promise to rise before dawn.) Robert Kee and Michael Parkinson stayed longer, Parkie most visible at weekends when he and his wife Mary were hosts on a magazine programme which combined chummy chats with their friends in showbiz, fairly embarrassing snippets of 'comedy' and pre-recorded items from Nick Owen, the station's sports reporter and soon to become frontman (chosen, he said, because unlike the others he was 'ordinary', which seemed to be pitching it a bit high).

In June, at a reception held by Lady Melchett, Anna Ford expressed her views on the way she and Angela had been treated by throwing a glass of wine over Jonathan Aitken, MP, her former boss. It may have been a waste of good Chablis but, whatever sort of Tory Aitken had been before, from then on he was a wet. The mission to explain was shelved as a mission impossible. Cosy, not too clever, celebrity-flavoured breakfast cereal was ordered. Among new recruits was one in grey nylon fur, Roland Rat, the only rat to join a sinking ship, with Kevin the gerbil and from BBC Birmingham Anne Diamond, whose perky girl-next-door manner made her a favourite with viewers (if not with all her female colleagues). Her partnership with Nick 'Ordinary' Owen proved more palatable with early-morning audiences than the porridgy partnership of soppy Selina and frumpy Frank. Selina left in March 1987, and in November 1988 moved to work in America, moaning that

'Widows' was a contemporary thriller serial about three women who inherited their late husbands' 'licence' to crime. Writer Lynda La Plante, who had quizzed helpful crooks in Brixton pubs about robbery planning and procedures, had the husbands, led by hard man Harry Rawlins, live and die in a taut opening sequence of violent robbery filmed in London's Aldwych underpass. Ann Mitchell was achingly convincing as dignified Dolly, devoted to the deceased Mr Big (who turned out to be alive and well and living with another woman), as was Fiona Hendley as the blonde beauty queen and Kate Williams as her mum. When the widows joined to carry out the next heist planned in the files they roped in Bella, a stripper played by Eva Mottley, who learned to act when in gaol on a drugs charge. For the sequel, two years later, Debby Bishop had replaced Eva who'd been found dead from a suspected drugs' overdose.

she had never been taken seriously. Frank Bough left in November 1987, then seemed to retire from television after a Sunday newspaper shattered his wholesome image by revealing his one-time use of drugs. He took them, he reportedly claimed, partly to counteract the strain of beginning work at unbearably early hours. (He made a sort of return to the screen early in 1989 as a presenter on Sky satellite television and later joined LWT.)

Six years on, a large section of the viewing population never watches breakfast television, stubbornly preferring to take their news and views with radio and newspaper. Changes on both programmes have been made to improve the news-gathering, but neither has achieved the snappy topicality of the American model, 'Today', which has been running since 1952. Undaunted by the relatively small audiences both programmes attract ('Breakfast Time' has around 1 million, TV-am around 2 million), Channel 4 launched its **'Daily'** breakfast programme in 1989 with the promise to offer not the lowest-common-denominator fodder of the other two but a diet to satisfy business people and the more discerning. There was no sofa, no chit-chat and not many viewers.

One group breakfast television served well was politicians. Coverage in news-bulletins, reviews of newspaper articles and interviews early in the morning softened viewers for onslaughts like 'Election Call' phone-ins later on. In 1983 there was a plethora of politics – little let-up between the February Bermondsey by-election, with the homophobic campaign against Labour's gay candidate Peter Tatchell, and the Alliance win and the June general election. This was the first without Robert McKenzie, the Canadian university professor and pundit who began covering elections on television in 1959. He had died in 1981. He was famous for his broad knowledge of British political parties and his puppy-like tenacity when interviewing politicians (Lord Hailsham had called his interrogation of him after the Profumo scandal in 1963 'a kick in the stomach'). He was enjoyed by viewers for his breathless enthusiasm for polling results and for his Swingometer, a brilliantly simple device of a pendulum to show how a swing in election voting from one party to another could affect an overall majority in the House of Commons. Of course there was more than one Swingometer; there were new ones (growing smaller and more colourful) for each election.

Election nights now are a spectator sport, and the BBC and ITV spend fortunes on fancy graphics, sending outside-broadcast teams, their top journalists and newscasters around the land with politicians, while hundreds of correspondents are employed to relay constituency results.

In 1983 politicians managed to involve themselves in one of the year's most talked-about imports from America: the 2½-hour documentary film **'The Day After'**, which showed what could follow a nuclear attack on an American city. The film – as politically neutral as a war film could be – cost £4.8 million to make in Laurence, near Kansas. Jason Robards led a cast of 2,000 local citizens as victims vaporised when their town went up in a giant puff of smoke. The random destruction had involved the careful arrangement of twenty truckloads of construction rubble and sackfuls of soot, flour and ashes blown by wind machines. Consequently the blasted buildings and the citizens – covered in white fallout dust, dead or dying, red-eyed and going bald, looting and killing, some digging mass graves before radiation sickness struck them, too – were a disturbing sight. When the film was shown in America, doctors and psychiatrists were warned to expect a rush of patients suffering depression the next day.

Secretary of State George Shultz appeared immediately after the screening to stress President Reagan's commitment to peace and argue the implications with commentators including Henry Kissinger. In Britain, Mary Whitehouse's call for it not to be shown because it would upset 'immature minds' was ignored, and after it was shown on a December Saturday night Michael Heseltine appeared to condemn peace campaigners who distorted the issues.

Another American drama about war left critics and millions of viewers depressed. The £26 million version of Herman Wouk's **'The Winds of War'** had more trailers than a caravan-park and ran for sixteen hours on ITV that autumn. The BBC seemed to wave the white flag, showing old films and darts as we learned how Robert Mitchum as Pug, an exceptionally elderly American naval attaché, travelled around Europe meeting Churchill, Hitler and Roosevelt, said what a man has to say and won the Second World War. On the way there were problems from his gee-whizz wife, a 'poetic' son called Byron, nutty Natalie (Ali McGraw), a Jewess who decided to go to Poland just as the Nazis invaded, and plucky Pam (Victoria Tennant), the English rose who tried to bowl Pug over. (Big, triangular men like Mitchum don't bowl that easy though. Mitchum moved as if on castors.) The series ended halfway through the book, with Pug up on a hill at Pearl Harbor. Threats of more ill Winds followed. A sequel, 'War and Remembrance', came in 1989.

Polished and well-written home-made drama series abounded in 1983. The true story of a legendary Russian agent working for the British to try to topple the Bolshevik régime before James Bond had sipped his first unstirred Martini, **'Reilly, Ace of Spies'**, was the most expensive series from Euston Films so far, at £4.5 million. Written by Troy Kennedy Martin, it had a fine performance from New Zealand actor Sam Neill, who wore a centre parting and a seductive frown as the cold-hearted killer and irresistible womaniser (in Moscow eight women claimed to be *the* Mrs Reilly before being rounded up by the Tsar's police). The sets of turn-of-the-century Moscow, Paris, Port Arthur were stunning. One error was spotted: as Sam undressed he displayed a white bikini-marked behind when Reilly would have worn a swimsuit down to his knees. And Reilly's death in the series had been guessed – accurately as it turned out. *Izvestia*, the Russian newspaper, reported three months later that he had been executed in 1925 by the Soviet Supreme Revolutionary Tribunal. Partly because the BBC had slotted *The Godfather* against the long opening episode the twelve-part series didn't make the Top Ten.

The ITV drama of the year was **'Auf Wiedersehen Pet'**, Central's thirteen-part comedy about a group of Geordie building workers on the lump in Germany, coping with krauts, with each other and without their families. The most popular was Oz, played by Jimmy Nail. Other lovable lads were Tim Healy's moderately sane Dennis, Kevin Whately's drippy Neville, Gary Holton's girl-mad cockney Wayne and boring Barry from Wolverhampton (stalwart of the West Bromwich and District Table Tennis League and fond of showing his snapshots of Bruges) played by Tim Spall.

Making the series in Germany proved tricky, especially for the Germans. One actor attacked a hotel porter and was chased by gun-toting cops who'd earlier had to separate rowing actors and locals in a bar. The producers hired a coachload of vice girls from Hamburg's red-light district to appear in a scene, only to find some were men a few of whom had cut themselves shaving. They also hired seventy squaddies from a nearby army camp to play extras in a bar, lads who promptly got into the mood by downing more than 600 bottles of beer before filming started and were so obviously drunk that the scenes had to be scrapped. One cast-member broke a leg, another broke a foot; but somehow episodes were made, and by February 1984 the show was challenging 'Coronation Street' at the top of the ratings. A new series was made in Marbella the following year, but halfway through Gary Holton died of a drugs overdose. With clever rewriting and re-editing and the occasional use of a double, Wayne was seen in every episode screened in the spring of 1986, and the series again proved a ratings triumph.

There were impressive plays. The best was **'An Englishman Abroad'**, the BAFTA winner, in which Coral Browne played herself twenty-five years earlier in Alan Bennett's play about her strange meeting with the spy Guy Burgess during an Old Vic tour in Moscow (Dundee did well decked out with eighty tons of salt). Alan Bates was mesmerising as the spy, stumbling into a dressing-room drunk and being sick in the washbasin, then inviting her to lunch at his flat to listen to his one record, by Jack Buchanan. Ironically Coral almost married Buchanan. Against this Thames Television slotted their big single drama of the year, **'Saigon, Year of the Cat'**, which cast Judi Dench in a would-be torrid tale of love during Vietnam's dirty war. Slow and so-so, someone should have told Frederick Forrest, her seemingly comatose co-star, that you're supposed to fall asleep *after*, not during.

The classical production of the year was undoubtedly Laurence Olivier's towering **'King Lear'**, made by Granada for Channel 4. For rehearsal of the storm scene a stagehand with an umbrella sheltered him from the torrent-making rain machine. But on the take the seventy-six-year-old actor withstood the deluge for fifteen minutes and spent the next two days in bed to safeguard against pneumonia.

There were several stinkers. The BBC's drama disaster was **'The Cleopatras'**, an eight-parter described as a horror comic about the incestuous murderous rulers of Egypt *circa* 145 BC. Amanda Boxer had a drastic haircut

The idea for 'Auf Wiedersehen Pet' came from a real Geordie brickie who had worked on a site in Düsseldorf. Writers Ian La Frenais and Dick Clement took him out to Germany for the filming, only to witness his being slapped into gaol for stealing a car on his last trip. The actors (all given a fortnight's course in bricklaying) soon became household favourites.

and appeared as a boiled egg, while a team of other actresses had to jiggle about topless dressed only in gold paint and black wire-wool wigs as handmaidens to the queens (there were umpteen Cleos, it turned out). Richard Griffiths, bulging like a stack of crumpets, with ice-cream cornets on his head and a pan-handle strapped to his chin, played the fiendish Potbelly. In one episode Potbelly killed the son of his sister Queen Cleo, married her and gave her a new son, raped her daughter, married her, discredited the mother and later cut up their son to send the mother the bits in a box. Richard was second choice for the charming chap. Roly-poly Roy Kinnear was first picked. Producer Guy Slater said: 'Potbelly was arguably one of the most evil people in the world, and Roy is arguably one of the least evil in Equity.'

The comedy of the year evolved from an agony column which John Sullivan read in one of his wife's magazines. He devised **'Just Good Friends'**, about Vince and Penny, a rough working-class chap and the prissy middle-class girl he jilted and met by chance five years later. Paul Nicholas was the cocky hero, now a rich bookie with a gorgeously grotesque family in scrap (can we ever forget Ann Lynn as his exotically common mum or the car with the bull-horns on the bonnet?) His lot were matched by Jan Francis as Penny with a snobbish mother and hard-up dad. After one series of foreplay Penny dropped. In the third Vince grew up and the couple married in a Christmas special.

In 'Coronation Street', Ken Barlow's wife Deirdre had her affair with Mike Baldwin. The nation took sides. *The Times* followed almost every other newspaper by giving a 'story-so-far' summary. John Betjeman, a fan of the soap, announced: 'Ken's a nice man; he deserves better.' Ken got Deirdre back, though.

Commercial Break

It was a great year for commercials. Lynda Bellingham and Michael Redfern arrived as the couple in the new Oxo family. Adam Faith appeared (free) at the end of a Family Planning Association film in which two teenagers talked about unwanted pregnancy. He said: 'Any idiot can get a girl into trouble – don't let it be you.' The Cinzano commercials starring Leonard Rossiter and Joan Collins were stopped by the company's directors in Italy who could see nothing funny about a man spilling his precious drink over a woman. And the Two Ronnies filmed a very funny series of commercials for Hertz car rentals.

Also Shown in 1983

There was plenty of transatlantic trash. 'The Blue and the Grey' was an epic that seemed to last longer than the Civil War. 'Matt Houston', millionaire detective with a jacuzzi and a Harvard-trained dolly-girl sidekick, failed to amaze us; as did Remington Steele, played by Pierce Brosnan as a detective cum moving tailor's dummy. 'T. J. Hooker' arrived featuring William Shatner of 'Star Trek' in a shaggy toupee as a sort of American Dixon of Dock Green – decent and boring; and 'Hotel' opened and closed quickly. The series which lasted and was wildly successful was 'The A-Team' – a bunch of certifiably insane Viet vet vigilantes led by cigar-chewing fancy-dress freak Hannibal Smith (George Peppard) with a vast black pudding in a Mohican haircut and necklaces, B. A. (for Bad Attitude) Baracus, played by former nightclub bouncer Laurence Tero (Mr T). Their weekly rescue missions ended in genocide (an average thirty-nine acts of violence a week, one watchdog group recorded) but didn't deter Boy George from applying to appear in an episode. He ended up paying £42,000 to appear as himself as a kidnap victim. By 1988 the knives were out for the show. Sir William Rees-Mogg, newly appointed chairman of the Broadcasting Standards Council, declared it too violent for young viewers.

The best American performances that year were in **'Kennedy'** – JFK's story from the election campaign to his assassination in Dallas. Martin Sheen managed to sound uncannily like the man, Blair Brown was excellent as Jackie, and the wonderfully ugly Vincent Gardenia was creep of the year as J. Edgar Hoover.

The best-lasting American series was Channel 4's **'St Elsewhere'**, a medicated soap set like **'Cheers'** (the brilliant Channel 4 comedy also to begin that year) in Boston and like 'Hill Street Blues' (both were made by MTM Television) juggling four or five stories each episode.

The British version of 'St Elsewhere' was G. F. Newman's four-part drama, **'The Nation's Health'**, attacking methods in the besieged National Health Service which cruelly mistreated patients and either wore out caring doctors or corrupted them. Also on Channel 4 was **'The Irish RM'** with Peter Bowles as a country magistrate and **'A Married Man'** turned out a triumph. It starred Anthony Hopkins and Ciaran Madden as a middle-class couple who seemed just bored with each other – they must have emptied a ketchup factory for the murder scene.

Anglia Television began making six-part thrillers from the straightforward classy whodunits of P. D. James. **'Death of an Expert Witness'** – the first of five screened up to 1988 – introduced Roy Marsden as the poetry-writing, mostly po-faced policeman Adam Dalgleish. Scottish Television introduced an even more sombre version with **'Killer'**, featuring Mark McManus as Taggart. Thames Television's thrillers featuring Antonia Fraser's gel detective **'Jemima Shore'** washed up early. Even Patricia Hodge as the heroine couldn't make up for a world of upper-class twits.

The BBC's record in drama series that year was not impressive. Workmanlike were the cockney caper **'Give Us a Break'** starring Robert Lindsay, **'Jury'** with twelve mediocre men, and **'My Cousin Rachel'** starring the Cornish scenery which stole the show in 'Poldark' and Geraldine Chaplin as Daphne du Maurier's heroine. Two other watchable serials were BBC2's **'The Old Men at the Zoo'**

from Angus Wilson's satire, starring Andrew Cruickshank, Marius Goring, Roland Culver and, unforgettably, Robert Morley as a power-mad millionaire, and **'The Mad Death'**, a horror story from BBC Scotland, showing how in a rabies outbreak our furry friends could become more deadly than the Alien.

As for the plays of the year, Maggie Smith was heart-rending as a meddlesome mum in **'Mrs Silly'**; Julie Welch took a backhanded shot at the prima donnas of women's tennis in her good play **'Singles'**; Tim Roth played the skinhead snarler you'd least like to meet in a dark alley in **'Made in Britain'**, David Leland's biased but brilliant quartet of plays; and Ian McKellen reappeared as the mentally handicapped tragic hero in **'Walter and June'**. Sarah Miles joined him as a nutty nympho who broke his heart again.

There were no excuses for Central's **'No Excuses'**, in which Charlotte Cornwell pulled sour faces and hit sour notes as an alleged rock singer. The series made history when Charlotte won £10,000 in a libel case against the *Sunday People*'s television critic who had written, among other things, that the actress had a big bum. Other bummers included the BBC's dire **'Dark Side of the Sun'**, a mishmash of occult goings-on in craggy Crete. Central's attempt at black comedy, **'The Home Front'**, in which Brenda Bruce played a monstrous battle-axe head of a frightful family, also sank. The BBC's nonsense-in-costume was **'By the Sword Divided'**, and the Corporation parted with many pieces of silver for the two-parter **'Peter and Paul'**. But it wasn't as awful as the hysterically historical **'Masada'**, which proved a joy for anachronism-spotters – polyester sheets, stainless-steel goblets, vestal virgins in white Crimplene, and the polystyrene pillars of Rome positively rocking with whispered lies.

Outstanding among the factual programmes was **'The Paras'**, a fly-on-the-barrack-room-wall series about the men on their way to become the élite 'red devils'. BBC Scotland's documentary series **'The Visit'** began with Desmond Wilcox tagging along asking ordinary people making life-changing trips anxious unctuous questions. By contrast the best things about BBC's **'Just Another Day'** were John Pitman's economical comments. The most memorable single documentary was BBC2's **'Simon's War'** about the continuing fight of Welsh guardsman Simon Weston, horribly burned during the Falklands War. He later made two more-heartening films.

Russell Harty began dropping in for tea with ordinary folk (we knew the BBC was hard up, but this seemed excessive); **'Name That Tune'** came out of 'Wednesday Night Out', emerging as Thames Television's most successful light-entertainment show next to 'This Is Your Life'. TVS gave us the ultra-noisy outdoor effort **'Ultra Quiz'**; and Yorkshire Television served up **'Just Amazing'**, a just appalling Saturday show featuring such stunts as a man eating worm pizzas with spiders and flies for afters.

High ratings (in Channel 4 terms) built up for **'Treasure Hunt'**, the game-show in which a contestant-controlled helicopter took Anneka Rice around the land shouting her head off and searching for a reward. Tennis's Annabel Croft took over in 1989.

Life wasn't so horribly cheerful in the soaps that year. **'Crossroads'** ran a plot involving a Down's Syndrome child, played by Nina Weill, who was so-afflicted. The worthy intention was ruined because the character chosen to befriend her was sexpot Sharon from the garage. In **'Dynasty'** Cecil Colby suffered a heart-attack during a stressful sex session with Alexis. Keeping his toupee on was not easy. When Alexis married him for his loot through a hole in his hospital oxygen-tent, he lost the will to live. In **'Dallas'** Sue Ellen took a toyboy, Peedurr. She found him, her son's counsellor, by the swimming-pool, so he was already wet but got wetter. Penelope Keith also took a toyboy in her least-successful comedy, **'Sweet Sixteen'**, and viewers could not forgive her. But there were far worse comedies. In **'Cuffy'** Bernard Cribbins wore a dirty mac and a dopey grin to play a tinker in a stinker of a series set in a village which looked about as rural as Kensington. Julia Foster smiled sweetly through a compost-heap effort called **'The Cabbage Patch'**; Nigel Havers and Tony Britton as father and son doctors started mugging their way through **'Don't Wait Up'**; **'No Place Like Home'** began with the worst sitcom nosy neighbour of all time Vera, the shrieking animal-lover.

Far better was **'It Takes a Worried Man'**, written by and starring Peter Tilbury, about a neurotic fool and his comically screwed-up psychiatrist, and **'Brass'**, Granada's send-up of all their ''Ee, lad, trooble at t'mill' series of the seventies. Timothy West's Bradley Hardacre, Caroline Blakiston's potty wife and Barbara Ewing's wretched mistress who'd been servicing his lust in the scullery these long years, were pure gold.

1984

That Was the Year When...

Policewoman Yvonne Fletcher was shot and killed during an anti-Gaddafi demonstration outside the Libyan embassy. □ *An IRA bomb blasted the Grand Hotel in Brighton where the Tory Party were at conference. Four died, and Norman Tebbit and his wife were badly injured.* □ *The long and bitter miners' strike started.* □ *The AIDS virus was discovered; eight months later it killed its first two people in Britain.* □ *Prince Charles called the National Gallery extension a 'monstrous carbuncle'.* □ *Heart-defect baby Fae lived for twenty days with a transplanted baboon's heart.* □ *Sarah Tisdall, a Foreign Office clerk, was gaoled for passing Cruise missile documents to the* Guardian. □ *A gas leak from a chemical works killed at least 2,000 in Bhopal, India.* □ *Sikh bodyguards shot dead Mrs Gandhi.* □ *In the Los Angeles Olympics, Mary Decker tripped over Zola Budd's heel and lost the 3,000 metres final. Torvill and Dean won a gold.* □ *Shares in British Telecom went on sale, the largest share issue in the world.* □ *Prince Harry was born.* □ *Frankie Goes to Hollywood's sexy single 'Relax' caused a row, but Michael Jackson's* Thriller *broke records for records, selling 37 million.*

Orwell's doom didn't dawn, but there were few smiles around the BBC at the start of the year. It was all very well winning high ratings for showing a trashy American version of a daft bestseller, but the commercial boys were giving 'em art – *and* pulling in sizeable audiences – and people were noticing. The fact that ITV launched 'The Jewel in the Crown' when the BBC's best bauble was 'The Thorn Birds' led to 'questions'. It also led to the bucking up of BBC ideas when later in the year

Michael Grade was appointed Controller of BBC1 and Jonathan Powell was promoted to the top job in the drama department.

Did **'The Thorn Birds'** really lay an egg? Most who saw it would say so. Here was Colleen McCullough's story of an Aussie priest who fell for a small girl, fancied her as a bigger girl, decassocked himself for some steamy love-scenes on weekend breaks from the Vatican every twenty years, and then (unknowingly) welcomed their son to the Church. Meanwhile an old rich woman yearned for him, and she and the other characters endured tragedies number 37, 24 and 18*b* in the pulp-writer's handbook. Richard Chamberlain got by as the priest – even under a white wig and with, at one point, jodhpurs under his cassock – while Barbara Stanwyck put her years of experience behind the old girl and concentrated on the fee. But Rachel Ward's playing of Meggie, the young girl, was quite outstandingly terrible. If she'd Sellotaped her mouth, merely shaken her pretty hair and pointed her pretty body at us, it mightn't have been so bad; but she *would* talk, each time in a monotone and in a different accent – English deb, strained Strine and cute Californian.

Perhaps American mini-series might benefit from the 'blessing' bestowed on Granada's fourteen-part saga **'The Jewel in the Crown'** – a customary ceremony before work on any film begins in India. There for four months to shoot half the saga based on Paul Scott's novels about the love–hate between India and Britain in the years to Independence and partition, the film crew had agreed to honour an aged holy man. He arrived at Udaipur complete with portable shrine, and above his Gandhi-style dhoti he wore a battered tweed jacket. The television gang were asked to remove shoes and squat, and were then invited to pelt the guru with flowers. In return he made to assault the camera with a coconut. At this rather worrying point, producer Christopher Morahan intervened to complete the task himself, tapping the shell gently on the tripod rather than battering the camera lens.

It was not the only worrying moment. Although three weeks had been allowed as a fair time for the crates of

Forbidden love between Harry (Art Malik) and Daphne (Susan Wooldridge) began 'The Jewel in the Crown', Granada's gem of a serial.

equipment to pass through Customs, forms for three crates among a batch of 300 had been incorrectly completed and Customs men politely proposed that all 300 should be flown back to Manchester and re-exported. With long and patient talking the problem was resolved, as was a later one involving beggars asked to be extras for a temple scene. Terms were agreed, and a coach was hired to take them to the town where the scenes were to be filmed. But when the coach arrived not only would the driver not accept such low-caste passengers, but the beggars themselves also refused – having decided that the true purpose of the trip was to whisk them to a hospital for vasectomies. A fate almost as humiliating befell actor Eric

Porter, there to play Count Bronowski, when he swam in the hotel pool in Delhi. His hair, carefully bleached silver for the old-man rôle, turned bright green on contact with the chlorine. Then there was extraordinary weather which delayed filming. Very high temperatures – 40° Centigrade in Mysore – affected everyone. Even after covering her face carefully, the sun caught the tip of Geraldine James's nose and she wasn't able to step in front of the camera for days. In Simla for the Rose Cottage scenes there was snow, so Dame Peggy Ashcroft and Rachel Kempson waited to be called for their scenes in bed with hot-water bottles. At one time, to conserve more heat, they shared the same bed.

The two most powerful scenes were among those left to be filmed in England. One was the Bibigar Gardens rape of Daphne Manners, the gawky English girl, gloriously played by Susan Wooldridge. Prejudiced reactions to the crime, blamed on her Indian lover Hari Kumar (played by handsome Art Malik), were a central theme, yet no suitable spot was found in India. The gardens had to be built in a disused quarry near Manchester. The final scenes of bloody riots between Muslims and Hindus at the railway station at the time of partition were filmed in a disused station at Quainton, Buckinghamshire, adapted with the aid of old photographs. In this case there had been suitable Indian locations, but Morahan feared faking such horrors might offend local people. Just as Europeans had been rounded up to play wartime Brits taking drinkies in Mysore, back home 130 people of Indian origin were employed as passengers and members of a murderous mob, most of them wearing dhotis for the first time in their lives. Magically the two sets of scenes were matched together. A party guest would step out of his car in India and arrive in Lancashire. A ball bounced by a child in a dusty India street was caught by Charles Dance's Sergeant Perron in Manchester.

Yet catastrophe awaited. An hour after filming ended one night in January 1983 a fire raged in the warehouse converted into a studio near the Manchester offices. All costumes and props (many brought back from India) were destroyed. Perhaps it was the benign effect of the guru's blessing that no one was injured, the items were replaced. Only the artificial arm worn by Tim Pigott-Smith as Ronald Merrick caused worry – until the Roehampton limb centre rushed up another.

Paul Scott's vision (adapted by Ken Taylor) of this 'damned, bloody, senseless mess' didn't please everyone. India experts including Enoch Powell and Salman Rushdie objected to aspects of 'The Jewel in the Crown'. Mary Whitehouse was shocked (as was the point) by a scene in which Judy Parfitt's mean-minded Mildred noisily made love with the fishy Captain Coley and was discovered by Dame Peggy's sad old missionary Barbie. But critics were almost wordless with admiration for something almost too good for television. It collected all the year's Best Drama

prizes; Tim Pigott-Smith won the BAFTA Best Actor award for his envious, sadistic and inadequate policeman Merrick, and Dame Peggy was garlanded for Barbie, the character she asked to play and whose tragic life became a judgement on events. Her portrayal of the simple, sincere yet not-quite the-right-class spinster, unwanted and finally unhinged, was outstanding.

Mind you, elsewhere on ITV new records in rubbish were being set. **'Surprise Surprise!'** was devised for Cilla Black – her first series in more than eight years – after the Liverpool singer appeared on 'Wogan' in 1983 and took over the show. Big Christopher Biggins, described as 'posh' to her 'dead common', helped explain to people (frequently addressed chummily by Cilla as 'chook') that surprises had been fixed for them – the result being a mixture of laughter and tears you found either heart-warming or stomach-turning. Cilla also appeared in little filmed stunts and sang. Critics booed, but letters poured in – 170,000 during the first series – from people hoping to set up a surprise for a relative, friend (or enemy). The second series dropped Christopher and boosted Cilla. Only when the show took her to Zeebrugge at Christmas

'The Price Is Right' was Central's high-decibel game-show in which the required skill was knowing the shop price of household goods. Leslie Crowther was the mahogany-haired host who, as the music blared, called 'Come on down!' to people picked from hysterical hooligan audiences who were then tantalised by the sight of 'the lovely Cindy' or 'the lovely Carol' draped across a lawnmower or a cocktail-cabinet. Only one contestant refused to come on down – the very first on the first show. 'My God, what have we let ourselves in for?' Leslie Crowther recalls asking himself. A man from Brixton won a holiday for two, making a girl from Liverpool the loser. The winner stunned everyone by promptly asking her to go along on the holiday. As with other game-shows, the prizes were often comically inappropriate. The winner of a set of garden furniture had only a window-box, and one little old lady almost won a windsurfer.

1987 to the hospital where ferry-disaster victims had been treated, and she led staff and survivors through the streets of Bruges singing 'Little Drummer Boy', were there a lorra complaints. This was bad taste, said some viewers.

There were some good comedies that year. Thames Television's **'Chance in a Million'** (for Channel 4) had this young fogey. Lumbering sort of fellow. Seemed sane. Not quite. Tight spots. Police. Wrong place, wrong car. Take your hands off my wife. Oops. Get picture? Trouble was talked like telegram. Simon Callow played him so well, hair stood on end. Brenda Blethyn played girl met on blind date. Wrong one, of course. Miss Mouse one minute, game girl next. Not everyone's cup of spilled tea. Caused speech problems length and breadth. Andrew Norriss and Richard Fegen were writer chappies. But comedy suffered a great loss in 1984. Appearing in **'Live from Her Majesty's'** in his famous red fez, Tommy Cooper keeled over with a fatal heart-attack. Viewers wondered if it was part of the joke. One of nature's funniest men, a star of the television age, kept them laughing to the end.

Michael Aspel proved he was more than the bland charmer he sometimes appeared to be when he began **'Aspel and Company'**, a Saturday-night chat-show for LWT. His touch was lighter and funnier than Parkinson's and more modest than Wogan's, whom he scooped on a number of occasions. In his first year he managed to lure Mrs Thatcher on to the show. She told the nation that she liked to potter around the house, turning out a drawer or two, and accidentally made a joke confessing: 'I'm always on the job.' In 1987, Oliver Reed appeared drunk, dishevelled and holding a jug of orange juice. He hijacked the band to sing 'Wild One' and accused fellow-guests including Clive James of being tipsy. Aspel stayed calm and James said later: 'It was one of the most exciting evenings I've had since World War Two when I was much further from the front.'

The best light-entertainment show to start in 1984 was **''Allo 'Allo'**, a send-up of 'Secret Army' and of all the series and films about zee Frennsh Rezzizztonce and zee Vee-haf-vays Gestapo. Its continuing strength is in its characters – all well drawn, well acted and very funny – in the continuing story (it's really a serial farce), in the clever production of elaborate and ridiculous escape-plots and in the central performance of Gorden Kaye as harassed café-owner René. (Gorden has now come a long way from his first television rôle as Elsie Tanner's skinny nephew Bernard Butler in 'Coronation Street' in 1968.) Belgian nobleman Count Axel du Monceau de Bergendal was probably the poshest person to be incensed by ''Allo 'Allo' – there was a call for it to be debated in the European Parliament. Many others have claimed that the series insults the memory of those who suffered in the war. But no nation is singled out. The Germans are shown as insensitive, lazy or kinky – a favourite running joke is black-leather-clad Herr Otto Flick's icy passion for Helga, the officer in whalebone corselette and black suspenders under her SS uniform. The French are shown as devious and immoral – René's nubile waitresses are always panting for his chubby body, and he is constantly on the point of betraying his battle-axe of a wife, Edith, whose singing in the café induces customers to plug their ears with Camembert. The show's catchphrase, 'I shall say this ernly wernce', is spoken deadpan by Michelle, Kirsten Cooke's raincoated Resistance fighter in every episode, usually after she has climbed into the café through a window. The British are perhaps most keenly insulted. Secret serviceman Crabtree has now been posing for five years as a gendarme and thinks he's speaking French by mangling and remangling his vowels. Because it is such a concentrated effort, he has never been seen to smile. When Arthur Bostrom who plays him (and actually speaks quite good French) had to play a scene in which he talked to the RAF twits in English, he dried up completely. While the series is loved in Spain and other European countries, and France bought it in 1989, an agreed deal for twenty-six episodes with the Americans fell through. But copiers of the famous painting, 'The Fallen Madonna with the Big Boobies' (which Hitler is desperate for), have managed to cash in. A Channel Islands firm produced a batch of £70 copies and sold them all.

The new heroines of the year were more worthy. Nerys Hughes was Megan in **'District Nurse'**, tut-tutting at 1920s Welsh miners' families. By contrast every appearance of Joan Hickson's **Miss Marple**, knitting and nodding her way around the villages of thirties and forties England, was like the arrival of a fairy godmother. Since 1984 eight Miss Marple stories have been filmed, some as three-part serials, many as Christmas treats.

Thames introduced some very common cockney coppers with **'The Bill'**, a drama which plodded like the sturdy feet of the WPC and her partner in the opening titles. The police who saw previews disliked it so much

---

A girl assists DI Burnside (Christopher Ellison) of 'The Bill' with his enquiries. What would Dixon have said?

they refused to go to the launch-party. Later Leslie Curtis of the Police Federation attacked the series for showing race prejudice inside the force. The very idea! The pace quickened and the characters developed over five series, and in 1988 the hour-long episodes were split into half-hours shown twice-weekly, fifty-two weeks a year. Again the series angered Scotland Yard, who objected to the extensive publicity campaign for it. Newspaper ads, they said, looked like recruitment notices, only they didn't like the suggestion that some policemen were 'liars, cheats and bullies'. But the new format, with its rule that there should never be a scene without a police character in it, and the use of hand-held cameras which gave the impression viewers were actually running on the chase, proved a success.

Meanwhile in a former banana-warehouse in Docklands a team of craftsmen, writers and actors were producing a series which, over the next five years, would 'denigrate what we hold most dear' according to one MP, outrage royalists and offend the famous. Central's **'Spitting Image'** made every other satirical show look cissy and every comedy since 'The Goon Show' seem well-behaved. At first the IBA censors asked for cuts – such as the deletion of a 'bugger' and a scene of a Harold Macmillan puppet spilling soup on himself. Conservative MPs fumed at their mocking of the royal family – the Queen Mum as a Brummie horse-racing fanatic, Princess Michael with a Hitler moustache or Prince Philip swigging Ouzo – because 'they couldn't answer back' and looked *so* ugly. Mary Whitehouse was disgusted that when Princess Margaret was in hospital 'Spitting Image' had her dancing and brandishing a gin-bottle. But no one complained at the sight of Colonel Gaddafi announcing the International Terrorist of the Year Award (and being blown up when opening the envelope). Gradually the audiences grew (to around 11 million for the Sunday-night shows) and protesters petered out, worn down by the cheek of modellers Peter Fluck and Roger Law, producer John Lloyd (who with Sean Hardie started 'Not the Nine O'Clock News'), the daring and topicality of the gaggle of writers mostly from the John Cleese, Peter Cook and *Private Eye* schools, and the skill of actors including Steve Nallon who provides Mrs Thatcher's booming butch voice, Chris Barrie, Enn Reitel, Kate Robbins and Jessica Martin. There were spin-offs, of course. Over 120,000 vinyl toy 'Spitting Image' Mrs Thatchers for dogs to chew were sold within six weeks, and chart success came with the 'Spitting Image Chicken Song', which topped the pops in May 1986. But, when a 'Spitting Image' book included a nude caricature of Prince Andrew, Prince Charles struck back by withdrawing a volume of his collected speeches from the same publisher, Faber & Faber.

Usually the show's victims pretended not to be stung.

In 1986 'Spitting Image' made a 'special' for American viewers. In it they could mock Ronald Reagan (who could not differentiate between ordering a pizza and a nuclear attack) but they couldn't 'do' Mickey Mouse, Walt Disney lawyers warned. In fact the show provoked a number of complaints to NBC second only to those about coverage of the Irangate affair.

Alastair Burnet was suave and unfazed by the puppet with the exploding nose. Ian St John said the puppets of himself and Jimmy Greaves looked better than the originals. Denis Healey, the only real person to appear on a show, pretended to be hurt that people mistook him for a dummy. Jeffrey Archer sent them a voice tape so that they could improve their version of him. But, while they weren't spending fortunes in libel damages, costs of making the half-hour shows still rose dramatically. By 1988 the £10,000-a-minute show's life-sized puppets were costing £2,000 a time to make. Economies were essential. Sue Lawley was a head with Cilla Black's bust; Kenneth Kendall was Magnus Magnusson in a mask; the newly deceased medium Doris Stokes proved there is life after death – she comes back regularly as someone's grannie.

A year earlier Michael Heseltine was poised to help their cash-flow. He offered £2,500 to buy his puppet and eventually agreed to pay £7,500; but after asking to whom he should make the cheque payable he stormed out. He'd been told: 'The Labour Party.'

Also Shown in 1984

There was plenty to embarrass us. 'All Star Secrets', a guessing game, made you cringe for celebrities. Meanwhile in 'Sex Matters' a model and her boyfriend were filmed making love (or pretending to) in one part of a six-part 'there, there' series officially supposed to help people with problems. Then LWT came up with a candidate for the Worst Situation Comedy of All Time – 'Bottle Boys' – about milkmen (a drunken Scot, a randy West Indian, a fusspot Welshman and an assortment of cavemen cockneys led by Robin Askwith of soft-porn fame). A runner-up was Granada's 'Poor Little Rich Girls', which had Maria Aitken and Jill Bennett as temporarily man-less upper-crust gels.

'Duty Free' was Yorkshire Television's soon top-of-the-ratings farce about two couples on the longest-lasting fortnight's holiday in travel history. Set on the Costa Quick Laughs, it was easy to enjoy the vulgarity. Another success was Channel 4's 'Fairly Secret Army', David Nobbs's comedy about Major Harry Truscott (Geoffrey Palmer), an unemployable, stupid yet strangely lovable member of the loony Right, rounding up a private army ready to fight when the Left tries to take over. Channel 4 also offered 'Who Dares Wins', an alternative-comedy sketch-show which proved that 'alternative' needn't mean not funny. Tony Robinson spent two whole shows naked. BBC2's answer, 'A Kick up the Eighties', came from Scotland and was almost as good. Mel Smith and Griff Rhys Jones began their sketch-and-gag series 'Alas Smith and Jones' on BBC2 and proved they were probably as talented, if dirtier, than the mainstream comics they said they disliked. Their regular 'man-talk' strand has been a lasting triumph.

'Fresh Fields' was a typical uninspired ITV sitcom saved by Julia McKenzie breathing a fresh-ness into her scatty-wife rôle and Anton Rodgers being lovable as her gruff sensible hubby. Those rôles were reversed in 'Ever Decreasing Cir-cles', the BBC's comedy which had Richard Briers as Martin, exactly the sort of pathetically precise know-it-all we've all had the misfortune to work with or live near, and Penelope Wilton as his absurdly nice wife. Among ITV's misses was 'Tripper's Day', set in a supermarket, which proved that even Leonard Rossiter could fail. So could the magnificent Ronnie Barker, who rolled his r's and flounced as a blundering bohemian photo-grapher in 'The Magnificent Evans' for the BBC.

Some new light-entertainment shows were not bad. 'Child's Play' combined the charm of Michael Aspel with that of small children in the serious process of defining words for celebrities teamed with contestants to guess. (Lyndon Nicholas, aged ten, said, 'Grown-ups do it when they're out of money from the bank and have run out of alcohol and haven't got any money for any more,' to define *worry*.) LWT also began 'We Love TV', a well-mannered quiz-show hosted by Gloria Hunniford. (It would have been better had the BBC allowed them to use clips of BBC shows.) Thames revived the BBC's parlour game 'What's My Line?', which never quite took wing, perhaps because George Gale and Jilly Cooper were never a match for Gilbert Harding and Lady Barnett, but Barbara Kelly returned looking and sounding unchanged after the twenty-one-year gap. Bob Monkhouse crossed to BBC to start 'Bob's Full House', a superior bingo game which allowed him to tell jokes and ad-lib. On some of the instruction-cards he would write key words to jokes but on others simply an exclamation mark indicating 'Get out of this'. Knowing he risked a whole show of exclamation marks helped whip up his adrenalin, he said.

Thames Television spent three years working on 'Crime Inc.', which showed such homely types as Jimmy 'The Weasel' Fratianno and other Mafia grasses, giving an ugly and frightening picture of the Sicilian secret society which organises America's biggest industry: crime. Better spent were the three years preparing 'The Living Planet', BBC2's sequel to 'Life on Earth'. 'River Jour-neys' was the BBC's sequel to its railway journeys series, in which explorer Christina Dodswell and others travelled down exotic rivers and won the BAFTA Best Factual Series prize. Best dramatised documentary was Channel 4's cool and chilling 'The Biko Inquest'. Albert Finney played the lawyer for the family of Steve Biko, the South African campaigner for people's rights, and Nigel Davenport played the brick-wall-brained police chief. There were two dramas about nuclear war and what might follow. Anthony Andrews appeared stripped in a stream in the first, 'Z for Zachariah'. There was little to say about it. The water was probably cold. Much more was made from 'Threads' – the BBC's go at creating the end of the world. It was made in Sheffield, with 400 locals as extras; and perhaps because it was so horrifying, few people watched the documentary sequel, 'On the Eighth Day'.

The heroes of 1984's drama series were mostly

apologetic, self-deprecating and a bit seedy. Stacey Keach was the most macho as **'Mike Hammer'** (until otherwise detained at Her Majesty's pleasure for a drugs offence). The show had us addressing our nearest and dearest as 'Hey, giant lizard breath'. Hammer's girls, all D-cupped in Bet Lynch cocktail dresses could have given Benny Hill a coronary. Powers Boothe, who looked like a baby Bob Hope, was Chandler's knight-in-tarnished-armour in **'Marlowe – Private Eye'**, walking the mean streets of Twickenham in a sadly short ITV co-production. John Thaw possibly wishes to forget LWT's **'Mitch'**, a screwed-up foot-in-the-door newspaper crime-reporter to whom Inspector Regan would not have given the time of day. Leigh Lawson played Granada's **'Travelling Man'**, Lomax, a framed copper, who did what a man's gotta do in a narrowboat, slowly but without getting wet. And Ray Brooks put believable anguish and charm into Robbie Box, dishevelled cardsharp and betting-shop shuffler, the hero of **'Big Deal'**, which became one for the BBC. In the BBC's **'One by One'** Roy Heyland played a zoo vet battling with elephants with bad bowels and keepers with bad tempers. For viewers missing 'All Creatures', this was something – but not much.

HTV's £2 million six-part **'Robin of Sherwood'** was a fresh throng of murky myths set in a glen where no man was merry but the 'hooded one' (a sort of talking hat-stand) guided the good. Michael Praed was a bedraggled, hairy and sweaty Robin until he was called to Broadway and thence to 'Dynasty' (as Prince Mince of Moldavia), so Jason Connery, son of Sean, took over for the third series in 1986.

Among the serials was the BBC's **'Diana'**, a leather-bound romance for which Jenny Seagrove should have won the Most Throttlable Heroine award for her rich tease. **'Sorrel and Son'** had Richard Pascoe's perfect performance as an ex-officer and gentleman left penniless after the First World War taking work as a lowly hotel porter to educate his son. Why Ray Lonnen plodded through Yorkshire Television's misnamed **'The Brief'** (it seemed to last a lifetime) as a barrister in a secrets case remained a secret.

Charles Dance dashed and dazzled in the BBC thriller serial **'The Secret Servant'**, and David Suchet baffled in BBC2's expensive serial about the shrink **'Freud'**. Yorkshire Television disappointed us again with **'The Glory Boys'**, a story of two assassins in search of a victim; but BBC2 delighted and titillated with the seven-part play series **'Oxbridge Blues'** from Frederic Raphael's stories of life after the glittering prizes. LWT's comedy film **'Blue Money'** with Tim Curry as a star-struck cabby on the run from the Mafia, the IRA and Billy Connolly as a head-banging hitch-hiker, was great value. Mona Washbourne was heart-warming as the old lady in ITV's Christmas play **'December Flower'**, and Harriet Walter was inspiring as aviator Amy Johnson in the BBC's play **'Amy'**. Laurence Olivier showed that even great actors can choose rotten plays when he starred in Granada's **'Ebony Tower'** as a painter with Toyah Wilcox ath one of hith playthingth.

There was a bumper crop of pre-packaged mini-series. Channel 4 brought us **'The Far Pavilions'**, an £8 million star-studded romance in the nineteenth-century Raj with John Gielgud, Omar Sharif, Ben Cross, and blue-eyed Amy Irving as the Indian princess. **'Master of the Game'** was a power-mad feuding-family saga with Dyan Cannon as Big Momma looking practically the same aged sixteen or ninety. ITV did better with the Aussie saga **'Return to Eden'**, in which Greg, a lip-curling former tennis star, threw rich wife Steff to the crocs. Much mauled, she survived. In the summer it was Reptiles versus the Olympics. While the BBC gave us running and jumping, ITV showed **'V'**, an American science-fiction serial about the Visitors who turned out to have green scales and black forked tongues.

In **'Coronation Street'** Mavis and Derek both bottled out of their wedding day, Elsie Tanner left for Portugal, and Stan Ogden died, prompting a brilliant performance from Jean Alexander as his widow, Hilda. In **'Crossroads'** David Hunter had an illegitimate child, and in **'Dallas'** Donna Reed took over the rôle of Miss Ellie.

Commercial Break

A new soap opera emerged in commercials. High-powered David told his glamorous wife Jo-anne that he was setting up his own business, and she was devastated it might mean goodbye to the Renault company car. Renault decided it was so successful that they launched a series of playlets about the couple, and Rosalyn Landor who played Joanne was inundated with marriage proposals. Henry Cooper appeared with his twin brother George eating Shredded Wheat, and snooker referee Len Ganley crushed a ball and was the first about whom one could 'bet he drinks Carling Black Label'. Victor Kiam II told us he was so impressed with an electric shaver that he went out and bought the company, Remington. Jimmy Tarbuck flogged us Sharp microwaves, and Cilla Black put the 'oo' in Typhoo (dressed as a waitress) – a personal best performance of the year for each of them.

1985

By the middle of 1985 an exclusive photograph of the Queen barbecuing a corgi would have had to make way on the front page of any popular newspaper for a story – any story – about a new twice-weekly television drama serial. **'EastEnders'**, the BBC's most spectacular success ever, had taken hold.

Throughout the history of the BBC, high-minded men had deemed soap operas not quite the thing, not 'proper' drama. Back in the sixties, daring producers had tried to compete with 'Coronation Street' by launching such running dramas as 'Compact', 'United!' and 'The New-comers', but these were all relatively short-lived and won little favour 'upstairs'. But by 1985, when ITV and Channel 4 were taking around 60 per cent of the viewing audience, attitudes were changing. A counterattack was needed, and this, important people decided, should be a popular serial, two episodes a week, fifty-two weeks a year – in other words a soap opera. Entrusted with this major breakthrough were producer Julia Smith and script editor Tony Holland who had worked together on 'Z Cars', 'Angels' and 'District Nurse'. They were offered a number of settings for their new project – including life in a shopping arcade and in a mobile-trailer park – and dumped them fast. In twenty minutes in a Shepherd's Bush wine-bar they thrashed out their format and sold it to BBC1 Controller Alan Hart in half an hour.

They decided to set the show in a decaying East London square, Albert Square, in the fictional borough of Walford. The principal families were the Fowlers, the Beales and the Wattses. Holland based the Fowlers and the Beales on his own relatives, while some of the character names were taken from East End cemeteries. There were the usual teething troubles. Ethel Skinner was supposed to have had a pet Yorkshire terrier and Den Watts an Alsatian, but suitable canine performers couldn't be found so they had to settle for a pug and an apricot standard poodle respectively. And the rôle of Angie Watts was to have been played by actress Jean Fennell, but she was sacked before the first episode and her place was taken by Anita Dobson.

The serial began on 19 February and soon became the most talked about show in the country – a good idea whose time had come. Newspapers learned that soap sold copies, and 'EastEnders' stars certainly made copy. A mere three days after more than 17 million had tuned in to the first episode, the news broke that actor Leslie Grantham (alias Den Watts) had served eleven years in prison for murdering a taxi-driver while he was a soldier in Germany back in 1966. Revelations followed about almost every other actor and actress in 'EastEnders'. The controversies may have upset the production team but they did wonders for the ratings. In October, three weeks after young mum Michelle told Den he was the father of her baby, 'EastEnders' ousted 'Coronation Street' from the top of the ratings (admittedly with the help of the Sunday omnibus edition). The programme went from strength to strength, and the two episodes screened on Christmas Day 1986 attracted an average of 30 million viewers – the highest-ever recorded figures. In fact bookmakers had been so convinced that 'EastEnders' would head the Christmas ratings that they had refused to take bets on it.

The characters became national heroes. Susan Tully, who played Michelle Fowler, was used to introduce the NSPCC's better-parenting campaign, and Bill Treacher (Arthur Fowler) became a symbol of the unemployed via the Hands Across Britain day. Both received a vast mailbag from those in similar predicaments. Prisoners at Dartmoor staged a mini-riot when they were unable to see whether Michelle married Lofty; couples rushed to marriage guidance councils after watching Den and Angie's break-up; a vicar spoke of forgiving Den in a parish magazine article; and 'EastEnders' even went on the school syllabus for thousands of inner-London children. As a result of this mass identification with the programme, Julia Smith as producer carried an extra burden. When Sue Osman (Sandy Ratcliff) had a cancer scare, Julia had to ensure that the story ended with a non-malignant tumour. 'Because I was sure that way we would send viewers

rushing out to their nearest clinic for breast-screening. If we'd had malignant cancer, they'd have all stayed at home worrying themselves to death, thinking they'd got it, too.' Women did indeed flock for screenings, and the story-line earned praise from junior health minister Edwina Currie.

The appeal of 'EastEnders' lay in its ability to deal with inner-city problems of the eighties. It didn't duck the important issues of the day – rape, unemployment, homosexuality, alcoholism, abortion and prostitution. Inevitably, there were numerous complaints. Salisbury coroner John Elgar made adverse comments about Angie's suicide scene, saying it was 'regrettable' and could lead to copycat attempts. Mary Whitehouse once said: 'It is at our peril that we allow this series. Its verbal aggression and its atmosphere of physical violence, its homosexuality, its blackmailing pimp and its prostitute, its lies and deceit and its bad language, cannot go unchallenged.' She also attacked the decision to repeat the show on a Sunday. Julia Smith countered: 'I think I'm just as moral as Mrs Whitehouse. And I care possibly more deeply. The difference is she generally believes in sweeping things under the carpet and pretending they don't exist. I believe

'EastEnders', the BBC's blockbuster soap opera, was never about happy families, but the Fowlers kept their miseries under their hats for a day in Southend.

in showing what does exist and preparing people for the world they live in. My prime aim is to entertain, my second is to inform.'

Despite the worthiness of 'EastEnders' the best soap of 1985 was undoubtedly 'Acorn Antiques' from **'Victoria Wood – as Seen on TV'**. With the cast continually fluffing their lines, the set in constant danger of collapse and the cameraman seeming to have had one too many in the pub at lunchtime, 'Acorn Antiques' was a joyous disaster, inexorably reminiscent of the halcyon days of 'Crossroads'. 'Victoria Wood – as Seen on TV' was comedy as not often seen on television – clever, original, her pictures and music coupled with a genuinely quirky personality. With Susie Blake as a condescending news-reader, Julie Walters as the crabby Mrs Overall, as well as a series of ratbags in café queues, the show was the obvious winner of the BAFTA Best Comedy prize.

Of course the King of Television was and is Terry Wogan. The year saw him graduate to a thrice-weekly live chat-show, **'Wogan'**. The new format began ignominiously when the host fell over on the very first edition, but Terry has picked himself up to confirm his standing as the most popular man on the box, attracting 3,000 letters a week. He appears permanently relaxed, although he admits that he doesn't like watching himself on screen if he's going through what he terms 'a fat phase'. Former producer Frances Whitaker said: 'He has a slim wardrobe and a slightly fatty wardrobe depending on how much weight he is carrying at the time.' Wogan was reported to earn over £350,000 a year, while guests on the show are paid between £200 and £500. When bestselling author Jeffrey Archer was a guest on the show, he was asked by Wogan: 'How much are you worth now?' He quickly replied: 'Not quite as much as you, Terry.' One of the least fragrant guests was Australian cultural attaché Sir Les Patterson, alias actor Barry Humphries. To capture that disgusting look of oral incontinence, Sir Les slapped his hand in the cheese dip in the hospitality suite and smeared it all over the front of his suit before going on stage. On another occasion, Edward Heath caused a panic among the production team when he was held up in heavy traffic on the way to the show. In the end, he just walked into the theatre and straight on to the stage, totally unruffled; but he did admit that he wished he still knew the phone number he'd had as Prime Minister which he could call to have every traffic light turn green. Wogan says his most disappointed guest was Omar Sharif. 'He told viewers he was interested in finding a wife. He got this tremendous postbag, full of naughty suggestions. The trouble was we mislaid the mail. Omar still lives in hope.' Wogan has his critics, most notably Prince Philip who once accused him of reading other people's questions off cards. 'People might not like me,' he says, 'but if they want to see a particular guest they'll switch on and tolerate me. I'm not offended by that.'

When Wogan took holidays his stand-ins sometimes floundered; Selina Scott had no problems with her star guest Prince Andrew. They flirted. One felt Prince Philip may not have been amused.

The best drama of the year was BBC2's eerie nuclear and political thriller **'Edge of Darkness'**, written by 'Z Cars' creator Troy Kennedy Martin. It won three BAFTA awards, with Bob Peck named best actor for his honest Yorkshire detective Ronald Craven. He was well equipped to play the part as his brother Geoff *is* a Yorkshire policeman. The story centred around Craven's search for the killers of his beautiful daughter Emma (Joanne Whalley), who was shot before his eyes in the opening episode.

She was a member of an underground ecology organisation, GAIA, and kept turning up as a ghost to direct her father's investigations. As a Save the Earther, Emma had been into heavier things than botany – she had raided a secret plant where illegal plutonium was being made to service America's Star Wars defence system. Enter CIA cowboy Jedburgh, played by Joe Don Baker who became Craven's one ally and eventually bestrode the show like a colossus. Baker, brought in to obtain American backers for the series and paid more than any of the British actors, said he liked the production so much that he would have

In 'Edge of Darkness', the brilliant if baffling BBC serial, a father (Bob Peck) avenged the death of his daughter (Joanne Whalley).

done it free. There were a number of intentional bloody deaths and the unintentional near-demise of Bob Peck. He was being pursued down a tunnel by two land-rovers while filming a chase in a mine when he tripped and fell. The driver didn't have time to stop, but Peck managed to roll out of the way and the vehicle missed him by inches.

Making his acting début in 'Edge of Darkness' was Labour's shadow social services minister, Michael Meacher, playing himself. His speech on nuclear energy to a students' union was worked out in collaboration with Troy Kennedy Martin. Meacher got the part because producer Michael Wearing's daughter attended the same school as his daughter and the two men met at a parent–teacher evening.

Despite its vision and power, 'Edge of Darkness' didn't please everybody. MI5 were annoyed at the disclosure of their precious security codes, while GAIA, the fictional underground terrorist group, was discovered to be the name of a respected ecological publishing firm backed by Prince Philip. They were not thrilled to be associated with the CIA, guns and sabotage.

The heroes of the American import **'Miami Vice'** might well be called trigger-happy. In one series alone, Crockett killed 32½ bad guys and Tubbs bagged 13½ (they both shot the same cocaine-dealer) whereas the genuine Miami police are responsible for only about eight deaths a year. Crockett and Tubbs can pass that total on a good night. As Crockett, Don Johnson started a trend for designer stubble and not wearing socks while it was probably advisable that men didn't imitate Philip Michael Thomas who played Tubbs. The former star of *Hair* is reportedly the father of eight children (six born out of wedlock) by several different mothers. 'Miami Vice' earned fifteen Emmy nominations in its first year as viewers latched on to its rock music, fast cars, expensive clothes and Crockett's pet alligator, Elvis.

But it topped the hate list among real American lawmen who had to wear tatty jeans to chase crooks, not flashy £400 suits. Gerald Avenberg, head of the 21,000-strong Association of Chiefs of Police, objected to the series giving the image that drug-dealing was a 'great career'. It also fell foul of the BBC when Michael Grade rejected four episodes (one was about an IRA terrorist) on the grounds that they were too violent. This didn't deter Phil Collins who played a British conman in one episode, Sheena Easton who appeared in four episodes as a singer whom Crockett married. George Michael and Andrew Ridgeley of Wham! turned down the chance to play waiters in 1986, and Princess Stephanie of Monaco was tested for a part but was judged to be inexperienced as an actress.

The BBC launched what it saw as a British version of Dynasty that year with the £3 million yachting saga **'Howards' Way'**. It told the story of Tom Howard (Maurice Colbourne) who began designing boats after being made redundant from his job in the aircraft industry

In the sailing soap 'Howards' Way', Jan (Jan Harvey) soon tired of Tom (Maurice Colbourne) and his boring mooring.

and bought into the Mermaid Yard, run by Jack Rolfe (Glyn Owen), one of the least convincing drunks in the history of television. Tom was about as wooden as Jack's boats, so it came as no surprise when wife Jan (Jan Harvey) had a fling with ghastly medallion-man Ken Masters (Stephen Yardley). For a woman with the brains to set up her own business, Jan Howard displayed an appalling lack of taste in men. She went on to have a romantic liaison with the near-geriatric Sir Edward Frere (Nigel Davenport) who bore a marked resemblance to Sam Eagle from 'The Muppets'. The Howards were blessed with two offspring: languid, goldfish-like Leo (Edward Highmore) and the huge-hulled Lynne (Tracey Childs), a spoilt brat who, after sailing solo across the Atlantic, married pigtailed Frenchman Claude du Pont (Malcolm Jamieson). Claude (pronounced 'Clod') was promptly mown down by a speedboat while water-skiing. The other member of the Howard clan was Tom's mother-in-law Kate (Dulcie Gray), a compulsive gambler but also an absolute treasure, prepared to help out any time, any place, anywhere. When she did a stint in Jan's clothes-shop, one critic dubbed her 'the world's oldest boutique assistant'.

As well as the many on-screen romances, Jan Harvey and Stephen Yardley became more than just good friends, as did Tracey Childs and Tony Anholt who played super-smooth tycoon Charles Frere. Stephen Yardley revealed that it cost a lot to make Ken Masters look tacky. Ken's clothes were bought in Savile Row and his shirts were specially made, but they were then deliberately put together in the worst-possible style. Yardley based Ken on someone he met in a bar in Benidorm. 'This guy was Ken,' he said. 'Everything was perfect – the white leather jacket, the medallions, even the gold-sovereign rings. I borrowed his style. Later, I had the idea of wearing sweaters without shirts underneath, the kind of thing Ken would think really cool. We got letters saying "It's too revolting for words", so I had obviously got it just right.'

The setting for 'Howards' Way' was the fictional Tarrant, really the yachting community of Bursledon on the River Hamble in Hampshire. The Mermaid Yard was in truth the Elephant Yard, whose owner Tom Richardson was paid £6,000 a season for filming at his premises.

Hampshire doubled for places all over the world as 'Howards' Way' fought to keep within budget. Southampton town hall became a Swiss bank, Rhode Island was re-created at Warsash on the River Hamble, and Claude and Lynne's romance in *QE2* was filmed partly on the Isle of Wight ferry and partly on a decidedly unglamorous dredger in the Solent.

Bursledon railway station became Tarrant on filming days. On one such day two elderly women passengers got out of a train but, on seeing that the sign said Tarrant, not Bursledon, thought they were in the wrong place, got back on the train and journeyed on.

'Dempsey and Makepeace' combined the 'talents' of a brash Noo York Lootenant (Michael Brandon) and an English chocolate-box blonde policewoman (Glynis Barber) who had a Cambridge degree and a titled deddy. The only interest stemmed from the real-life romance between Brandon and Barber which seemed to be on and off more frequently than a hot-water tap.

Commercial Break

Old film clips were a popular trait of commercials being screened in 1985. Griff Rhys Jones promoted Holsten Pils in a whole series of black-and-white movies opposite the likes of Barbara Stanwyck and later Marilyn Monroe, while Julie Walters was shown how to make tea by an old fifties battle-axe who looked like an urn. Silly songs proliferated, including 'Hello, Tosh, gotta Toshiba?', based on Alexei Sayle's 'Hello, John, Gotta New Motor?', and an inane housewife cavorted around the lounge doing the Shake 'n' Vac. Was that what Emmeline Pankhurst fought for?

Also in 1985

Granada launched two new soaps to compete with 'EastEnders'. The £3 million **Albion Market** began in August amidst a blaze of publicity, but a year later, while 'EastEnders' was topping the ratings, it was wound up after just a hundred episodes. Even the introduction of sixties pop star Helen Shapiro as Viv the hairdresser hadn't halted the slide. **'The Practice'**, the latest in the line of medical soaps, fared somewhat better despite a shaky start when executives scrapped the first six episodes made, claiming they were substandard. There were some original story lines such as Kev, the vasectomy-shy bus driver being driven by his wife to live in the garden shed. However, in 1986 'The Practice', too, got the snip.

Dawn French, Jennifer Saunders, Ruby Wax, Tracey Ullman and the late Joan Greenwood teamed up for the manic flat-sharing comedy **'Girls on Top'**; Alf Garnett returned for **'In Sickness and in Health'**; Richard Vernon stole the honours as the crusty father in the music teacher (Liza Goddard) and rock star (Nigel Planer) romance **'Roll Over Beethoven'**; and schoolboy Gian Sammarco starred in the first-rate television adaptation of Sue Townsend's bestseller **'The Secret Diary of Adrian Mole, Aged 13¾'**. Other new comedies were less inspiring. **'Up the Elephant, Round the Castle'** was a vehicle worthy of the talents of Jim Davidson; **'Full House'** was a dire effort about two couples who shared the same home; and **'Troubles and Strife'**, involving a young vicar and a gaggle of silly women, was marginally worse. Carla Lane wrote **'The Mistress'** in which Felicity Kendal flitted between her flower shop and her pink flat to woo lukewarm Luke, played by Jack Galloway. Teetotal Carla also penned **'I Woke Up One Morning'**, an alleged comedy about the perils of drink.

Noel Edmonds tested families' television knowledge in **'Telly Addicts'**; android **'Max Headroom'** (alias actor Matt Frewer) hosted his futuristic video show on Channel 4; Julian Pettifer presented the occupational quiz **'Busman's Holiday'**; and Cilla Black provided a 'lorra lorra laughs' on **'Blind Date'**, a show that owed much of its success to the fact that Cilla never sang on it. Sadly, its appeal began to wear thin as the contestants' carefully rehearsed ad-lib answers started to grate.

The most harrowing serial was **'The Price'** in which Peter Barkworth played an emotionally blank, work-obsessed computer millionaire whose wife and daughter were kidnapped by the IRA. A far lighter tale was Alan Plater's delightfully idiosyncratic **'The Beiderbecke Affair'**, in which two schoolteachers (James Bolam and Barbara Flynn) joined forces in a wreck of a car to solve a story of deep-rooted corruption, encountering some truly bizarre characters *en route*.

The mysterious machinations of Fleet Street were the subject of two new series that year. Peter Bowles starred as the suave rat-like gossip columnist Neville Lytton in **'Lytton's Diary'**, while David Warner played Ken Wordsworth, 'the poet laureate of sport', in **'Hold the Back Page'**.

The BBC spent £2.8 million on **'Bleak House'** with Diana Rigg and Denholm Elliott, only for it to clash with ITV's hugely popular second series of **'Widows'**. Prunella Scales and Geraldine McEwan teamed up in that delightful comedy of Edwardian manners **'Mapp and Lucia'**, Michael Gambon in **'Oscar'** showed the importance of being Oscar Wilde in all his forbidden fruitiness, and George Cole temporarily abandoned Arthur Daley to play Sir Giles in Tom Sharpe's **'Blott on the Landscape'**. Among exquisite verbal jokes were Sir Giles – body like a half-defrosted chicken – in sex games with his mistress, and mad Lady Maud (Geraldine James) yanking out her left boob to ensure that a motorway hearing became a riot. It brought new meaning to the phrase 'a titter went round the court'. David Suchet was superb as her Ladyship's loyal gardener-cum-handyman, Blott.

A series that lost its way was **'Connie'**, the female JR of the title played by Stephanie Beacham in Central's tale of passion and fashion. Stephanie was quoted as describing 'Connie' as ' "Dallas" for grown-ups or "Dynasty" with joined-up writing'. To make her heroine so aggressive, she ground her teeth enough to alarm her dentist who fitted her with a gum shield. Ironically, the series enabled Stephanie to conquer America – in 'Dynasty' spin-off **'The Colbys'**. Meanwhile, naturalist Sir Peter Scott had his reservations about Trevor Griffiths's depiction of his father, Captain Scott (played by Martin Shaw), in Central's £7 million epic **'The Last Place on Earth'**. And Dr John Hemming, director of the Royal Geographical Society which helped fund both Scott and his rival Amundsen, accused the series of being 'hysterically anti-patriotic'. Shaw's Scott, a snobbish blinkered fool, could have done with help from the actor's old colleagues in 'The Professionals' to head off Amundsen at the glacier.

Channel 4's most successful ever mini-series, **'A Woman of Substance'**, told the story of Emma Harte, a tough Victorian kitchen maid who made big. There was trooble on t' moors, trooble in t' big house, trooble in t' shop, and then trooble in t' boardroom. Alas, there was also trooble at t' script and trooble at t' cast. Jenny Seagrove played Emma between fifteen and eighty but succeeded in looking a vacant twenty-three throughout. Deborah Kerr took over at eighty, but looked only fifty and had all the grit of a cuddly pink teddy. Another forgettable drama serial was **'Maelstrom'**, set in a Norwegian fish-processing factory, with Tusse Silberg as a heroine with the liveliness of a frozen fish finger. Dyan Cannon dressed up as Deputy Dawg for the dreadful Second World War mini-series **'Jenny's War'**, and when the last episode of Jackie Collins's **'Hollywood Wives'** was shown minus fifteen crucial minutes, none of the 10 million viewers noticed! **'Drummonds'**, ITV's story of a private boarding school, was enough to send anyone off to a comprehensive, while **'The Winning Streak'**, a tedious saga of garages and rally cars, was enough to send anyone off to sleep. It would have won the worst-drama-of-the-year award but for those two preposterous all-action series **'CATS Eyes'** and **'Dempsey and Makepeace'**.

The BAFTA award for best play deservedly went to the moving **'Shadowlands'**, the story of writer C. S. Lewis's late-in-life marriage, starring Claire Bloom who duly won the Best Actress award; while Peter Watkins's banned work about an imaginary nuclear attack, **'The War Game'**, was finally transmitted, nineteen years after originally intended. The makers of **'Comrades'**, BBC2's twelve-part profile of 'ordinary' Russians, went to great lengths to obtain the footage they required. For eighteen months the Russians refused producer Olivia Lichtenstein a visa to go and see underground jazz musician Sergei Kuryokhin. Eventually, she went anyway on a holiday visa with a small video-camera hidden in a handbag. Her boyfriend prevented it from being searched by engaging the Customs man in conversation about the novels of Graham Greene. At home, John Cleese recorded a party political broadcast on behalf of the SDP and we mourned the death of courageous liver-transplant boy Ben Hardwicke whose cause had been championed by Esther Rantzen on **'That's Life'**.

For younger viewers, Gudrun Ure starred as the magical **'Supergran'** with Iain Cuthbertson at his villainous best as Scunner Campbell. Meanwhile, in the soaps, David and Barbara Hunter got the boot from **'Crossroads'**, and Miranda Pollard was raped; Bet Lynch took over the Rover's Return in **'Coronation Street'**, and Terry Duckworth got Andrea Clayton pregnant; the Free George Jackson campaign was mounted in **'Brookside'**; Thames Television tried unsuccessfully to snatch **'Dallas'** from the BBC; and the Moldavian Massacre drastically reduced the actors budget on **'Dynasty'**. Steven Carrington's lover Luke was the only one to stay dead though.

And finally 1985 was the year that snooker really captured the public's imagination with an incredible 18 million viewers staying up until the early hours to watch Dennis Taylor defeat Steve Davis in a dramatic final to the Embassy World Championships in Sheffield. By 1987, 344 television hours were devoted to the sport, with 70 per cent of its fan mail coming from women. Television made snooker. By 1988 the prize for the winner was £95,000, while Joe Davis, the first world champ, pocketed £6 10s in 1927. Just thought you'd like to know.

1986

That Was the Year When...

The American space shuttle Challenger exploded seconds after lift-off, killing its crew of seven. □ Cabinet ministers Michael Heseltine and Leon Brittan resigned over the Westland Helicopter Company's future. □ Fire damage at Russia's Chernobyl power station caused several deaths, large-scale evacuation and a rise in radiation levels in Western Europe. □ Former Nazi Dr Kurt Waldheim was elected Austria's president. □ Colonel Oliver North's arms-for-hostages deal with Iran put President Reagan in a row. □ American planes from British bases bombed Libyan terrorist-camps. □ Prince Andrew married Sarah Ferguson in Westminster Abbey. □ Junior health minister Edwina Currie told Newcastle people fry-ups, drink and cigarettes were bad for them. □ Jeffrey Archer resigned as deputy chairman of the Tory Party after an allegation that he gave a prostitute £2,000. □ The Government went to court to stop Peter Wright's book Spycatcher. *□ An AIDS campaign was launched. □ And Halley's Comet made its first visit for seventy-five years.*

This was the year in which ITV's big guns misfired. Like Halley's Comet, their two blockbuster drama serials, 'Lost Empires' and 'Paradise Postponed', both lost viewers as they went along. Celebrating its fiftieth birthday, the BBC flexed its experienced muscles and won battles on all fronts. Their posh dramas were more thoughtful, daring and controversial; their everyday dramas more durable; their soaps washed dirtier; and their comedies had rounded characters not gag-shooting dummies.

The BBC's Saturday series about harassed hospital staff was **'Casualty'** – 'Juliet Bravo' with spots, chest pains and bloody cuts (government ones and others). It had a nice touch of rôle reversal. One heroine was the beautiful gifted doctor, Baz (Julia Watson), who was having an affair with the main male nurse; but Baz was upstaged by the motherly Irish nurse, Megan (Brenda Fricker), who dispensed common sense, TLC plus TCP, to her frequently bolshie patients and raddled colleagues. As the ward was usually awash with entrails, the medical staff popping pills or booze and the consultant apoplectic with rage at the latest decision of the money-saving bureaucrats, 'Casualty' collected complaints like germs. Edwina Currie called it left-wing propaganda, the Casualty Surgeons' Association condemned it, and nurses' organisations called it a slur. Audiences grew as it grew braver and more angry. With stories about AIDS, terrorist bombings, race riots, domestic violence and every awful accident, it has become our best home-grown carbolic soap.

The cult American series of 1986 introduced a new Beatrice and Benedick in **'Moonlighting'**. Cybill Shepherd was Maddie Hayes, ladylike model turned detective-agency boss. Bruce Willis was David Addison, the swaggering and streetwise sleuth she inherited with the business. Together with excellent one-liners, elaborate stunts and elegant clothes, they made much ado about not much and said they detested each other so much we knew it was real love. As the credits came up each week, we had usually forgotten the crime but were still chuckling at the jokes. While the two stars were reported to detest each other off-camera (and Bruce Willis became a major heart-throb and recording star), the 1987 series had them falling finally between the sheets. This development was not unconnected with the fact that Cybill was pregnant with twins and the producers wanted her to stay but to have an explanation for her rapidly expanding waistline. An unsatisfactory third series had her marrying a man on a train and breaking David's heart. From then on 'Moonlighting' became moonshine.

Few of the heroes of 1986 were the sort you took home to mother. The most traditional featured in adaptations of two Jeffrey Archer novels which the author was able to watch in his unscheduled free time. **'Kane and Abel'** was

'Emmerdale Farm': Matt (Frederick Pyne), who usually showed as much life as a leg of lamb, got to grips with Harry Mowlam (Godfrey James) and was accused of murder.

an American-made mini-series about star-crossed rivals (Peter Strauss and Sam Neill) which brought relief to the many millions of women suffering from wall-to-wall World Cup football. Later came Granada's expensive production of **'First among Equals'**, which gave us a magnificent replica of the House of Commons (so realistic that visiting MP Joan Lester found herself bowing to the Speaker as she entered) and four fictional MPs starting out in 1964. One of them would become Prime Minister: the principled Tory, the complete Conservative swine, the deeply dull Labour man or the Scottish socialist who seemed to have it made (so we knew his world would be the first to collapse). There was an additional intrigue when producer Mervyn Watson made two endings and ruled that only he and Granada's managing director, David Plowright, would elect the Prime Minister in the final week. There were many sighs of 'If only he, too . . .' from Archer fans when halfway through the serial the dull Labour man brushed with a prostitute but ignored her blackmailing attempt and nothing happened. In the end it was the now not so dull Labour man Gould (Tom Wilkinson) rather than the decent Tory, Kerslake, who walked into Number Ten. (Archer had picked him in the British version of the book, but Kerslake won in the American one.)

David Plowright had had another hard decision to make, too: whether to blow up the House of Commons. Their £200,000 set, complete with Leader of the Opposition's office, smoking-room, whips' office, Members' Lobby and corridors with statues had to go to make room for the sets of 'Lost Empires'. It would have gone up in flames had not the producers of Yorkshire's parliamentary comedy **'The New Statesman'** heard about it at the ninth hour and sent up their lorries.

The hero of J. B. Priestley's last work, which became Granada's £5 million serial, **'Lost Empires'**, was twenty-year-old Richard Herncastle, forced to join a troupe of magicians touring the music-halls as the First World War took its toll. Colin Firth played him as a huffy Yorkshire lad, shyly in love with Beatie Edney's lovely dancer Nancy, then recklessly undone by Carmen du Sautoy's worldly drink-sodden Julie. Seven episodes began with a stage-show opening out to the trenches as shells dropped, a stunning set-piece, reminiscent of *Oh What a Lovely War!*. The story then moved with the troupe, much of the filming done in the palatial theatres of the North-West. Extras had the unusual task of booing Laurence Olivier when he played the eccentric old comedian Harry Burrard. To everyone's alarm he actually slipped and fell on the Buxton Opera House stage, but he staggered up and carried on. Brian Glover was frightening as the terribly violent Tommy Beamish and Pamela Stephenson's cameo as showgirl Lily, teamed with Alfred Marks as her pianist-manager Otto, was nicely controlled. John Castle, taught his stage tricks by magician David Hemingway, triumphed as the glowering cold-hearted Nick, though he fell victim to one of Pamela's jokes. After she had watched him being served plate after plate of roast beef in the retakes of one scene she arranged for the hotel to call him to the lobby that night for a special supper. There he found a whole live cow waiting. June Howson's production was faultless, everything looked sumptuous – almost too good: lushly upholstered trains, lavish spreads at restaurants, lodgings with mahogany furniture aglow. But somehow the total 'Lost Empires' was less than the sum of all these splendid parts.

It was hard to tell who the heroes were in John Mortimer's **'Paradise Postponed'**. Thames Television's blockbuster about Simeon Silcox, the 'Red rector', and how he left all his money not to his family but to Leslie Titmuss, a local lad turned Tory minister, seemed more of a blockbluster, all stop-starts with too much talk and too little action. The problem with the flashbacks was that the actors always looked the same age. Perhaps Fred, the doctor son, was the character we should have liked. He had Standards – but no spine. Most people enjoyed David Threlfall's unscrupulous Titmuss more – if only for his Edward Heath vowels.

Other heroes that year were on the peculiar side. Everyone except Peter Davison's bashful decent Dr Stephen Daker in **'A Very Peculiar Practice'**, Andrew

On Channel 4 the agonies of sagging skin, wobbly thighs and sex for the over-sixties were being explored in the American show 'The Golden Girls', probably the best-written comedy on television in the late eighties. Actresses Bea Arthur (dry Dorothy) and Betty White (dim Rose) with Rue McClanahan (man-mad Blanche) and Estelle Getty (cynical Sophia) have more than a hundred years of television experience between them. Susan Harris, who also created 'Soap', said: 'At eighty-two Cary Grant could still have been a romantic lead, but a woman over fifty was cast as an axe-murderess.' 'The Golden Girls' changed that and set a new standard for jokes. Blanche, for instance, felt bound to comment on her date (young enough to be her son): 'Dirk's nearly five years younger than me.' To which a disbelieving but not sneering Dorothy replied: 'In what, Blanche, dog years?'

Davies's brilliant satire for BBC2 about doctors at Lowlands University, was funny peculiar. In that year's series the main story was an epidemic of VD – what David Troughton's gleefully beastly Dr Bob Buzzard called 'a bit of tool trouble'. Boozy Dr McCannon (Graham Crowden) told one stuttering youth, 'Out with it!' – only to be instantly sorry. Dr Daker and Barbara Flynn's Dr Rose Marie ('Illness is a thing men do to women') worked overtime treating infected parts and broken hearts, sewing up the catering manager's trousers and telling the Vice-Chancellor what he'd caught. In the second series two years later, the mood blackened as a group of American businessmen took over Lowlands, turfed out non-profit-making activities like learning and ran a germ-warfare station. It again won first-class honours.

Not everyone celebrated the BBC's success in 1986. Tory MP Norman Tebbit – then a regular star of 'Spitting Image' as a grey-faced punk headbanger – alleged bias in Kate Adie's reports and other aspects of the BBC's news-coverage of the American bombing of Libyan camps. His long list of complaints was knocked down by the BBC's news boss Ron Neil, but 'Get the Beeb' became a regular

sport enjoyed by Tory MPs, some businessmen and right-wing newspapers.

They had a field-day when BBC2 began **'The Monocled Mutineer'**, a four-part £3 million serial about Percy Toplis, small-time crook turned impersonator of officers, set against the background of the harsh treatment and large-scale mutiny of raw recruits shipped to Etaples, France, in 1917. Unwisely perhaps, the BBC hyped it as a true story. But Alan Bleasdale – inspired by the idea of a young miner who beat officers at their own game until the Establishment took revenge and had him hunted and killed – had written an imaginative version based on the facts. The *Daily Mail* began a campaign to smear it as a 'tissue of lies', citing the scenes where an officer, played movingly by Nick Reding, was executed for cowardice. Bandleader Victor Sylvester, a seventeen-year-old soldier at Etaples, confirmed before his death in 1978 that he was haunted for years after taking part in several such executions. But historians and old soldiers protested to the papers that this and much more was preposterous.

Whatever the historical truth, 'The Monocled Mutineer' was magnificent television drama, and Paul McGann (the star of 'Give Us a Break') perfectly conveyed Percy's amoral charm. Scenes with 200 unemployed young men at the Tonfannau redundant military camp on the Colwyn Bay coast graphically suggested the horrors of trench warfare, and those in which Percy visited the executed officer's mother to tell her the lies she needed to hear (and borrow money) and called on his own blind mother pretending to be a doctor were quite brilliant.

BBC-bashing continued with **'The Singing Detective'**, a television triumph perhaps outranking even 'The Jewel in the Crown' and 'Brideshead Revisited'. Probably the best of Dennis Potter's works, it was certainly the most personal. Filmed in a fully equipped but closed-through-the-cuts NHS hospital ward, this hero, Philip Marlow (an award-winning performance by Michael Gambon) was covered in the scales and sores of a crippling psoriasis – Potter's own disease for nearly half his life. Mostly Marlow lay prostrate in a hospital bed racked with rage and pain.

More complex than any television drama tried before, with the skills of Kenith Trodd and John Amiel as producer and director, 'The Singing Detective' worked on the level of a human story – a writer crippled by illness, feverishly dreaming about his wife's betrayal of him, surrounded by dying men and patronising doctors. It worked as a thriller – the detective (also played by Gambon), a crooner in a sleazy wartime club, was the hero of one of Marlow's novels in which a beautiful girl was dredged from the Thames. It worked as a chunk of autobiography of Potter's childhood in the Forest of Dean – with potent scenes of a hateful old schoolmarm and a short-trousered boy high in a tree in a sea of green leaves. And it worked as a musical, better even than 'Pennies from Heaven'. The sound of Fred Waring's Pennsylvanians' 'Dem Bones, Dem Bones, Dem Dry Bones' as the throng of doctors and nurses at the foot of Marlow's bed began miming and dancing was one of its superbly comic set-pieces. And finally it worked as a philosophy lesson, an attempt to define reality. Were Marlow's imaginings – in particular the long love-scene in the grass, featuring his bare-bottomed villain Mark Binney and his mother (Patrick Malahide and Alison Steadman), observed by the boy – less real than happenings in the hospital?

Many people didn't hold with art from old scabs. Mrs Whitehouse for one. She wrote to Mrs Thatcher complaining about the love-scene linking sex with death. Harry Greenaway, MP, said it was 'upsetting and horrid'. Mr Tebbit's watchdog committee looked into it. Every newspaper carried stories reporting how disgusted viewers had been put off their Sunday-night cocoa. But writer Fay Weldon sprang to Potter's defence, calling him 'the best television playwright in the world'. Revenge seemed to be taken when the BAFTA awards came up. 'The Singing Detective' was not picked as best drama. Fay Weldon's **'Life and Loves of a She-Devil'** won that.

Generally, whether ugly or old, heroines seemed to fare better that year. Jean Boht's over-fifties Liverpool heroine Nellie Boswell, in Carla Lane's **'Bread'**, wasn't an instant success. Some people thought this frowzy Catholic mother and her family of scroungers who knew all about fiddling the Social took the biscuit. But in two years 'Bread' had risen, and become a part of the nation's life. The comedy that was almost a soap toppled our top soap, 'EastEnders'.

It was a year of new heroines. Good looks got girls nowhere. Ruth in the BBC's cartoon-horror serial 'The Life and Loves of a She-Devil' was a giant with shoulders like the back of a sofa, boobs like barrage balloons, four hairy moles on her face, a moustache and, when threatened, the red eyes of Hell. She was writer Fay Weldon's champion of what men call 'dogs' and Julie T. Wallace played her to perfection. As she burned down her house, ruined her runaway husband and tormented her rival, women cheered and men cowered. Tom Baker played one victim.

Commercial Break

The most talked-about commercial in 1986 was one for AIDS, a depressing forty-five seconds shown on both BBC and ITV which featured a couple in bed together and ended with a tomb and the slogan 'Don't Die of Ignorance'. (The young actors asked not to be named for fear people would associate them with the virus.) It signalled the start of a spate of worthy discussion programmes.

Stars of advertisements that year included Nick Kamen who stripped off his clothes in a launderette to advertise Levis. Most young women watching didn't mind what make of jeans they were. A mysterious and never-seen Sid was the man they told us to 'tell' in a campaign for British Gas. Leo McKern began his Lloyds Bank series, and the voice of Geoffrey Palmer ('Yours truly' in 'Fairly Secret Army') told us about 'Vorsprung durch technik' in the Audi Quattro.

Peter Howitt as Nellie's black-leather-clad eldest son Joey had become a heart-throb; Gilly Coman's squeaky bird-brained Aveline was loved for her baubles, bangles and falsies; Kenneth Waller was a card as Grandad (who cursed so much in one episode his own mother wouldn't talk to him for a week); and Pamela Power, who played Martina, the tight-lipped lady at the DHSS, said she had not needed to do any research, having drawn the dole herself often enough at the start of her career.

There was no such success for the former siren of 'Coronation Street', poor Pat Phoenix, who was to die of lung cancer in 1986. Central's **'Constant Hot Water'** was a tepid comedy written for her new life after soap. Although she joked about possessing a pensioner's bus-pass (and, with her new mature wisdom, even did a little amateur agony-aunt work on TV-am), she looked her usual glamorous self playing busybody Phyllis Nugent, a seaside landlady, disrupting the life of her younger landlady neighbour played by Prunella Gee. Recording at a real boarding-house in Bridlington brought back bitter-sweet memories of days in digs as a struggling actress. 'I remember creeping downstairs starving one night and raiding the larder,' she said. 'I had a feast of rice, Ovaltine, mustard, gravy browning and a scrape of Cherry Blossom boot polish for good measure.'

Coverage of the wedding festivities of Prince Andrew and Sarah Ferguson started at six a.m. and ITV and BBC teams vied with each other to cover every aspect, from the first early-morning shots of Major Ferguson's bristling eyebrows to the carpet-sweepers at the Abbey. Cameras caught Prince William fiddling with his hat-strap, the Queen chasing an erring page-boy and the new Duchess of York winking at friends as she walked back down the aisle. The BBC's relaxed no-gimmicks coverage beat ITV's aerial shots and Sir Alastair Burnet's holier-than-thou comments from on high. By then Sir Alastair had become chief kneebender to the royals. His deeply respectful, hushed-voice interviews with Charles and Diana in **'The Prince and Princess of Wales, in Private, in Public'** had so promoted him. The ITN documentary aided the Prince's charities trust but hardly helped HRH's image. It was in this that the heir to the throne admitted talking to his plants. Diana had also been filmed joking that she had a 'brain the size of a pea', but that was edited out.

Also Shown in 1986

Among a new breed of heroines, Hazel O'Connor starred in **'Fighting Back'**, a serial about a penniless Bristol mother fighting to keep body and soul and her two kids together; Francesca Annis was the career-girl heroine, Fleet Street's first woman editor, in Anglia's **'Inside Story'** (Roy Marsden wore his worst wig yet as her boss and Lord Harold Wilson played himself presenting her with an award); and **'Bluebell'** bloomed before the spring. This was a small-budget BBC serial based on a true story, with strong-faced Carolyn Pickles as Margaret Kelly, the Liverpool chorus dancer tapping away and not letting the club-owners or the Nazis get her down in wartime France.

One tough liberated lady (Amanda Redman) had a baby for her more traditional sister, plus a dis-astrous affair with the brother-in-law in LWT's **'To Have and to Hold'**, a well-intentioned women's weepie; and Thames Television brought us a twee but tolerable series set in the 1920s about three Girl Fridays, **'Ladies in Charge'**.

Among the heroes, Denis Lawson's petty crook in BBC2's **'Deadhead'** caused some sharp intakes of breath when he was tied to a bed and a yuppie lady had her wicked way with him. Lovely was how most women viewers judged **Lovejoy**, Ian McShane's antiques-dealer, trying to make ends meet among odd East Anglians (a bought-in series on BBC1). And Michael Maloney's baby-besotted hero in the Channel 4 four-parter about divorce, **'What if It's Raining'**, went down well with women who wanted to mother him and smother the wandering wife. Ken Hutchinson's Colin, the weasel-like hunched crook on the run with his wife and daughter in BBC1's **'Hideaway'** serial was heroic only in comparison with the nastier crooks he was running from. In **'King and Castle'**, Thames Television turned tubby Derek Martin into a cockney heavy who had decided to give up a life of crime by leaving the police force. They teamed him with lanky Nigel Planer as a martial-arts-practising moped-riding genealogist. But the Laurel-and-Hardy-like debt collectors they became in this sub-'Minder' series were never lovable. The same company's new Troy Kennedy Martin police drama, **'The Fourth Floor'**, hardly got off the ground floor. One three-part difficult story starring Kenneth Haigh was its lot – sadly. Central found a stayer in **'Boon'**, a blessing for fans of slow-smiling Michael Elphick. Ken Boon was a fireman, invalided out and able to fulfil a dream to be a cowboy or – the next best thing, apparently – to run the Texas Rangers motorbike messengers around the Mid-lands prairies. The actor's drink problems almost sank the series in 1988 (ironically while he appeared in commercial breaks advertising alcohol-free lager). LWT's **'London's Burning'**, which was a colourful stirring single film in 1986 and a series for 1988, should have smoked Ken off the screen. Jack Rosenthal's firemen, with nicknames like Charisma (because he had none), Sicknote (because he was always ill) and Vaseline (because he was slippery), were lazy loafers, doing odd jobs, taking the mickey out of each other, cheating on their wives. But when the bell rang they were transformed into valiant life-savers.

There were excellent plays. Ben Kingsley was a fine **Silas Marner** for the BBC. Timothy West's Eastbourne poisoner in **'The Good Dr Bodkin Adams'**, again for the BBC, was a hit. Maureen Lipman made up for her dismal sitcom **'All at Number 20'** by a super performance as a cabdriver in **'Shiftwork'**. Anna Massey made drama *de luxe* of **'Hotel du Lac'**. And **'Brick Is Beautiful'**, about Manchester teenagers, was solidly built and well pointed by Andy Armitage.

Some fairly ordinary new game-shows emerged. Paul Daniels's **'Every Second Counts'** was perhaps better than Roy Walker's **'Catchphrase'**, which in turn pipped **'Pass the Buck'** with George Layton as host.

Sid Jenkins, an RSPCA inspector whose often distressing work was featured in BBC1's **'Animal Squad'**, became one documentary hero that year. Joe Horsley, a five-year-old with brain damage who went to the Peto Clinic in Hungary and learned to walk, in **'Standing Up for Joe'**, Ann Paul's unsugared film on BBC, was another. The four Hooray Henrys having a bloody good laugh in a **'Forty Minutes'** film, **'The Fishing Party'**, were the critics' favourites.

Soaps were supreme that year. In **'EastEnders'**, Andy the nice Scottish nurse fell under a lorry; in **'Dallas'** Bobby Ewing came back from the dead; and 'Dynasty' gave birth to **'The Colbys'**, another Aaron Spelling saga of the super-rich, starring Charlton Heston as Jason Colby with Stephanie Beacham as Sable, his wife. Neither their acting nor the millions spent on the clothes and sets could counteract viewer fatigue and the show closed after two seasons with Fallon (Emma Samms) being wafted away in a UFO. Unfortunately she came back the next year in **'Dynasty'**. In **'Coronation Street'**, Brian Tilsley divorced Gail because she had an affair. Working-class corny old **'Crossroads'** changed to middle-class witty new **'Crossroads, Kings Oak'**. The writing was on those walls, too.

The chat-show host everyone talked about in 1986 was Jonathan Ross, who couldn't sound his r's, was as sharp as his £800 designer suits, and teased his cultish guests on Channel 4's **'The Last Resort'**. A former Labour MP was his only rival. Robert Kilroy-Silk's **'Kilroy'** became a daily discussion show when the BBC's daytime programming started in the autumn.

The most impressive import was the eleven-part saga **'Heimat'**, the story of three families in a German village between 1919 and 1982. Shown every day for nearly a fortnight on BBC2, it drew five times the expected audiences for a (mostly) black-and-white subtitled film. Critics hailed a masterpiece. No one who watched wanted it to end.

Edward Woodward turned up in a depressingly successful avenging-angel series, set in New York, **'The Equalizer'**. Other imports included the growing mass of mini-series: **'George Washington'** starring Barry Bostwick, **'North and South'** starring half of Hollywood in ten-second snaps, **'Mistral's Daughter'** and **'Deceptions'**, both wasting the talents of Stephanie Powers.

In the comedy department George Cole appeared as the father of a family of beetroot-eaters in a 'communism' comedy, **'Comrade Dad'**. Big Brother was supposed to be watching. He was probably the only one. Ralph Bates played wet and well-meaning teacher John in **'Dear John'**, the sitcom which topped the television comedy league in the spring. The idea came to writer John Sullivan when his sister visited a Divorced and Singles club, once. All the members of his One To One club, mothered by Rachel Bell's 'any sexual problems?' Louise, needed a shake and a hug. But the BBC should have foreseen a short life for **'The Clairvoyant'**. Despite Roy Kinnear's comic dithering as a used car salesman with psychic powers and Roy Clarke's script, it sank. ITV's **'Room at the Bottom'**, with Keith Barron playing a televisionstation tyrant, stayed where there was room for it. LWT's **'Hot Metal'**, Marshall and Renwick's painfully accurate satire took the p's and q's out of Fleet Street – the *Daily Crucible* was a soaraway success. Thames Television's **'Executive Stress'**, supposedly about a marriage with both partners in publishing, showed again that Penelope Keith is no picker of parts. **'Hell's Bells'** brought Derek Nimmo back to ecclesiastical life, blinking and blithering, and must have made a few more atheists. The actor had a heart by-pass operation only weeks afterwards, so we must be merciful. Richard Briers also took the cloth in **'All in Good Faith'**, which needed a miracle to give it life.

1987

Herald of Free Enterprise, *a Channel car-ferry, capsized after leaving Zeebrugge, its bow door left open: 187 people died.* □ *Terry Waite, the Archbishop of Canterbury's representative, was kidnapped in Beirut.* □ *In Hungerford, Michael Ryan shot fifteen strangers before killing himself.* □ *'Madame' Cynthia Payne was acquitted of controlling prostitutes.* □ *Lester Piggott was gaoled for three years for tax fraud.* □ *More than 200 children examined by Cleveland paediatrician Dr Marietta Higgs were taken from their parents.* □ *Margaret Thatcher began a third term after a general election.* □ *Wilberforce, the 10 Downing Street cat, resigned after catching mice for four prime ministers.* □ *An IRA bomb at a Remembrance Day service at Enniskillen killed eleven and injured sixty.* □ *A fire at the King's Cross Underground station killed thirty-one.* □ *Prince Edward resigned from the Marines.* □ *Manchester police chief James Anderton announced that God may be using him as a prophet.* □ *A hurricane hit southern England, killing eleven people and destroying 15 million trees, and a record fall on the New York Stock Exchange led to the worst day for shares in Britain.*

Predictably television caught AIDS in 1987. As deadly diseases go, this one offers everything: sex and more sex; homosexuality and moralising about same; the gruesome but unfailing dramatic appeal of fatal illness; black comedy and the chance to be ever so rude and wave condoms about.

In the first three months of the year we had AIDS the pop show, AIDS the panel game, AIDS the serious news-bulletin and AIDS the drama. As a result most viewers could have gone on 'Mastermind' answering questions on safe sex. No you cannot catch AIDS from sharing a television set – but you could be painfully embarrassed. So for safe telly it was advisable not to watch anything after 'News at Ten' with your children or your parents.

LWT didn't wait till after ten for their pop-star-packed **'First AIDS'** hosted by Mike Smith. It was the first

---

Had a plague struck most of the year's comedy output, no one would have mourned. Probably the worst was ITV's 'High and Dry', starring Bernard Cribbins, with a set purporting to be a seaside pier so cheap you could see the creases and a tape-recording of a seagull.

television show to pass condoms round the audience for twiddling, twanging and blowing up, and to have Rik Mayall hang one outside his trousers. Two experts fitted one over their fingers, but later discussion programmes used plastic models of the more appropriate organ. (On Swedish television a man put it on – er – himself, but we're not that brave yet, thank goodness.)

In a rare show of co-operation ITV and BBC collaborated on an AIDS week. BBC2's 'Horizon' reported on how scientists were chasing a cure, the 'Bodymatters' doctors explained what happens, and 'Spitting Image' had Willie Whitelaw with a condom over his head.

'Intimate Contact' was Central's AIDS drama serial, well written by Alma Cullen and about shame and sadness more than about sex and symptoms. Daniel Massey played a married man who lost his job, his social standing, the love of his wife (temporarily) and his life after joining a businessmen's orgy with a couple of whores. Without lurid voyeurism (a flashback to the orgy was essential to show he hadn't caught AIDS off a lavatory seat) the serial won a healthy number of viewers, most drawn to Claire Bloom's fine performance as the wife, at first more horrified that he might be 'queer' (her word) than that he was going to die. The production was Central's bestseller abroad that year and the next.

'Tutti Frutti' was John Byrne's drily funny story about the Majestics, a group of Glaswegian fifties rockers in drainpipe trousers and crêpe soles. Robbie Coltrane as the big fat slob singer fell for Emma Thompson's toughie, Suzie Kettle, who made him sleep in the bath. Memorable, too, was Maurice Roeves as unhappy Vincent, who set himself alight on stage. Although the rock 'n' roll hits in the series were sung by the actors, the fact that the songs were originally recorded by Elvis, Chuck Berry, Little Richard and others caused problems when the BBC planned to sell the series abroad. The copyright fees would have pushed costs through the roof. But sales fell through, the thick Scots accents perhaps to blame.

Royalty were on television so often in 1987 we half-expected Bob Monkhouse to introduce Prince William doing impressions of Dirty Den or singing 'You Need Hands' as an act on his new BBC talent series **'Bob Says Opportunity Knocks'**. (Hughie Green, credited as a consultant for that series, is still fuming that he has never been consulted.)

Prince Edward teamed up with sister Anne, brother Andrew and sister-in-law Fergie to dress up as vegetables and do silly things on **'It's A Knockout'**. He also wrote and presented the worthy but dreary two-parter **'The Duke's Award'** about the Duke of Edinburgh Award scheme. He interviewed his dad, the Iron Duke, who had recently appeared on **'Wogan'** terrifying viewers and cracking the whip about carriage-driving. Wogan barely got a word in edgeways. Princess Anne appeared on **'A Question of Sport'** and hit Emlyn Hughes only once, so demonstrating her powers of restraint. And the Queen Mother starred in her first documentary **'Royal Champion'**, talking about horses, flirting girlishly with the cameras, wise to every angle and trick. Meanwhile, we waited to see if the temporary replacement for TV-am's Anne Diamond, who took leave to deliver her first child, would be Princess Michael. She had made an unforgettable appearance on that programme, tearfully talking about her Nazi father.

The best new comedy was Yorkshire Television's **'The New Statesman'**, for which Rik Mayall was given a perm and promoted from yukky (in 'The Young Ones' and this year's sequel **'Filthy Rich and Catflap'**) to yuppy as newly elected rampantly right-wing MP Alan B'Stard. This sado-masochist, married to a lesbian, who won his seat after arranging for his opponent to be maimed in a car crash, armed the police and dumped nuclear waste in a children's playground. No one, least of all the writers Laurence Marks and Maurice Gran, thought it would be taken seriously. But Tory MPs hated it. Many called it 'disgusting', and Teddy Taylor the Member for Southend said: 'It was so immature and childish it reminded me of a Neil Kinnock speech.' B'Stard's aide Norman Bormann gradually revealed that he was changing sex. The actor billed as R. R. Cooper turned out to be Rowena Cooper. It wasn't hard to spot, but the joke still worked.

The only reason to watch BBC1's **'Divided We Stand'**, a comedy about a warring greengrocer and his wife living in separate parts of the house divided by a wall, was to spot the lapses in the accents. Originally the series was to have been set in Liverpool, but what with the 'Bread' family, Cilla Black and other invaders from outer Mersey seeming to take over our screens it was changed to Birmingham. Between the 'Yow's and the 'ectually's there were a lorra gaffs.

The shortest-lived sitcom of 1987 was Central's school romp **'Hardwicke House'**, launched in an hour-long episode followed by a half-hour episode the next day. The anarchic comprehensive school made Grange Hill seem like a kindergarten for angels. Complaints flooded in. Viewers felt that, for instance, it was a bad idea to show a child deliberately electrocuted by Mr Fowl (Granville Saxton) the geography master at eight in the evening. The rest of the series and work on the sequel were abandoned. A pity; some of it was very funny.

Comedy sketch-shows were excellent in 1987. Dawn French and Jennifer Saunders, joking about the bossiness, spite and weediness of women, flanked by game guests and their resident musicians Raw Sex (the seediest pair of deadbeats) in their BBC2 **'French and Saunders'** series

were superb. Stephanie Beacham gave one of her finest performances as the secret love of Elvis Presley's life (with large Dawn and Jennifer looking larger in white rhinestone-covered suits as his love-children).

On the chat-show front, Wogan seemed to be more fun when he wasn't there. The BBC's wonderboy now took so many holidays, the substitutes were the stars. Derek Jameson, the Marf of the Sarf, was the noisiest; Ronnie Corbett was the gushiest; Bruce Forsyth was the jumpiest; and Sue Lawley was the best. By 1988 her holiday relief-work had brought her success enough for her to leave the 'Six O'Clock News' and put her temp rates up. Michael Parkinson came back with a Yorkshire Television chat-show on to which he seemed to invite only old men. By the second series in 1988, his guests had cottoned on to the fact that they could say more with him. Several, including Adam Faith, Richard Harris and Boy George, proved excellent talkers. By contrast Dame Edna Everage gave no one a chance to upstage her in **'An Audience with Dame Edna'**. In her brilliant LWT Saturday-evening series she pulled trapdoors to consign Kurt Waldheim and others to the abyss and shot Cliff Richard into outer darkness. He came back – but still . . .

Imports were up again. NBC's made-in-Russia $30 million epic **'Peter the Great'**, shown by the BBC, was billed as the most extravagant and magnificent Hollywood mini-series ever. Later it transpired that there had been a problem. With Austrian heart-throb Maximilian Schell in the title rôle of the seventeenth-century Russian Tsar, co-stars who included Omar Sharif and Vanessa Redgrave and half the Red Army as extras, they had much to boast about. But what they tried to keep secret was that Schell had walked out four weeks before completing his contract and the producers had hired a double to replace him.

The double was unknown English actor Denis de Marne, who was flown to Rome where an Italian make-up artist took a mould of his face. From this he built a false chin and false nose, and back on the set in Russia, after daily make-up sessions lasting from three to five hours, de Marne became Schell as the Tsar. This was not just for long shots. De Marne had to learn fifty pages of dialogue and filmed for fourteen hours a day for three weeks, eventually appearing in the leading rôle for over one hour of the eight-hour serial. Until he blew the gaff trying to improve his fee, the switch was undetected. It made little difference, of course. The series seemed to last as long as the Romanovs themselves. Peter the Great it wasn't. All that money, all those miles of film and it rated just Peter the So-So.

There were good ITV series – although you had to search hard. The best was Central's **'Inspector Morse'** in which John Thaw became a man alone, a breaker of rules, a sort of Jack Regan with culture, finding corpses in Oxford. For the rôle John had to drink Real Ale often and in pints. For most actors that might be a bonus, but for

'Yesterday's Dreams' was Central's gorgeous gooey stuff with Judy Loe torn between a greasy garage-man and diddy but dishy Paul Freeman forever missing planes and trains.

desiccated estate agent trying to catch him, but Rosemary Leach outshone them all as the tweedy tease Joan Plumleigh-Bruce. In Channel 4's **'Brond'** we learned what Stratford Johns had been doing since he stopped playing Barlow in 1975 – eating. The now very big actor was excellent as the supersized sinister killer in this serial set in Scotland. Scotland seemed to be *the* place that year for original drama. **'The Houseman's Tale'** was a two-parter about the bug-ridden lives of junior doctors in a chaotic Scottish hospital. Sadly it had been doctored itself, pubic hair surgically removed and the whole thing postponed and hidden away late in a nasty case of BBC censorship.

Peter Egan continued as the smoothie of **'Ever Decreasing Circles'** on autumn Sundays; but on Wednesdays on BBC2 he was aiding and abetting his lying bombastic father Rick and betraying his country as Magnus Pym, John Le Carré's **'A Perfect Spy'**. At times it seemed as if Ray McAnally's rheumy-eyed Rick would steal the show. Even lying dead in a bath of ice-cubes fittingly fetched by two old tarts from the pub across the road, his presence was powerful. Jane Booker was superb as Magnus's misused wife, and Peggy Ashcroft sublime as his dotty seaside landlady. But it was Peter with his faked joviality, his pain at being cheated who made 'A Perfect Spy' perfect.

If the year began depressingly with condoms as the answer to *that* disease, at least condoms provided the best joke in the best comedy drama of the year. As politicians pontificated on every television station during the June election, David Jason was priggish porter Skullion in **'Porterhouse Blue'**, Tom Sharpe's super satire of Oxbridge life. In the most fantastical and strangely beautiful scene of the four-part Channel 4 serial, troubled student Zipser had to dispose of several thousand condoms. His solution was to fill each with gas from his fire and push them up the chimney. From there the teated balloons floated and settled on the college lawn, forcing a horrified Skullion to rush around frantically trying to puncture them.

But it wasn't quite like blowing bubbles for producer Robert Knight. First Durex had refused to supply the condoms because they disapproved of the frivolity of the project. Luckily Duet, a rival firm, saw the joke and sent ten thousand. Then the dons at Cambridge where they planned to film objected. A suitable scholarly square in Peterborough had to be used. Finally the hoped-for still moonlight in which the balloons, filled with a little water, would hang 'like lost sperm in the air' turned out a night of gale-force winds. What viewers didn't see were about twenty people releasing fifteen condoms each, while others sewed dozens into the lawns. In the event the wind made things funnier. David won the BAFTA best actor award, and the night of the flying condoms lives in television history.

John it's hell. He likes vodka, loathes beer. The Morse stories are well written and have a quality feel to them, but perhaps at two hours a time are a little too long. The BBC introduced another rule-breaking copper at around the same time. Ian Hogg became the tough-talking sergeant in charge of young crime-fighters making their marks and mistakes on London streets in **'Rockcliffe's Babies'**. The following year in **'Rockcliffe's Follies'** he had moved to the country where the scenery was greener but the criminals weren't.

Probably the best-loved serial was LWT's prettily staged thriller **'The Charmer'** starring Nigel Havers as Gorse, a thirties conman, flashing his last fiver to win over rich suburbanites. Bernard Hepton was excellent as the

The BBC's £6 million 'Fortunes of War' began slowly but turned out to be our good fortune. Olivia Manning's story set in Bucharest at the outbreak of war acquired a deft delicious script from Alan Plater and the world's most irritating hero, Guy Pringle, played by Kenneth Branagh. It also had Emma Thompson, struggling under some awful wigs, as his sensible wife Harriet finding to her anguish that her husband, a naïve lecturer working for the British Council, was all things to everyone but quite insensitive to her needs. As Harriet and Guy reaffirmed their love high on a pyramid (with a friend he'd invited along for good measure) you knew this was the Harrods class of drama.

Commercial Break

Jonathan Ross's 'Last Resort' chat-shows continued to attract the younger viewers, and that cramped his style as the star of an advertising campaign for Harp lager. His contract was terminated halfway through because it was feared his cult image might encourage under-age drinking. Other commercials of 1987 were the Carling Black Label spoof on the Levi jeans ad and the skilful Brooke Bond Red Mountain coffee series in which the hostess of a dinner-party disappears to her kitchen to make strange gurgling noises to 'take the grind out of ground coffee'. Volvo began running a commercial for their cars 'tested by dummies, driven by the intelligent' in which a robot drove a car through a first-floor plate-glass window. Inside the robot's plaster cast was robotic dancer Andy Sinclair. Apt casting, it turned out. Andy had failed his driving test seven times. That year scriptwriter Wilfred Greatorex tried to ban the commercial for the British Airport Authority which starred Roy Marsden and Polly Hemingway. It had hijacked the idea, characters, wardrobe, even Roy Marsden's wig from his 1982 series 'Airline'. In the commercial Roy and Polly Hemingway looked at a tatty airfield which was to become Heathrow. Greatorex tried to sue the agency J. Walter Thompson but failed.

Also Shown in 1987

Soap opera caught AIDS and the panic about it early. The 'EastEnders' gay man Colin Russell and his younger lover Barry each went down with (gasp, suspense) . . . a cold. They had the tests and were clear. (In 1988, Colin was more seriously ill; he feared AIDS but got multiple sclerosis.) The 'Brookside' producers boasted they would 'do' AIDS properly; unfortunately Ian Bleasdale, the actor introduced as the sufferer, had other acting commitments and disappeared. (In 1988 their gay Gordon Collins feared he might have it but didn't.) 'St Elsewhere' went to town with the 'waste' of it. Their best-looking doctor, the plastic surgeon played by pinup Mark Harmon, contracted AIDS after casual sex. He had to stop work and leave.

'Emmerdale Farm' was immune – it was busy with perhaps an even more serious issue, that of nuclear waste with a fine story-line about a plan to dump on the dales. 'Coronation Street' will probably stay clear for ever – no one has had cancer yet – and they had Hilda's departure (Jean Alexander left) and Bet and Alec's wedding to arrange. 'Casualty' gave AIDS to the boyfriend of one of its nurses. In 'Dallas' JR mentioned it obliquely to a young buck off to see a woman. 'Dynasty' did it worst when Blake lectured his bisexual son Steven in a tiny scene swamped by the cliffhanger ending of Alexis's 'drowning' in a car.

The disease was a ghostly presence in many other series that year. Channel 4 thought they were being daring with the first British sitcom about gay people, 'The Corner House'. Christopher

Eymard's Gilbert, the proprietor, gave little lectures on such things as the desirability of bidets in gay café loos. A scene of a couple in bed (a sort of drunken accident) opened the BBC's **'Life without George'** starring Carol Royle and Simon Cadell. There was crude language, much drinking in a wine-bar with a gay bartender and no mention of the dangers of sex with estate agents.

Mollie Sugden, once as well loved as the Queen Mum, disappointed us with **'My Husband and I'** – it was her real spouse William Moore, too. Ken Jones and Liz Smith tried valiantly in Central's **'Valentine Park'**, about a harassed park-keeper and a dotty landlady. And sitcom men were weedier than ever. Tim Brooke-Taylor's man in bathroom fittings, unhinged by the contents of his wife's lurid bestseller in the BBC's **'You Must Be the Husband'**, was the wimpiest. Keith Barron and Nanette Newman as a 'gosh, we're middle-aged and we're having a baby' couple in **'Late Expectations'** pulled the shortest sitcom straw. For **'Father Matthew's Daughter'** James Bolam should have been unfrocked, and BBC2's **'Small Problem'**, a grey comedy about short people being run out of town, should have been run off the screen.

LWT took two BBC stars and tried to build sitcoms around them. They had some success with Nicholas Lyndhurst, transplanted from 'Only Fools and Horses' to become the conventional half of a couple (he wants marriage, she doesn't), in **'The Two of Us'** which began in 1986. But Ray Brooks, taken from 'Big Deal' to **'Running Wild'** as a hopeless husband, rooted in his sixties habits, ran right out of jokes. Kate Robbins was in good form with her knockabout show **'Kate and Ted'**, although Ted got knocked out of most of the sketches. Rory Bremner proved a cut above most impressionists with his **'Now Something Else'** BBC2 series. Lenny Henry introduced Brixton's spondaciously crucial disc-jockey Delbert Wilkins in **'The Lenny Henry Show'**, a series which was almost a sitcom and improved as it went along.

An unexpected hit was **'Batman'**, the sixties American children's series, slipped into TV-am's half-empty output when technicians went on strike. It drew 100,000 more viewers than Anne Diamond. When Adam West visited Birmingham for a record-shop promotion in 1988, he insured his 'Batman' mask for a million dollars against damage.

Channel 4 gave Ruby Wax a chance with her late-night alternative to chat-shows, **'Don't Miss Wax'**. Most viewers didn't miss it when it went. Pamela Armstrong, former ITN newscaster, was given a BBC daytime chat-show which was not a success. In her pregnant and perhaps unsettled state, Anne Diamond co-hosted **'The Birthday Show'**, otherwise known as the Donkey Show, with Benny (brilliant on radio, bore on television) Green. It was almost the worst game-show of the year, but that prize went to **'Sweethearts'**, the who's-telling-the-truth-about-their-romance guessing game that was supposed to be Larry Grayson's comeback but was more of a coffin. Gloria Hunniford hosted **'The Newly Wed Game'** in which couples still shaking confetti from their luggage answered questions such as 'What was the most interesting thing you did in bed on honeymoon?' And Noel Edmonds launched **'Whatever Next?'** in which contestants had to guess the sequel to filmed stunts. The BBC decided whatever it was for Noel next it wasn't more of this rubbish.

On ITV **'LA Law'** was enforced. Set in a legal firm, this was another perfectly packaged, fashionable cocktail of sob stuff, shocks and 'it's not a perfect world' philosophy washed down with wise-cracks. It was soon a cult among 'Hill Street' and 'St Elsewhere' fans. Sentimentalists preferred Michael Landon as a musclebound probationary angel in **'Highway to Heaven'**. Transatlantic mini-series included the 'back story' of Dallas: **'Dallas – the Early Years'**, a great deal more gripping than the current year's in which the main character was Pam Ewing's bandages.

More melodrama came in the blood-and-guts-ridden **'Blood and Orchids'**, a story about prewar Americans being beastly to Hawaians. Don Johnson fared better in **'The Long Hot Summer'**, as the barn-burner lighting up three hours of Deep South power and passion. **'Ellis Island'**, about immigrants to turn-of-the-century New York, gave us Richard Burton's last performance – one of his worst. **'Hold the Dream'** was a sequel to 'Woman of Substance'; Jenny Seagrove – back as the grand-daughter – took the 'dream' bit literally and acted as though asleep. From Australia came **'Fields of Fire'**, about half-cut cane-cutters in dirty vests in northern 'Stralia, and **'The Last Frontier'** about an American divorcee alone in the outback. But it was a g'day when the BBC bought **'The Shiralee'**, starring Bryan Brown as a tough sheep-shearer trailing his young daughter as he searched for work, and **'Whose Baby?'** based on a true story of a baby mix-up with a splendid moving performance from Lisa Crittenden.

Among the travellers delayed for carrying illegal substances by **'The Duty Men'** in BBC2's fly-on-the-wall Customs-hall series was the actress Judy Carne. Also on BBC2 was **'The Edge of Life'**, a series following the difficult lives of premature babies; and in the year when reported cases of child abuse rose Esther Rantzen's campaigning work on the subject on **'That's Life'** and **'Childline'** earned her the Richard Dimbleby Award. Radio's Roger Cook began being biffed and bashed by villains on television, too, in ITV's **'The Cook Report'**. Among several excellent **'Forty Minutes'** reports was one about young prostitutes, **'Street Girls'**; another **'Home from the Hill'**, followed Colonel Hilary Hook, an old hunter back in Warminster after 'the right bugger' of being kicked out of his house in Kenya. Dramatised documentaries in 1987 were first-rate. Fine low-key performances from John Stride and David Calder set the tone for **'The Trial of Klaus Barbie'** – screened only a couple of weeks after the 'Butcher of Lyons' was sentenced to life in prison. **'Life Story'**, about the scientists who discovered DNA, with a superb performance by Jeff Goldblum, rightly won the year's best play award. There had been plenty of competition. Ian Richardson was a spookily believable **Blunt** in Robin Chapman's play about the spy, with Anthony Hopkins as an ebullient Guy Burgess. Dennis Potter's **'Visitors'** brought 'Dempsey and Makepeace' Michael Brandon and Glynis Barber back with John Standing and Nicola Pagett. Timothy West was convincingly gruesome as a double-crossing double-glazing man in Ron Pearson's **'Harry's Kingdom'**, and people who saw Michael Fitzgerald as the fey peroxided killer in Malcolm

McKay's chilling police-station drama, **'The Interrogation of John'**, did not forget it in a hurry. HTV remade Alfred Hitchcock's **'Suspicion'**. The old film worked because Cary Grant's charm was irresistible, but Anthony Andrews's charm in the same rôle was undetectable. ITV's best single drama was LWT's stylish no-expense-spared **'Scoop'**, Waugh's wicked satire on Fleet Street. It starred Denholm Elliott and Donald Pleasence as the *Daily Beast*'s editor and proprietor, and Michael Maloney as a polished Boot, the paper's 'Nature Notes' writer accidentally sent to cover an African war which had not happened.

'Floodtide', Granada's serial about a doctor working in a small French village embroiled in the murder of a British MP, had Philip Sayer as an appealing hero. **'Lost Belongings'** was Thames Television's authentic and unsettling serial about a Romeo and Juliet pair in Northern Ireland, notable for the stunning performance from Catherine Brennan as Deirdre and the ghastliness of her fanatical Loyalist uncle played by Harry Towb. The most passionate performance was Kenneth Cranham's as a man cracking up and at times disastrously drunk after divorce in **'A Sort of Innocence'** on BBC2. David Andrews's hero was rarely sober in Roy Clarke's complex series within a series, **'Pulaski'**; Susan Penhaligon, pouting and perplexed, was wonderful in Fay Weldon's **'Heart of the Country'**; and everyone went right over the top in **'The Bretts'**, Central's serial about an acting dynasty in the 1920s. Despite lashings of melodrama – homosexuality, drug addiction, suicide, cancer, passion – no one was interested. By the end it was screened after eleven at night.

1988

Earthquakes in Armenia killed 50,000 and made millions homeless. ☐ George Bush was elected President of the United States. ☐ Three IRA members were shot by SAS marksmen in Gibraltar. ☐ And 167 died in the Piper Alpha oil-rig fire. ☐ A virus killed vast numbers of North Sea grey seals, but a million-pound rescue operation freed two of three whales trapped in Alaskan ice. ☐ The Iran–Iraq war ended. ☐ Soviet troops left Afghanistan. ☐ Lesbians protesting an 'anti-gays' clause 28 of the Government's Local Authorities Bill invaded the BBC's Six O'Clock News; newsreader Nicholas Witchell sat on one. ☐ Canadian athlete Ben Johnson was stripped of his 100 metres Olympic gold medal after drugs tests proved positive. ☐ A kiss-and-tell barmaid earned Mike Gatting the sack as England's cricket captain. ☐ Three trains collided near Clapham Junction and thirty-four died. ☐ A Pan Am 747 crashed at Lockerbie in Scotland, killing 259 passengers and eleven from the town. ☐ Junior Health Minister Edwina Currie resigned after a salmonella-in-eggs row. ☐ And Bros were the teens' rave.

Perhaps we'd been laughing too much, too knowingly at Dame Edna Everage and her send-up of life in Moonee Ponds. Perhaps revenge was being taken for all the rotten shows we'd dispatched Down Under for years. Whatever the reason, in 1988 the Empire struck back. The trickle of Australian soap operas and mini-series into our schedules changed to a flood. It was no use our pleading: 'Look, we let Rolf Harris *stay*' – **'Neighbours'**, created by Reg Watson, the man who gave the world 'Crossroads', became an addiction for more than 16 million viewers. And not once or twice a week but every weekday.

The soap, made by Australia's biggest producer of brash game-shows and 'soapies', Grundy, had made a few false starts over there before becoming a hit with 5 million Aussies. It had been a popular daytime distraction here since the autumn of 1986 for children and women at home. It might well have remained so. Then sixteen-year-old Alison Grade told her dad that she and her friends couldn't always get to the school television set for the lunchtime episode. Her father, the Controller of BBC1, ordered the morning repeat to be moved to a 5.35 teatime slot from the New Year to help all children deprived like his daughter. In so doing, Michael Grade, the man who had cosseted 'EastEnders' until it grew big and strong and number one, gave the Aussie import all it needed to sweep its way into the ratings and to make television history. (He then left the BBC to run Channel 4.)

No one says 'Neighbours' is art. It's the cheapest brand of soap the BBC can buy – a week's worth costs about half one half-hour of home-made drama. It washes cleanest, too – there's no smoking or swearing, the characters rarely drink anything stronger than orange juice or mineral water (even in the Waterhole pub) and sex is in its infancy in Ramsey Street. Nothing nasty will ever be found in the woodshed. Because the scripts are corny, the acting is often heroic, the action funny for the wrong reasons, and the most moving thing is sometimes the scenery. Fiona Corke, who plays Gail Robinson, recalls asking the director to stop a wall wobbling for one of her scenes, expecting a bit of quick carpentry. After filming it, she found two stagehands spreadeagled behind the troublesome wall, trying to hold it still. But, for all that, 'Neighbours' works. Babies are soothed by the theme tune (composed by Tony Hatch). There is standing room only in university common rooms when it's on. Vicars use it as texts for sermons and headmasters wake up pupils in assembly by commenting on what young Scott and Charlene may have done to upset Gentleman Jim or mother Madge or Mrs Mangel, the show's absurd old busybody who speaks with an English accent to show she's supposed to be comic.

Everybody needs good Neighbours – but we got Madge (Anne Charleston), Henry (Craig McLachlan) and Charlene (Kylie Minogue) from Ramsey Street, Soapland, Australia.

'Neighbours'-knockers form alliances, too. Comedians no longer able to jibe at 'Crossroads' have found a substitute ('You know why they show it twice each day? Because people can't believe it the first time!'). Most teachers call it rubbish. And Michael Caine, who came back from America to live in Britain in 1987, spoke for puzzled parents everywhere when he said: 'I find I'm the father of someone who watches (*face contorted in pain*) "Neighbours".' But the fact is that 'Neighbours' supplied what many home-made soaps do not: a show for kids and about kids, a sunny setting and a sunny philosophy of 'she'll be right, mate'. It also supplied the world with a new poppet pop star – Kylie Minogue, who played cheeky

Charlene, garage mechanic, girlfriend and bride of school-boy Scott.

By contrast most drama from America came in two parcels to fill gaps between the ends of one home-made series and the start of another. The BBC gave us **'Anastasia'** with Amy Irving as the woman who believed she was a Russian princess. Convincing though her story was, with the variety of accents in this Tsar's family – British, Brooklyn, Omar Sharif's Cairo – all the Romanovs were clearly fakes. Arguing her case on ITV at the time was another pretender to the Russian throne: Katrina Petrovina, heroine of **'Monte Carlo'**. This was a four-hour schlockbuster produced by Joan Collins, starring Joan Collins and bearing the stamp of Joan Collins. To wit, Katrina, the tantalising princess/world-famous singer/incredibly brave spy living in France was Alexis from 'Dynasty' with garlic. Hitler was a big fan of Katrina's, so someone said in a Cherman accent. He might have gone into the bunker a lot sooner had he heard, with us, her rendition of 'The Last Time I Saw Paris'. It recalled the singing of that other heroine of the Resistance, Edith in ''Allo 'Allo'. While Katrina was tapping Morse code on her jewel-box, flouncing in polka dots, enduring such torture as lip-gloss denial at the hands of the Gestapo and winning the devotion of George Hamilton as a famous blocked writer, Leslie Phillips was Carrying On Against Jerry at the War Office.

Euston Films decided to celebrate the centenary of the horrific **Jack the Ripper** prostitute murders and make a killing with sales *to* America. Michael Caine was Scotland Yard's Detective Inspector Abberline in curly bowler and too-small jacket for this two-part film – a co-production with Lorimar (the 'Dallas' people). For it they built a dinky Whitechapel in Virginia Water in which floozies floozed and urchins urched speaking the sort of Dick Van Dyke cockney with which American housewives would have no problem. Red herrings weren't simply slipped in – there was a drum-roll first. 'Oh, Lord luv us, isn't that Prince Albert Victor, Duke of Clarence, grandson of Queen Victoria, known to frequent these parts?' Caine's copper perusing a succession of ketchup-covered corpses was naturally brighter than his snooty superiors and, despite his fondness for whisky, was nifty at unbuttoning bodices. Jane Seymour playing an artist-sleuth obliged. The producers improved the publicity by claiming Tests Proved their culprit – Queen Victoria's surgeon Sir William Withey Gull – was the real Ripper. Historians begged to differ.

Home-made drama series managed to hold up well. Who needed an orchestra, a cast of thousands, superstars and spectacle when Alan Bennett had written monologues about frumpy failures? His **'Talking Heads'** series for BBC2 in which lonely women and one man (a sad homosexual living with his mum, played by Bennett himself) told their life-stories in sets which comprised perhaps one chair and the edge of a table, was a triumph.

Thora Hird's crippled Doris, slumped by her door, remembering how they wrapped her stillborn babe in newspaper, refusing to shout to the postman for fear they'd cart her off to a home where 'they mixed the teeth', brought the biggest lump to the throat.

LWT's major serial of the year, **'Piece of Cake'**, about the wartime RAF and based on Derek Robinson's controversial book, failed to be the triumph they had hoped for. Because the Air Force and the Ministry of Defence refused to co-operate, and the right planes (Hurricanes) weren't available – those which survived are now priceless antiques – it almost didn't get off the runway. War veterans were outraged that Robinson's pilots weren't patriotic heroes but ill-prepared immature boys often cruel to each other and usually frightened out of their wits. Sir Christopher Foxley-Norris, chairman of the Battle of Britain Association, was among many angered to learn the serial would be made. 'This is not a warts-and-all portrayal but a warts-and-nothing-else,' he said. But a six-part serial was made, at a cost of £4.6 million using five Spitfires, a few other planes unearthed in unlikely places (a Heinkel 1-11 was found in bits in a Cambridge coalyard) and some replicas. Months of planning went into the flying scenes, daredevil swooping under bridges and other potty missions, notably the enemy's dropping of a chamberpot from a Messerschmitt on the British base. In such aircraft the cockpit and windows are tiny, so only a small object could be used. It also had to be light, because a heavy object might damage the tailplane and the Civil Aviation Authority expressly bans the dropping of dangerous objects. Eventually a two-ounce potty of ping-pong-ball plastic was made, approved by both the pilot and the Authority. The chances were it would float away, but miraculously as the cameras rolled it hit the ground on the spot marked X. Yet, despite wizard flying sequences and dashed good performances from Tim Woodward, David Horovitch, Richard Hope and others, there was too little romance, the comedy was too black and, as each twisted and unpleasant young man bought it, it was hard to shed tears.

Granada spent even more money, £5 million, on **'Game Set and Match'**, a thirteen-part serial of Len Deighton's trilogy of thrillers not only about secrets and moles but also about the relationships between spies in the *glasnost* era. Ian Holm, who'd been fascinated by spies ever since he went to Moscow in 1958 and met Guy Burgess ('he was a sad pathetic figure'), took on the rôle of Bernard Samson, the disgraced British spy. His devoted wife Fiona (Mel Martin) turned out to be a KGB agent who had to flee to Moscow leaving their small children as pawns in a tense battle of nerves and loyalties. Small, serious and growing more grim-faced by the week, Ian appeared in 660 scenes out of 664. The year-long filming schedule included work in the sub-zero temperatures of Berlin where East German border guards photographed every member of

the crew, arrested, stripped and searched two of them for wandering off the main autobahn, and popped up everywhere in the director's viewfinder with binoculars and machine-guns trained on their groups. It also involved filming in Mexico where everyone suffered from the intense heat, seasickness and the trots. But as with 'Piece of Cake' the response was cool. One mistake, producer Brian Armstrong later decided, had been to screen the first two hours together, which included several difficult-to-grasp 'back-stories', flashbacks and a somewhat sombre escape 'over the wire' back to the West (actually they were crossing farmland in Cheshire). By 11.30 on a Monday night most viewers had gone off both Berlin and

In 'Tumbledown', Colin Firth was perfect as Lawrence, half stupid sod, half lovable boy wounded as much by the fact that the Army he loved let him down as by Argy bullets.

Bernard. Philosophically Ian Holm said: 'If it's not a success . . . well, I'll go back to what I was doing the year before – voiceovers for adverts like Duracell, Condor and Red Mountain Coffee.'

Plays caused stinks in 1988. George Younger, the Defence Secretary, was 'deeply unhappy' about **'Tumbledown'**, the first major drama about the Falklands War, and tried to persuade the BBC not to screen it without major changes. Charles Wood's play was based on the experiences of Scots Guardsman Lieutenant Robert Lawrence, half of whose head was blown away in an assault against 'Tumbledown' mountain the day before the end of the war was declared. It was in the firing-line partly because another play about the war, by Ian Curteis, had been dropped in 1987 (too right-wing, said the author, too boring said the BBC) and partly because Lawrence's account blasted the forces for showing a lack of care and concern for the injured. Threats of injunctions were flying. Finally lawyers made only a two-minute cut and most viewers judged it a necessary play, if somewhat heavy-going in its dizzying flashbacks to miseries in the mud and flash-forwards to polite lunches in the country for the partly paralysed ex-soldier played by Colin Firth. David Calder as his father, saying he was proud, showing he was shattered made it almost unbearably sad. Anthony Hopkins's portrayal of aristocrat Donald Campbell, who died in 1967 breaking his own world speed record, in **'Across the Lake'** brought a different kind of protest. The actor learned days before shooting in the Lake District was due to begin that someone had pledged to kill him. Hopkins suspected the would-be killer was an actor jealous of his success, who once accosted him in the street. He hated the fuss and police presence over the next weeks but he also admitted to being 'bloody frightened'. Filmed next to a replica of Campbell's 297 m.p.h. *Bluebird* (made for £35,000 and top speed 25 m.p.h.), Hopkins's likeness to the driven, desperately unlucky Campbell was uncanny. There seemed to be an edge to his disturbing performance – a sense of the closeness of death.

There was also a fuss when ITV pulled the plug on thirty-three years of grapplers devising complicated ways of sitting on each other's faces. Kent Walton's velvet voice of wrestling no longer had its Saturday-afternoon home. But there was an alternative. Channel 4 brought in even bigger mounds of flesh with a weekly series of Japan's national sport, Sumo wrestling. In the summer sports fans had to give up sleep as ITV, BBC and Channel 4 swamped our screens with Olympics for sixteen nights. South Korea is nine hours ahead of us, so most of the events took place early in the morning. Barry Norman was the Channel 4 anchorman – his first stab at live television. On the first night he heard on his earpiece that he was to interview former diving champ Brian Phelps just before a group of people came on screen. He had no idea which was Phelps. Luckily, in a moment when the camera wasn't on him,

The most popular righter of wrongs to come from America in 1988 was Vincent, half man, half make-up department, a hero who lived in the New York sewers, wore weird medieval clobber and proved that not everyone in America opts for plastic surgery, however badly they need it. The rôle of the Lennie the Lion lookalike in 'Beauty and the Beast' went to towering gravel-voiced Ron Perlman, who submitted to hours of preparation to emerge in a ginger Tina Turner wig and a furry face. Vincent read meaningful passages from Dickens or Kipling, and commented on the evils of the modern world when not killing baddies to save Linda Hamilton, as the caring lawyer who was the Beauty.

Barry collared the director to point Phelps out. Football commentator Alan Parry could have done with a little help like that. ITV won the contract to televise all league football matches in 1988. After a cup-tie match between Nottingham Forest and Leicester the 'Midweek Sports Special' producers wanted Alan to chat to a Nottingham star, either Brian Clough or his son Nigel or player Franz Carr. A nineteen-year-old apprentice who happened to be black like Franz was pushed forward. Parry solemnly interviewed him. Only later was he told he'd been set up.

A special star of the year was the hairy baby of **'First**

Born', BBC1's preposterous but hugely enjoyable serial based on Maureen Duffy's *Gor Saga*, a stern warning about the dangers of genetic engineering. Charles Dance played the scientist with a rosary in one hand and a scalpel in the other, who felt a godlike mission to improve the human race. One experiment led to the birth of a human-gorilla hybrid he called Gordon (presumably for 'Gor! what have we Don?'). At first five-week-old Jack Dymond played Gor. (While the fictional baby survived against the odds, the little actor was a tragic cot-death victim only months afterwards.) Later in the serial twins Josh and Tom Robinson, eight months old, took turns to play him, transformed into little monkeys, with whiskers glued all over their bodies. 'They ended up with more hair on their chests than their father,' said their mum, Claire. At the end of the first part, Dance had to try to drown the infant on the orders of his boss. One of the twins was placed in a baby-basket and, in the dead of night and in the rain, floated like Moses down the River Wye. Even with ten divers on hand in case the stunt went wrong, everyone was nervous when the wind sent the basket cascading downstream. The babe was fine, the scene was absurdly moving. And the heavyweight gorilla from Longleat who played his mum in a special set at a disused airfield sulked only briefly. Then she was given a television set in her cage and calmness returned. Ah, the power of television!

Commercial Break

More and more commercials took soapy treatments. The most hyped was a series for Gold Blend coffee featuring Anthony Head as a smoothie and Sharon Maughan as his cucumber-cool neighbour from whom he borrows jars of instant. Ironically they earned Sharon as much fanmail as her husband Trevor Eve received when he played Shoestring. Funniest were the commercials for British Telecom in which Maureen Lipman played a Jewish mother fussing over her grown son (played by Lional Haft, actually three years older than her) and nagging her husband. Most enjoyed were those for the Leeds Permanent Building Society, featuring George Cole as Arthur Daley in all but hat. This time he wore a flat cap instead of the trilby; the Leeds did so well from it – 20,000 new customers a month – that other building societies complained to the IBA that George was cashing in on his 'Minder' rôle. As if . . . Most disliked (by the Jewish Board of Deputies) was Midland Bank's commercial showing a Jewish clothing-firm boss. It was taken off after claims that it 'depicted Jews as being mean and hypocritical'. Sneakiest was the commercial for Batchelors soups using the same characters, grandad (actor Johnny Maxfield) and grandson (Adam Sunderland, now two feet taller), used by Heinz and dropped five years before. Heinz were quite steamed up by it. Boldest was the Rumbelows Option Three television commercial using film of Mikhail Gorbachev in the Kremlin asking comrades: 'Have you rumbled it?' The campaign was shown at the Russian embassy and approved before it was screened. And the best-loved commercial of 1988 was one for Real Fires, featuring a dog, a cat and a mouse, snoozing in harmony in front of a blazing hearth.

Also Shown in 1988

One Aussie hit was not enough for the BBC. They imported 'The Flying Doctors'; while ITV, who had been screening other Aussie soaps including 'Sons and Daughters', 'The Young Doctors' and 'A Country Practice', bolstered up their afternoons with 'Richmond Hill', a country police series (also made by Grundy and a flop in Australia), and bought 'Home and Away', a soap about teenagers set in Sydney, a rival to 'Neighbours', to slot it opposite the BBC show from 1989. By then there were nine shows with characters wishing each other 'G'day'. They sent us mini series, too. The best was 'Vietnam', showing their country's involvement in the war, and following the fortunes of a politician and his increasingly divided family. Next-best was TVS's American-financed story about an IRA man set in Australia – 'Act of Betrayal' starring Elliott Gould as an assassin who discovered killing people was wrong.

America sent ITV half-hours of 'Hooperman', the nicest policeman in the history of law-enforcement, played by John Ritter (son of Tex), inheritor of a crumbling apartment building and attracted to a beautiful plumber who like all plumbers, wouldn't come out at night. The BBC's only retaliation was to buy up a job lot of secondhand episodes of Peter Falk as 'Columbo', a hit on ITV fifteen years before. 'In The Heat of the Night' brought us Howard Rollins's version of Virgil Tibbs, the educated black city cop Sidney Poitier made famous in the film. His wasn't so handsome or so het-up, but this was at least different. **Maigret** – a long film, in a series of HTV co-productions in which Richard Harris played Simenon's famous Parisian detective as an elderly, wheezing Irish scarecrow – was absurd.

Not many people know my name's Inspector Abberline – Michael Caine impressed upon Jack the Ripper's coach-driver (George Sweeney).

American money paid for Anthony Andrews and Jane Seymour as a passionless Edward and Wallis Simpson in 'The Woman He Loved'; Mia Sara played the Merle Oberon Anglo-Indian stripper-turned-film-star with a seemingly embalmed Kirk Douglas as her Svengali in 'Queenie'. Stephanie Powers was the Kenyan pioneer horsewoman, aviator and bagger of handsome male specimens Beryl Markham in 'A Shadow on the Sun'.

'Blind Justice' was the BBC with bite. Five films produced by Michael Wearing (who also produced 'Edge of Darkness') showed radical lawyers (Jane Lapotaire, Jack Shepherd and Julian Wadham) beating their bewigged heads against the limitations of our legal system. 'South of the Border' was a jaunty low-life thriller series starring the Oxfam version of Cagney and Lacey, Pearl and Finn (Buki Armstrong and Rosie Rowell). The fact that most of the characters were black yet ordinary was important. Nothing about life in darkest Deptford was whitewashed. The BBC also brought us a jokey serial about Subbuteo fanatics, 'Playing for Real'; a satirical serial about advertising, 'Campaign'; two thrillers about the IRA – 'Crossfire' and 'Final Run'; and a local radio reporter striving against devious developers, drug-taking colleagues and a tetchy news-editor in 'Thin Air'. The costume drama of the year was Anne Devlin's adaptation of 'The Rainbow', prettily set in D. H. Lawrence's Nottinghamshire village of Eastwood. Imogen Stubbs played the teenager wrestling with her passions, while Kate Buffery played her lesbian schoolteacher. The nipple-count seemed to have soared since most of us read the book at school.

Dennis Potter's 'Christabel' – a four-part adaptation of Christabel Bielenberg's account of her life with her anti-Nazi German husband during the war – was deeply moving. Despite fine performances from Elizabeth Hurley and Stephen Dillon (the yuppie in Midland's 'new kind of bank account' ad), the slow treatment, omitting so many of the book's incidents, made it somehow a letdown.

It was a medium year for ITV drama. 'The Fear' brought us designer gangsters, and as one wit said: 'The criminals didn't shoot till they saw the whites of the victim's socks.' Robert Powell, so strong in sackcloth and sandals as Jesus, stepped into a hairy suit for 'Hannay', John Buchan's brave chappie. Granada's serial about academics, 'Small World', saved on costumes by making all the women strip. All the academics were hateworthy – even the little leprechaun hero (Barry Lynch) who simply wouldn't stop smiling. TVS gave us 'Gentlemen and Players', a glossy soapy series about Bo and Mike, rival whizzkids living in the shires and carving each other up in the City. Scottish Television gave Maurice Roeves the lead rôle in 'Bookie', a three-part series about the tough times of a Glasgow turf accountant. 'Wipe Out', the secret-agent-and-psychological-research-station thriller, was a washout for Granada. Central tried harder with 'Hard Cases', about probation officers, and LWT went back to the war for 'Wish Me Luck' – adventures with Resistance heroes and gritty Brits.

'**A Very British Coup**', Channel 4's short serial based on Chris Mullin's book, was a fast, exciting and highly enjoyable success which picked up the BAFTA best drama award. The plot put Ray McAnally's perky Harry Perkins, a former steelworker, into Number Ten as a left-wing Labour prime minister and proceeded to take the P out of politics as it's apparently played – a war game between cabinet members, uncivil servants and cynical press people. Among the plays, '**Airbase**' on BBC1 provoked a storm by suggesting that most USAF personnel are continuously injecting themselves with drugs, drinking heavily and precipitating the Third World War. Mrs Whitehouse sent a letter of apology to Ronald Reagan about it. '**The Great Paper Chase**', Keith Waterhouse's script from Anthony Delano's book about the discovery of train robber Ronald Biggs in Rio, finally came to the screen after Jack Slipper, the policeman who trailed him and failed to bring him home, made enough objections about the way he was portrayed to fill a book on its own. Other outstanding plays were '**The Most Dangerous Man in the World**', a thriller with Ian Sears and Martin Shaw about the shooting of Pope John Paul II in 1981; Central's '**Closing Ranks**' about a wife-battering policeman; and '**A Vote for Hitler**' by Paul Bryers on Channel 4, about the 1938 Oxford by-election.

Each new situation comedy seemed to be worse than the one before. Ronnie Barker was a clot to write and star in '**Clarence**' on BBC2, a farce about a clumsy clueless furniture-remover in pebble glasses. Mr Magoo was funnier years before. David Essex took the rôle Paul Nicholas did not want of a lock-keeper with an 'all you have to do is be' line in '**The River**'. He spoke his silly words in a dry monotone; everything else was wet. '**Double First**' with Michael Williams as N. V. Standish, Oxford literary lion, turned hamburger chef until discovered by two twee sisters, was doubly so. There was no studio laughter, so we never knew where the joke was. The studio audiences howled in '**Wyatt's Watchdogs**', about fuddy-duddies in a Neighbourhood Watch scheme. Perhaps they were in pain. '**No Frills**' had Kathy Staff as a Northern grannie disrupting the life of her lecturer daughter and punk grand-daughter. Each of the women seemed to come from a different planet. In '**Streets Apart**', Amanda Redman spent six episodes not telling James Hazeldine that she'd become a successful publisher since they had met as kids, while he was still a humble cabbie. Then he found out by accident. Zzz. Only '**Colin's Sandwich**' on BBC2,

with Mel Smith as a British Rail complaints clerk, would-be writer and coward, had any decent dialogue. Thames Television did better with a version of Simon Brett's stylishly written BBC radio success '**After Henry**', starring Prunella Scales. '**Andy Capp**', with James Bolam as the idle boozer, didn't survive the switch from cartoon to series even with scripts by Keith Waterhouse. Central's '**A Kind of Living**' teamed Richard Griffiths and Frances De La Tour as a bungling married couple with a cherubic baby called Og. Odd but not off. Comedians who shone were **Hale and Pace** (despite a cat-in-a-microwave sketch which had switchboards jammed). Emma Thompson was rewarded for 'Fortunes of War' with a song-dance-and-joke series of her own, '**Thompson**', which many people hated. Those clever writers Renwick and Marshall and that 'ugly fat bastard' Alexei Sayle were responsible for BBC2's '**Alexei Sayle's Stuff**', the wittiest joke-show of the year. But the best single comic character was Harry Enfield's loud loathsome plasterer Loadsamoney who first appeared with his Greek kebab cove Stavros ('Hhhallo peeps!') on '**Friday Night Live**'.

Several old series acquired new hosts. Angela Rippon became the bossa nova of '**Come Dancing**'; Michael Aspel relaxed into '**This Is Your Life**'; and Sarah Kennedy began a counterattack with '**Classmates**', reuniting celebrities with their real schoolchums. Esther Rantzen took to the streets each week dressed up as a series of aged damsels in distress in BBC's '**Hearts of Gold**'; much better was their showbiz version of 'A Question of Sport' – '**A Question of Entertainment**'. Tying for worst new game-shows were Scottish Television's version of the American hit '**Wheel of Fortune**'; the BBC's '**Brainstorm**' in which Kenny Everett tried to be the new Ted Rogers; LWT's '**You Bet**', with Bruce Forsyth; and TVS's '**Concentration**' whose host Nick Jackson talked like a ruminating camel. Thames began a brash popular consumer programme, '**The Bottom Line**' which was far from the bottom except when Danny Baker, a professional cockney, presented items. At the same level, Jimmy Greaves stumbled through a short shoddy chat series, speaking v-e-r-y s-l-o-w-l-y, and Derek Jameson spluttered 'Hope and Glory, what's your story?' throughout his terrible hotchpotch '**The People Show**'.

Among documentary series, Alan Whicker's '**Living with Waltzing Matilda**' was the most popular. David Dimbleby's series about America,

'**An Ocean Apart**', was perhaps the most thoughtful. The most disturbing was the BBC's five-part investigation of racial prejudice, '**Black and White**', using two reporters. Doors closed to black Geoff Small opened for white Tim Marshall. The most exciting was BBC's animal-experience series '**Supersense**', thanks to novel filming techniques. Stunning shots inside an angry lioness's mouth were lucky accidents. A lion cub sniffed a radio-controlled camera in a toy buggy covered in fur and fetched its mother. To the dismay of the camera crew, she ran off with the buggy in her mouth, but when they finally retrieved it – they had victim's-eye pictures.

Documentaries to commemorate the death of President Kennedy abounded, each one with a different theory about the real assassins. The fawning film was Tony Palmer's '**In from the Cold**' about Richard Burton. Liz Taylor would not share her thoughts on the flawed genius. Luckily Lauren Bacall and his daughter Kate did.

The Bitter End came to '**Crossroads**'. The motel was taken over by nasty Daniel Freeman (Philip Goodhew), Jill Chance (Jane Rossington) ditched awful Adam and chose jolly John Maddingham (Jeremy Nicholas), and the pair whizzed over the hill in his sports-car to that great soap in the sky. Partly taking its place were '**Jimmy's**', a fly-on-the-wall series from St James's Hospital Leeds, and round-the-year twice-weekly half-hours of the police series '**The Bill**'. '**EastEnders**' lost its best bint – alcoholic Angie Watts who went off with her fancy man to the Costa Del Sol when actress Anita Dobson left. Lofty and punky Mary also went; Lou died; Kathy was raped; Den went to gaol. In '**Coronation Street**' Mavis finally married dreadful Derek, and Annie Walker, eighty-four-year-old Doris Speed, popped back for an Easter special.

Meanwhile the BBC's '**Nine O'Clock News**' took on some soapy features. A million-pound relaunch resulted in one rather than two newsreaders, a new thunderbolt symbol and new graphics designed for £200,000 by an outside firm to the fury of members of the BBC's own design department who claimed they could have produced better for £15,000. It also placed the newsmen in front of a live background of a newsroom with television sets and computers. Viewers keenly watched what was going on behind them. Who was that girl on the phone to? Her mum? 'News at Ten'? Was that man rummaging for the latest employment figures or his car keys? That woman slumped over her desk – was she dead?

1989

A sudden overcrowding on the Hillsborough football stadium terracing led to the death of ninety-five Liverpool team supporters. ☐ Salman Rushdie was forced into hiding after Muslims outraged by his book The Satanic Verses *threatened his life. ☐ In a second earthquake in Armenia a thousand people died. ☐ President Bush sent American troops into Panama. ☐ Forty-four died when a jet crash-landed on the M1 in Leicestershire. ☐ Wartime prisoners of the Japanese protested when Prince Philip went to Emperor Hirohito's funeral ☐ The Christine Keeler-like life of Pamella Bordes, model and parliamentary researcher, embarrassed her many famous men-friends. ☐ Soft cheeses and cooked meats were declared health risks, concern for the damage to the earth's ozone layer increased and Mrs Thatcher joined the Greens. ☐ Heinz recalled jars of baby food after blackmailers added glass fragments and draw-ing pins to the ingredients. ☐ Pop hysteria reminis-cent of Beatlemania occurred at Jason Donovan concerts. ☐ Ayatollah Khomeini, Salvador Dali and Lord Olivier died. ☐ Massive student demonstrations in China ended when the People's Army opened fire killing many thousands. ☐ Mike Tyson beat Frank Bruno, but there were better fights among some boxing fans who'd paid to see the bout on the new Sky satellite: in many areas it didn't work.*

Large grey wok-like objects began appearing on the sides of houses. These were the signs that 1989 was the year of the television revolution, the year that should bring twelve new channels, the year of the dish. Were they status symbols, the envy of the neighbours? Not as it turned out. Alexei Sayle wondered if a dustbin lid and a pair of jump leads might work as well. Many of the people who in February had believed the advance advertising for Rupert Murdoch's Sky Television, battled to find a supplier who actually had a satellite dish to sell (most had to wait about two months) and paid the £250 to get tuned in probably wished they'd tried a dustbin lid, too. An early highlight on the Sky sports channel was Baltic handball. Sky entertainment channel offered Dolly Parton, pop shows from Holland, sixties favourites 'The Lucy Show' and 'Skippy', Australian soaps (also available on ITV) and versions of 'New Faces', 'The Price Is Right' and 'Sale of the Century'. Their 'heavyweight' stars turned out to be Keith Chegwin, Derek Jameson and the resurrected Frank Bough. Labour MP Austin Mitchell was sacked from his Shadow Cabinet job for partnering Norman Tebbit in a Sky discussion series. It was a far better plug than the show deserved. Even the commercials were disappointing. Many were aimed at the housewife in Luxembourg.

Sky boss Andrew Neil was frank about the poor quality of the programmes: 'I'm sure the Sky staff were worried at first that we didn't have many viewers. But there were some nights when I was perfectly happy that no one was watching,' he was reported as saying.

By June only half the hoped-for million-strong audience had been attracted. Sky's rival, British Satellite Broadcast-ing due to start in the autumn and already over budget, suffered from the bad reactions to its competitor and delayed its launch. And there was some doubt whether there would be sufficient advertising to pay for programmes of any quality, programmes likely to tempt us viewers away from what we're used to.

But several tedious discussion programmes at the start of the year on BBC and ITV hammered home the news, deeply depressing to most, that the Government planned to change what we were used to. British broadcasting had 'outgrown its suit of clothes', said Home Secretary Douglas Hurd. As had been outlined in the White Paper the previous year, franchises for the ITV companies would be up for grabs in a few years' time and in a few more the BBC would also be forced to change.

'Disgusting', they called it – and not only in Tunbridge Wells. 'Trick or Treat' was the joke game-show with Julian Clary (in the eyeshadow) and Mike Smith.

Happily television was still wearing its old clothes for most of 1989. Broadcasters were still making the old endearing mistakes. The **'Brits'** pop awards, screened live on BBC1 with Samantha Fox and Mick Fleetwood as a kind of Mick and Montmorency team of hosts, was a delightful shambles with the wrong people turning up under the spotlights. The keen-eyed viewers to **'News at Ten'** one night in March noticed that weatherman Alex Hill did not predict snow, sleet and rain for the north as had rival forecasters on BBC (where the forecasts are always live). He was also wearing the same clothes, using the same gestures and indeed delivering the same weather as he had the night before. When ITN's bosses found out that technicians had played yesterday's tape, the outlook was said to be overcast with outbreaks of thunder.

There were also scandalous treats from **'Trick or Treat'** on LWT. With Mike 'Mr Personality' Smith and the clever camp comedian Julian Clary, dressed to kill (usually in the glitziest frocks), as hosts, this game-show's publicised aim was to be 'whacky' by having the prizes fall off the display shelves and the hostesses busy eating a banana or fiddling with their tights at those moments when they should have been pointing and grinning at the prizes. Sunday newspapers soon alleged the show was more tacky than whacky. Three of the hostesses were former stars of pornographic films as its producer Michael Hurll (late of the BBC's 'Top of the Pops') well knew, they said. One of them, Erica Lea, also arranged clients for House of Commons call-girl Pamella Bordes. Jimmy Greaves shared with TV-am viewers his belief that Julian Clary was 'a prancing poofter' unsuitable for family entertainment. Julian replied that he never pranced – he 'minced'. Greaves said 'sorry' with a dozen red roses. LWT dropped

the frankly feeble series, but Channel 4 offered the now adored mincer a £50,000 contract to present a new 'outrageous' series, **'Sticky Moments'** in the autumn. Rory Bremner was soon impersonating Julian, the sure sign he'd 'arrived'.

'Groovy Fellers' was another whacky show which won't be returning. In it the large naked rump of Rowland Rivron, formerly Dr Scrote of 'The Last Resort', was seen as he, a naked Martian (with aerial on head), was shown around Britain by Jools Holland. Motormouth Ruby Wax took to the road in a clapped-out bus for **'Wax on Wheels'** and was spectacularly rude to people, and Clive James justified his enormous BBC salary with a serious Friday discussion series and **'Saturday Night Clive'**, in which he welcomed wits from other lands and showed a few clips of foreigners' television. (Food-series presenter Keith Floyd took over Clive's old post at LWT but seemed ill at ease without a wine-glass in his hand.)

Other comedy efforts in 1989 seemed tame by comparison – even **'A Bit of a Do'**, which had sex before, after and during the wedding (the bride's mum and the bridegroom's dad at the reception, to be precise). David Jason played the dad, a toasting-fork tycoon in this David Nobbs serial for Yorkshire Television set around the highspots of the social calendar of two Northern families – parties, dinner-dances and the crowning of Miss Frozen Chicken UK (sponsored by Cock-a-Doodle Chickens). Jason's performance in this was overshadowed by the best-ever series of **'Only Fools and Horses'** running at the same time and written under such pressure by John Sullivan that he was sending the producer a scene at a time.

Gwen Taylor, Jason's 'A Bit of a Do' co-star, turned up as a poverty-stricken vet's assistant, living in a grotty flat with her newly widowed once-rich sister, in **'Sob Sisters'**. For one scene of this sitcom a double-decker bus, driven by a stunt driver, was filmed crashing into the garden of a house in suburban Nottingham. It was then supposed to stop. Instead it hurtled through the bay window and into the front room. Nothing in the rest of this uneven series was that exciting. Wendy Craig had only herself to blame for **'Laura and Disorder'**, the BBC1 comedy in which she played a daffy divorcee back from the States. The situation and the script were woefully weak. She was the show's creator and co-writer with her son. Wee Hannah Gordon was teamed with the admired Peter Egan, she as a bank manager, he as a house-husband, in the BBC's **'Joint Account'**, but the idea was soon bankrupt. Only Nichola McAuliffe as a surgeon who bit off male heads during operations in Granada's perhaps too clever **'Surgical Spirit'** had decent jokes written for her. Anita Dobson, much missed from 'EastEnders', starred in the Granada sitcom **'Split Ends'** playing a hairdresser. It was scripted by several writers, and was about as funny as dandruff.

American Roseanne Barr became the biggest woman in comedy (if not in television) in 1989. The jumbo-sized comedienne's Channel 4 show **'Roseanne'**, was as rich in one-liners as 'The Golden Girls' and broke new ground, being about a poor American family, with a messy flat where Roseanne, as the slovenly but cheery factory-worker, demonstrated mother love through abuse. She told her three whiny kids she was not their real mother and would probably change the locks once they had gone to school. Meanwhile her even bigger-bellied builder-husband (John Goodman) was (rare for sitcoms) neither a bully nor a wimp.

Colourful epics co-produced with Australian companies did well. In **'The Heroes'**, which recounted the revenge mission by British army officer Ivan Lyon (Paul Rhys) and thirteen comrades to blow up the Japanese navy, Jason Donovan put aside his 'Neighbours' skateboard to play (excellently, as it turned out) a scared but brave young sailor. Singapore harbour was a tank in a Sydney warehouse. In Noel Barber's romping **'Tanamera'**, Singapore's colonial splendour was re-created in the Sydney hills, but some war scenes were filmed in Singapore. There the locals so loved the specially built grand house (actually a British army barracks) that after it was spectacularly set on fire the Tourist Office preserved the burned-out shell with a notice telling tourists that these were the ruins of the famous Tanamera, bombed in the war. A more serious Aussie mini-series was **'A Dangerous Life'**, with American Gary Busey as a reporter covering the end of the Marcos era in the Philippines. Tessie Thomas as the snivelling Imelda upstaged everyone including Ronald Reagan who appeared in inserted news-footage.

On BBC1, **'Midnight Caller'** became a Saturday-night success. It featured Gary Cole, the American actor who turned down the Crockett rôle in 'Miami Vice', as a cop turned radio talk-show host, so hip he never seemed to wear earphones. Victoria Tennant partnered Lindsay Wagner in the slushy **'Voice of the Heart'** and then turned up in **'War and Remembrance'**, romantically entwined again with Robert Mitchum, now seventy-two and still doing an impression of a tree. It was early spring when ITV bought this thirty-hour sequel to 'Winds of War' which had taken longer to film than it took the Allies to win the war. They delayed showing it because it was so embarrassingly bad. Advertisers in America reportedly got refunds on their commercials because it was such a flop there.

Drama in the first half of the year was never embarrassing but rarely worth raving about. If you liked wildly over-the-top gothic horror, Peter O'Toole's evil rheumy-eyed Uncle Silas and Jane Lapotaire's grotesque French governess, high on laudanum and sin in BBC2's serial **'Dark Angel'**, was the ticket. Jonathan Hyde looked somewhat sinister, too, as the arrogant and fearless lawyer of legend, Edward Marshall Hall, in **'Shadow of the Noose'**, the melodramatic Victorian courtroom series which followed. Hyde, whose career in television must surely flourish, made him a hero.

Both ITV and BBC produced thirties detectives for Sundays and had them zipping around pretty country lanes in Lagondas with stupid sidekicks in tow. Peter Davison was the lead in the BBC's **'Campion'**, who might have been called Campy One, being a silly ass who made irritating jokes. David Suchet starred in LWT's **'Poirot'**, or rather, 'Agatha Christie's Poirot', the fuss-pot Belgian sleuth with the ridiculous curly moustache and 'little grey

Sheila Hancock was the suicidal widow, David Threlfall was the murderer in the BBC's weird and wonderful 'Jumping the Queue'.

cells' in need of stimulation. The BBC's props were probably classier, but 'Poirot' won bigger audiences.

The Sunday success on ITV was **'Forever Green'**, an unashamedly sentimental drama with fashionable conservation plots – everything from saving badgers and banning pesticides to alternative medicines – and with Pauline Collins and John Alderton as the Boults, a townie couple who move to a Gloucestershire cottage. We watched them slowly renovating a wreck. In fact a beautiful Cotswold farmhouse had been carefully aged with lorry-loads of dust, cobwebs, broken furniture and a scurrying rat. The story also had that ace ingredient – illness. The Boults' daughter Freddy suffered from asthma; her doctor predicted it would worsen in the country. Instead her health improved – but not in the way intended by the series' writers Terence Brady and Charlotte Bingham. Their daughter Candida had been so badly affected by asthma that at eleven, after two bedridden years, she weighed only three stone. In the series Freddy Boult threw away her inhaler and was all but cured by a cranky old aristocrat and her 'black box' treatment. Brady and Bingham had their names removed from the credits; the Asthma Research Council was appalled; but viewers loved it.

Friday nights perked up with **'Making Out'**, a sort of female 'Auf Wiedersehen Pet', centred on the far-from-ladylike antics of women in a Liverpool electronics factory and suggesting that Scouse poverty isn't the fun it's cracked up to be in 'Bread'. Its star Margi Clarke's Queenie could have gone a few rounds with Ma Boswell. The most compelling Friday drama was **'Jumping the Queue'**, which came to be made after Sheila Hancock had read, liked and bought the rights to Mary Wesley's novel, then met BBC producer Sally Head in the street and suggested the BBC made the serial with her in the lead. Down in Cornwall for filming, Sheila spent the first four days in intensive care with a suspected heart-attack. It turned out to be wind. There was nothing so normal about the thriller's heroine Matilda, a woman in her fifties whose chance meeting with a young man on the run for killing his mother helped her face the ugliness in her family's life – and with incest, cocaine addiction, murder and adultery there was plenty to face. David Threlfall played the fugitive, and Don Henderson was her quirky neighbour. In the novel Matilda had a dog and a pet goose. On television she had a dog, a goose and a duck. The actor goose (Bertie) was deeply attached to the scruffy duck, so they had to be hired together.

Judi Dench bagged probably the year's next-best woman's rôle: dowdy decent Bridget in **'Behaving Badly'** on Channel 4. After years of meekly accepting her lot as a callous businessman's dumped first wife, Bridget moved back into the marital home and eventually took off for California with her daughter's bisexual flatmate. Meanwhile she did the cooking and the washing-up,

No longer Dirty Den and Bulman, actors Leslie Grantham and Don Henderson became brothers in Brixton, jointly running 'The Paradise Club', BBC1's drama series.

smiling. Behaving not badly enough, many viewers thought.

Keith Barron made a truly tragic figure of ordinary taxi-driver Tom in Tony Marchant's three-part BBC1 love-story **'Take Me Home'**. Married to a cheerful frump, superbly played by Annette Crosbie, his love for a sulky if stunning young bitch, played by Maggie O'Neill, led to a chain of ordinary but excruciating misery. The setting was a new town, actually Telford, all roundabouts, mudbanks and Japanese-owned factories with remote-control cameras in the carparks. Telford tourist board must have loathed it.

The new Glasgow (just as scary as the old, but with flash buildings, health clubs and sports-cars) was the setting for the exciting Friday thriller **'The Justice Game'**, starring Denis Lawson as lawyer and tough chappie Rossi who stumbled on a conspiracy by Scots American businessmen to buy up the city. The same mcsmoothies and mcyuppies were found in Scottish Television's three-part **'Winners and Losers'**, which had Leslie Grantham, conveniently out of 'EastEnders' (his character, Dirty Den, was shot dead – apparently by a bunch of daffodils working for the Mafia), as a rich London boxing promoter Eddie Burt. The highlight for Grantham fans should have come in the second episode when ever-ready Eddie made passionate love to his accountant (Denise Stephenson). But while Scots viewers saw the long steamy coupling, a freak break in reception robbed English viewers of all but a glimpse of the Grantham rear. This may or may not have been a shame. A blonde policewoman seemed the next most likely screen bedmate for Grantham in the autumn in **'The Paradise Club'**, a ten-part crime-adventure series on BBC1 which the independent makers hoped would fill the gap left by 'Minder'. Grantham, as upwardly mobile Danny Kane, lives with his family in the docklands, running a seedy dance-hall with his brother, a disgraced priest played by Don Henderson, and trying to go legit.

More yuppies arrived in Malcolm Bradbury's **'Anything More Would Be Greedy'** for Anglia, a sort of modern day 'Glittering Prizes', about the lives of six students, one of whom became a whizzkid inventor, another a Tory MP involved in dirty tricks during the Falklands War. Meanwhile Frederic Raphael traced the lives of two boys, one English, one a German Jew, from their forties schooldays to the sixties world of television and the theatre in the superb ten-part Granada serial **'After the War'**. Anton Rodgers, Susannah York and Denis Quilley were among the stars.

Russell Harty's old house in Giggleswick, North Yorkshire, was bought by newspaper proprietor Eddie Shah to provide the setting for his first venture into television drama. **'Capstick's Law'** was 'All Creatures Great and Small' without animals. Instead there were stuffy fifties folk, solicitor Edward Capstick (William Gaunt), whisky-mellowed widower-brother Henry ('Poldark' star Robin Ellis) and, playing the bosom of the family, the well-qualified Wanda Ventham. Christopher Villiers and Lesley Dunlop played the would-they-wouldn't-they young lawyers in love. Gaunt, who'd attended Giggleswick school only yards from the house, modelled the part on his father, a country solicitor in practice at that time. He even borrowed dad's specs. Critics renamed the series 'Capstick's Snore'.

Eric Sykes takes golf very seriously, but his 1989 comedy, 'The 19th Hole', didn't.

Among the documentaries of the year, a controversial film by Norwegian Odd Lindberg showing that seal pups are still being clubbed to death and illegally skinned, **'Seal Mourning'** in the **'Fragile Earth'** series, provoked a record response. Thousands of distressed viewers rang the Channel 4 free phone-line as many more jammed the switchboard to complain. Dramatic pictures of an armed robber being shot dead by police and lying in a pool of blood in Thames Television's fly-on-the-wall series **'Flying Squad'** caused hardly a ripple of protest. The series aimed to show that London's crack crimebusters weren't like the hard men of 'The Sweeney'. It didn't succeed.

Marcel Orphul's long unforgettable **'Hôtel Terminus'**, by and about the people who knew, suffered under, helped and exploited the sadistic talents of Nazi torturer and killer Klaus Barbie, shown on BBC2, was probably the outstanding factual film of 1989. The May report for **'First Tuesday'** focused on another mass killer in wartime: William Calley, who'd led the boys of Charlie Company to slaughter 500 villagers in My Lai, Vietnam, in 1968. Calley, who now runs a jewellery business, wouldn't talk on the film. But many of his men, some literally sick with guilt, and some of the surviving villagers did; the effect was chilling.

What was cheering was the BBC's second Comic Relief day spearheaded by Lenny Henry and pals. It raised £16 million for famine victims, and cars sported red plastic 'noses' for the rest of the year.

Also Shown in 1989

It was 'in' to be arty. 'Late-Night Line-Up' returned better as BBC2's **'The Late Show'** most weekday evenings. Seriously laid-back presenters included Sara Dunant and Michael Ignatieff. Central Television took the plunge and 'sold' seventeen children in 1989. Their **'Find a Family'** fortnight was a daily spot for children in care to giggle at the cameras and talk about their ideal new parents. David Steel, MP, Colin Welland and others who had successfully adopted children, and Derek Jameson and others who'd been adopted, chipped in with their experiences. It worked for the kids and for hundreds more to whom interested viewers were referred and proved wrong viewers who thought it would be 'in the worst possible taste'. Channel 4's controversial drama for the end of the year was Peter Brook's medieval masterpiece, **'Mahabharata'**, but the series most likely to displease Mrs Whitehouse was **'Black Eyes'**, Dennis Potter's sexy serial about a model called 'Sugar Bush'. It was based on real events related to Potter by his niece. Carol Royle and Michael Gough starred.

British television celebrated the 200th anniversary of the French Revolution with **'A Tale of Two Cities'**, a French-English co-production of Charles Dickens's novel. In our version the peasants sounded like extras from ''Allo, 'Allo', and the whole thing was revolting. Screening was to have been on Bastille Day, but as too many people went on holiday in July history lost out to ratings. The two-parter went out in May. Channel 4 made amends, clearing the 14 July decks for programmes about France from France. They also showed a far far better version of the Dickens classic, made in 1935, starring Ronald Coleman.

Among notable factual programmes was the often amusing history of birth control in Channel 4's **'In the Club'**. *Glasnost* opened the door to the year's best-researched factual series, Central's twelve-part **'The Nuclear Age'**. The powerful men in the history of Soviet events, as well as their American counterparts, talked openly. Comedy drama series later in the year included **'Stay Lucky'**, with Dennis Waterman playing a new cockney geezer sparring with Jan ('Just Good Friends') Francis, as a new widow; Diana Rigg and James Fox teamed up for Andrew Davies's **'Mother Love'**, and Sir John Gielgud and Susan Wooldridge were father and daughter in John Mortimer's **'A Summer's Lease'**. A Yugoslav taxi-driver who's a dead ringer

for Gorbachev played the Russian leader under threat of assassination in the first of six Frederick Forsyth stories lavishly filmed for LWT. Keith Carradine and Robert Lindsay were the heroes of the Jack Higgins adventure **'Confessional'**, and Cathy Tyson and Karl Johnson starred in the TVS serial about the threat of nuclear war, **'Rules of Engagement'**. Real heroes included Joss Ackland who filmed Anglia's **'The Quiet Conspiracy'** in Strasbourg with pneumonia and Ben Kingsley who lost twenty pounds and had nightmares about the concentration-camp horrors while making **'Murderers among Us'**, the TVS film about Nazi-hunter Simon Wiesenthal. Kingsley consoled himself that he, the script and the background details had been approved by Weisenthal who'd earlier vetoed a version to star Kirk Douglas. **'Shalom Salaam'**, written for BBC2 by Gareth Jones, explored the racial tensions of multicultural Britain through a complex love-story set in Leicester. The five-part series offered Asian actors their first real opportunity in television drama and Manta Kaash as the Muslim girl was particularly impressive. The political drama of the year was BBC's **'Fellow Traveller'**, with Ron Silver and Daniel J. Travanti, about the McCarthy witch-hunting era in Hollywood. Among outstanding single plays on BBC2 were **'Death of a Son'** in which Lynn Redgrave brilliantly played the mother who prosecuted the pusher who sold her son lethal drugs; **'Virtuoso'**, the account of deeply depressed musical genius John Ogdon, starring Alfred Molina; and **'Defrosting the Fridge'**, a jaunty film about a rubbishy American football team in an East Anglian fishing town and starring the marvellous Joe Don Baker. Thames adapted Kingsley Amis's black comedy of old age, **'Ending Up'**, into a drama. Yorkshire Television gave us two first-rate plays: **'A Day in Summer'**, the beautiful, slowly unfurling picture of a war cripple (Peter Egan) in a town of tortured souls on feast-day; and **'Comeback'**, the true, funny but awful story of a film producer who tried suicide and ended up in the weird 'graveyard' ward of a hospital. Anton Rodgers, who starred in this, also cropped up in one of the few other decent sitcoms, **'May to December'**, as a Scottish solicitor in love with Eve Matheson as a games mistress who cracked corny jokes when nervous – the perfect excuse for the scriptwriters. Johnny Speight wrote **'The 19th Hole'** to star Eric Sykes, the comedian whose scripts he wrote in the early sixties (Sykes wrote his own for the next twenty years). Actor Simon O'Brien, the late lamented Damon from 'Brookside', turned up in Central's **'Young Gifted and Broke'**, about a Youth Training Scheme. Norman Beaton and Carmen Munro were reunited for Channel 4's **'Desmonds'**, a jolly comedy about a hairdressing salon full of philosophising West Indians; but if there was anything jolly or comic in LWT's **'High Street Blues'** it was well hidden.

Dynasty died but yuppie soap arrived with **'thirtysomething'** on Channel 4. Built around seven friends from college, it had the misery, guilt, uncertainty and irritation you can get at home but was better-dressed. Being American, there was also more Meaning in every comment, from 'I can't handle that right now' to 'Want me to fix you a salad?' **'Coronation Street'** was repeated on Sundays and resumed top place in the ratings. A plan to run it on Fridays as well was leaked in May. ITV imported the Sydney soap **'Home and Away'** and had it overlap **'Neighbours'**. But Scott and Charlene reigned supreme. **'EastEnders'** lost Den, Donna, Colin and its Godmother, Julia Smith, and upset the Brownies by suggesting that in Walford at least the junior guides were more like little lager louts.

Commercial Break

Madonna was paid £3 million to advertise Pepsi, but the commercial had a short life. Because of protests that the video to promote her song 'Like a Prayer', heard on the commercial, was blasphemous, the company dropped it. The Weetabix bovver boys were sacked for looking too aggressive; Frank Bruno and his daughter Nicola, aged six, advertised Champion bread; former prime minister Edward Heath sold cheese; and Karl Howman, star of the sitcom 'Brush Strokes', plugged Walls sausages for not being what the health-conscious would approve of. The ITV companies advertised themselves with clips of past glories run to the song 'Just the Way You Are' and also carried the costly campaign for Sky, starring Rosemary Leach and Tony Doyle.

You Have Been Watching...
THE EIGHTIES

In its golden maturity British television became more powerful than ever before. With satellites in place, news reports became instant and the world shrank. Television made us see more and made some of us care more. Time differences meant television could bring us terrifying pictures of earthquakes in South America before people in the rest of that continent had got out of bed. When the Chinese students were trying to democratise their world we saw it happening live. We knew of events in Tiananmen Square before people elsewhere in Beijing.

Each screened disaster – the Zeebrugge ferry sinking, the Falklands War, the Hillsborough tragedy – brought us a cast of goodies and baddies. Television made politicians work harder, making them campaign for our votes with each appearance. The royal family couldn't beat showbusiness so they joined it – most of them becoming chat-show guests. And as the box in the living room (and the ones in the bedroom and the kitchen) became unquestionably the main source of our entertainment, we were able to have more control of things by using what became the new necessity, the video recorder (it also gave us the chance to become vidiots when we couldn't work the timer).

There was more television. Channel 4, daytime and breakfast television arrived. And thanks to a government determined to break up what it sees as too tight a marriage between ITV and BBC, the 1990s will bring one, perhaps two more 'earth' stations. For those who buy a Sky dish or a 'squarial' for British Satellite Broadcasting, and pay a monthly subscription, there will be a whole new family of entertainment channels beamed from outer space to our inner space.

Will more mean worse? Will bad television drive out good? We would like to suggest that this need not be so. Not yet anyway, not while the BBC is allowed to live, driven by the idea of making good programmes, not simply of making money.

But, to put the lid on our Box of Delights, let us look back at a few highs and lows. At the start of the decade the BBC was not very lively while the newly franchised independent companies were showing how highbrow they could be. Posh drama was not easy, of course. Derek Granger at Granada spent nine years making his version of Evelyn Waugh's *Brideshead Revisited*. It proved worth it. 'The best piece of fictional television ever made,' was how Anthony Burgess described it. He praised Jeremy Irons and said Olivier and Gielgud, 'not rushed into dramatic tricks', gave the best performances of their lives. By the time it was shown, the same company were taking even greater risks. They had sent an army of actors

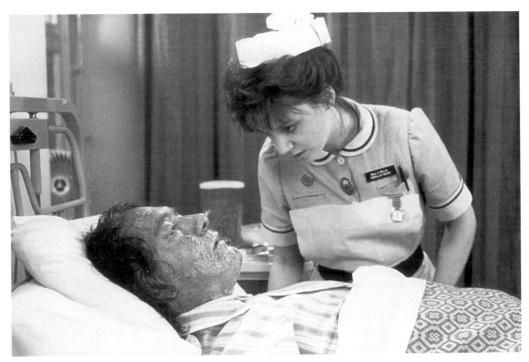

The Singing Detective (Michael Gambon), skin and mind diseased, braced himself for a pleasing treatment by Nurse Mills (Joanne Whalley).

and production people to India to make 'The Jewel in the Crown'. That proved to be worth it, too. The BBC were beside themselves with envy. Sadly, Brian Armstrong, producer of Granada's last multi-million pound drama serial 'Game, Set and Match', confirmed recently that with the dissolution of the IBA, Granada would not be making any more expensive 'prestige' dramas.

Central Television brought us coarser heroes, labourers on the 'lump', with high-quality comic drama, in 'Auf Wiedersehen Pet'. The story goes that Jimmy Nail (real name Bradford), with broken nose and absent front teeth, a singer rather than an actor, heard that the television people were looking for Geordie-speaking extras. So he walked in and said to the first person he met: ''Ey, you with the face. 'Ow do I get a part in this fookin' play?' He was talking to the director and he was hired.

By 1984, Michael Grade, nephew of Lew, came back from America to work for the BBC rather than for his old company LWT, first as Controller BBC1, then as Director of Programmes. 'There was a feeling that the BBC had lost its way,' he said. 'I hadn't seen any British television for three years and I imagined it was because BBC programmes weren't any good. I discovered there were wonderful things.'

Grade says his job was simply to work out where to put the wonderful things – 'Tenko', 'Big Deal', 'Only Fools and Horses', 'Just Good Friends', for example – because nobody at the BBC had noticed what a difference Channel 4 had made. Given this extra choice, viewers didn't know what they wanted – until given the 'map' of his new schedules. With a twang of his red braces, Grade moved Wogan's new chat-show to 7 p.m. instead of the 10 p.m. slot planned for it. 'Panorama' went out later. Plays came back on Tuesdays. Dennis Potter's angry, sexy 'The Singing Detective' was slotted on BBC1 at peak time on a Sunday, and Grade calmly puffed his cigars as a row about ten minutes of bare buttocks raged. He also nursed 'EastEnders', the BBC's first proper soap opera, which the whole of ITV was praying would flop, through its post-natal fevers. 'It was my idea to do the Sunday omnibus, but we could only afford it for six months,' he said. 'I knew I had to keep "EastEnders" in the Top Twenty for that time or it would be finished.' Few people know that after a few months its audiences went down to only 5 million. Without the omnibus (for whose continuance money was miraculously found) and Grade's inside-out knowledge of ITV's schedules – such things as the summer break of 'Emmerdale Farm' – the Corporation's most successful ever series would not have survived.

As BBC1 shows began filling the Top Ten, BBC2 risked dramas which tried to make sense of life in depressed 1980s Britain. Yosser's breakdown in 'Boys from the Blackstuff' was a searing metaphor for the economic scrapheap. Another timely dramatic experiment, 'Edge of Darkness', added uranium to politics and money to make nightmare, death and doom. It frightened and enthralled, and Grade repeated it quickly on BBC1. He said 'Yes' on the phone to the idea of a story about a batty band from Glasgow, 'Tutti Frutti', before Robbie Coltrane or Emma Thompson had been signed to star in it. He fought and won with Tory politicians and, more important, with the BBC's board of governors to get the Falklands War play 'Tumbledown' to the screen. He also wrote the memo establishing 'The Late Show', which turned out to be the best thing to happen to arts programming in 1989. By this time Grade had left the BBC to greyer men and had joined Channel 4.

One mistake Grade made was passing the advertising copy on the drama about atrocities inside the British army during the First World War, 'The Monocled Mutineer', which suggested it was all 'true'. He said: 'I was sorry because it took the gloss off Alan Bleasdale's brilliant story. But the same people who were kicking the BBC every day for screening faction were the people saying we *had* to show Ian Curteis's pro-Thatcher Falklands play. I kept trying to point out that that was also faction.'

Bill Cotton, Grade's colleague, recalls those BBC-bashing years of the middle and late eighties. 'We were being chased by the press, by the Government, by a whole load of real toe-rags; it became a national sport and made some of us quite ill. I mean, I hadn't joined the BBC to listen to the load of codswallop I had to listen to from backbenchers on both sides.'

In the end the bashing stopped. Cotton said: 'Everybody loves the BBC, but it's a funny sort of relationship. I think they'd gone so far down the line, people thought they were going to destroy us so the best thing to do was leave us alone.'

What the politicians did not complain about were the public services carried out by both the BBC and ITV companies during the 1980s. In many different ways, television became the doer of good deeds. Massive, noisy and hugely enjoyable fund-raising efforts began: Live Aid, then Comic Relief and the regular 'telethons' – marathon nights of nagging which featured sponsored silliness by groups of people secretly hoping it would get them on television and celebrities haranguing viewers to 'pledge' donations. Esther Rantzen's dogged and often doggy years on 'That's Life' has done social work for years, campaigning for transplant donors, against child abuse and for dozens of other worthy causes. ITV has enjoyed being worthy, too. Beefy Roger Cook became a real-life Equalizer tackling child pornographers, organised black crime, badger-baiters and paramilitary protection racketeers in Northern Ireland among others. The same ITV company, Central, also boldly advertised children for fostering with the 'Find a Family' series. It resulted in a national register of adoption agencies, some cutting-away of red tape, and thousands of happier kids.

Television's love-affair with the police continued. Heroes were still mostly law-enforcers. But women – Cagney and Lacey, Juliet Bravo and others – joined the men from 'The Bill' and the much missed, hard-boiled officers from the MTV series 'Hill Street Blues'. This was one of the polished well-scripted series – with slick comedies such as 'Cheers' and 'The Golden Girls' and soaps such as 'St Elsewhere' and 'thirtysomething' – which stopped us complaining of transatlantic trash.

British policemen, including the real ones exposed (mostly to their credit) in fly-on-the-wall documentaries such as 'Police', 'Operation Carter' and 'Flying Squad', could not match the colourful procedures of Hill Street where cigar-chewing Belker might well bite the 'perp' before booking him and bad-tempered Buntz might easily beat up an informant – well, as he said 'leanin' on a snitch ain't exactly Hiro-freaking-Shima'. At times television did the police's work for them. In the BBC1 series 'Crimewatch', respectable presenters Nick Ross and Sue Cook introduced reconstructions of recent unsolved crimes to prompt witnesses to come forward, satisfying the public's appetite for violent crime-stories at the same time. In five years their programmes have led to more than 200 arrests, 118 convictions and the recovery of mountains of swag.

There have also been some more doubtful developments. With many more hours to fill there has been a proliferation of studio discussions on a range of topics which seem increasingly desperate ('Are traffic wardens a good thing?', 'Does incontinence matter?'). Series such as 'Kilroy', 'The Time the Place', the LWT agony-column 'A Family Affair' and Thames Television's late-night counselling programme 'A Problem Aired' have revealed that many people will confess to weaknesses in a studio that they would be far too embarrassed to talk about with their doctor or their mother.

The decade has not matched the previous one for comedy, but the early eighties brought us the start of 'Yes, Minister', 'Only Fools and Horses' and the short-sketch shows of Victoria Wood with her friend Julie Walters – certainly not bad going. Wood and Walters, like most new comics, were not instantly accepted. A multiple-birth joke in their 1982 Granada series in which the girls were surrounded by seventy babies even provoked complaints from viewers who pointed out that some of the babies were crying and that this may have been cruelty on a vast scale. In fact all the small stars were out of their mothers' arms for minutes only and all their names were listed on the credits. Still, outraged viewers seemed par for the course with many young performers – Rowan Atkinson, Mel Smith, Griff Rhys Jones, Alexei Sayle, Lenny Henry, French and Saunders – and absolutely essential for the satirists of the decade, the 'Spitting Image' puppets. Farce returned with the splendidly well acted ''Allo, 'Allo', set in a French café in the forties. Subtle it wasn't – but, then, neither was the Gestapo.

How different will television be in another ten years' time? Wendy Nelson, producer of Central's 'Find a Family', is pessimistic about changes for the better within the independent companies. Mass-appeal programmes, series which sell well abroad may continue, but regional programmes and daring documentaries look threatened. She says: 'Series like ours which help people only ever won brownie points for the company with the IBA. Now the companies don't need brownie points, only profits.'

Michael Grade believes viewers will hardly notice the changes for the next few years. 'If the BBC is preserved to the end of the century with an adequate licence fee, viewers will stay happy,' he said. 'But I talk to television-company executives all over the world, and they think this country is taking leave of its senses even to contemplate interfering with the BBC.'

Anthony Simonds-Gooding, chief executive of British Satellite Broadcasting, naturally does not believe more means worse. 'I don't care what's going to happen to the next "Brideshead Revisited",' he said. 'If you want high-quality drama, look at our films. I think it's all going to work out rather well.'

Well, he would, wouldn't he? But let's hope he's right.

WHERE ARE THEY NOW?

WHERE ARE THEY NOW?

Australia doing concerts and television, performing on the instrument that made her a household name and which she once swore she'd never touch again – the zither.

Anne Aston achieved fame (or was it notoriety?) as the dizzy blonde who couldn't add up on 'The Golden Shot'. Yet for someone who appeared to have absolutely no head for figures she is doing very nicely now running a property business around the New Forest area of Hampshire. 'I've got people to look after my accounts, so I don't have to use maths,' says forty-one-year-old Anne. 'It was only really mental arithmetic I couldn't do – I've always been able to count numbers with a pound sign in front.' The young actress from West Bromwich was working in her father's travel agency, under her real name, Anne Lloyd, when she heard about 'The Golden Shot'. She applied for the job, got it and changed her

Shirley Abicair was known as the Queen of the Zither in the fifties days of jive and skiffle. The Australian musician appeared on numerous television shows before discovering that as far as teenagers were concerned the good old zither came a distant second to the electric guitar. Shirley dropped out in the early seventies and spent three years in an American log cabin. 'I lived on Ken Kesey's farm in Oregon – he wrote *One Flew Over the Cuckoo's Nest* – and this enabled me to reflect and develop as a person.' She then embarked on a new career designing T-shirts based on Idi Amin's array of medals. But now, aged fifty-six, Shirley resides in America and surname to the location of the studios at Aston. But her trademark came about unintentionally. 'As I went to add up on my first live show in 1969, someone told me there were sixteen million people watching at home. My mind just went blank, and I turned round and started adding up the scores on my fingers. I thought I'd get the sack, but the producer loved it and we decided to keep it that way. Mind you, it wasn't easy to add up, anyway, with apple juice from the targets dripping all over me!' Anne's showbusiness career is strictly part-time now. 'I still do panto in winter but, although I get offered plenty of touring plays, I just want to enjoy myself without thinking: I've got to be in Norwich next week.'

Raymond Baxter, tall, straight, with a strong plummy voice, was always every inch the RAF fighter pilot he'd once been. Viewers knew him as the no-nonsense presenter of 'Tomorrow's World'. He was also one of the BBC's top commentators and experts on motor racing.

He made newspaper headlines in 1977 when his former gardener claimed he was unfairly dismissed from Baxter's thirty-two-acre estate in Denham, Buckinghamshire. The same year he walked out of 'Tomorrow's World' after bitter differences with the new young producer Michael Blakstad. Blakstad allegedly called Baxter a 'dinosaur', Baxter allegedly commented that he couldn't work with someone who rode a bicycle to work. A year later Baxter sold his estate and began making commercials for British Leyland and promotional films and videos for business conferences. These days he lives in Henley and, when not busy with business, works as Honorary Admiral of the Association of Dunkirk Little Ships.

Robert Beatty was the popular Canadian star of the late-fifties police series 'Dial 999', but he believes the series had an adverse effect on his career. 'It put me out of television for ten years. I was type-cast – my face was too well known for being a cop on TV.' His long and outstanding film career has seen him work with names of the calibre of Gregory Peck, Richard Burton, Rock Hudson and Clint Eastwood, and on stage he has appeared with the likes of Douglas Fairbanks, Jnr, and Peter O'Toole. One of his most recent television credits was as President Reagan in Granada's 'Breakthrough at Reykjavik'. The affable Beatty now lives in London but has relatives in Canada as well as son Michael who is a television presenter in Australia. Even at the ripe old age of eighty, Beatty says: 'I still enjoy working – besides, no actor can ever afford to retire.'

Bernie the Bolt was the mysterious character who loaded the crossbows on 'The Golden Shot'. In total there were three 'Bernies': Derek Young who did twelve shows at Elstree, and then Alan Bailey and Johnny Baker who used to alternate when the programme moved to Birmingham. When Bailey left, Baker did the loading alone for the last three years and became the face most readily associated with the name. 'I rarely said anything on the show and I suppose I became something of an enigma.' For the past twelve years, Baker has worked as a grip in the film unit at Birmingham, first with ATV and now with its successor Central Television. Aged fifty-one, he is single, lives in Birmingham and says he is still recognised

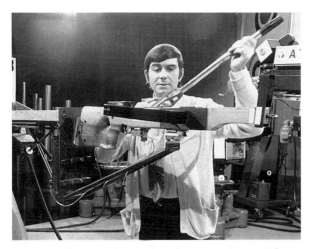

occasionally. 'But not like the old days when even if I was on holiday in Cornwall people would approach me and say: "Aren't you Bernie the Bolt?"'

Terry Brooks

Terry Brooks starred as the original Milky Bar Kid back in 1962, playing the weedy cowboy in NHS glasses between the ages of nine and fifteen. Before the Milky Bar commercials Terry had made commercials for Walls Ice Cream, Kellogg's Corn Flakes and Smarties. He also appeared in films like *The Young Ones, Half a Sixpence* and *A Hard Day's Night.* On leaving school, Terry, like most actors, was in and out of work but he then found steady

employment for six years as a Pontins Blue Coat at Christchurch, Hampshire. Eventually, he packed in show-business altogether, and after a spell as a lorry-driver he set up his own air-conditioning business which he now runs in Basildon, Essex. Aged thirty-eight, Terry has four children; he took his seven-year-old son to audition for the latest Milky Bar Kid in 1988, but Tony was a bit too young. 'The national press did some pictures of us. Tony thought he really was the Milky Bar Kid. I must admit with the glasses and the cowboy hat he looked the spitting image of me when I did it.'

Barry Bucknell is still as keen on do-it-yourself as he was over thirty years ago when his programmes were compulsive viewing for millions. Barry admits: 'I'm always trying to design improvements to existing products. Last year I finished work on a new catamaran, specially designed to cater for elderly people like my wife and

myself, and we moored it by my house at St Mawes in Cornwall.' Barry is also justifiably proud of a boat he designed in the sixties, the *Daily Mirror* dinghy. 'There are 70,000 *Mirror* dinghies in Britain alone,' says Barry, 'and over twenty-five years after its launch it is still the most popular family dinghy in the world.' In addition, Barry finds time to help out with the London family building business, Bucknells Ltd, and he has also designed caravans and houses. At seventy-seven he still does the occasional broadcast and is amazed that people remember him from shows like 'Bucknell's House'. 'I really can't believe it', he says, 'when they come up and ask me for advice just like they used to all those years ago.'

Gerald Campion has come a long way from the tuck shop at Greyfriars School. For the man who starred as Billy Bunter back in the fifties now earns rave reviews as the owner of the Campions' Woodmans Arms Auberge at Hastingleigh, near Ashford. Gerald retired from acting in 1968 to run a succession of restaurants around the Home Counties. In 1986 he bought the Woodmans Arms and began what he terms 'a minor acting comeback' with a voiceover for a butter commercial, a rôle in the film *Little Dorrit* and work on television series such as 'Sherlock Holmes' and 'The Bretts'. Now sixty-seven, Campion reflects: 'In the old days, people used to send me cakes through the post and even playfully kick me around if they saw me because that was what always happened to Bunter. But now they are very complimentary, and I suppose it is fitting that the man who played Billy Bunter should end up in the *Good Food Guide* . . .'

Jillian Comber left her rôle as 'Crackerjack' hostess in 1970 and hasn't worked in showbusiness since. Her only real link with that world is her actress daughter Beverley Adams who appeared in the comedy series 'No Place Like Home'. 'I was never particularly ambitious,' says Jilly (now known as Jilly Adams). 'If I had been, I don't think I would have stayed with "Crackerjack" for so long. When I left, I thought it would be nice to be at home with my three daughters, and my ex-husband was very big in advertising so a lot of time was devoted to entertaining. But I found that I was turning into one of the cabbages that we used to have in "Crackerjack" on Double or Drop. And after my divorce I needed to work again for financial reasons, so for the past seven years I have been working for Telemac, a London raincoat company.' Now a fifty-three-year-old grandmother, Jilly lives in Walton-on-Thames, Surrey. She adds: 'People often come up to me and say, "Don't I know you?" but I think that is probably because on screen Beverley looks just like a younger version of me.'

Russ Conway was the darling of mums everywhere when he appeared on 'The Billy Cotton Bandshow' in the fifties and sixties. It was hard to know which were whiter – the teeth in his dazzling smile or the keys of the piano he played so brilliantly. For someone who has sold tens of millions of records throughout the world, it comes as a

shock to learn that Russ has had only one piano lesson in his life and that was at the age of four. He believes he inherited his talent from his mother. A former sailor, Russ was at his peak with Billy Cotton, but illness (he suffered two strokes) seemed likely to curtail his career. However, he has recovered and, at the age of sixty-three, still presents 'An evening with Russ Conway' at theatres all over the country. He has a home in Eastbourne but departs to his residence in Spain to escape the British winter. Russ's fans have remained loyal to him over the years – not only do the mums still flock to see him but he also finds that their daughters come along, too.

Michaela Denis was the beautiful half of husband-and-wife 'On Safari' team Armand and Michaela Denis whose wildlife programmes were much loved in the fifties and sixties. Armand died in 1971, and in the seventies Michaela married Sir William O'Brien Lindsay, the last English Chief Justice in the Sudan. Tragically, he died of a heart attack only a few weeks after their wedding. Now aged seventy-five, the charming Michaela leads a very active life (she is a vegetarian, non-smoker and virtually teetotal) and still loves to go on safari in Kenya: 'It is always a thrill.' But a lot of her time is taken up by the spiritual healing clinic she runs in Nairobi. 'I have had this gift for years,' says Michaela. 'Armand had Parkinson's Disease yet he could walk and talk right up until the last few days of his life thanks to my healing powers. By putting my hands on the foreheads of people and animals, I have been able to cure cancer victims, asthma, migraines, and enabled people who have had strokes to walk again. I treat between thirty and forty patients each afternoon, and I can also cure myself, which explains why I am able to enjoy such a busy life.' Even when she visits London, Michaela is constantly interrupted by long-distance phone calls, patients and fan mail. But, 'when the sun comes out in Britain, I run out of the house so as not to miss it!'

Patricia Driscoll was known to millions of fifties children, first for brightening up Monday afternoons by reading 'Picture Book' on the BBC and then by giving the Merrie Men something to smile about on a Saturday afternoon when she played Maid Marian in ITV's 'The Adventures of Robin Hood'. Now sixty and a widow (she was married to actor Duncan Lamont) with two grown-up daughters, Patricia still acts, 'but not as much as I'd like to'. However, she became very excited last year when she heard that 'Watch with Mother' was being released on video. 'I was on the point of signing the contract when I discovered that the clip from "Picture Book" was taken from after I'd left to do "Robin Hood".' Patricia lives in an old house near East Grinstead. 'I've got a smallholding with cattle and chickens and I used to have a house-cow which I milked. There are even some horses – you see, the Robin Hood tradition carries on.'

Keith Fordyce was the grown-up on the pop-music show 'Ready Steady Go!' in the early sixties. He'd started in radio in Germany with Cliff Michelmore and Raymond Baxter, and had graduated to working as a disc-jockey. He was booked for 'Ready Steady Go!' because he could handle the interviews and could hold things together. 'They were such exciting shows, though,' he said. 'We never knew what would happen.' Keith went on to become what he calls 'an avuncular anchorman' in a long list of shows. Keith presented 'Come Dancing' and for fourteen years was the host of WestWard Television's quiz 'Treasure Hunt'. He liked working in the West Country

and has no intention of ceasing teaching. 'I don't think I'm even the oldest keep-fit teacher in Britain – after all, keep fit is for all ages. But I am older than my pupils.' Eileen is currently hard at work writing her autobiography.

and moved there in 1969. There were several gardening series – 'Kitchen Garden', 'Greenhouse Gardens' and 'Star Gardens' – and Keith was always busy with radio programmes, too. From 1969 to 1974 he presented 'Late Night Extra', did 'Sounds of the Sixties' for three years and masterminded long-running radio game-shows such as 'Town and Country Quiz' and 'Beat the Record'. In the eighties he has introduced 'Movie Go Round', appeared on chat-shows and quizzes and made guest appearances. Last year he turned up with Harry Secombe on 'Highway' reading poetry, and Alexei Sayle pulled him into one of his comedy shows in the 'Alexei Sayle's Stuff' series. Now sixty, a family man with four daughters and three grandchildren, his main work is as curator of the Torbay Aircraft Museum. Pop music today? 'Very rarely do I hear anything in the current pop music scene that I find appealing. I always look for an element of sound entertainment and it usually doesn't exist.'

Eileen Fowler

was Britain's keep-fit queen from the moment she first came to television in 1954. And even at the age of eighty-three she still holds two classes a week at Frinton Lawn Tennis Club on the Essex coast where she has 120 pupils on her books. A regular contributor to radio as well as to television, Eileen was awarded the MBE in 1975 and was a founder member of the Keep Fit Association. Right up until the early 1980s she held major rallies throughout the country. Over the years, Eileen has managed to keep her weight at just under 8½ stone (she is 5 feet 5 inches tall). She is President of the Eastern Counties Keep Fit Association

John Freeman

has enjoyed a distinguished career since his powerful series of interviews, 'Face to Face', ended in the early sixties. The former MP for Watford became editor of the *New Statesman* from 1961 to 1965 and was then British High Commissioner in India for three years before accepting the post of British Ambassador to Washington from 1969 until 1971. He returned to this country as chairman of LWT for thirteen years, and during the late seventies he was also chairman of ITN. In 1985 he went to the University of California where he lectures part-time as a visiting Professor of International Relations. Aged seventy-five, Freeman is surprised that so much significance is still attached to 'Face to Face'. 'It sounds awful, but the series was a good deal less important to me than to all the people who criticised it.' He adds modestly: 'I feel gratified that anybody should remember me for anything. They always recognise my voice not my face. And when I think of my silly voice I'm astonished.'

Simon Groom has certainly led a varied life since leaving 'Blue Peter' in 1986. He has appeared in *Aladdin* with Anita Dobson, been breeding Wensleydale sheep on his farm in Derbyshire, and has made two documentaries about Ken Russell! After leaving Birmingham University, he taught English for a year and worked as a disc-jockey for two before joining 'Blue Peter' in 1978. He made some 700 appearances, filming all over the world, and he also interviewed Prince Charles about the raising of the ship *Mary Rose*. Following his departure from 'Blue Peter', Simon filmed six 'Countryside Special' programmes for the BBC and worked as a reporter on 'Country File' at Pebble Mill. Aged thirty-nine, his great passion in life, apart from wife Ann, farming and Ken Russell, is Derby County Football Club.

Robin Hall and Jimmie Macgregor captured the nation's imagination as the regular folk-singers on the 'Tonight' programme in the early sixties. The Scottish duo, whose best-remembered song was probably 'Football Crazy', went on to host 'The White Heather Club' for five years before splitting up in 1979 after twenty-one years together. They were a couple of working-class lads from Glasgow singing in Hampstead coffee-bars when they were approached for a special Burns Night edition of 'Tonight'. 'The only problem was', says Robin, 'that we didn't have a Burns song in our repertoire. So we hastily wrote one and finished rehearsing it in the taxi on the way to do the show. It must have gone down well because, after a week's trial, we stayed for nearly five years on "Tonight".' They became the best-known folk singers in the country. Eventually, Robin tired of London and moved back to Glasgow. 'I'd had enough of performing. I've always been a very nervous performer whereas I don't think there's a nerve in Jimmie's body! I was fed up with living out of a suitcase so I said to Jimmie "this is it" and gave him a year's notice. But we parted good friends and still are.' Now fifty, he recently recorded a series of Scottish music programmes for the World Service. He sings in folk-clubs from time to time and has an occasional partnership with another Macgregor, classical guitarist Fiona.

Former teacher Jimmie Macgregor is, at fifty-seven, one of Scotland's leading television and radio personalities. Since 1981 he has hosted a highly successful live daily programme on Radio Scotland entitled 'Macgregor's Gathering' – a mixture of music and chat. He has also made four series of the television show 'Macgregor's Scotland' in which he pursues his great love of hill-walking. 'I've never worked so hard in my life,' says Jimmie.

Hans and Lotte Hass were the German husband-and-wife diving team who popularised undersea programmes in the fifties and sixties. They made 105 films in total and they still dive for pleasure even though Hans is now seventy. They are based in Vienna where Lotte helps Hans in his scientific research. Hans says: 'We may do more films one day, but at the moment I am busy with books on management strategy and on giving advice to businesses. Businessmen are like sharks. Whereas I used to study sharks underwater, I am now interested in sharks on land.' Hans Hass is only too happy to encourage younger divers. 'I am very concerned about pollution in the sea . . . . Divers can help clean the oceans by taking samples from the waters of the world.'

Jeremy Hawk was the Old Harrovian questionmaster of the popular late-fifties game-show 'Criss Cross Quiz'. Born Cedric Lange, he had made his West End début back in 1939 and was straight man to stars of the calibre of Benny Hill, Arthur Askey, Norman Wisdom and Arthur Haynes before he sprang to fame in his own right in 1957. As television's quiz king (he also hosted 'Junior Criss Cross Quiz' for a while), he was reportedly earning £300 a week but after some five years of success a long-running television strike hit him badly. 'Television producers pigeon-holed me as a quizmaster,' he says, 'so I went back to theatre.' And he has been there since, performing with great distinction all over the world. He took *No Sex Please, We're British* to the Middle East and the Far East and appeared in *Not Now Darling* in Toronto. In 1988 he played Charles in *Me and My Girl* at the Adelphi Theatre, London. Since those halcyon days, Jeremy's television appearances have been few and far between, but he found that his seventies commercial for Cadbury's Whole Nut ('nuts whole hazelnuts') jogged people's memories. 'I was amazed that I was being stopped in the street afterwards. People are just obsessed with TV.' Now seventy-two, Hawk keeps a keen eye on the progress of one of his daughters, actress Belinda Lang, who starred in 'Dear John'.

Pip Hinton was adored by millions of children in the sixties as resident singer on 'Crackerjack'. It's a long way from Peter Glaze to *Macbeth*, but Pip successfully made the transition in 1988 when she played a witch in the Royal Shakespeare Company production at Stratford. Since leaving 'Crackerjack' in 1966, Pip has put her classical training to good use with many seasons at the Bristol Old Vic and a recent West End appearance in *Nunsense* where she did a tap-dance routine with Honor Blackman, the pair of them dressed as nuns. Pip, who admits to being 'in my fifties' says: 'We all had such fun on "Crackerjack", and even now I still get recognised by ladies in Marks and Spencer. Thankfully, nobody yelled out "Crackerjack" when I was in *Macbeth*!'

Mary Holland spent eighteen years giving 'a meal man appeal' as Katie in the famous Oxo commercials. She and screen husband Philip were dropped in 1976, but Mary soon started doing commercials for Electrolux. 'By 1981, my family, one daughter and three sons, were fairly grown up, so I felt I could return to the theatre where I had started twenty-nine years earlier.' She played the blind character made famous by Audrey Hepburn in *Wait until Dark* and toured in *Gaslight* with Tony Adams (Adam Chance from 'Crossroads') as her husband. She did a few more commercials, including one for Bovril, but when

Mary's husband retired from television direction early in 1988 they moved to Spain. 'Should another commercial be offered to me, I would be delighted to return to England, though ever so briefly. For it's a wonderful life here and suits us extremely well. I think the prize remark was made to me on the boat coming over here to Spain. A lovely old chap came up and, taking my hand in his, he said: "You are my favourite girl. I'd know you anywhere. I loved those Bisto commercials. And your Hoover ones were very good, too!"'

Tony Holland thrust his way to national prominence in 1964 as television's first musical muscle-man. Performing to the strains of the 'Wheels Cha-Cha', he won for six successive weeks on 'Opportunity Knocks' and eventually retired undefeated. Tony Holland's story is a tribute to his courage and faith. Following his 'Opportunity Knocks' success, he continued muscle-dancing for seven years and appeared on such shows as 'Sunday Night at the London Palladium'. 'But the glamour of showbusiness faded into long periods of unemployment between bookings,' recalls Tony, 'and so in 1971 my wife and I became houseparents in a community home for adolescent boys. Eight years later, we ran a children's home in Birkenhead,

but our marriage broke up and I left.' Tony worked at a nearby health club for some fifteen months, but then spent a miserable year unemployed. 'I was claiming dole money but I was also doing a muscleogram act. I knew it was wrong to claim while I was working – I have strong principles – and when I heard that Billy Graham was speaking at Liverpool's Anfield Stadium in July 1984 I felt drawn to go and see him. I left the football-ground knowing I was saved, loved and changed. Four months later, I went to the DHSS and confessed to cheating them and incredibly when I got home that night I received a phone call from my daughter Andrée telling me that there was a job going at a children's home in Clitheroe, Lancashire. And that's where I am now, as a residential social worker. I firmly believe that God opened this door for me.' Nowadays fifty-year-old Tony is thrilled when he is asked to perform his muscle routine, to Christian gatherings, keep-fit groups and so on. 'I keep saying I'll give the act up, but somehow I never get round to hanging up my costume for good. Obviously, I don't train as hard as I used to, so the biceps aren't as big these days – but they're still twitching.'

Mary Malcolm, grand-daughter of Lily Langtry, was, in company with Sylvia Peters and the late McDonald Hobley, one of the BBC's regular announcers in the post-war period. Mary was famed for occasional slips of the tongue, particularly when reading the weather. Among her forecasts were 'drain and rizzle', 'frog and fost' and 'shattered scowers'! On another occasion, while testing the sound channel before the start of the programme 'Mainly for Women', she jokingly said: 'Good afternoon,

here is a programme mainly for morons.' Alas, it was accidentally broadcast. Mary left her £1,500-a-year job to go freelance in 1956, stating that she never wanted to do announcing again. In 1960, she was divorced from Sir Basil Bartlett and later married lawyer Colin McFadyean. In the early sixties she made a series of light-hearted documentaries about Britain for German television, but now Mary and Colin lead what she describes as 'an ordinary life. I still get recognised by taxi-drivers – they know the face but usually guess at Sylvia Peters or, some years ago, Isobel Barnett.'

Ray Martine was best-known as the outrageous cockney host of television's sixties pub entertainment 'Stars and Garters', but these days he's buying and selling antiques. Back in 1963, Martine was top of the nightclubs with an act which he himself describes as 'very rude for the time'. He loved the razzmatazz, but when he was axed from 'Stars and Garters' in a mass shake-up he began to get disillusioned with working the club circuit. 'I didn't drive and so I travelled everywhere by train. It just got too much. I'd pass houses where families were eating their Sunday lunch and I'd think: What am I doing? I went through a bad period as clubs turned into discos and also I found that humour was becoming too violent. I don't find

swearing funny – I like innuendo. Anyway, in 1973 after thirty-five years in showbusiness, I decided I'd had enough of the clubs and became a recluse.' In 1986, thirteen years after he had last performed on stage, Martine was persuaded to try his act in Spain. 'I started off: "I know you haven't seen my act since 320 AD . . . ." It fell on stony ground – mind you, they were Spanish. But I got a centre-page spread in the *Costa Blanca News* and it got the old adrenalin going.' Now sixty-one and living on Tyneside, Martine is hoping for a comeback while still keeping the antique business going. 'Early in 1988 I did *The Tempest* at Salford for a month with Freddie Garrity of Freddie and the Dreamers and Jack Smethurst, and it was great. From that I went to Blackpool as a barker on a plate-breaking side-show, but I'd really like to get into comedy acting. I did a couple of British clubs not long ago, but the atmosphere's just not the same.'

Janice Nicholls shot to overnight fame as the 'Oi'll give it foive' girl on the sixties pop show 'Thank Your Lucky Stars'. She was working as an office clerk when she was suddenly plucked from obscurity in 1962, and her distinctive Black Country accent made her a national celebrity. When she was eventually axed from the programme, viewers protested at the loss of their favourite, but Janice retreated into the more sedate world of chiropody. 'I was a chiropodist for twenty-one years and I had my own practice in Hednesford for ten years. Examining feet wasn't as glamorous as the telly, of course, but I enjoyed it.' Now forty-three, Janice has given up chiropody but still lives in the West Midlands, at Hednesford. She has been married for twenty-three years to Brian Meacham. 'I was only fifteen when I met him at Wednesbury Youth Centre. He was Gulliver, the singer with Gulliver and the Travellers!'

John Noakes was the one-man SAS team of 'Blue Peter'. He climbed Nelson's Column, stepped out of an aeroplane at 25,000 feet and was generally more concerned with action-packed adventures than nursing the show's pet tortoise. A former RAF mechanic, office cleaner, and 'feed' to Cyril Fletcher, Noakes had his own series, 'Go with Noakes', after leaving 'Blue Peter'. Over the past few years, his television appearances have been infrequent, although his voice has been heard on a number of commercials, notably ones for Farleys Rusks and Everest Double Glazing He now spends most of the time on his boat in Spain with wife Vicky and son Mark. He owns a villa there, too, and runs a boat charter company. Indeed, he only returns to Britain for occasional television assignments.

Sylvia Peters was a dancer in a show with Bud Flanagan at the Coliseum in 1947 when her mother spotted an advertisement in the paper. The BBC were testing girls for the job of television announcer. Sylvia went along, did 'lots and lots of tests', including reading a children's nursery story, was chosen but then balked when she heard the pay was a miserable £8 a week, considerably less than she'd earned dancing, and she'd have to buy her own clothes, too. 'But they said: "This is different; it's *television*. You'll be famous."' And they were right. It was a long working day, starting around 10.30 a.m. writing and learning the scripts, announcing the programmes until 'Children's Hour' when she read the famous Bengo stories and then came a gap (the Toddlers' Truce) during which she changed into evening dress for the night's announcements.

Sylvia also used to host 'Come Dancing' ('very funny, still is'), introduced 'Dancing Club' with Victor Sylvester and appeared in the annual BBC pantomime, always playing the principal girl. And she was the girl in the royal enclosure at Ascot talking about the fashions until the Duke of Norfolk complained and she had to sit up in the stands.

After leaving the BBC, she freelanced 'for the other side', doing the advertising magazine 'Buy Lines' for Southern Television. It led to a lady in her High Street gasping at the sight of her and explaining: 'When I saw you, I knew I'd forgotten the fish.' Sylvia had advertised kippers the day before. She was then asked to promote sausages but declined. 'Kippers were bad enough. I didn't want to become a subliminal sausage.' Later she bought and ran a dress boutique near her London home which she ran happily until her husband became ill. He died in 1982 after they had been married for thirty-two years. She spends her time now gardening, recording talking newspapers for the blind and making occasional television appearances. Her one regret? 'No one ever took me seriously. I always wanted to do a series talking to successful women, but no one gave me the chance.'

Conrad Phillips has just turned the clock back over thirty years, for he appeared as Stefan, elderly friend and mentor of William Tell, in the French–American production 'Crossbow', shown on ITV in 1989. And it was as William Tell back in 1958 that Conrad first achieved fame. 'It was like going back in time,' says the genial fifty-eight-year-old Phillips. 'Fighting in the River Loire at my age was ridiculous – I thought I was dreaming. I had a big beard in "Crossbow" and looked slightly different from the slim young thing of the old William Tell series.' Simon Oakes, executive producer of 'Crossbow', added: 'Conrad loved the idea of being in it. I think he would have liked to play Tell again, but he hasn't got as much hair as he used to have.' Phillips also appeared as NY Estates managing director Christopher Meadows in 'Emmerdale Farm' – an appropriate rôle as after the original William Tell tales he packed away his crossbow and took up hill farming in Scotland for six years. 'I milked forty cows a day as well as doing all the ploughing, but I found that trying to combine farming and acting simultaneously was physically too demanding.' Phillips now lives in Chippenham, Wiltshire.

Leslie Randall made his name in the fifties television series 'Joan and Leslie', in which he starred with his wife. They also did nine years of Fairy Snow commercials, after which Leslie went to New York to work in nightclubs and to star on the prestigious 'Ed

Sullivan Show'. He moved on to Hollywood to appear in 'The Monkees' and 'I Dream of Jeannie' and then to the University of California to study film production. Leslie's next stop was Australia as Director of Programme Development for Channel 7. Since returning to England in 1972, he has combined performing with writing. His plays have included *Forty Love* with Bernard Cribbins and *Death of a Comic*, and he wrote two radio series for himself and Warren Mitchell called 'This is Living?'. He also scripted a television series, 'Rogues Gallery', and in 1988 he toured the country as the vicar in *Fur Coat and No Knickers* with Jack Douglas. He is now divorced from Joan.

Anthea Redfern, once the twirling hostess of 'The Generation Game' when it was presented by her former husband Bruce Forsyth, now leads 'a very private life'. She lives near Bracknell in Berkshire with her second husband, property developer Freddie Hoffman, and her three daughters. 'I was never really in showbusiness in the first place,' says Anthea. 'I got the job on "The Generation Game" by pure chance. I was a model and I met Bruce when I was compèring a beauty competition. I was just lucky to be in the right place at the right time.' These days, thirty-seven-year-old Anthea makes only occasional television appearances. 'I've guested on "Give Us a Clue" and "Blankety Blank" and I've done the odd chat-show like "Open Air", but in truth I'm not sorry to be out of the

limelight. I think it's so important for a mother to be with her children while they are growing up. And that's what I'm happy to be doing.'

Joan Regan was chosen as one of the ten most beautiful women in Britain by the world-famous photographer Baron, and in her heyday in the fifties she was one of the country's most popular artists. She made a string of television appearances, including her own BBC series, 'Be My Guest'; but in 1984 her singing career seemed to be over when she fell in the shower of her Florida home, hitting her head against the tiled wall. It caused a blood clot on the brain resulting in an operation that left her paralysed and unable to speak. She undertook both speech

and physical therapy in order to overcome the problem and regain her confidence. Her courage and determination helped her pull through, and now she assists others who have been in a similar predicament. Joan is able to sing again and divides her time between entertaining around the world, her home in Florida and visiting her family in Britain.

Monica Rose decided to give up her job as a junior accounts clerk to become the best-known cockney kid in the country, a hostess on 'Double Your Money' in 1964. Pint-sized Monica isn't rich or famous now, but she doesn't regret her brief flirtation with stardom. She'd earned £8 as a contestant on the show in 1963 and had stars in her eyes. Hughie Green, who had taken a chance and let her chatter away for an unedited eighteen minutes that first time, believed she had a bright future. 'She was a natural, an exciting personality,' he said recently. 'She wasn't trying to be sexy; she was just lovely – every mum's kid. People began telling me that they watched the show for her rather than for Hughie Green.' Stardom and money came like a sudden heady dream to the sixteen-year-old daughter of an Underground-train driver and a cleaner at the White City Stadium. 'Can you imagine a chauffeur arriving at that scruffy old estate, me getting out and the driver walking after me carrying boxes of wonderful clothes from Harrods and places like that?' she said. 'In some ways it was quite difficult. My friends and my brothers and sisters didn't know how to treat me. On the whole, my television career was one big laugh. I never worried much about what I was going to say or do – I was

just myself.' Monica went on from 'Double Your Money' to Hughie's next show 'The Sky's the Limit', again the chirpy hostess; but the show's producer, Jess Yates, didn't value her as Hughie did. She left to try her hand as a comedy-singer, and after that came pantomime which she loved best of all. Personal problems soon began to impinge. 'I'd been living with a guy. The relationship faded. I was left alone with very little money and ended up in a psychiatric hospital suffering from depression.' But there was a silver cloud. In hospital she met Terry Dunnell whose wife was also a patient. His wife died, but Terry, youth officer of a religious group called the Frontier Trust, continued to visit Monica. Later they married. Monica became a Christian and now works in a supermarket near their home in Leicester. She sings in the Trust's singing group and is the least-depressed person you could meet. 'I don't really hanker for the old days,' said the forty-one-year-old veteran. 'I like my new life, but I'd like to do a bit of entertaining now and then. It's lovely when people recognise me.'

Jonathan Routh has left the world of 'Candid Camera' far behind. The sixty-one-year-old arch-joker now lives in Jamaica with his second wife Shelagh (his first wife Nandi was killed in a car crash) and works as a painter and writer. Jonathan had to stop doing 'Candid Camera' because he was becoming too recognisable. He started painting in 1970 and now has a semi-permanent art exhibition at San Lorenzo's Bar in London's Beauchamp Place. Back in the sixties, he wrote the *Good Loo Guide*, a tour of London's lavatories, and he produced an updated version in 1987 where he decided that loos aren't as interesting as they used to be. He has also written a spoof diary, *The Secret Life of Queen Victoria*, and *Recipes of Leonardo da Vinci*, based on the premiss that all of Leonardo's designs were in fact kitchen utensils for making pasta! Another of Jonathan's more bizarre recent activities has been dwarf-tossing – an annual competition in Jamaica where locally carved wooden dwarfs are thrown for charity. Jonathan is actively championing this pastime and is hoping that it will discourage the practice of tossing human dwarfs which apparently exists in America.

Sabrina drove men to distraction in the fifties with her version of the fuller figure. With vital statistics of 42–19–36, Sabrina (real name Norma Sykes) was an enormous hit on Arthur Askey's television series 'Before Your Very Eyes'. Aged just seventeen and the daughter of a Blackpool landlady, she was the original dumb blonde. Indeed, part of her gimmick was that she never said a word on screen. In 1965 she tired of her image and went to the States with the intention of becoming a serious actress. Instead she married a successful young Beverly Hills surgeon, Dr Harold Melsheimer, who had never heard of her. This, she said, was part of the attraction. However, they were subsequently divorced. Now fifty, Sabrina still lives in California and only rarely visits this country.

in London but left in 1986. Now fifty-six, Chris continues to busy himself with various projects and has an ambition to write comedy. Does he ever regret leaving 'Blue Peter' at the height of his and the show's popularity? 'No not really. I felt I needed a change at the time.'

Jack Scott has at last said goodbye to troughs and depressions. He finally retired from weather forecasting in 1988 after forty-seven years working for the BBC and for Thames Television, and he has since been enjoying a new career as a presenter and interviewer for 'Years Ahead', Channel 4's magazine programme for old people. Sixty-five-year-old Jack says: 'I joined the Met. Office when I was seventeen and I suppose I do miss the embarrassments of the weather. I think I took the jokes well – I even did a Carling Black Label advert last year which took the mickey out of weathermen. But I don't miss some of the complaints we used to get from people who claimed we were always putting rain symbols over their town.' In addition to his new television work, Jack likes nothing better than a round of golf. 'But I make sure I listen to the weather forecast first.'

Christopher Trace was one of the original stalwarts of 'Blue Peter', presenting 550 editions of the show from its inception in 1958 until 1967. Since then he has been through a variety of jobs as well as the odd bout of unemployment. He spent seven years with the BBC at Norwich, and in the late seventies he got a job at Hemel Hempstead as a stock controller with an engineering firm, from which he was given time off to train would-be BBC presenters. He then worked in the press office of SSAFA, the Soldiers', Sailors' and Airmen's Families Association,

Bert Weedon has made over 5,000 radio and television shows, including children's programmes like 'Tuesday Rendezvous' and 'The Five O'Clock Club'. But Bert is best known as 'The man who taught the world to play the guitar'. Bert wrote the world-wide bestseller *Play in a Day* in 1958 after his father bought him a battered guitar from Petticoat Lane market. When he got it home,

Bert realised he hadn't a clue how to play it and years later resolved to write a tutor that anyone could understand and so learn without a teacher. People like John Lennon, Paul McCartney and Eric Clapton all learned to play from Bert's book, and in all he is said to have influenced 4 million guitarists. He has backed such diverse singers as Tommy Steele, Marty Wilde, Billy Fury, Frank Sinatra, Nat 'King' Cole, Judy Garland and Paul Robeson. Now in his sixties and living in Beaconsfield, Bucks, Bert is still going strong. He recently made a video on guitar-playing – 'I hope to influence another four million' – and regularly tours all over the world. 'I think I'm probably busier now than I was in the sixties,' says Bert. 'I get paid for what I love doing – I'm the luckiest man in the world.'

Wally Whyton used to be one of the most familiar faces on children's television through his appearances with Pussy Cat Willum and on shows like 'Tuesday Rendez-vous' and 'The Five O'Clock Club'. He also created the characters of such favourites as Ollie Beak, Joe Crow and Spike McPike and has still got his own music show on Radio 2. Whyton became a professional entertainer at the start of 1957 when he led the Vipers skiffle group who scored their first chart success with 'Don't You Rock Me, Daddy-O'. With the skiffle boom over, Wally turned solo and after a season busking in the South of France was invited on to a children's show to deputise for Rolf Harris. This led to numerous programmes throughout the sixties

and into the seventies where he appeared on 'Lift Off with Ayshea'. Wally's radio career dates back to 'Skiffle Club', 'Guitar Club' and the legendary 'Saturday Club' and went on to encompass such favourites as 'Country Meets Folk' and 'Country Club'. Now in his fifties, Wally reflects: 'Ever since I turned professional, I've been lucky enough never to have been out of work. It's a miracle that I've managed to keep going through all the changing trends in music. I only hope I'm still working at eighty.' Some people say, "Weren't you embarrassed about doing all those kids' shows on TV?" Why should I be? After all, I got a house out of Pussy Cat Willum . . .'

Leila Williams had the distinction of being the first presenter of 'Blue Peter', along with Christopher Trace. She co-hosted the show through its first four years before leaving in 1962 following a row with the new producer. 'He wanted us to write all our own material,' says Leila. 'I protested, we had a big argument and he sacked me.' She then packed up showbusiness altogether and stayed at home to look after husband Fred Mudd of the Mudlarks singing group and their young daughter Debra. 'But Fred was away singing a lot, and I eventually got fed up with being stuck at home, so in 1970 I got a job as assistant manageress at Dorothy Perkins in Harrow.' Five years later, she and Fred took over the Liverpool Arms at Kingston-upon-Thames before moving to the Royal Oak, Surbiton, in the early eighties. And they are still there. Now fifty-two, Leila doesn't miss showbusiness at all. 'I've still got a stage in the pub really – behind the bar. In fact I think this is a natural progression from showbusiness. All the locals know what Fred and I used to do but, to be honest, they don't bother that much. And we just get on with our work.'

Kenneth Wolstenholme was the voice of football for twenty-three years. Born in Worsley, near Manchester, Ken was a bomber pilot during the war and was awarded the Distinguished Flying Cross and then the Bar. He was under contract with the BBC from 1948 until 1971, during which time he covered twenty-two FA Cup Finals, five World Cups, all the European Cup Finals up to and including 1971 and countless international matches all over the world. He was also heard on television programmes like 'Sports Special' and, from 1964, 'Match of the Day'. Many people feel that Ken should have been kept on by the BBC long after 1971, but instead he was allowed to drift to Tyne-Tees Television. Now sixty-nine, Ken has retired from commentating. 'I spend my time doing a spot of writing, after-dinner speaking and playing golf.'

Jess Yates was fifty-four when he was sacked by Yorkshire Television in 1974. He had made over a thousand shows as presenter, writer, producer or director, and as host of 'Stars on Sunday' he was one of the best-loved television stars of his day. His life changed when his relationship with Anita Kay – what was called the Bishop and the Showgirl Affair – became public knowledge. Despite applying to all the television companies, to his disappointment he has found that a 'defrocked' bishop is almost unemployable. The only work he has done in the fifteen years since has been to play the organ on a few television shows, record a series of radio programmes for a hospital in North Wales and appear as a victim of the media in programmes where the methods or values of the press have been discussed. Now aged sixty-nine, he receives a pension of £17 a week from Yorkshire Television and says this and his state pension are all he has to live on. He is proud of his daughter Paula Yates, wife of Live Aid fund-raiser and rock star Bob Geldof, but rarely sees the couple and says he would never ask for a handout from them. His former wife Hellen Torens has remarried, and Anita Kay and he parted in 1983. She married another man and has a child. He said: 'I am so keen to work, I would look after the toilets if they asked me.'

Muriel Young has recently carved out a whole new career for herself as an artist. Famed for her appearances with Pussy Cat Willum and on sixties children's shows like 'The Five O'Clock Club', Muriel stayed as an announcer

with Associated Rediffusion until 1968 and then went to Granada to set up children's programmes. She was there for twelve years and was responsible for such shows as the film series 'Clapperboard' and pop series like 'Shang-a-Lang', 'Lift Off with Ayshea' and 'Get It Together'. In 1982 she joined Mike Mansfield's independent company and worked on the series 'Ladybirds' about girl singers. 'At the end of "Ladybirds", I was exhausted,' says Muriel. 'I had never worked so hard in my life. So I decided to take some time off from producing and renewed an old hobby of mine, painting. I studied oil painting at Winchester Adult Education College and I simply haven't looked back. I've got a whole new career at sixty-one. I've managed to sell a lot of paintings and I've had an exhibition at Liberty's in London.' Muriel, who was often confused with Sylvia Peters ('we used to sign each other's names'), only makes occasional television appearances these days. But she is still in the public eye thanks to the frequent repeats of the Peter Sellers film *I'm Alright Jack* in which she played a television announcer. 'The trouble is, people think the film's only just been made and write to me saying how glad they are that I'm back on television.'

Select Bibliography

Alvarado, Manuel, and Stewart, John, *Made for Television: Euston Films Limited* (London: British Film Institute, 1985).

Black, Peter, *The Biggest Aspidistra in the World* (London: BBC Publications, 1972).

Buckingham, David, *Public Secrets: 'EastEnders' and Its Audience* (London: British Film Institute, 1987).

Buckman, Peter, *All for Love* (London: Secker & Warburg, 1984).

Cantor, Muriel, and Pingree, Suzanne, *Soap Opera* (New York: Sage, 1983).

Cockerell, Michael, *Live from Number 10* (London: Faber & Faber, 1988).

Crowther, Bruce, and Pinfold, Mike, *Bring Me Laughter* (London: Columbus Books, 1987).

Ferguson, James, *'Emmerdale Farm': The Official Companion* (London: Weidenfeld & Nicolson, 1988).

Gable, Jo, *The Tuppenny Punch and Judy Show* (London: Michael Joseph, 1980).

Glaister, Gerard, and Evans, Ray, *'Howards' Way'* (London: BBC Publications, 1988).

Halliwell, Leslie, and Purser, Philip, *Halliwell's Television Companion*, 3rd edn (London: Paladin, 1986).

Katter, Suzy, *The Complete Book of 'Dallas'* (New York: Abrams, 1986).

Kingsley, Hilary, *Soapbox: The Papermac Guide to Soap Opera* (London: Macmillan, 1988).

Moss, Nicholas, *BBC TV Presents: A Fiftieth Anniversary Celebration*, with a foreword by Bill Cotton (London: BBC Data Publications, 1986).

Norden, Denis, *Coming to You Live* (London: Methuen, 1985).

Nown, Graham (ed.), *'Coronation Street': 25 Years* (London: Ward Lock, 1985).

Radio Times (1936–89).

Oram, James, *'Neighbours': Behind the Scenes* (London: Angus & Robertson, 1988).

Passingham, Kenneth, *The Guinness Book of TV Facts and Feats* (London: Guinness Superlatives, 1984).

Smethurst, William, *The New Official 'Archers' Companion* (London: Weidenfeld & Nicolson, 1987).

Smith, Julia, and Holland, Tony, *'EastEnders': The Inside Story* (London: BBC Publications, 1987).

Tinker, Jack, *'Coronation Street'* (London: St Michael/Octopus, 1985).

TV Times (1955–89).

Figures in **bold** type refer to pages containing illustrations.

Magicote, 106
'Magnificent Evans, The', 123, 224
'Magnum for Schneider, A', 94
'Magnum PI', 204
Magnusson, Magnus, 133, 182, 210, 223
'Magpie', 43, 101
'Mahabharata', 261
'Maigret', 57, 130, 251
Mahoney, Jock, 26
'Main Chance, The', 105
'Mainly for Women', 277
'Making Out', 258
Malahide, Patrick, 178, 237
Malcolm, Mary, 4, 14, 48, **277–8**
Malden, Karl, 154
'Malice Aforethought', 181
Malik, Art, **220**
Malin, Edward, 100
'Mallens, The', 181
Malone, Dorothy, **82**
Maloney, Michael, 238, 246
Mamta Kaash, 261
'Man', 90
'Man about the House', 141, 160, 167
'Man Alive', 83
'Man Called Ironside, A', 96, 146
'Man Called Shenandoah, A', 90
'Man from UNCLE, The' 84
'Man in a Suitcase', 94
'Man in Room 17, The', 85
'Man in the Kitchen, The', 14
'Man of Our Times, A', 102, 138
'Man with a Flower in His Mouth, The', 3
Manahan, Anna, 119
Mancini, Al, 66
'Manhunt', 119
Mankowitz, Wolf, 43
Manning, Bernard, **124**, 147
Manning, Hugh, **91**
Manning, Olivia, 244
Mansfield, Jayne, 33
Mantovani, 4
'Mapp and Lucia', 233
Marchant, Tony, 258
Margaret, Princess, 59, 171
'Marie Curie', 167
'Marigold', 4
Mark, Sir Robert, 176, 183
'Mark Saber', 36
Mark Vardy, 63
'Market in Honey Lane', 96
Marks, Alfred, 24, 80, 235
Marks, Laurence, 211, 242

'Marlowe – Private Eye', 225
'Marriage Lines', **74**
'Married Man, A', 217
Marsden, Betty, 45
Marsden, Roy, 173, 217, 244
Marsh, Jean, 120–2
Marshall, Andrew, 239
Marshall, Bernard, 155
Marshall, Bryan, 82, **83**
Marshall, E. G., 70
Marshall, Jonathan, 143
Marshall, Peter, 15
Marshall, Tim, 253, 254
'Martian Chronicles, The', 197
Martin, Derek, 238
Martin, Dick, 99
Martin, Ian Kennedy, 203
Martin, Jessica, 223
Martin, John Scott, **72**
Martin, Kerry, 37
Martin, Kingsley, 35
Martin, Len, 38–9
Martin, Mel, 163, 249
Martin, Millicent, 66–7
Martin, Steve, 159
Martin, Troy Kennedy, 66–7, 214, 229, 238
Martine, Ray, 75, **276**
Martini, 118
'Marty', 102
Marvin, Lee, 80
'Mary Tyler Moore Show, The', 145
'Masada', 217
'M*A*S*H', **135 -6**, 187
Mason, David, 179
Mason, James, 105, 162
Massey, Anna, 174, 181, 239
Massey, Daniel, 241
Massey, Raymond, 63
'Master of the Game', 225
'Mastermind', 132–3
'Match of the Day', 79, 127, 285
Mathie, Marion, 171
Matheson, Eve, 260
'Matt Houston', 216
Matthew, Brian, 65, 73
Matthews, Bernard, 202
Matthews, Francis, 80, 106, 154, 167
Matthews, Stanley, 22
Mattingley, Hedley, 89–90
Maugham, W. Somerset, 59
Maughan, Sharon, 251
'Maverick', 47
Maw, Janet, 174
'Max Headroom', 232

Maxfield, Johnny, 251
Maxwell House, 195
'May to December', 260
Mayall, Rik, **205**, 241, 242
'Maybury', 203
Maynard, Bill, 154, 159
'Mayor of Casterbridge, The', 174
'Me Mammy', 119
Meacher, Michael, 229–30
Medwin, Michael, 34
'Meet the Wife', 80
'Meeting Point', 31, 109
Melba, Paul, 131
Melford, Frank, 14
Mellow Birds, 142
Melville, Alan, 31
'Men of Our Time', 75
Mercer, Tony, 37–8
Mercier, Sheila, 127, **128**
Meredith, Burgess, 90
Merriman, Eric, 144
Merryfield, Buster, 202
Mervyn, William, 96
'Metal Mickey', 182
Metalious, Grace, 81–2
Meyer, Hans, 130
'Miami Vice', 230, 257
Michael, Princess, 223, 242
'Michaela and Armand Denis', 18
Michell, Keith, **117**
Michelmore, Cliff, 15, 20, 32–3, 83, 106, 107
Michener, James, 174
'Mick and Montmorency', 26
'Mickey Dunne', 96
Midland Bank, 195, 251, 252
'Midnight Caller', 257
'Midweek Sports Special', 250
'Mike Hammer', 225
Miles, Bernard, 63
Miles, Michael, **23**, 107
Miles, Sarah, 217
Milk Marketing Board, 148
Milky Bar, 69, 271
Miller, Gary, 43
Miller, Joan, 3
Miller, Jonathan, 170
Millican and Nesbitt, 28
Milligan, Spike, 84, 107, 111
Mills, Annette, 12
Mills, Freddie, 22, 33
Mills, Hayley, 150, 200
Mills, John, 99, 147, 182, 196
Mills, Mrs, 147
Mills, Roger, 210